# THE COUNTRYSIDE OF EAST ANGLIA

The countryside we enjoy today has a very long history, but many of its key features were created in the relatively recent past – as this book shows. It investigates how the landscape of one particular area of England, East Anglia, developed in the period of relative agricultural depression which began in the 1870s and which lasted – with only a few short up-turns – until the period of war-time intensification after 1939. It considers how fields, farms and villages developed in this period; examines the fate of country houses, gardens, and landed estates; and looks in some detail at the character of habitat change – at the development of hedges, woods, wetlands and heaths. It also considers how new kinds of landscape, ranging from vast conifer plantations to holiday resorts, came into existence. The period was not simply one of stasis and decay. It was, instead, a time in which there were fundamental changes in the rural environment, changes which were not always beneficial to wildlife and biodiversity.

This book will be essential reading for all those interested in the history of the countryside (in East Anglia and beyond), landscape history, agricultural history and historical ecology.

# The Countryside of East Anglia

## CHANGING LANDSCAPES, 1870-1950

Susanna Wade Martins
Tom Williamson

THE BOYDELL PRESS

First published 2008
The Boydell Press, Woodbridge

ISBN 978-1-84383-417-5

The Boydell Press is an imprint of Boydell & Brewer Ltd
PO Box 9, Woodbridge, Suffolk IP12 3DF, UK
and of Boydell & Brewer Inc.
668 Mt Hope Avenue, Rochester, NY 14620, USA
website: www.boydellandbrewer.com

A CIP record for this book is available
from the British Library

This publication is printed on acid-free paper

Designed by Tina Ranft
Printed in Great Britain by
CPI Antony Rowe, Chippenham, Wiltshire

# CONTENTS

# LIST OF ILLUSTRATIONS

## Colour Plates

# ACKNOWLEDGEMENTS

We would like to thank, first and foremost, the Leverhulme Trust, whose generous financial assistance made possible the bulk of the research on which this book is based. We would also like to offer our thanks to all the people who provided advice, ideas or information – in particular: Ivan Ringwood, who undertook a vast amount of invaluable research in local record offices; Clare Dobbing and Matt Williamson, who spent many hours meticulously counting trees on Ordnance Survey maps; Peppy MacDonald, who provided information from her unpublished research on Thorpeness; and Patsy Dallas and Gerry Barnes, for being (as ever) helpful in a wide variety of ways. We have also drawn heavily on MA dissertations and PhD theses produced by past students of the Centre of East Anglian Studies and the Landscape Group at the University of East Anglia, especially those by Alec Douet, Kathryn Allen, Edward Bujak, Carole King, Barbara Linsley, Sarah Birtles and Elise Perciful. We would also like to thank the staff of Norfolk Library and Information Services and Suffolk Record Office, Elizabeth Rutledge at Wolterton Hall and Christine Hiskey at Holkham Hall, for all their assistance; and an anonymous reader for a number of very helpful suggestions on draft chapters of this work. Matt Williamson provided Plates 1, 2 and 3; other maps and diagrams are by Phillip Judge. Figures 2, 18, and 27 are from the Norfolk Local Studies Collection and are reproduced with the permission of the Norfolk and Norwich Millennium Library and Mrs Flowerdew. Figures 3, 17, 26, 28 and 34 are from the Suffolk Local Studies Collection, Figures 21 and 40 from the National Monuments Record, Swindon, Figure 35 from *Old Tractor Magazine*, Figure 37 from the Stapleton Collection, and Figures 16 and 41 from Norfolk Landscape Archaeology, and are likewise published with permission. We would like to offer particular thanks to the Scarfe Foundation, and to the Anne Ashard Webb bequest, for generous subventions towards the costs of producing this book.

# ABBREVIATIONS

| | |
|---|---|
| CPRE | Council for the Protection of Rural England |
| *EDP* | *Eastern Daily Press* |
| ESRO | East Suffolk Record Office, Ipswich |
| *JRASE* | *Journal of the Royal Agricultural Society of England* |
| LRO | Lowestoft Record Office |
| MERL | Museum of English Rural Life |
| NRO | Norfolk Record Office |
| TNA: PRO | The National Archives: Public Record Office |
| WSRO | West Suffolk Record Office, Bury St Edmunds |

# CHAPTER 1

# Context

## INTRODUCTION

This book is about the landscape history of East Anglia – strictly defined as the counties of Norfolk and Suffolk – in the period between 1870 and 1950. It examines the development of the region's fields and hedges, woods and commons, roads and villages, farms and cottages, mansions and parklands over a period of some eight decades. Although landscape history and landscape archaeology are now well-established disciplines, few practitioners have so far turned their attention to the relatively recent past. Indeed, the main emphasis of the subject has always been on medieval and early modern times, with even the eighteenth and nineteenth centuries generally receiving only limited attention.[1] There are signs that this is beginning to change, and the recent publication of Trevor Rowley's wide-ranging and erudite *The English Landscape in the Twentieth Century* marks a welcome departure in this respect.[2] But for the most part, in so far as the English rural landscape of the late nineteenth and twentieth centuries has received academic attention, this has mainly been from members of other, related disciplines. Several geographers – most notably David Matlass – have been keen to examine the countryside of the twentieth century, although mainly in terms of its cultural significance, and the ways in which it has been represented.[3] And environmental historians like John Sheail have discussed the complex impact of industrial and urban expansion, and changes in farming practices, on the environment of Britain.[4] The history of the countryside during this period has primarily, however, been the preserve of agricultural historians and – of necessity when studying an essentially rural region – much of what follows in this book comprises fairly conventional farming history.

We begin our story with the final years of the intensively managed 'high farming' era of cheap labour, high commodity prices and tidy arable fields. These were followed after 1870, as most readers will be aware, by a long period of depression in agriculture, and especially in cereal farming, during which many farmers diversified into alternative enterprises. A brief period of prosperity during the First World War was followed by an even greater slump, and further diversification. Our study ends with the campaign to be self-sufficient in food during the Second World War, a return to intensive farming which continued into the 1950s. The period was a roller-coaster ride for the agricultural industry.

As we shall see, there has been much academic argument over the details of this story, and about the varying experiences of farmers operating in different sectors and in different regions: some of these important debates will be revisited here. But since the 1980s, in the work of rural historians like Alun Howkins, a wider cultural and social history of the English countryside in the period since the late nineteenth century has begun to be written.[5] Attention has recently turned, in particular, to the inter-war years, most notably in a collection of essays, *The English Countryside Between the Wars: Regeneration or Decline?*, which argues forcibly, in part by shifting the focus away from the economics of farming to a wider consideration of social issues, that the 1920s and 30s were not – as has usually been thought – a period of unremitting gloom in the countryside.[6] In addition, the release of material in the early 1990s from the wartime 1941–43 National Farm Survey has enabled more detailed work on the agrarian history of the Second World War to be undertaken, again producing a wealth of new perspectives.[7] The research presented in this book thus builds on a growing interest in the wider rural history of the relatively recent past. But its focus – on the physical environment, and on how this was experienced by those who inhabited the countryside – is different from that of earlier studies. Indeed, as far as we are aware, this is the first detailed study of the history of one region of Britain, in the period between 1870 and 1950, written specifically from the standpoint of landscape history.

As in earlier periods, farming was the main force moulding the physical structure of the countryside. But, to an extent which increased decade by decade, the activities of farmers and their workers were only one of several influences. As a result of significant changes in patterns of disposable income, and improvements in personal transport, an urban-based and increasingly mobile sector of society visited the countryside on a larger and larger scale, in some cases began to settle there, and took an increasing interest in preserving it from the insidious effects of modernity. Moreover, as employment in agriculture declined and rural crafts gave way to manufactured goods, both the structure of the village and the aspiration of the villagers changed, in some ways dramatically. Above all, the landscape was affected by the development of new structures of political power at both a local and a national level. Successive political reforms shifted the control of public affairs away from an oligarchy of large landowners, and both local and national government increasingly took over roles which landowners had traditionally exercised, providing rural housing, acquiring extensive tracts of land and leasing it to agricultural tenants, and planting vast areas as national forest. In short, the development of the landscape was not solely moulded by the fortunes of farming, but by a diverse range of forces.

## THE NATURAL FRAME

Farming nevertheless remained the most important influence on the character of the countryside, and local and regional variations in the agricultural economy were to a significant extent structured, as they had always been, by environmental factors: by climate, and by soils and topography, which are themselves largely a product of geology. Chalk is the dominant element in the solid geology of the region, but is exposed on the surface only in the west, as a low escarpment on the edge of the Fens, together with a number of older formations – Gault Clay, Greensand and Kimmeridge Clay.[8] It dips towards the south and east and becomes buried ever deeper beneath more recent 'Crag' deposits, a varied collection of clays, gravels and shelly sands dating from the late Pliocene and early Pleistocene periods; or, in south Suffolk, beneath sands and clays of Tertiary date. But for the most part all this solid geology is blanketed by a diverse range of glacial deposits. The most important is the so-called 'boulder clay', formed from a wide range of detritus – especially Kimmeridge clay and chalk – dragged up by an ice front moving, during the second (Anglian) glaciation, across northern England and through the Midlands. The character of the clay varies greatly, generally being more sandy in northern and central Norfolk and more clayey in south Norfolk and Suffolk. Equally important are the areas of sands and gravels laid down in part in the Anglian but mainly in the succeeding (Devensian and Wolstonian) glaciations. Across much of north and central Norfolk extensive areas of outwash gravels, laid down by streams flowing out of the ice fronts, were deposited; similar deposits occur along the Suffolk coast, here lying directly above the equally sandy Crag. And across a very wide area of north-west Suffolk and south-western Norfolk the high winds blowing close to the ice fronts during the Devensian laid down extensive sandy deposits in the area called Breckland. Lastly, these same high winds also deposited a thin layer of silty material called *loess* across much of the region, most notably in north-east Norfolk and in a scatter of places between Colchester and Ipswich.[9]

Not all of the superficial geology of East Anglia dates to the period of the Ice Ages. Large areas of post-glacial deposits were laid down in valleys and coastal basins as water levels changed and as the structure of the coast was altered by complex processes of erosion and redeposition.[10] Some of these low-lying, wetland deposits – in the lower valleys of the Broads, and in the areas of Fenland lying near the Wash – were silty and clayey in character, and these were mainly drained and farmed, as pasture or arable, from early medieval times. In contrast, various kinds of peat characterise the southern parts of Fenland and the upper valleys of the Broadland rivers, and are also scattered more widely in river valleys throughout the two counties. These areas were generally used as common land in the Middle Ages, when they were grazed in the summer and cut for a variety of products, but many were drained and reclaimed in the course of the post-medieval centuries.[11]

These varied geological formations, coupled with idiosyncrasies of local climate, gave rise to a wide range of soil types which presented the region's farmers with a variety of problems and possibilities (Figure 1).[12] The boulder clay soils, for example, are difficult to cultivate and often poorly draining; yet at the same time they hold lime and nutrients well. The region's sandy soils, in contrast, are freely draining and easy to work; but lime and nutrients are rapidly leached from them, so that they become acid and infertile. Most of the region's soils can, however, be exploited in a number of different ways, and these tended to change over the centuries, partly in response to changes in agricultural technology and partly as a result of wider social and economic developments.

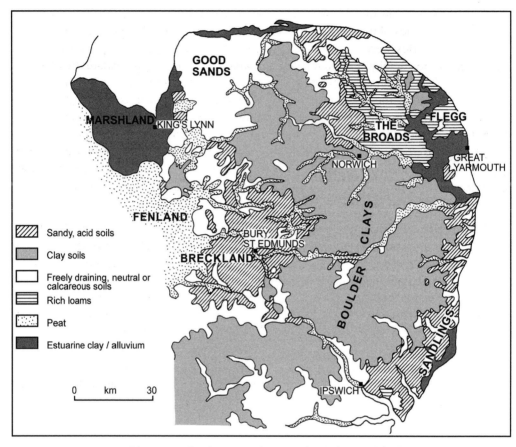

Figure 1. The principal soil regions of East Anglia, as discussed in the text.

In the early Middle Ages all areas of Norfolk and Suffolk were exploited by a multitude of small peasant producers in a variety of mixed-farming systems which everywhere prioritised the production of grain. East Anglia's gentle topography, smoothed and softened by glacial action, its soils, mostly at least moderately fertile and/or easy to cultivate, and its comparatively dry climate together ensured that the region was well suited to the cultivation of cereals, and in the eleventh, twelfth and thirteenth centuries East Anglia was one of the most densely settled areas of England.[13] In the period between the late fourteenth and early eighteenth centuries, in contrast, as a more complex system of market exchange developed, farmers on different soils began to specialise to a greater extent in the production of particular commodities – cattle on the heavy clays, for example, or barley on well-drained calcareous loams.[14] In the course of the eighteenth and nineteenth centuries, in response to improvements in transport systems, industrialisation, urbanisation and other changes in the national economy, there was a further significant shift, and all parts of East Anglia began to concentrate once again on the production of cereals, especially wheat. The various new crops and techniques of the 'agricultural revolution' period of the late eighteenth and early nineteenth centuries were mainly directed towards overcoming problems of soil quality, such as infertility, acidity and water-logging, which held back this expansion of cereal production.[15] The region was at the forefront of agricultural change, and was acknowledged widely at the time as the birthplace of 'modern' farming. In the succeeding 'high farming' period of the mid-nineteenth century, as farming became more industrial and intensive in character, and more dependent on manufactured animal feed and fertilisers, the region may have lost its position at the cutting edge of agriculture, but it remained the breadbasket of England, with production of bullocks now rivalling the cultivation of cereals as the main source of farming profits in many districts. Farming continued to enjoy relatively good fortunes in a period of rising population and rising prices.

The late eighteenth and early nineteenth centuries witnessed a transformation of the East Anglian countryside. In particular districts the removal of open fields was important, but of greater significance was the enclosure of common land. Somewhere between 150,000 and 200,000 acres of common grazing, heath and wetland were converted to private property in the course of the eighteenth and nineteenth centuries, and often 'improved' from rough grazing to arable. This, however, can also be seen as part of a wider shift in the agrarian economy, as pasture of all kinds steadily gave way to arable. In 1700 Norfolk and Suffolk, like most of England, had constituted a complex mosaic of farming regions, some largely pastoral in character, some predominantly arable. By 1850 arable farming dominated the region and, although certain branches of livestock farming remained important, ploughland reigned supreme.

## THE REGIONS OF EAST ANGLIA

Within East Anglia, as elsewhere, local societies and their landscapes tended, to a significant extent, to develop along their own trajectories. They were crucially affected, of course, by national and international trends, but moved nevertheless with a measure of autonomy. At any one point in time systems of farming and land use were not simply structured by economics, communications and the natural environment; they were also a consequence of patterns of settlement, agrarian organisation and property inherited from the past: 'antecedent structures', as landscape historians often call them. Spatial patterns and relationships (and their associated institutional forms) persisted as active and structuring forces long after the circumstances that engendered them had changed beyond recognition. By the nineteenth century the differences between the various regions in Norfolk and Suffolk had been considerably eroded by the overwhelming dominance of arable agriculture and by improvements in communications, yet they remained significant, and in some respects regional variation actually increased once again in the years of the Great Depression.

It is possible to break East Anglia down into a myriad of farming districts, but for the purposes of this book we can reduce this complexity to a few broad regions. The first – small in area but immensely important by the late nineteenth century in terms of image and reputation – is north-west Norfolk, the area described as the 'Good Sands' by the eighteenth-century agriculturalist Arthur Young. Traditionally, this was an area of 'sheep-corn husbandry'.[16] Before the eighteenth century, settlement here was largely concentrated in nucleated villages; arable open fields occupied the more calcareous soils and extensive heaths the poorer ground, where the land was blanketed by thin layers of sandy drift. Fertility was maintained by feeding large flocks of sheep during the day on the heaths and close-folding them at night on the arable, when this lay fallow. This was the landscape transformed by the classic agricultural revolution of the history textbooks. From the early eighteenth century open fields were progressively enclosed, the size of farms was increased and a range of new techniques was adopted, especially the cultivation of turnips and clover in regular rotations with cereal crops in the famous 'Norfolk four-course rotation', or one of its variants. These new crops could be fed off in the field by sheep, or used as fodder for cattle over-wintered in yards. Either way, they increased the number of stock that could be kept, and thus the amount of manure available for the ploughlands, so that cereal yields rose. Moreover, because half the arable land was now devoted to fodder crops, the rough grazing of the heaths was no longer required as a 'nutrient reservoir'. Heathland was enclosed and reclaimed wholesale, a process which involved marling – excavating the chalk and other calcareous material lying beneath the thin layers of sandy drift, and spreading it on the surface to reduce soil acidity. The open prospects of heath and common field were replaced by landscapes of large, rectilinear fields, defined by neat hawthorn hedges – classic 'planned countryside', to use Rackham's term.[17] New breeds of sheep were adopted, designed to stand around getting fat on turnips and grass rather than for eating the rough heathland vegetation and walking long distances each day from grazing to fold and back again.[18] All these developments were closely associated with large estates like Holkham, Houghton and Raynham, which grew steadily in size throughout the period. This was a land of large landowners, large tenanted farms, and landless labourers, whose toil, in return for low wages, was the precondition for agricultural improvement. Only with cheap labour and high grain prices could the fields be marled, the turnips weeded, and the manure spread on the fallows.

The classic techniques of the agricultural revolution – new crops, new livestock breeds, enclosure and marling – worked well in north-west Norfolk. In other areas of light land and sheep-corn husbandry they were less successful. Lying to the south of the Good Sands is Breckland, an extensive but thinly populated district of poor acid soils extending over much of north-west Suffolk and south-west Norfolk. Here the sands lay thick above the underlying chalk, and while many landowners embarked on heroic schemes of reclamation and enclosure, especially when prices were high during the Napoleonic Wars, much heathland survived, and the worst of the arable continued to be farmed in the traditional manner, with short periods of cropping interspersed with long fallows or 'brecks' of eight or more years.

Some of the land reclaimed from heaths, moreover, was abandoned again with the cessation of conflict. Much the same was true of the other heathland areas of East Anglia. In the 'Northern Heathlands' (the intermittent band of poor soils extending northwards from Norwich to the sea), on the Greensand ridge to the north of King's Lynn in west Norfolk, and in the 'Sandlings', or 'Sandlands' (the strip of outwash sands overlying crag which runs all along the Suffolk coast), a paucity of material suitable for marling limited the scale of reclamation, although some inroads were made into the heaths.[19] All these districts of light land had, like the Good Sands, long been characterised by large or medium-sized landed estates, and in most places mansions and parks were prominent features of the landscape. Farms were often even larger than in the Good Sands: the 1851 census shows that the average farm in the Brecklands covered 450 acres, and some holdings cultivated over 1,000. But the economic health of owners and tenants in these districts depended on high grain prices, without which the worst land would not repay cultivation.

The bulk of East Anglia comprises not light land, acid sands and gravels, but a broad belt of boulder clay, characterised by soils which are generally fertile if poorly draining. The nature of landscape and farming across this extensive area varied considerably, depending in particular on the extent to which the clay plateau is cut by valleys, in which soils were generally lighter, and on the proportion of sand incorporated within the clay.[20] In general, the soils are particularly poorly draining on the level plateau of south Norfolk and north-east Suffolk. In south-west Suffolk they are generally heavier, but are interspersed to a greater degree with bands of lighter valley soil, and the landscape in general is more undulating and thus easier to drain. In central Norfolk, at the northern end of the plateau, the clays were often intermixed with pockets of sands and gravels. Despite these differences, all these districts were, however, areas of 'ancient countryside', characterised by dispersed settlement (isolated farms and common-edge agglomerations), early enclosure and frequent woods and commons. Large estates, mansion and parklands were never as prominent as they were in the light soil, sheep-corn areas. It is true that, by the nineteenth century, large landowners had managed to acquire much of the land here, but often only as scattered blocks. In part, this essential difference in tenurial and social structures between light lands and heavy dates back to the early Middle Ages, but it was accentuated by the fact that in the fifteenth, sixteenth and seventeenth centuries the clays had become cattle-farming country, with only small areas of arable, an agricultural bias which tended to favour the survival of comparatively small units of production and of ownership. By the middle of the nineteenth century there were some large farms on the claylands, usually where land had been acquired by major landowners, but the most characteristic feature of the district – especially on the heavier clays of north Suffolk and south Norfolk – was the plethora of small farms, those covering fifty acres or less. Indeed, across much of the claylands the average holding size in 1851 was below 100 acres.

The development of livestock husbandry on the claylands in the early modern period was encouraged not only by the nature of the soils, which produced reasonable grass, but also by the character of the local field systems inherited from the medieval past.[21] In some areas there were extensive commons where cattle could be grazed, especially where the plateau was most level. More importantly, in some areas enclosed fields – suitable for livestock husbandry – had always dominated the landscape. And where open fields existed these were usually of highly 'irregular' form, easily enclosed – in this district of weak manorialisation – piecemeal, through informal agreement. These 'wood-pasture' landscapes of hedged pasture fields, numerous farmland trees and damp commons were, however, transformed once again in the course of the agricultural revolution period. By 1850 the claylands had become wheat-growing country. Versions of the 'new rotations' were widely adopted in clayland districts, albeit with local variations, but the other classic techniques employed on the light lands, such as marling, were here of minor importance. Instead it was the adoption of under-drainage, using bush drains and subsequently tile pipes, which was the key improvement, together with the large-scale simplification of the ancient, 'bosky' landscape through field amalgamation and the thinning of pollards and other hedgerow trees.[22]

The other distinctive landscapes of Norfolk and Suffolk are the various wetlands, the largest of which is Fenland, in the west of the region. This actually comprises two distinct areas. The silt Fens – close to the Wash – have been settled and farmed since the Middle Ages.[23] It was the wide expanse of the peat Fens, to the south, which was the object of the great drainage campaigns of the seventeenth century. These had been only partially successful, and both peats and silts lay, in the eighteenth century, largely under pasture.[24] From the 1790s, however, both went the same way as the clays. Enclosure of the remaining Fenland commons, improvements in arterial drainage, and above all – from the early nineteenth century – the spread of steam drainage allowed more and more of the area to be cultivated as arable. By the 1870s most of this fertile land was under the plough, producing vast quantities of wheat and, increasingly, potatoes.[25] Some large farms existed, but here too the landscape was dominated by substantial numbers of small family enterprises, especially on the old-enclosed siltlands, where over 40 per cent of holdings were under fifty acres.[26]

Fenland was, however, in some respects unique. As well as being, by a long way, the most extensive wetland area in East Anglia, it was also the only one which, during the course of the eighteenth and nineteenth centuries, fell wholesale to the plough. The others – the silt marshes of the eastern Broads, the ribbons of peat fen in the upper valleys of the Broadland rivers and in various other valleys scattered across the region, the coastal marshes of north Norfolk, and those all along the Suffolk coast – all these remained largely unploughed even after enclosure and were used as grazing marsh or, in the case of the valley fens, as a source of rough grazing, marsh hay, reeds, sedge and peat.

Of the many other minor districts, with their own distinctive character and agrarian histories, only one needs to be noted here. In the north-east of Norfolk, immediately to the north of the Broads – on the former island of Flegg and in the adjacent areas – the soils are particularly fertile and tractable. Since the early Middle Ages this district had been characterised by a plethora of relatively small estates and relatively small arable farms, some of which also held land on the adjacent marshes. As in the Fens, over 40 per cent of farms in 1851 covered less than fifty acres. There were very few large estates, mansions or parklands here, and the settlement pattern was dispersed, like that of the claylands to the south. The soils of this district, combined with its distinctive tenurial structure, destined it for a particular role in the new agrarian economy which emerged from the late nineteenth century. As we shall see, to some extent the other regions briefly described above continued to follow their own trajectories of agricultural and landscape development into the twentieth century.

## ON THE BRINK OF THE DEPRESSION

In the early 1870s, on the brink of the Great Depression, East Anglia was an overwhelmingly rural region. Only King's Lynn, Ipswich and Norwich, and to a lesser extent Bury St Edmunds, were substantial population centres. Norwich had lost most of its traditional textile industry by this time but it continued to be a centre for leatherworking and brewing, and it supplied a wide variety of services to its hinterland.[27] Its population grew significantly, from around 37,000 in 1800 to 68,000 in 1850. By the 1840s it was already beginning to expand beyond its medieval walls.[28] Ipswich also grew rapidly in the course of the nineteenth century, especially following the construction of the Wet Dock in the 1830s and the arrival of the railway in 1846. This was the home of Ransomes, manufacturers of agricultural machinery and, by the later nineteenth century, lawnmowers.[29]

Smaller market towns were scattered across the region, generally at intervals of around 20 km, and provided the range of services essential for their rural hinterlands. Their businesses and facilities included manufacturers of agricultural implements (such as Garrett's of Leiston, Randells of North Walsham, Plowrights of Swaffham and Burrells of Thetford, to name but a few); elegant corn halls in which agricultural business could be transacted; and the corn merchants and maltings to which farm produce could be sold. These smaller urban centres were linked to each other, and to many villages, by a particularly dense railway network: following the last additions to the system in the 1880s few settlements lay more than 10 km from a station, except in parts of west Suffolk.[30]

For the most part, however, the landscape of Norfolk and Suffolk was a rural one, of fields, farms and villages, and the bulk of the underpaid workforce was engaged in farming. It was, moreover, by now a primarily arable region, with around 80 per cent of the cultivated acreage of both counties being devoted to crops or rotational grass. Barley was the most important crop on all the lighter land, but on the claylands and the Fenlands especially wheat held pride of place as the main commodity produced by farmers. Livestock were by no means neglected, however. Not only were sheep and cattle indispensable producers of manure but the production of bullocks, in particular, had intensified in the Victorian 'high farming' period as the penetration of the railways deeper into the two counties allowed easy access to distant urban markets. The animals were mainly fed in yards during the winter on manufactured feed and on fodder grown in rotation with the cereal crops, and in summer they were grazed on rotational grass rather than on permanent pastures.[31]

Crops and rotational grass did not dominate everywhere. Some areas of permanent pasture existed, principally in Broadland and on the coastal grazing marshes of north Norfolk and along the Suffolk coast; and a scatter of wet fens, cut for peat, reeds, sedge and marsh hay, remained in the valleys of the Broadland rivers, and dispersed more widely across the region. A surprisingly large area of heathland had also survived the reclamations and mania for 'improvement' which characterised the later eighteenth and early nineteenth centuries. Small pockets of pasture and meadow existed everywhere and, on the claylands especially, numerous ancient, semi-natural woods remained, mostly still managed on traditional lines, as coppice-with-standards. But it was, nevertheless, the broad expanses of arable which contemporaries considered the most distinctive feature of the East Anglia countryside, and in this respect at least the landscape of the two counties in the 1870s resembled that of today. Yet, in many other ways, it was radically different.

Apart from the existence of the numerous areas of heath, fen and other rough grazing, the land surface was divided into a plethora of small fields: there was, almost everywhere, an abundance of hedges and hedgerow trees. Nowhere would we have found the vast expanses of undivided cereals, stretching to the far horizon, which characterise many parts of the region today. Country houses – more numerous than today, standing in elaborate, manicured gardens and within spacious parklands – would have been present to some extent almost everywhere but especially, as we have noted, in areas of poorer and lighter land. Even major roads had only rudimentary surfacing, council houses were non-existent, village halls a rarity, and no memorials had yet been erected to commemorate the dead of two World Wars. Many features which we now think of as characteristic of the East Anglian landscape, such as the vast conifer plantations of Breckland and the Sandlings, had yet to make their appearance.

Rural life would have seemed even more unfamiliar than the landscape. Tractors, combine harvesters, cars and buses were all absent; most people worked on the land, their social and geographical horizons circumscribed; inequalities of wealth were stark, extreme and obvious, for although in 1870 farming remained profitable, most of the wealth produced went not to those who worked the land but to the larger farmers and to their landlords, some of whom owned estates covering 30,000 acres or more. In many parishes, life was still dominated by the squire and the church. Where it was not, the influence of the nonconformist chapels was usually strong.

# CHAPTER 2

# Farming in Depression

## THE ONSET OF DEPRESSION: 1870–1900

Most historians agree about the overall pattern of agricultural change in Britain in the late nineteenth century. From the mid-1870s prices fell and farming began to slide into a long period of depression. The principal cause was the expansion of the American railway network into the prairies of the Midwest, which meant that European markets were flooded with large quantities of cheap grain. Prices, rents and land values all fell steeply in the course of the 1880s. After a brief period of stabilisation a further intense depression occurred after 1896, this time affecting not only arable farmers but also livestock producers, as cheap meat and dairy produce were imported, on refrigerated ships, from the New World and Australia.[1]

Both later historians and commentators writing in the early years of the twentieth century – such as Lord Ernle – presented an extremely gloomy picture of British farming as a whole in this period,[2] but from the 1960s historians began to question the ubiquity of the late nineteenth-century depression. In 1961 Fletcher demonstrated that the arable regions of the east suffered more than those devoted to livestock husbandry,[3] while in 1974 Perry used the evidence of farming bankruptcy rates to suggest that this distinction was too simplistic, not least because most English farms were in fact mixed enterprises; a division between 'breeders' and 'feeders' might be more accurate.[4] Thompson, in 1990, using the evidence of rents and of percentage changes in gross farm outputs, concluded that 'The notion that there was a general and chronic depression in English Agriculture throughout the period, or even between the mid-'70s and '90s, must be abandoned'.[5] More recently, work by Hunt and Pam in Essex, and by Brown in Lincolnshire, has suggested that while there was enough distress amongst farmers and landlords to merit the description of 'depression', this did not mean that 'high' farming was entirely abandoned.[6] It would perhaps be more accurate, in the light of recent work, to describe the period as one of irregular downward movements necessitating painful adjustments, with occasional ameliorations.[7] Cereal farmers were certainly suffering badly from cheap imports but profits from livestock, although declining, were never as seriously hit. Most profitable were perishable goods such as fruit, vegetables, poultry, pigs and milk: cereal producers who could diversify at least part of their enterprises into these areas, particularly if they were within reach of urban markets, did not suffer anything like as much as their fellows.

Wheat prices dropped steadily through the late 1870s and East Anglian farmers and landowners certainly entered the 1880s with some trepidation. Their anxiety is evident from diaries and letters, although it is interesting that most people initially blamed a run of poor weather for the problems in farming, rather than shifts in the economics of world agriculture. The dry summer of 1870 meant that the light land on the Rope family's farm at Blaxhall in east Suffolk, for example, produced only a poor crop, although that on the heavier lands, and on the ploughed marshes, could be described as 'fine'. In 1875 the corn on all descriptions of land was very promising until the beginning of July, when the weather changed: both wheat and barley on the heavy ground was then beaten down by the rain and became mildewed. There was another wet season in 1878 and the grain sprouted in the shocks, while 1879 was the wettest year since 1860 and the grain sprouted as it stood. Land was flooded in July and hay washed away. Corn was carted in a poor condition and stacks had to be taken down because they were overheating.[8] A farmer at Green Farm, Stowupland (Suffolk), simply described 1879 as 'the black year'. There was snow at rye-seeding time, and the clover and hay were spoilt by a very wet summer. The corn contained more weeds than ever before and the harvest was late and bad. As if this wasn't enough, 1880 was another wet year in which only the root crops did well. In 1881 there was a good hay crop, but the corn harvest was again spoiled.[9] Only sheep kept up their prices to some extent, and this was partly because of a scarcity of stock caused by disease. There was disease, too, in cattle. In the autumn of 1882 George Gladden of Hickling in east Norfolk reported foot and mouth in sixteen bullocks, and the markets were closed until April the following year.[10] A more serious outbreak occurred in 1886.

This series of natural disasters tended to obscure the true cause of the deepening depression, and Lord Monson's Lincolnshire agent was not entirely atypical when he wrote, in 1879, that 'notwithstanding all that is said of the competition with America, I can not doubt that two or three good harvests would restore the previous state of things'.[11] However, by 1884 Henry Chaplin realised that 'low prices rather than bad seasons were the root of agriculture's difficulties'.[12] Wheat prices were halved between 1873 and 1893, while those for barley and oats fell by a third. Meat went down by between 15 per cent and 20 per cent, and butter and cheese by 15 per cent. In the case of Norfolk and Suffolk, Thompson has calculated that the fall in value of gross farm output between 1873 and 1894 was 14 per cent.[13] This figure, which includes all types of agricultural produce, does not indicate the total collapse of farming in the 'arable' east.[14] Nevertheless, an agricultural industry experiencing falling prices and abrupt changes in relative commodity values was certainly facing the need for radical and uncomfortable changes.

Livestock production, and other alternatives to arable farming, could still be profitable. In 1884 George Gladden bought sixty-five bullocks for £591, spent £131 on cake and also fed them with the roots grown on thirty-one acres. He sold them for £1,022, making a profit, not counting labour costs, of £300. In 1892 he bought stock for £750, spent £305 on feed and sold for £1,233, leaving a profit of £178. In the 1890s his yearly profit was usually over £200, but by the 1900s was between £400 and £700. He was also selling pigs and Christmas turkeys.[15] Many farmers, like the Fishers of Letheringsett, made reasonable amounts of money from eggs and poultry, and market gardens and orchards remained profitable.[16] But in the 1880s and 90s the vast majority of farmers in the region continued to specialise in arable production, and therefore did badly as the price of wheat continued to fall. Many owner-occupiers were forced to sell up, but notes on sales catalogues in a variety of archive collections suggest that prices fell from between £30 and £50 an acre in 1870 to £20 or less by 1900. On the Earl of Stradbroke's estates in east Suffolk land values fell by between a half and a third between 1873 and 1894.[17] Rents also fell. At Holkham, rental income peaked at nearly £60,000 in 1880 after being between £55,000 and £58,000 for most of the 1870s, only to fall away rapidly to just over £43,000 by 1888.[18] Tenants were becoming hard to find, and were in recalcitrant mood. The situation on the Hare estate in west Norfolk was probably typical: while seeking a new tenant for Fincham Hall Farm in 1893 the agent candidly admitted that 'A man needs a good bit of courage to take land at any price at the present time'. The new tenant, Mr Mason, took up the holding only after protracted negotiations, during which he forced the estate to accede to most of his demands.[19] When Mr Clifton, another tenant, was obliged to give up his tenancy of the mill at Shouldham in 1896 he informed the estate that he could not make a living out of farming alone. 'The mill being stopped makes a difference to me as I have only coming in what the land produces and that is not enough to pay labour and has not been for the last few years. If rent could be reduced and I could have twenty or thirty more acres at the same expense, I could manage.'[20] Everywhere on the estate tenants were leaving and farms proving difficult to let.

What was true on the Hare estate was true more or less everywhere. In 1883 Mr Marshall, one of the Duke of Portland's tenants at West Lynn, was anxious to leave: 'Things are looking so serious now on the farm from the wet weather that we have quite made up our minds to leave as soon as we possibly can.' This would have meant breaking the terms of their lease, but it 'cannot be the Duke's wish to keep us here losing money year after year as we are now doing'. After protracted negotiations, the Marshalls stayed with a reduction in rent from a high farming peak of £1,075 to £620 per annum.[21] In 1888 a tenant in Thompson, on the Merton estate in the Norfolk Breckland, could not afford a rent of more than £200, a reduction of £60 on the previous year. As the agent, Henry Wood, noted: 'Even this reduction is much less than many persons have had to make and many more would be willing to make if they could keep their farms occupied.'[22] Like agents everywhere, he advised keeping farms tenanted, even if this meant reduced rents, although 'There are now more people anxious to get out of farming than go in.'[23] 'The fact is farmers have little or no money. More than three fourths of the farmers in this and other counties are kept afloat by the bankers.'[24] 'Few farmers have capital and those there are do not want to risk it in farming'.[25]

Turner, Becket and Afton's research suggests that rents across England as a whole averaged 28s per acre in 1875, an amount which dropped to 22s in 1890 before rising slightly by 1900.[26] Not surprisingly, in arable East Anglia the decline was slightly greater, rents falling by 38 per cent in Suffolk and by 31 per cent in Norfolk between 1879 and 1895.[27] This meant, in turn, that there was little money available for building or land improvements at a time when these were most needed to enable farmers to change direction – and when farmers were most in a position to demand them. Lord Monson's agent voiced the feelings of many when he wrote to his employer in 1884 that 'the demand for expenditure on the estate grows daily while the means of meeting it diminishes.'[28] Nevertheless, it is clear that on many estates the proportion of income spent on improvements was maintained, or even increased, at this time. On the Holkham estate, for example, expenditure on buildings remained constant, at over 10 per cent per annum, through the 1880s and 90s, and new ranges of cattle sheds were built on many farms.[29] The Kentwell Hall estate spent £200 on new buildings at Stanstead Hall in 1874 and £191 at Broom Farm, Glemsford, in 1879.[30] On the Heydon estate in Norfolk new bullock and implement sheds and turnip, hay and manure houses were erected in many places in the 1880s: at Churchgate Farm, Wood Dalling, for example, a six-stall cowhouse, with a calf box and turnip house on one end and a feeding passage behind, was built in 1882.[31] When East End and Wickmere farms were leased by Lord Orford in 1900 the agreement stipulated that new buildings were to be erected on both holdings.[32] Some owners, such as Lord Cadogan at Culford in west Suffolk, continued to erect farmsteads as flamboyant as anything seen in the years of 'high farming' prosperity. Built in 1890 as an extension to an earlier Home Farm, the new buildings here included two covered yards and a cow house for forty-eight prize Jersey cows. Tramlines ran along the feeding passages with turntables at the corners to allow the trucks carrying feed to be turned through ninety degrees. The walls were tiled, and patent cast-iron stalls and sliding doors installed.[33] Building projects were sometimes aimed at encouraging particular tenants to stay on. In 1891, when John Hastings of Longham threatened for the third time to leave his Holkham farm, he was persuaded to stay by the offer of a new field yard for cattle, which was duly erected at a cost of £184 the following year.[34]

Expenditure on drainage also increased on many estates, particularly those on the heavier clays. A farm at Rumburgh on the Adair estates in Suffolk was completely tile-drained in 1882–3.[35] On the Kimberley estates in Norfolk there was a spurt of activity in the 1880s, when over £100 was spent in most years on drainage (with a peak of £306 in 1883).[36] Many estates turned to the Government Loan Companies for help and nearly £40,000 was lent to owners in Norfolk and Suffolk between 1875 and 1900.[37] By far the largest borrower was the Adair estate at Flixton, receiving £20,000: £7,606 was spent on farm buildings and on six new pairs of labourers' cottages, the rest on roads and land improvement.[38] Other major borrowers included Lord Stafford, who, between 1879 and 1894, received £3,273, half of which was for buildings and half for the improvement of watercourses on his Costessey estate near Norwich. In the 1880s the Marquis of Townshend of Raynham in Norfolk borrowed nearly £1,000 for drainage and land reclamation, and £1,666 for buildings, while in the 1890s over £2,000 was borrowed by the Raveningham estate.[39]

But it was not only the large landowners, borrowing heavily from the government, who invested in drainage schemes and similar improvements even as the depression deepened. Small owners were also involved, although their activities are, of course, less well documented. John Baxter, owner-occupier of Grange Farm at Pulham Market in south Norfolk, kept a careful account of all his drainage work between 1887 and 1895.[40] In 1888 First Low Field and Eleven Acres were drained at a cost of £5 10s. Two men spent five days digging drains on Station Meadow and laying 850 pipes. New hedges were planted and fields cleared of stones. And he was not alone: George Gladden bought 800 pipes to drain land at Hickling in 1889 but was also busy 'brushing' (bush draining) in 1892 and 1893.[41]

This admittedly rather circumstantial evidence suggests that the gloomy picture painted by the Royal Commission into the 'depressed state of agriculture', which reported in 1881, may have exaggerated the extent of rural decline: indeed, it is now widely accepted that its findings were heavily biased towards the problems of the large cereal producers of the east. Two substantial East Anglian farmers, Henry Overman of Weasenham, Norfolk,[42] and Herman Biddell of Playford, Suffolk,[43] both gave evidence to the Commission. Although their farms were very different (Henry Overman farmed 1,300 acres of mainly light land in north-west Norfolk and Herman Biddell 440 acres near Ipswich, 120 acres of which was low meadow), their evidence agreed on many points. Overman reported that Lord Leicester (of whom he was a tenant) had four farms amounting to 3,000 acres in hand, while seven farms near Biddell had recently become vacant. Both men agreed that rents had been too high, although they were now everywhere being cut in order to keep farms occupied, sometimes by as much as 30 per cent. They also thought that rates, tithes and agricultural wages had risen – Overman somewhat bizarrely claiming that the labourers 'lived in affluence'! Both men were convinced that crop yields were going down, and that more manure was needed than previously to maintain productivity. The five and a quarter bushels of barley an acre which had often been reached in the high-farming years were never now attained. Another witness, Sir E.C. Kerrison, blamed the decline on the 'injurious and unscientific use of artificial manures', and on the fact that 'straw was being cut into chaff for feed and therefore was not available to make into farm yard manure'. Edward Beck, the agent to the Sandringham estate, similarly believed that land reclaimed from sheepwalk in the previous century had now lost its fertility 'owing to the instrumentality of artificial manures'.[44]

The Commissioner for the eastern counties, Mr Druce, visited Norfolk in 1880 and concluded that external indications of depression were not as great as in many other districts. There was no lack of livestock in the yards, no uncultivated fields. Unlet farms were usually taken in hand: most landowners farmed their home farm, together with another. But land was being farmed less intensively, with fewer artificial fertilisers being used.[45] A year later he reported again. Farmers with capital made in the good years could still afford to fill their yards with cattle; but the smaller landowners and farmers were suffering more. Most land remained in cultivation, but fences, ditches and drains were being neglected.[46] The situation in Suffolk was rather worse, according to Druce's report of 1881, in part because the opportunities to diversify in west and central Suffolk were hampered by a lack of railways. In one parish of 3,200 acres, 300 acres were unlet and 175 acres had recently been given up.[47] By 1895, when a second Commission reported, things were said to have deteriorated further. Wilson Fox's report described, in particular, increasing problems in Breckland, where 5,000 acres lay untenanted, huge farm premises stood unlet, and game preservation was taking precedence over farming.[48] Rider Haggard painted a similarly depressing picture in 1902. For £1,000 a man could be put into a profession, whereas to farm he needed £3,000. In the Suffolk Sandlings, and in Breckland, tenants were giving up and their land was being used for training racehorses or shooting. The heavier lands also presented a dismal appearance. In the area round Lavenham in Suffolk the country was 'bleak, lonesome and undulating. The parishes in this area were badly farmed and full of misery.'[49] The only profits were to be made either in intensive production for the urban market, as in the case of Mr Dyer, who kept 1,000 geese, turkeys and ducks on his seventy-acre farm, or in farming on a large scale. Mr Carlton of Great Waldringfield, for example, farmed seven farms as one – 'thus land that had supported seven farms now supported one'. Mr Beck of Ormsby told Haggard that farmers 'didn't go bankrupt, but they vanished and some of them died broken-hearted'. Farms were not being taken on by farmers' sons.[50]

Whilst the evidence submitted to Royal Commissions and the views of writers like Haggard provide useful information, it will be apparent that they need to be treated with caution. Much of the former was given by large farmers and landowners hoping for some form of government action to relieve the situation; Haggard and others had their own political agendas. Other observers were certainly more sanguine: Edmund Beck's report on the Hare's fen-edge Stow Bardolph estate in 1883 stated that in spite of 'this difficult season when agriculture has been turned upside down … I deem it impossible to find in Norfolk or any other county a similar area of land wearing the same prosperous appearance and being held by such a body of tenantry', all of whom were farming well.[51] In Norfolk and Suffolk, as in the areas of Essex studied by Hunt and Pam, farmers displayed a high degree of resilience and sought a number of ways out of their troubles.[52]

One possible reaction was to cut labour costs by turning to mechanisation,[53] but in East Anglia this policy seldom seems to have been adopted. True, new technology was regularly displayed at the county agricultural shows: at King's Lynn a prize was offered in 1872 for the best stacking and elevating machine, and throughout the 1870s the air at both the Norfolk and Suffolk shows would have been thick with the smoke from traction engines.[54] Fowlers (London), Robey (Lincoln), Woods (Stowmarket), Burrells (Thetford), Garrett (Leiston) and Eddington (Chelmsford) were all exhibiting traction and portable steam engines at the Suffolk show in 1876.[55] Oil engines first appeared at the Suffolk show in 1898 and Holmes and Sons of Norwich brought a 'collection of oil and gas engines with food preparing machinery and pumps in motion' to the Norfolk show in 1900.[56] But prices, particularly those for traction engines, were high: in the last decades of the century most were priced at between £200 and £400,[57] but Howard of Bedford's Farmers Locomotive with 'self-moving

Figure 2. Getting in the harvest at Bracon Ash, Norfolk, c.1905. Steam traction engines were only very sparingly adopted by East Anglian farmers.

automatic anchor and self-lifting cultivation apparatus designed with detachable windlass for use for thrashing, hauling and ploughing' was offered for sale at £750 in 1877.[58] While traction engines had already, before the start of the depression, been widely employed by contractors for threshing, they were too expensive for the average farmer, and few seem to have been used for ploughing or other routine tasks (Figure 2).

Other than labour, the two main expenses for East Anglian farmers were feed and artificial manures, and, at some places, as on the Holkham estate, expenditure on these declined markedly in the last thirty years of the century.[59] For most farmers, however, a shift of emphasis away from wheat production was the most promising course. Between 1880 and 1895 the area under wheat decreased in Norfolk from 184,284 to 106,812 acres, and in Suffolk from 139,538 to 88,204. True, the area under barley rose slightly (from 203,387 to 203,980 acres in Norfolk, and from 203,387 to 203,980 in Suffolk), reflecting continuing demand from an expanding brewing industry; as did the area under oats, a consequence of the expansion of horse-drawn transport in urban areas. Overall, however, the total cereal and pulse crop was down by 40,187 acres in Norfolk and 42,503 in Suffolk. In contrast, the total area of both rotational and permanent grass rose from 424,912 acres to 467,790 in Norfolk and from 251,457 to 298,383 in Suffolk.[60] As Fox put it in his report on Suffolk, 'a newly laid out paddock of permanent grass is not an uncommon sight'.[61] At the Norfolk Agricultural

Show of 1888 Suttons offered a free booklet entitled 'Full information for laying down new and improving old grasslands'. The following year Webbs offered 'An essay on permanent pasture'.[62]

Not all forms of livestock farming were equally profitable, however, although the pattern varied from district to district, even from year to year. On the Home Farm at Holkham profits from sheep dropped significantly after 1870, while those from cattle remained relatively steady.[63] On the Merton estate in west Norfolk, in contrast, Lord Walsingham's prize sheep continued to be sought after, and became the most profitable enterprise on the Home Farm, sales realising as much as £3,200 in 1888.[64] As late as the 1890s they were still the most profitable part of the home farm enterprise, making over £1,000 in most years.[65] This was unusual. On the whole, profits from sheep and beef cattle declined, income from livestock sales on the Home Farm at Holkham continuing to fall into the 1900s.[66] Indeed, throughout the region the numbers of livestock decreased, with those for sheep falling by 220,790 in Norfolk and by 215,791 in Suffolk between 1880 and 1895, in spite of the expansion of the area under pasture.[67] In part this was because it was the worst land which was generally laid to grass, land which also made relatively poor pasture ('what people call grass, but what we call weeds', as the *Eastern Daily Press* reporter noted in 1895, quoting from the Essex report to the Royal Commission).[68]

It was dairying, more then other forms of livestock husbandry, which expanded significantly in this period, especially on farms in the vicinity of railway stations.[69] Already in 1886 the entries for the Farm Prize Competition suggest that increasing numbers of farmers were moving in this direction.[70] Mr Garrett Taylor at Whittlingham, near Norwich, was able to utilise town sewage to produce rich grass crops which he both sold as forage and fed to a dairy herd.[71] On heavy land near Hingham in Norfolk dairying had become the basis for one farming business; milk was sent by train twice-daily to London, having been refrigerated at the nearby station.[72] The Eastern Counties Dairy Institute was set up in 1888 to provide education and encouragement for dairy farmers, and in the same year prizes began to be offered in a dairy section at the Suffolk Agricultural Show, where from 1891 the Institute, based at Akenham, had a stand which included a working dairy.[73] A capillary refrigerator which cooled 125 gallons an hour was also demonstrated. By the 1890s, the London-based Dairy Supply Company felt it worthwhile to have a stand at the Norfolk Show, and one of the products it displayed in 1897 was a 'milk filter to clear milk of the finest sediment … most important for all those who deal with milk in transparent vessels'.[74] There were frequent articles on the subject in the local press, and milking machines in particular were seen as having an important future. The *Eastern Daily Press* urged farmers to 'make the most of their opportunities in the dairy' and described the grand opening of a model dairy on Mr Blyth's farm at Stanstead in Suffolk where 'everything was on most approved principles' and worked by electricity.[75] Many East Anglian farms were let to tenants from Scottish dairying areas, who came with their Ayrshire cows:[76] the only person offering to take on two farms at Saxthorpe in Norfolk in 1897 was a Scotsman.[77]

The increased importance of dairying led some to consider the possibility of making silage, a technique already widely practised in Europe. It was the publication of a book by the French agriculturalist Auguste Goffart which brought the technique to the attention of British farmers and landowners, some of whom dubbed the 1880s, rather over-enthusiastically, the 'decade of ensilage'.[78] In 1884 the Royal Agricultural Society commissioned an investigation into the technique. Questionnaires were sent out to British farmers and replies received from, among others, Lord Walsingham at Merton, Norfolk, Col. Tomline of Orwell Park and the Duke of Hamilton at Easton, both in Suffolk. Some silos were placed partly below ground or built into slopes; others were constructed within redundant barns, partitioned off into cement-lined sections. Generally the grass was tipped in, trodden down by horses and then topped with weighted boards.[79] The *JRASE* reported on a 'silo and silage stack competition' in 1886, and in the same year Mr Garrett Taylor's silo at Whitlingham was described and illustrated in the report on the Farm Prize Competition.[80] Lord Walsingham was one of the most enthusiastic promoters of the system, building a new silo at Merton in Norfolk in 1885 which he claimed would be 'one of the best if not *the* best in the kingdom';[81] ten acres of sorghum and a crop of buckwheat were grown on the estate experimentally as silage crops.[82] Walsingham offered a prize of ten guineas at the Norfolk Show for 'the best plan and specifications and estimated cost of a silo of 50 tons capacity',[83] and in 1886 became president of the short-lived Ensilage Society. Unfortunately, it proved difficult to keep the clamps airtight and there is no record of silage being made on the Walsingham estate after the very wet summer of 1880. Other farmers seem to have lost interest around the same time. Nevertheless, the story suggests that innovation and enthusiasm, as much as apathy and despair, were displayed by East Anglian farmers in the early years of the depression.

The seriousness of the problems faced by farmers in the late nineteenth century depended on a range of factors: how far they were able to diversify into dairying or the other new forms of agriculture, especially poultry production and horticulture; the attitudes of their landlord, where they had one; and, perhaps above all, on the location of their holdings. Areas of poor, light, acid land were particularly badly hit, especially Breckland. On the heavier soils the situation was more patchy. Some farmers were able to devote themselves to milk production, especially where their enterprises lay close to a rail station, and thus kept their heads above water: men like Mr Mclauchlan, a defaulting tenant of the Flixton estate, who in 1894 was reprieved from eviction and wrote to the agent that 'With the increase in milk, I should be able to keep matters from getting any worse and hope to remain here for a time if allowed'. Others failed: when the tenant of Oaklands Farm on the same estate left his farm in 1896 the arable was foul and the ditches, marshes and hedges had been neglected.[84]

The size of the farming enterprise was also perhaps a factor, and there was much discussion nationally about the relative merits of small and large farms. Clare Sewell Read undertook a survey for the Royal Agricultural Society on the subject.[85] Although smaller farms were typically found in the pastoral areas of the country, Read reckoned that there were 12,000 farms under fifty acres in Norfolk in 1897 (the 1895 Agricultural Returns record

8,950 for Norfolk and 3,602 for Suffolk). Read concluded that in arable regions small farmers were less able than their larger neighbours to stock their farms adequately in these bad times.[86] This rather traditional view of the essential superiority of larger holdings did not, however, take account of a changing emphasis in farming towards market gardening and new livestock enterprises such as dairying, pigs and poultry. Nor was it a view shared by everyone. In 1894 Thomas Rose undertook a survey of the Gunton estate in north Norfolk and argued that it was a mistake to amalgamate farms, partly because this resulted in one set of buildings being under-utilised. The house would be used by a labourer or bailiff, and the buildings not properly looked after. Low Farm, South Repps, should 'never have been allowed to be farmed off-hand especially in such bad times as the present – all neglected'. Goulders Farm, Felmingham, covered only eighty-six acres but Rose considered 'these small holdings of great importance and if a good tenant has been found, it would be worth while considering the improvement of the buildings'. 'The day of the large farm is over'.[87]

Many observers believed that those who were prepared to accept the life of a working rather than a gentleman farmer were also more likely to succeed. 'The tenant at Tuckwell Hall Farm [on the Walsingham estate] gets up at five every morning to feed his large herd of pigs and is not ashamed of speaking of it'.[88] The agent at Wolterton in Norfolk thought that £10 an acre was the capital required, although 'if a man intends to work himself, he might deduct two pounds'.[89] Part-time farming may also have experienced something of a comeback. Edward Scutton of Brandeston, Suffolk, who won a second prize in the Farm-Prize Competition of 1886, farmed forty-seven acres, but was also a wheelwright, carpenter and timber merchant.[90] A farm at Waldringham in Suffolk was run at a loss in the late 1870s and 80s, but its owner made good profits digging coprolites for Edward Packard's fertiliser works in Bramford.[91] Rider Haggard stated in 1902 that 'nearly all the landholders' in the area around North Walsham in north Norfolk 'had a trade which they combined with their farming'.[92]

It would thus be wrong, as Hunt and Pam have already pointed out, to accuse farmers of not being prepared to change, of being passive victims of economic crisis. The agricultural statistics make it clear that late nineteenth-century farmers were moving out of the main loss-making commodity, wheat, and taking up new forms of production. Farmers were aware that they were being accused of being slow to adapt, 'but gradual change is usually more satisfactory than violent measures'.[93]

## THE EARLY TWENTIETH CENTURY

1896 was the worst farming year of the nineteenth century, but the following years saw a noticeable recovery in farming fortunes, in East Anglia as elsewhere. The author of the preface of *Webb's Farm Account Book* noted in 1905 that much land in the region was as well cultivated as it had been thirty years before and that the deep soils of east Norfolk had 'held their own'. Herman Biddell's essay on Suffolk agriculture of 1907, while less optimistic, nevertheless suggests a picture of relative vitality. Cattle were being improved by importing

North Country bulls, while on clayland farms milk production was continuing to increase in significance. Potatoes were also becoming more important, as were pigs and eggs. 'The co-operative at Framlingham has given an enormous boost to the egg industry and thus to the small farmer.'[94] The accounts of some individual farms support this cautiously optimistic picture. Spencer Symonds of Shackerland Farm, Badwell Ash, Suffolk, made a loss of £56 in 1896 but his fortunes gradually turned thereafter, so that by 1900 he was making an annual profit of over £200.[95] The unnamed Suffolk farm whose history was reviewed by Carson in 1935 showed a profit in all but three of the years between 1900 and 1914, giving an average yearly profit of £160 and a return on investment of 6.3 per cent. This was a significant improvement on the previous ten years, when the average return had been only 3.6 per cent.[96] By the early 1900s total factor income in England as a whole had returned to the levels of the early 1880s, and, by 1911–1914, those of the late 1870s.[97] One indication that the condition of farming was improving was the increased interest shown by the press in new agricultural machines. Accounts of and advertisements for root cleaners, horse-drawn hay rakes, and turnip hoeing and singling machines appeared in some numbers, along with descriptions of such innovations as a 'power-driven fruit spraying plant' and an 'agricultural oil tractor'.[98]

The production of milk, eggs, poultry, fruit and vegetables continued to expand. Even on the majority of farms, which continued to be involved primarily in arable husbandry, there was often some deviation from established practice. One Suffolk heavy-land farm, described in detail in an article in the *JRASE*, was still run according to a fairly strict four-course rotation at the start of the century, but there was a noticeable shift after 1910 from sheep and bullock fattening to pigs and dairying.[99] While nationally the income from wheat was five times that from liquid milk in 1870, by 1914 milk income was three times that from wheat.[100] This period still, however, 'remains a grey area, thinly researched and … lacking a clear historical identity'.[101] Certainly, the extent of recovery should not be exaggerated. Mr Buck of Raveningham in Norfolk thought that 1903 was the worst year on record and obtained a 10 per cent rent reduction from the estate. In January 1904 he went to Norwich market to try and sell some grain, but there was no demand. 'I never saw trade so bad.' He bought fertiliser but wondered whether he would ever see his money back. He nevertheless hired another 156 acres of land, at 17s an acre, in the autumn, noting in his diary: 'I sincerely hope this venture will prove all right'. But 1906 was another bad year, with a cold and frosty spring and summer droughts, and there followed a further 10 per cent rent rebate.[102] There were further episodes of abnormal weather: the summer of 1911 was the hottest on record and exceptionally dry. There was a thin harvest on the light lands and also frequent fires, such as that which, in August, ravaged a 25-acre field on a farm at Hoveton in east Norfolk.[103] Milk yields plummeted through July and August, with those on a farm at Langley in Norfolk said to be more than 500 gallons less than in the previous year.[104] Incomes were still well below those of the 1860s and as long the psychologically important price of wheat remained low, the fact that other new ventures were becoming profitable did not entirely dispel the gloom.

There is, moreover, little evidence that levels of landlord investment in farming infrastructure increased to any significant extent. Expenditure on repairs on the Holkham estate rose from an average of around 10 per cent of income in the last decades of the nineteenth century to between 14 and 15 per cent in 1906–9 and 16–18 per cent in 1912–15,[105] but on most estates investment remained low, and a sample of sales catalogues analysed for the period suggests that very few farms yet possessed the types of buildings already being advocated by agriculturalists in the days of high farming. Covered yards, for instance, remained the exception up to the First World War.[106] Mr Channell of Hardley noted in his diary in 1907 that he hoped his landlord 'would take it into his head to do the premises up'. In the margin he added 'hope deferred'.[107]

The Inland Revenue surveys of 1910–12, which describe all farms in East Anglia parish by parish, suggest that fortunes continued to vary greatly from place to place, but that, overall, agriculture was in a poor but by no means disastrous state. In the South Elmham group of parishes, on the heavy clays of north-east Suffolk, some of the arable was described as 'foul' but most of the pasture was 'fair'. Milk production had evidently expanded in recent years and housing for cows and cattle was to be found on all farms.[108] The loams of south-west Suffolk were generally faring better. Buildings, arable and pasture were all described as 'fair' or 'very fair', and farmhouses were generally 'good' or 'very good'.[109] The light lands of the Sandlings also come across as rather less of wilderness than we might expect from the writings of men like Rider Haggard or Biddell. The 500 acres of arable at Valley Farm, Boyton, were described as 'good', as were the smaller acreages at Collins Marsh, Frogs Hall and Mill Farm.[110] Similar descriptions applied to the farms in the neighbouring parishes. Only at Stonebridge Farm, Butley, and Buttons Farm, Capel St Andrew, were the buildings 'old and bad', and even here the cultivation could be described as 'fair'.[111] Although several farms on the Sudbourne estate had been taken in hand the general picture is of a rather well-cultivated arable district, albeit with extensive areas of open heath.[112] Less surprisingly, farms on the fertile loams of east Norfolk were doing reasonably well, especially where horticultural pursuits were important, although the reports were not always complimentary about the condition of buildings.[113] The overall impression is that on the light lands – with the exception of Breckland, an area of singularly appalling soils – where large estates dominated, land was on the whole well cultivated and farms reasonably well equipped with buildings. On heavier land and more fertile land, where a higher percentage of farmers were owner-occupiers, many had diversified into horticulture or milk production but little was being spent on buildings.

By 1913, on the eve of war, the consensus among agricultural commentators was that conditions were improving, but the industry still faced significant challenges. The author of the Preface to *Webb's Farm Account Book* for 1913–14 thought that 'British agriculture has, within the last 20 years, passed through a terrible crisis and it is still passing through a fiery ordeal; for while admitting with cheerfulness and gratitude that the corn crops of recent years have been better, and that at the present moment, the price of most farm crops is satisfactory, the bulk of arable farmers have sustained such heavy losses that it will take many years to restore them to their former prosperity.'

## THE FIRST WORLD WAR

The declaration of war, however, meant an immediate change of fortune for East Anglian farmers. The normal supply routes with America were broken and wheat prices rose from 34s 2d a quarter in August 1914 to 55s 11d a quarter by the following May. The Board of Agriculture initially saw 'no occasion whatever for public concern about food supplies', and believed that the rise in prices would be sufficient incentive for farmers to increase production.[114] But the government soon adopted a more proactive approach, encouraging the cultivation of cereals at the expense of livestock. The response of the local farming community was mixed. In January 1915 cattle were being prematurely sold for slaughter on Norwich market, 'a bad thing for the country and a bad thing for arable farmers' in the opinion of the *Eastern Daily Press*,[115] which also considered that the ploughing-up of poor pastures was a step in the wrong direction. Given the wartime labour shortage, the only realistic way of achieving this was by steam ploughing, but this was very expensive. Instead, it was argued, the state should be encouraging dairy and meat production.[116]

More coercive measures soon followed. The Milner Committee, set up in May 1915 to report on what actions might be desirable to increase production if the war should continue beyond the harvest of 1916, recommended that the Board of Agriculture set up War Agricultural Committees for each county, responsible for organising supplies of labour, fertilisers, feeds and implements and generally promoting the cause of increased food production.[117] Members were chosen for their knowledge of local farming, and included representatives from the National Farmers' Union, the Central Chamber of Agriculture, local farming clubs and agricultural trading societies, as well as from the labourers' unions. By the spring of 1917 almost every landowner, occupier and worker was affected by the activities of these bodies. Norfolk is one of the few counties for which the records of the 'War Ag.' survive. The committee was formed in January 1917 and comprised members of major landed families (such as Edward Fellowes of Shotesham), leading farmers (like Henry Overman) and the leader of the farm workers' union (George Edwards).[118] Below them were twenty District Sub-Committees whose role was to survey their areas and report back, identifying and forecasting local difficulties and shortages.

The committee ordered farmers to plant at least 62 per cent of their tillage land with cereals and potatoes, but this ruling proved difficult to enforce. The Flegg District Committee, for example, responsible for the dairying regions around the Broads, warned that farmers needed to grow root crops to sustain their milking herds during the winter and would thus be unwilling or unable to comply.[119] The committee also strove to maintain standards of farming, and levels of production, in the county. Many farms were a cause for concern. In Broadland in 1917, for example, eighteen acres of land in Somerton lay uncultivated and 240 acres in Hemsby were neglected, while Mr Charles Fabb of Thrigby needed to improve his farming. The Committee demanded that land at Dairy Farm, Burgh, be brought into 'proper cultivation', and twelve acres in Rollesby 'into better cultivation'.[120]

Similar problems were encountered, and similar instructions issued, in other districts. In the south of the county, for example, there were two derelict farms at Brooke; farms at Reedham and Loddon were 'not properly cultivated'; while a strong letter was sent to the farmer at Earsham Hall asking him to cultivate his land.[121] Orders for the ploughing-up of small areas of pasture were frequently issued. Restrictions were put on the acreage of mustard grown, and no more land was to be cultivated for soft fruit until the end of the war. The cultivation of flowers and bulbs was, understandably, frowned upon. The Committee even considered the state of allotments, criticising those at Barnham Broom, South Acre, Winterton, Repps and Ormsby for being 'insufficiently cultivated'.[122] Hedges at Dunston, Ketteringham, Shotesham and elsewhere were ordered to be trimmed; rabbits were to be cleared at Cranmer; and landowners were generally instructed to reduce game and vermin.[123]

The main excuse put forward for poor farming, overgrown hedges, weedy fields or lack of ploughing was a shortage of labour, exacerbated on some small farms by the fact that occupiers' sons were now in the army. Such men were generally unable to pay for outside help. It was sometimes possible for the Committee to provide additional workers in the shape of prisoners of war, although a lack of suitable accommodation was often a problem. Many farmers complained that ploughing up all that was expected of them would mean reducing their dairy herds, and this was sometimes accepted as an excuse. Mr Moore of Street Farm, Forncett St Peter, thus agreed to all the conditions set by the Committee, but wanted to leave 161 acres of pasture for his cows, a request to which they assented.[124]

In extreme cases, the Committee could actually take over particular holdings. Mr Formby's farm in Long Stratton was a continuing problem and it was finally taken over in February 1917.[125] The Collings family's farm in Bacton was also taken over at the same time, together with forty acres in Hingham, and Manor Farm, Tibenham, was acquired in this way in April the following year.[126] In total, about twenty farms were temporarily confiscated in Norfolk.[126] Most places where land was either uncultivated or badly farmed were on the claylands of mid and south Norfolk, where there were large numbers of owner-occupiers of small farms, many of whom depended for their survival on a dairy herd.

Machinery was available for hire from the Committee and over 4,000 acres of land were tractor-ploughed in 1918; the number of 'government tractors' hired to farmers in England and Wales as a whole rose from 1,550 in November 1917 to 3,240 the following spring and 3,925 in October 1918.[127] Indeed, the demands of the war years saw the first widespread adoption in East Anglia of tractors in the modern sense of the word – ones powered by internal combustion engines, rather than by steam. They had been displayed at the county agricultural shows since 1904, when Ransomes' 'agricultural tractor suitable for ploughing, driving, mowing, binding or cultivating as well as working barn machinery and taking goods on the road' appeared at the Suffolk show,[128] but the depressed state of agriculture had ensured that, until the war years, few had actually been purchased. Even then, many farmers and landowners remained suspicious of this new technology, not least because the machines often proved unreliable. Prothero appealed to farmers 'not to put tractors to impossible tasks, and then throw them to one side as useless'.[129] Lord Stradbroke's agent bought a tractor and a 'motor plough' at this time but they gave nothing but trouble, and he was afraid that they would break up the pipes of the land drains unless the soil was very hard. 'The motor tractor plough seems quite useless and it looks as if we will have to rely on horses or steam ploughs for real ploughing.'[130]

The government was continually asking for more ground to be ploughed up, a policy doubted even by some members of the Committee. Given the shortage of labour and fertilisers, many thought that it would be more practical to cultivate existing arable more intensively. As Mr Sapwell wrote in the *Eastern Daily Press* in January 1917: 'To plant wheat on newly ploughed old pasture gives no wheat, but only straw and rubbish'.[131] In the Freebridge Lynn district farmers declared that they could not break up any more grassland because of a shortage of labour.[132] The War Ag. minutes have not survived for Suffolk but here, too, there was opposition to the expansion of tillage. In 1917 Lord Stradbroke's agent suggested ploughing up a few fields on the Home Farm for oats, but hesitated because of the shortage of labour. Later in the year Stradbroke himself proposed breaking up the fields by 'Day's Wood on Valley Farm' but urged the agent to do nothing until he was sure he had the workforce. He might even have to resort to female labour: 'women can do a lot in a hay field with modern appliances'.[133] Stradbroke was also concerned that he should receive a share of any increased profits arising from a change in land use, and that his interests should not be adversely affected, writing in 1917 from his war-time posting:

> If the tenants want to break up land, I should have compensation, either in a share of
> the profits, or in increased rents and perhaps some agreement as to the laying down to
> grass again. You must always bear in mind that the tenants will want to break up land
> and take all they can out of it and then, when the war is over in two or three years' time
> and prices fall, they will throw up their farms with the land run out.

In March 1918 he enquired whether arrangements had been made for compensation to be paid when pastures were broken up.[134]

In spite of some opposition and backsliding there were 17,000 additional acres of cereals in Norfolk by the end of 1917 (a 4 per cent increase) and 3,000 acres of pasture had been ploughed up.[135] But yields were often disappointing, partly because of the lack of fertilisers, but also because of the weather.[136] The government wanted a further 95,000 acres ploughed and expected 62 per cent of arable to be in grain, but this meant breaking rotations and further reducing fertility, for the obvious reason that a reduction in pasture and fodder crops meant a decline in the numbers of livestock, and thus in the amounts of manure being applied to the land. Livestock numbers certainly declined in East Anglia in this period, especially those of pigs and sheep: the former fell in Norfolk from 181,672 in 1913 to 140,646 in 1917, the latter from 98,957 to 91,487. In Suffolk, similarly, sheep numbers fell from 142,558 to 113,608 and pigs from 157,460 to 129,585. The number of cattle kept in Norfolk rose slightly, however (by 1,180), and the number of dairy cows within that number increased. In Suffolk the number of cattle kept rose more sharply, by about 5,370, again including a slight increase in dairy cows.[137]

With the end of the war the War Ags did not immediately relinquish control of farming. In the autumn of 1918, a farmer in Hingham asked if he could grow six acres of bulbs: his request was granted on condition that he planted an extra six acres of corn on his other farm at Terrington.[138] Orders continued to be issued for the cleaning of drains and even for more land to be ploughed. Mr Rush, who farmed at Denver Sluice in west Norfolk, was ordered to clean five acres of land, on which he had grown beans the previous year, for a spring crop.[139] The War Ags remained in existence throughout 1919, and although all ploughing orders were rescinded at the start of that year the Norfolk Committee continued to concern itself with the maintenance of good husbandry. The main concern now was how to organise the return to a peace-time system as farm labourers came back from the front and as exhausted land was restored to normal rotations. Land that had grown grain for more than two years was ordered to be planted with roots.[140] Permission was granted for land to be returned to grass in both Hilgay and Swanton Novers and in March the Committee declared that 'complete freedom of cropping was now compatible with the public interest'.[141] The provision of labour, horses, tractors and other supplies ceased, but drainage schemes continued to be promoted, including a plan to drain the Cley Marshes on the north Norfolk coast. The scheme came to nothing as the Committee was soon disbanded, but the threat led to the foundation of the Norfolk Naturalist (now Wildlife) Trust in 1923, the marshes being their first acquisition.[142]

The scale of the War Ags' success in increasing food production remains unclear because of a lack of detailed statistics, especially concerning the extent to which yields declined as rotations were broken and as the supply of artificial fertilisers was reduced. In national terms it is probable, in fact, that increases in production only served to raise the amount of home-grown food from 38 per cent to 40 per cent of the total consumed in the country.[143] In East Anglia the wheat acreage increased significantly – from 119,727 in 1913 to 126,194 in 1917 in Norfolk and from 110,686 to 119,712 in Suffolk – but this was partly at the expense of barley and roots, rather than of permanent pasture and derelict land.[144] In Norfolk the area devoted to barley declined by 6,918 acres, in Suffolk by 1,519: the acreage of fodder crops fell by 11,694 in Norfolk and 8,177 in Suffolk. The loss of rotational grass was less, however, with the acreage in Norfolk actually increasing by 277 and that in Suffolk only declining by 1,278.[145]

Whatever the scale of the achievement in terms of food production, the war years undoubtedly saw farming fortunes reversed. Not only did prices rise but rents, controlled by the Board of Agriculture through the local committees, remained static. Income on the Everington's farm on the light chalky soils at Castle Acre in Norfolk reached a peak in 1919–20 of £12,001, rising from £6,500 in 1913–14. The income from wheat alone increased from £139 in 1914–5 to a peak of £913 in 1916–17. Between 1910 and 1919 the price rose from 15s 9d to 38s per comb. Barley profits also rose, from £2,188 in 1914–15 to £5,646 in 1918–19, partly as a result of a climb in prices from 12s 6d per comb in 1909 to 31s in 1917.

Income from cattle, on the other hand, rose less dramatically, from £1,344 in 1914–15 to £2,787 in 1919–20.[146] Heavy-land farmers also did well. On the unidentified Suffolk farm described by S.H. Carson the average net annual profit as a percentage of capital invested in live and dead stock for the war years was 24.4 per cent, three times the pre-war level. The percentage of receipts from wheat was 25 per cent, roughly double the percentage of the previous ten years.[147]

## BETWEEN THE WARS

The end of the First World War, however, brought renewed uncertainty to the farming community. Nationally, one million extra acres of arable had been ploughed up between 1914 and 1918: the area under arable in East Anglia as a whole had risen from 2,697,000 acres in 1914 to 2,803,000 in 1918, an increase of 106,000 acres.[148] More wheat had been grown but the future prospects for this crop were very unclear. Rotations had been broken to increase production in the short term, but this meant that fertility had been allowed to decline: flock numbers had been depleted and urgently needed to be built up again, a challenge not helped by the severe winter of 1919/20. However, alongside these negative results of the war years, there were some more positive ones. Government intervention in agriculture had begun, and this had included, besides the kinds of coercive and restrictive measures resented by many farmers and landowners, guaranteed prices and the provision of scientific and technical advice, both of which were to increase in importance during the inter-war years.

To begin with, government protection for agriculture was continued. The 1919 Royal Commission into farming was split over what action was necessary to sustain agricultural profitability, but the majority thought that price guarantees should continue. The Agriculture Act of 1920 maintained minimum prices for wheat and oats and farmers were promised four years' notice of any change. The government had good reason to believe that this policy would not be too expensive to implement. Indeed, the minority report of the Royal Commission had concluded that the guaranteed prices of the war years were no longer necessary ('the evidence submitted to us does not show any prospect, for some years to come, of a fall in cereal prices to a level unremunerative to the farmer').[149] Indeed, prices rose by 26 per cent between 1918 and 1921 as a result of poor harvests and economic disruption in Europe. At Wicken Farm, Castle Acre, west Norfolk the value per acre for wheat peaked at £4 15s per quarter in 1918.[150] East Anglian farmers were in an optimistic mood, and farming seemed set for a promising future.

The return of agricultural profitability led to a strong revival in the land market and large landowners, burdened with the debts accumulated during previous decades, were often keen to sell. Even before the war ended the Duke of Portland was considering selling farms at Lynn 'to take advantage of the present increased price of agricultural properties'.[151] Early in 1918 Lord Stradbroke asked his agent whether any of the tenants wanted to buy their farms. 'If the tenants wish to buy, they had better offer me prices for their farms, and if I could settle all the farms I could dispose of the property that way without an auction.'[152] Histories of twentieth-century England often reiterate the contemporary belief that a quarter of the land in England changed hands between the end of the war and 1927. The significance of this figure, if indeed it is reliable, is easily exaggerated[153] – after all, three-quarters of the land did not – but between 1917 and 1921 at least 51,000 acres were sold within Norfolk and at least twelve of the 100 largest estates in the county changed hands.[154] In Suffolk the picture was similar: Hollesley, Thorndon, Livermere, Rendlesham and Easton were all sold between 1918 and 1922, and many other estates divested themselves of outlying portions. Most were divided into lots and bought by their tenants. Farmers invested their war-time profits in buying farms and average prices rose from £17 an acre in 1916 to £28 in early 1920.[155] Many were unwilling buyers, forced to purchase in order to ensure continued occupation and spurred on by a feverish atmosphere. In 1920 the *Eastern Daily Press* argued that purchase was the only way in which they could secure their future: although they would be worse off in the short term, it was a good investment in the long run and should not be delayed because, as the supply of land coming on to the market slowed, prices might well rise further.[156] A report on the condition of the Lee Warner estate at Walsingham in Norfolk in 1917 stated that it would be better for the tenants if the estate was sold. They had been suffering 'by reason of the inadequate repairs and the whole thing slowly lapsing into a bad state'.[157] The 1919 Royal Commission reported that 'most Norfolk farmers prefer to be tenants than owners', but in spite of this the number of farmers working their own land in the county more than trebled (from 11.8 per cent to 37.2 per cent) between 1914 and 1924.[158] The problem for the new owner-occupiers, however, was that their capital was tied up in the purchase; they had nothing left to spend on bringing the land back into good heart after the over-exploitation of the war years, and so their debts mounted.

Moreover, the boom was short-lived. As cereal imports began to rise again, symptoms of the pre-war depression began to return: at the same time, farmers increasingly resented the terms of government support laid down in the 1920 Agriculture Act, which as well as guaranteeing minimum prices for wheat and oats also ensured that the Wages Boards, established during the war to ensure reasonable agricultural wages, should continue.[159] Both the *Eastern Daily Press* and the *East Anglian Daily Times* frequently spoke out against the Act, and against state intervention more generally: 'If only we were left alone we could get along' was a typical sentiment.[160] 'What with Wages Boards, the Corn Production Act, labour agitators, government interference and now foot and mouth disease, the lot of the farmer in the eastern counties is not a happy one.'[161] Wheat, which had fetched nearly 18s a hundredweight in 1920, made only 10s in 1923;[162] the price received per comb of wheat on the Home Farm at Holkham halved between 1921 and 1924.[163] The government found itself unable to afford the commitments made in the Agriculture Act and in 1924 financial support, and at the same time control over wages, was withdrawn.

At the time, many farmers seem to have been relieved to be free of government controls. It was only later that the move came to be seen as 'The Great Betrayal'. The rest of the 1920s saw little revival in farming fortunes. Carslaw and Venn's study of twenty-four East Anglian farms suggests that returns in 1927, at 5s an acre, were catastrophically down on the £3 16s an acre calculated for the previous year,[164] while the area of wheat in Norfolk and Suffolk fell from 200,392 acres in 1925 to 168,560 in 1930.[165] There were some slight signs of recovery in the late 1920s and in 1927 the price of wheat could be described as 'not really bad',[166] but the Baldwin government's White Paper on Agriculture of 1926 continued to reject subsidies and protection in favour of free trade, with some investment in agricultural education and research, contributions towards pest control and land drainage, and improved marketing arrangements; and any slight remission in farming fortunes ended with the Wall Street Crash in the autumn of 1929.[167] 'The cumulative effect of 1930–32 has resulted in the exhaustion of both the farmers' credit and private savings.'[168] By 1933 prices were down to such an extent that 'the position of the large producer is impossible and of the small producer precarious.'[169] The *Eastern Daily Press* reporter claimed to know of one estate on which every farmer had given notice to quit.[170] Once again, landlords were obliged to reduce rents or offer other inducements. In 1931 the Fisher family at Dairy Farm, Gunton, Norfolk, gave in their notice to Lord Suffield who replied by offering them a £50 rent rebate on a total rent of £160 'so long as notice to quit is withdrawn'.[171] The general situation was serious, and Claudsley Breton predicted in the *Eastern Daily Press* the complete collapse of village life, the desolation of the countryside and the return of much of Norfolk to the 'state of heath and moorland from which "Turnip" Townshend and Coke of Norfolk had reclaimed it'.[172] In April 1930 the *Press* reported that seed merchants were selling 'exceptional quantities' of seed for permanent pasture. 'Whether the policy that is being pursued is a wise one remains to be seen, but there can be no doubt that a drastic reduction of the arable acreage is being brought about with the specific object of reducing labour charges on the farm'.[173]

In these circumstances, and facing a wider economic recession, the new Conservative government was forced to act. In 1931 both free trade and the tying of the pound to the gold standard ended, and in 1932 a general system of protection was implemented. A tariff of 10 per cent was put on all foreign goods, but imperial preferences were put in place which meant that farming did not benefit as much from the move as manufacturing. Nevertheless, the Wheat Act of 1932 guaranteed prices and the Agricultural Marketing Acts of 1931 and 1933 resulted in statutory marketing schemes for all major products, providing deficiency payments and subsidies. The Milk Marketing Board was the most comprehensive and successful of these schemes, and ensured that a common price was paid to all producers.[174]

In 1935 the *Eastern Daily Press* could state that 'The day is very far distant when wheat will realise a price anywhere near approaching the cost of production.'[175] But in fact the new policies – coupled with changes in world trade – seem to have had some positive effects. Having fallen rapidly between 1920 and 1922, and then steadily until 1933, agricultural prices in general, and those for wheat in particular, now began to rise again. The acreage devoted to wheat in Norfolk increased from 82,600 to 123,500, and in Suffolk from 85,600 to nearly 109,000, between 1930 and 1935. Nevertheless, the overall arable acreage continued to decline, from 1,252,898 to 1,202,050 between 1930 and 1935, a fall of just over 4 per cent, due to the steady reduction in the acreage devoted to oats and rye, and to a lesser extent barley.[176]

With cereal farming in the doldrums – although evidently not in the completely collapsed state often depicted – throughout the inter-war years, East Anglian farmers effectively had two options. They could continue to grow cereals, but on a large scale, cutting labour costs by mechanising; or they could diversify. The most significant form of diversification, adopted on the majority of farms in Norfolk and Suffolk, was the cultivation of sugar beet. The industry already had a long history in the region; a factory had opened in Lavenham in Suffolk as early as 1868 but had soon failed, partly because it was under-financed but mainly because not enough beet was grown locally to make it viable. It reopened in 1884, but encountered the same problems. Plans to build a similar factory at King's Lynn were mooted but dropped in 1873.[177] In 1900 the *Eastern Daily Press* reported that sugar beet was to be grown experimentally on thirty-three sites, one of which would be in Suffolk.[178] By the early 1900s, a small but regular trade existed through King's Lynn and Great Yarmouth, with beet cultivated in the region being sent to Holland for processing. Dutch factories provided the seed and paid for transport.[179] In November 1910 the *Eastern Daily Press* was reporting that 'The time is approaching when we will be asked to sign contracts for future years to induce the Dutch capitalists to build a factory at Loddon or elsewhere in Norfolk.'[180] The first factory was in fact opened by the Anglo-Netherlands Sugar Corporation at Cantley in 1911. The following years were wet, however, and the crop was almost impossible to harvest: the factory closed in 1915.[181] More importantly, beet was distrusted both by farmers, who were wedded to a rotation that included a fodder crop, and by landlords, who feared it would exhaust the soil. Pilot trials by the Norfolk Chamber of Commerce from 1910 showed, however, that beet pulp made good animal feed, and the advantages for the farmer of growing crops under contract were considerable.[182]

As the price of sugar rose steadily on the world market in the inter-war years interest in the crop increased, and in March 1920 the English Sugar Beet Corporation was founded by a group of English and Dutch refiners. They agreed to take over the Cantley factory and interest in beet-growing spread rapidly, not least because the owners were prepared to pay the rail freight costs for crops grown as much as 100 miles away. Advertisements for contracts appeared in the local papers, and the proffered price, £4 a ton, was a good one. Three thousand acres were contracted for, but 5,000 were needed to make the factory viable: the next few years were difficult ones, with less than 3,000 acres being grown annually, but the withdrawal of excise duty on sugar in 1922 finally allowed the industry to take off. Although duty was reimposed in 1924, a sugar-beet subsidy was also introduced 'to revive British agriculture and restore rural England'.[183] In Suffolk, the establishment of a factory at Bury St Edmunds by was also dependent on enough beet being available, but by Christmas 1924 the necessary 4,000 acres was contracted for and United Sugar's factory opened in November 1925 (Figure 3). In 1925, a rival company owned by Dutch industrialist J.P. Van Rossum

Figure 3. The Bury St Edmunds sugar beet factory at night, c.1930.

opened another factory in Ipswich, with one at King's Lynn following in 1927.[184] In 1923 Van Rossum himself began to purchase land near Cantley for beet-growing and by the end of the Second World War the East Anglian Real Property Company owned 5,000 acres in east Norfolk, across which the landscape was transformed. Large, regular fields were laid out and old buildings were replaced by substantial, brick-sided Dutch barns. A three-course rotation of sugar beet or potatoes, wheat and barley was employed, and the sugar beet tops were ploughed back in as a green manure.[185]

The cultivation of sugar beet was the great success of inter-war farming in Norfolk and Suffolk. In 1926 the total East Anglian acreage reached over 67,000 acres; ten years later it had exceeded 136,000.[186] By the start of the Second World War beet had replaced turnips and mangolds as the most important root crop in the region.[187] One mid-Norfolk farmer stated emphatically in 1935 that 'If it had not been for the sugar beet and wheat subsidies the whole of this district as far as Lynn would have gone out of cultivation.'[188] Because the crop was grown to contract, the price was fixed and the market certain; moreover, the sugar beet pulp was returned to the farmer at a reduced price, providing valuable feed, as did the tops on the fields. The substitution of beet pulp and tops not only reduced direct feed costs, but also cut out the time-consuming chores of carting and cleaning more conventional root crops.[189]

There were, however, a range of other ways in which farmers could diversify. Fruit growing and market gardening, pigs, poultry and eggs were important growth areas, more so than in the pre-war period. Although many of these activities were more suited to smallholdings than to the kind of large and medium-sized arable farms which dominated the East Anglian countryside, these often adopted one or more such enterprises. Many, in particular, began to keep pigs on a large scale. By 1936 there were over 211,000 pigs in Norfolk, 'a figure which is higher than that for any other English county' according to Mosby, who was evidently mistaken, as 255,637 were recorded in Suffolk in the same year and pig production was described as the 'prominent livestock industry' there.[190] By the late 1920s some huge enterprises existed: one in Suffolk was reported in 1927 to have 1,000 head.[191] But most pigs were kept on mixed farms as one arm of the enterprise. On the Home Farm at Holkham numbers increased from under 100 in the years up to 1919 to as many as 300 in 1927.[192] On the 201-acre Clay Hall Farm in Great Witchingham in Norfolk their numbers rose from seventy-seven in 1929 to 235 in 1937, with the value more than quadrupling during the same period.[193] When the farm was sold in 1940 the particulars described 'An exceptionally fine piggery 38 feet by 40 feet for a hundred, with fattening pens and feeding passage', together with other ranges of piggeries.[194] Local processing facilities developed. A bacon factory was opened at Elmswell, near Bury St Edmunds, in 1911, and lasted throughout the inter-war years. Another was opened in North Elmham in Norfolk in 1924 beside the railway line. The industry was thus buoyant, although not without its problems. Prices fluctuated; swine fever appeared in Norfolk in the summer of 1924;[195] in 1935 there were complaints about the serious increase in the import of chilled pork; and numerous difficulties were reported with the government's pig marketing scheme.[196]

Milk production, already expanding rapidly before the war, continued to be a growth area, especially where there was easy access to markets. These could be as far afield as the metropolis – as early as 1912 Welford and Sons of London were advertising at the Suffolk show for 'well-cooled milk'. Churns would be provided and, most importantly, a weekly cheque paid.[197] The size of milking herds continued to rise, especially after the establishment of the Milk Marketing Board in 1933 reduced price fluctuations and the extent to which farmers were at the mercy of price-fixing milk combines. The number of milking cows on the Elveden estate increased from 120 in 1927 to 335 in 1931, 549 in 1935 and 734 in 1938: on many relatively small farms herds of sixty, hand-milked, had by the mid-1930s been replaced by herds of up to 300, milked by machine. James Alston of Uphall in south Norfolk milked seventy cows in 1924, but by 1931 had 240.[198] On the Suffolk farm studied by Carson the proportion of farm income from the dairy herd increased steadily from 20 per cent in 1918 to 50 per cent in 1933.[199] Overall, the number of milkers across the region rose from 45,000 in 1917 to nearly 72,000 in 1935.[200] By 1935 dairying was regarded as the 'most stable aspect of farming practice' in the region.[201]

The inter-war years saw a revolution in milk production, as improved standards of cleanliness were introduced to meet the buyers' demands for greater purity. The Dairying Act of 1926 laid down minimum hygiene standards, encouraging the installation of purpose-built milking parlours.[202] Rupert Guinness (later Lord Iveagh) of the Elveden estate in north-west Suffolk pioneered the testing of milk for tuberculosis and in 1920 was co-founder of the Tuberculin Tested Milk Producers' Association. From 1927 systematic efforts were made to ensure that all the cows on the estate were clear of TB: by 1936 all had 'attested' status.[203] In 1920 Earnest Batten of Nayland in Suffolk began earmarking cows for the Essex Milk Recording Society,[204] and by 1927 the Suffolk Milk Recording Society had a stand at the county show for the first time and an 80-gallon milk refrigerator was exhibited.[205] A variety of milking machines was shown at both county shows from 1919. The marketing of milk was also addressed, with a display of non-returnable paper milk cartons appearing at the Suffolk show in 1933.[206] In all, this amounted to a veritable revolution in dairying: every cow had a number, its milk yields were recorded and it was fed accordingly; milkers wore overalls and used machinery.

Many landlords, such as Captain Meade at Earsham in south Norfolk, installed new dairies for their tenants.[207] When the Kemp's estate at Gissing, in the same area, was sold in 1936, Old Hall Farm was described as having fifty-one acres of 'rich dairy pasture' and the buildings included a 'recently erected cow house for 30 cows'. There were a number of smaller cow houses and the barn had been converted to accommodate a further twenty.[208] All three of the farms on the Worstead estate in north-east Norfolk, sold in 1938, had 'model' cowsheds for seventy, seventy-three and fifty-five cows respectively.[209] Generally, milking parlours and cooling rooms are more frequently noted in sales catalogues after about 1933.[210] There were other innovations; interest in silage revived, and in 1923 a model of a 'creosoted wood and patent steel spring frame silo was shown at the Suffolk show,[211] while in 1927 the Gasgoine 'economic' silo was shown at the Norfolk. By the late 1920s the availability of reinforced concrete tower silos ensured that silage-making began to spread among East Anglian dairy farmers. The popularity of the tower silos was short-lived, however, as silage pits soon gained popularity as a cheaper alternative: 'The outstanding success of modern methods of inexpensive storage in pit or trench silos … or in clamps above ground … have rendered costly permanent tower silos unnecessary.'[212]

Sheep numbers, which had fallen drastically during the war, never returned to their pre-war levels. In Suffolk numbers declined from 210,280 in 1919 to 179,592 in 1930, before rising again to 220, 873 in 1933, then slowly declining once more to 173,000 on the eve of the Second World War. In Norfolk the inter-war peak came at 311,000 in 1926, with numbers then declining steadily, falling below 200,000 by 1938.[213] What these raw agricultural statistics do not show is the changes in the relative proportions of flocks fed off arable and off pasture. The availability of sugar beet tops as winter feed meant, as Rayns suggested in 1935, that grassland sheep were 'now tending to decrease, and there is some indication that the arable flocks are regaining some of their lost popularity'.[214] In part this may have been a response to the high costs of artificial fertilisers. As the *Eastern Daily Press* put it in the same year, 'Men who during the bad times have tried to do without sheep have found that the resulting deterioration of both land and crops is bad policy. For without question, large stretches of the light land are more easily and cheaply fertilised by sheep than any other method.'[215]

Although cereal production remained the core activity on the majority of East Anglian farms, alternative sources of income were thus increasingly explored through the 1920s and 30s, especially those which could be fitted in well with arable husbandry. Sugar beet, vegetables, dairying, pigs and poultry everywhere increased in importance. Indeed, on some farms, especially the medium-sized ones, a wide variety of enterprises was adopted. The Fishers at Gunton, for example, were selling milk and butter, eggs, sheep, cattle, pigs, wool and poultry in the 1930s, with a particularly good trade in Christmas turkeys.[216]

The other strategy adopted in the inter-war years was to farm on a large scale, on highly mechanised holdings, something which seems to have been a particular feature of the light lands of west Norfolk. Raynes described how Messrs Parker and Proctor acquired a farm at Congham and Middleton in 1917 and by 1934 had taken over eleven more farms, two of which might otherwise have become derelict, and thus worked over 14,000 acres.[217] Their success was based on mechanisation, sugar beet, long temporary grass leys and a productive livestock system. The Alley brothers of South Creake gained much publicity from their efforts to farm mechanically in the early 1930s. They took over the 1,113-acre Blue Stone Farm, allegedly in a very run-down state, in 1930. Because yard feeding of cattle was expensive the brothers relied on artificial fertilisers, and the rotation was limited to two years of cereal followed by one year of fallow, with mustard being planted on the fallow. Only four men were employed on a regular basis, with extra labour being brought in at harvest. There were three tractors, a variety of tools all designed to be tractor-powered, two combine harvesters and grain dryers. There were no horses on the farm and 'the system approaches most closely to the ideal farming on factory lines.'[218] They realised that maximum profits could be obtained by seeing their produce right through the processing stage to the market, and they began to produce 'Morning Glory' wheat flakes in a small factory in the parish. They then expanded and opened a further mill, but in this they overstretched themselves and had left the farm before the start of the Second World War.[219]

Another example was James Keith, who took on Wicken Farm at Castle Acre in 1923. Like the Alley brothers, he believed that cereals could still be grown at a profit; but unlike them he kept livestock, although changing the traditional Norfolk regime from fattening bullocks to dairying. He took over further farms and by the mid-1930s was cultivating no less then 14,000 acres. Neglected land was limed, deep ploughed and planted with corn and sugar beet, and in 1935 he began reclaiming 136 acres of heathland between King's Lynn and Swaffham, land which he described as 'covered variously with bracken, gorse and ling, all liberally interspersed with thorn trees, and, of course, infested with rabbits.' 'These wastes undoubtedly give an added charm to the countryside and have their uses from a sporting point of view', he later wrote, 'but are a curse to the surrounding arable' because of the cover they provided for vermin.[220] In 1938 he brought 170 acres of Harpley Common into cultivation, and in 1939 130 acres of Massingham Common.

Modern historians often quote the activities of such agribusiness pioneers, but they seem to have been rare. In general the number of large farms gradually fell, in both Norfolk and

Suffolk, during the 1920s and 30s, and for medium-sized arable farmers an increased reliance on mechanisation was not a very realistic option. As we have seen, a limited number of tractors were employed during the First World War and a few were shown at the Norfolk Show in 1919, but interest then lapsed, and no more appear in the catalogues for either county show until 1927. After this the variety of makes displayed increased but, to judge from the available evidence, take-up was limited. Mechanisation made little sense at a time of relative depression. In 1935 a Fordson tractor cost £140, the same as a pair of good horses and their tackle: moreover, horses had a working life of ten years, while that of a tractor was only four or five; and a horse's fuel could be grown on the farm. Added to this, gateways might need to be widened to provide access for a tractor, changes that an owner-occupier, but not a tenant farmer, was free to make.[221] Such evidence as there is suggests that tractors only made a significant impact in those districts (most notably the Norfolk Fenland) in which market gardening and fruit growing increased in importance through the inter-war years, and were more sparingly adopted on normal arable farms. The 1940–41 Farm Survey, for example, shows that in the Fenland parishes of Terrington St John and Walpole St Peter there were twenty-eight and thirty-eight tractors respectively: one farm had as many as five.[222] In the Sandlings parish of Hollesley, in contrast, there were only six, while neighbouring Butley and Capel St Andrew could boast only two.[223] Companies such as Baldings of Dereham, who at the Norfolk show in 1931 advertised the 'usual display of International tractors, power-driven binders and power-driven equipment, together with horse-drawn agricultural machinery', continued to sell both horse- and tractor-drawn machines long after the end of the Second World War. Combine harvesters made a very hesitant appearance at the shows; the first at the Suffolk (a Case Combine) in 1936, the second at the Norfolk in 1937, with others appearing in the following years. It was really only after the Second World War that tractors came to replace horse teams on most arable farms, and not until well into the 1950s that combines become a normal part of farm equipment.

Whatever kind of farming was adopted in the 1920s and 30s capital was required, for stock, buildings, and equipment: contemporaries were clear that a paucity of capital, more than anything else, held back the development of agriculture in East Anglia, as elsewhere. As Bensusan put it in 1927, 'There is no doubt that a lack of capital could be a serious setback for farmers. Farming today demands sufficient capital, sound judgment, hard work and good luck.'[224] These sentiments were echoed by the *Eastern Daily Press* three years later: 'It often happens when we see a farm neglected, and that is a rare occurrence, the reason is, not that the farmer is incapable, but that he lacks capital'.[225] The fact that a greater number of farmers were now owner-occupiers saddled with debts from the purchase of their properties exacerbated this problem. But even where they were tenants, the poor finances of landowners ensured that there was now little money to invest in improvements or even maintenance.

In many ways the state of East Anglian farming in the inter-war years mirrored that during the pre-war depression, but the extent of diversification was now considerably greater: so, too, was the scale of government intervention, although this was seldom much appreciated by the local farming industry. Indeed, right-wing propagandists like Henry Williamson were keen to lay much of the blame for the depression on the expanding role of the state. 'Landowners, who have looked after their tenants for years, cannot do so as much now as they might wish because they are crippled by taxation and in many cases have let or sold their homes. The farmer who bought his land, in many instances to save his home, finds himself in a very serious position, and the ordinary tenant farmer is hit by high prices.'[226] Opinions like this were widely expressed in the farming press. As the *Eastern Daily Press* put it in 1925, following the repeal of guaranteed wheat prices in the previous year: 'Bad as the present prospect is, I would far sooner that the present government left us alone than gave us a subsidy, which, however, is unlikely – it would be accompanied by a control, which would remain if the subsidy were withdrawn.'[227]

While the inter-war period was generally an unprofitable one for farmers, who again had to face stiff foreign competition in the production of staples like wheat and lamb,[228] the 1930s in particular can also be seen as a major watershed in farming history. Rather than being a time of unremitting gloom, there were clear signs of recovery. Both the number of cows and the wheat acreage were increasing and in a number of ways the preconditions for subsequent expansion were being laid.[229] Much of the impression of total depression which has passed into the folklore of farming was the creation of the contemporary farming press, and of polemicists like Henry Williamson and Adrian Bell, the latter keen to portray a 'decent way of life blighted by government inactivity and urban neglect'.[230]

## ON THE EVE OF WAR

As in earlier periods, however, it is hard to generalise about East Anglian farming. There was much variety in agricultural fortunes, depending on the type and size of the farm in question, and where it was located. Indeed, the evidence of the *Land Utilisation Survey* reports for Norfolk and Suffolk – published in 1938 and 1941, by Mosby and Butcher respectively – emphasised the continuing importance of regional variations.[231] They described how, on the heavier clays, where wheat had traditionally been the principal crop and farms were often small and owner-occupied, the area of grassland had increased significantly in the inter-war years, although this process had been halted or even reversed in a few places as the price of wheat recovered through the 1930s. A reasonable living could, they suggested, be made from growing wheat and sugar beet, and between two-thirds and three-quarters of the land was in tilth. But dairy farming using permanent pastures was increasing at the expense of bullocks reared on roots in yards. On the fertile loams of east Norfolk, in contrast – again a land of small farms and owner-occupiers – only around 2 per cent of the land was in permanent pasture. The rich soils were intensively cultivated for cereals and beet, and as market gardens. Very different were the light, poor soils of Breckland. Here, sporting rents were often higher than agricultural ones and rabbit warrening was the most profitable activity on many farms, providing fur for the Brandon hat factory. Only half the land was under the plough, with the rest being used as grazing. The farms, mostly still the property of landed estates, were large and sugar beet was the main cash crop, with barley the second. Very little wheat was grown, but rye still accounted for 6 per cent of the arable. Crops such as carrots, asparagus, lucerne and sainfoin did well. Not surprisingly, this was the least heavily stocked region in East Anglia, and although the number of dairy cows were increasing, this was really sheep and sugar beet country. The Suffolk Sandlings were similar, but less badly affected by the depression. Much of the arable was deficient in lime, however, in spite of the fact that – with proper investment – this problem could have been remedied fairly easily by using either lump chalk or the residues from sugar beet factories. In spite of these problems, the general standard of farming in the Sandlings was described in 1939 as good, and 'the skill of those engaged in agriculture in the district reaches a very high standard.'[232] The Good Sands district of north-west Norfolk, another area still dominated by large estates, was less badly affected by the depression (the soils were more fertile, less acidic) and here malting barley and sugar beet were the most important crops. It was in this district, as already noted, that men like the Alley brothers and Keith experimented with large-scale, mechanised agriculture, and Mosby in 1938 described how 'several large farms with enormous fields grew one crop of wheat after another, using combine harvesters and in general adopting the methods used by the prairie farmer.'[233] The Fens were different again: here a massive change in husbandry had occurred, with a huge reduction in both the area under grass and the wheat acreage, and an expansion in the cultivation of fruit and vegetables, which we will examine in more detail in the following chapter. Every soil region was thus different, in part because of the character of the soils themselves and the potential they presented to, and problems they posed for, farmers, but also in part because of the structures of landownership and tenancy, and the essential character of the landscape (in terms of settlement patterns, field sizes and the like) inherited from the past, and often the distant past.

But soils were no longer, as they had been in the eighteenth and nineteenth centuries, the overwhelmingly dominant factor determining regional farming specialisation. Patterns of contact and communication were more important then they had been before the start of the depression. Proximity to a railway line would thus encourage, and remoteness discourage, heavy-land farmers diversifying into dairying; proximity to large urban areas like Norwich or Ipswich was a major determinant of the extent to which land could be profitably used for market gardens or orchards; while the nearness to beet factories at Lynn, Cantley and Ipswich, more than any intrinsic qualities of the soil, determined the concentration of beet-growing in south-west and east Norfolk, and in south-east Suffolk. During the inter-war period, however, as road transport improved, all this perhaps became less true, and beet production in particular was increasingly dependent on local lorry companies, whose impact on farm lanes became legendary.[234]

Overall, the picture of East Anglia that emerges from the two *Land Utilisation Survey* volumes is notably more positive than that presented by commentators like Henry

Williamson or A.G. Street. True, there were long-term problems, especially regarding soil quality. Although soil fertility had recovered from the hammering it had taken during the First World War, there were still difficulties in a number of areas, and lime-deficiency in particular was common in many districts because marling and liming had been widely neglected over the previous decades. A report on the farms in hand of the Earl of Stradbroke's 15,000-acre estate in east Suffolk, compiled in 1937, was not untypical in suggesting that soil fertility was not being adequately maintained. Too much grain had been grown on light soil, not enough fertiliser was being used, and too few youngstock were being kept. The report suggested that more young animals should be maintained on the farms and more use made of both fertilisers and lime.[235] But overall the two *Land Utilisation Survey* volumes do not give an impression of an agricultural industry on its knees, and instead of gloom and dereliction we get an impression of a fairly vibrant economy adapting to new challenges, and certainly not one which – to quote Street in 1936 – was 'suffering from its past greatness', its farmers simply surviving on unfair government subsidies.[236]

## AN OVERVIEW

It will be evident from what we have said above that the 'Great Depression' in East Anglia was not a period of pronounced and unremitting gloom. As historians before us have pointed out, in studies of other regions, it was a long and complex period of change, in which the fortunes of particular branches of farming, and of individual farmers, fluctuated in a bewildering variety of ways. Nevertheless, there are some broad overall trends in this period; and it is these, rather than the 'noise' of the short-term or very localised fluctuations, which were perhaps most important in shaping the character of the rural landscape.

The main feature of the depression, in terms of land use, was the decline in the area under cereals and the expansion of pasture, and while this has not in itself left an enduring mark on the East Anglian countryside (the trend was more than reversed in the period following the Second World War) it would certainly have been the most noticeable aspect of landscape change at the time. Bell in 1932 described how 'Year by year the choppy sea of ploughland was being superseded by grass. A green sameness, which was like a stillness after the various earthen geometry of the plough, possessed the place.'[237] Between 1894 and 1936 the area of permanent pasture, including rough grazing, rose from 536,500 acres to just under 630,000 in the two counties. This development was not constant and linear, it must be emphasised. The area under grass expanded steadily until the last years of the nineteenth century, then remaining fairly stable until the First World War. During the war it declined, although rather less dramatically than we might perhaps expect, and continued to fall into the early 1920s. It then expanded again until the middle years of the 1930s, before stabilising once more (Figure 4 and Plates 1–3).

Of rather less importance, but locally significant, was the retreat of cultivation from marginal land, mainly light, acid sands and gravels, especially in Breckland and the Suffolk

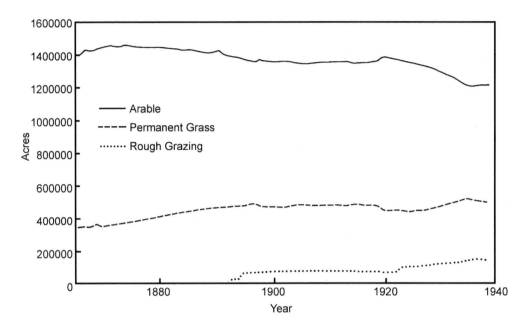

Figure 4. The relative area of arable, pasture and rough grazing in East Anglia, 1870–1936. Source: MAFF Agricultural Returns. NB: rough grazing is not included as a category in the Returns before 1894.

Sandlings but also, to a lesser extent, in the district to the north of Norwich. The extent of abandonment likewise probably fluctuated over time and, as we shall see (below, pp. 119–122), was evidently exaggerated by contemporaries. It is certainly difficult to quantify, owing in particular to problems of definition. Abandoned land, land cultivated on the basis of long fallows and rough grazing are hard to distinguish in the documentary record and indeed, divisions between them are to a large extent arbitrary. But some poor land certainly went out of cultivation or was cultivated less intensively in these heathland regions, reversing the developments of the agricultural revolution and high-farming periods.

When prices were high such land repaid the heavy costs required for successful cultivation in terms of fertilisers, marling and the movement of manure. As prices fell, inputs were reduced and yields declined, although it is difficult to demonstrate the scale of this because the Agricultural Returns produced by central government give only the overall yields for the two counties, and these seem to have remained relatively stable (at around eight combs per acre for wheat and slightly more for barley) until around 1920, then rising slightly to around nine combs by the early 1930s before levelling out again (Figure 5).[238] It is hard to break these figures down and look at the experience of different regions within East Anglia because – somewhat surprisingly – local yield data are far rarer for the late nineteenth and twentieth centuries than they are for the eighteenth or early nineteenth. A good series of figures for Holkham Home Farm, however – and a rather shorter series for Devas

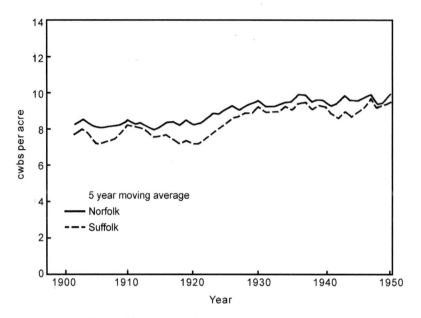

Figure 5. Wheat yields in East Anglia, 1900–1950. Source: MAFF Agricultural Returns.

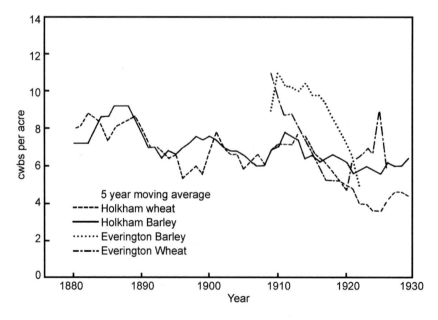

Figure 6. Wheat and barley yields in north-west Norfolk, 1880–1930. A long sequence of figures from the Home Farm at Holkham, and a shorter run from the Everingtons' farm at Castle Acre, suggest that on light land cereal yields may have declined significantly in the late nineteenth and early twentieth centuries (compare with Figure 5).

Everington's farm in Castle Acre – suggest that in north-west Norfolk at least both wheat and barley yields may have declined, if erratically, from the 1880s until at least the mid 1920s (Figure 6).[239] This was light but moderately fertile soil, calcareous but easily leached and in need of regular inputs of manure and fertiliser. The levels applied appear to have dropped significantly at Holkham as the depression intensified, and the decline in yields evident in Figure 6 was presumably the consequence. On the more marginal and more acidic soils of the heathland districts a decline in yields resulting from these factors would presumably have been steeper. On the other hand, given that the *average* cereal yields for East Anglia remained relatively buoyant in this period, in districts with more fertile soils productivity must presumably have increased, perhaps because the higher numbers of cattle being kept on many farms ensured that greater inputs of manure were available for land that remained in tilth.

If patterns of land use changed significantly across the period, there was more stability in farm size. Government statistics purporting to give the number of agricultural holdings in different size categories need to be treated with caution because of problems such as knowing what was meant by a 'holding' when two or more farms were amalgamated under a single management. The figures certainly display sporadic inexplicable short-term fluctuations. Nevertheless, they leave little doubt that this was not a period in which there were major changes in farm size (Figure 7). In Norfolk there were 5,438 holdings covering between five and fifty acres in 1885. In the period up to the Second World War this number fluctuated erratically, but not significantly, around a mean of 5,714, reaching a peak of 6,101 in 1921 before falling back to 5,247 in 1939. In Suffolk the pattern was slightly different, with a very gentle decline from 2,822 in 1885 to 2,498 on the outbreak of war: overall, across the two counties, there was a fall in the number of holdings in the 5–50 acre range of just 4.6 per cent. The number of medium-sized farms, those of between 50 and 300 acres, also

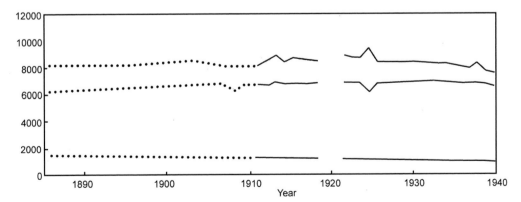

Figure 7. Changing farm size in East Anglia, 1885–1939. Top, 5–50 acres; middle, 50–300 acres; bottom, above 300 acres. Before 1912 information is not available for every year. Source: MAFF Agricultural Returns.

remained fairly stable, fluctuating only slightly throughout the period and, overall, rising in the two counties between 1885 and 1939 by 5.6 per cent, from 6,395 to 6,754. Only the number of large farms, those of over 300 acres, displays a more constant pattern, falling gradually but steadily from 1,574 in the two counties in 1885 to a low point of 1,169 in 1934, before recovering slightly, to 1,175, on the eve of war – an overall decrease across the whole period of just over a third. The fact that this decline in numbers is only partially mirrored by a corresponding increase in the number of medium-sized farms suggests that it may be related to the abandonment (and eventual coniferisation) of some of the very worst soils, especially in Breckland and the Sandlings – districts in which, as we have seen, the very largest farms tended to be concentrated (above, p. 7). Here, some holdings disappeared entirely: others, abandoning the most marginal land to heath and plantation, fell below the 300-acre level, and thus reappear in the statistics as 'medium-sized' holdings.[240]

Global figures thus disguise some complex variations in the agrarian fortunes of different districts, variations which are also manifest in the development of farm layouts. There are three periods at which these can be mapped: c.1840, using the tithe award maps; c.1910, when a survey was undertaken by the Inland Revenue Valuation Office in order to establish the value of land, so that any increase in value when land changed hands could be taxed;[241] and 1940–1, when the National Farm Survey was undertaken to establish the state of cultivation on individual farms as a basis for planning increases in food production. All these surveys, although undertaken for rather different reasons, recorded patterns of farm occupancy, as well as a variety of other information. In practice, direct comparisons are difficult: tithes were commuted on the basis of individual parishes, whereas the 1910 surveys were organised on the basis of 'income tax parishes' (usually groups of contiguous ecclesiastical parishes) and both they and the 1940 surveys used the existing OS 6-inch sheets as the basis for mapping. All sources, moreover, often omit individual holdings, for a variety of reasons which are not always apparent to the modern user. Perhaps because of such difficulties, while the value of studying changes in farm layout using these three sources has been recognised by a number of researchers[242] it has so far been used only to trace the development of individual farms (by John Godfrey and Brian Short in Sussex); no studies of larger areas have yet been published.

An examination of sample areas suggests that farm layouts in East Anglia developed in three main ways in the depression period. Firstly, there were those areas of particularly fertile soils, well suited to horticulture and market gardening, in which the number of small farms and smallholdings increased, a process often accompanied by extensive if piecemeal changes to boundaries. On the rich soils of the Fens around the Terringtons and Walpoles the field pattern shown on the tithe award maps (Plate 4) was an ancient one, created by the piecemeal amalgamation and enclosure of strips in the old medieval open fields. Many farms in 1840 still, nevertheless, consisted of fairly scattered, strip-like parcels. A large number cultivated between five and twenty acres, slightly fewer between twenty and fifty acres; a minority extended over 200 acres or more. By 1910 the number of allotments and smallholdings had increased, partly through the activities of the South Lincolnshire Small Holdings Association, which had acquired over thirty acres of land in the area in the 1890s. These changes in farm size were accompanied by many piecemeal alterations to boundaries: some holdings had been subdivided during the intervening years, some combined, and only a minority boasted the same boundaries as they had had sixty years earlier. By 1940 further consolidation had taken place: there was a further slight increase in the number of holdings, and farms were now more compact.[243] This general pattern of development was mirrored across much of the Fens, and also on the fertile loams of north-east Norfolk, as in the parishes of Rollesby, Repps and Bastwick (Plate 5), although here there was less change in farm size until the development of county council smallholdings, largely through the purchase and division of Church Farm and Sowells Farm in Rollesby.[244]

Secondly, there were areas of moderately fertile land, especially on the claylands, where there was less change in farm size, and less proliferation of smallholdings, in the depression period. In the parishes of Forncett St Peter, Aslacton, and Moulton St Michael in south Norfolk, for example, there was some subdivision of the largest farms in the period between 1840 and 1910, and a consequent increase in the number of smaller units.[245] The 170-acre Neville Farm in Aslacton, for instance, was subdivided to form the 105-acre Somerset Farm and the 59-acre Neville Farm; The Rookery, in the east of Forncett, 125 acres in 1840, was divided up into three holdings; while Limetree Farm, covering 182 acres in 1840, became two. Overall, the number of farms cultivating upwards of 100 acres was halved between 1840 and 1910, and only the smaller farms remained relatively unchanged in terms of size and layout. Yet this trend did not continue, and between 1910 and 1940 there was some limited consolidation of holdings, accompanied by numerous piecemeal changes to farm boundaries (Plate 6).[246]

Other clayland districts display variations on this theme of essential stability. In parts of north Suffolk, for example – as in the parishes of the South Elmhams – amalgamation rather than subdivision was the key development in the period between 1840 and 1910: many small farms, of between five and twenty acres, disappeared but the number of larger farms, in excess of 150 acres, more than doubled. Between 1910 and 1940, in contrast, there was little change in holding size, although there was with some further amalgamation and numerous piecemeal changes to farm boundaries.[247]

The third way in which holding layout might develop in the depression period was especially evidenced in areas of relatively poor, light land, especially in Breckland and the Suffolk Sandlings, where the number of farms frequently declined through the amalgamation of holdings. This was not, however, reflected in any general increase in the average size of farms, because much of the poorest land reverted to heath, was used as game cover, or was planted up as woodland or plantations. The precise development of such areas varied widely, however, depending on how far such poor soils were interspersed with more fertile land, or – in the case of the Suffolk Sandlings – the extent to which farms included areas of coastal marsh as well as inland heath.

In short, while there were significant changes during the depression period in holding size and layout on the most fertile, and to some extent on the poorest, land in the region – changes on both soil types being in part a consequence of government initiatives which we shall explore in the following chapters – for the most part this seems to have been a period of comparative stability in farm size, especially when compared to the great changes of the eighteenth and early nineteenth centuries, and in spite of the massive transfer of land from large estates to owner-occupiers which took place in this period.

# CHAPTER 3

# Alternative Agriculture

## INTRODUCTION

So far, we have discussed the fate of 'mainstream' agriculture in East Anglia during the Great Depression – the way in which most farmers in this land dominated by grain production were affected by, and responded to, the changing economic conditions of the later nineteenth and early twentieth centuries. In this chapter we will concentrate on more idiosyncratic, less 'mainstream', aspects of the agricultural industry. Our chapter title comes from the famous book by Joan Thirsk, which is concerned with the multifarious ways in which farmers innovated and experimented with new forms of husbandry during the various depressions which British agriculture has suffered over the centuries, and in the pages that follow we will pay some attention to new crops and new forms of production which were adopted in Norfolk and Suffolk after the 1870s.[1] But 'alternative' also implies other forms of deviation from the mainstream of medium-sized and large farms held by owner-occupiers or estate tenants, and we will also be concerned here with communes and co-operatives; with the fate of commoners and common land; and, above all, with the appearance of a new class of smallholders, brought into existence in part by the conscious exercise of political power at a national level. These two broad aspects of 'alternative agriculture' were, in fact, closely linked to each other, in that for the most part smallholders and their ilk were primarily involved, not in grain production, but in horticulture, poultry-breeding, market gardening and a range of similar enterprises which expanded phenomenally as mainstream farming endured depression.

## NEW CROPS AND ENTERPRISES

As prices of grain and, to a lesser extent, livestock declined, farmers and some landowners experimented with new crops. The most important of these, sugar beet, was adopted on such a scale in East Anglia that it can be regarded as part of the 'mainstream' of agriculture, and was for this reason dealt with in some detail in the previous chapter. Others, however, were adopted on a smaller scale, in limited areas, or by particular kinds of farmer. Some were positively cranky, such as tobacco. In 1782 its cultivation in Britain had been prohibited by law, but in the 1880s limited trial crops were permitted and in 1886 Lord Walsingham was granted permission to grow it experimentally on his estate at Merton in the Norfolk

Breckland. A security had to be paid and then, when the tobacco was dried, the customs duty was levied or the crop deposited in a bonded warehouse. Walsingham was one of a small number of growers in England led by Faunce de Laune of Sittingbourne in Kent, an individual with whom he frequently corresponded. A quarter of an acre was sown and was said to be 'growing well, but not a very heavy crop'.[2] By September the crop had been hung in drying houses but a later note in the estate archives states simply: 'I believe that the experiment will show that tobacco cannot be grown profitably in England.'[3] The following year Faune de Laune himself contributed a long article to the *JRASE* extolling the virtues of the crop,[4] but no further attempts seem to have been made to grow it at Merton, although there were trials elsewhere, most notably around Methwold and at Croxton (also in Breckland). Seventeen acres of the crop were being cultivated by ten growers in 1916, falling to twelve acres and eight growers in 1917 and twelve and a half and nine in 1918; Mr Meade of Croxton alone grew ten acres in 1921 and 1922.[5] Experiments were not confined to Breckland. The sale of £2 worth of tobacco is recorded in 1911 on the Earl of Stradbroke's home farm at Henham in east Suffolk.[6] Less successful were attempts at cultivating rice. In the 1880s Charles Ellis of Maidstone tried to interest Lord Walsingham in seed, and letters were exchanged discussing whether it should be grown under glass or under water. Whether any rice was actually planted at Merton is not clear, but Ellis's own crop failed entirely, although John Morton, agricultural writer and land agent to Lord Ducie at Tortworth in Gloucestershire, was said to have 'got quite a good crop'.[7]

These attempts were clearly on the lunatic fringe of husbandry. Of far more significance was the steady expansion of horticulture, market gardening and related activities which, as we have already noted, took place from the late nineteenth century. Articles on the cultivation of soft fruit and vegetables, as well as on the production of eggs and poultry, were a regular feature of the *Eastern Daily Press* in the 1880s and 90s, together with reports on such things as the planting of Dutch bulbs in the 'wasteland district around Wereham'.[8] The growing importance of these concerns was reflected in the exhibits at the county agricultural shows. Ploughs designed for smallholders were increasingly displayed from the 1890s, fruit- and potato-spraying equipment regularly shown from 1910.[9] Although these new enterprises were widely distributed across East Anglia they were a particular feature of the Fens, and especially the northern silt Fens, and of the light, fertile loams of north-east Norfolk. In the former district it was thought in 1893 that horticulture 'had been the means of enabling people to escape the depression, as they had been able to grow the best class of potatoes, vegetables and fruit'.[10]

Poultry production expanded steadily in these districts, although also to some extent in all parts of East Anglia. By 1902 flocks of 1,200 hens were said to be common in the Fens.[11] Turkey production, in particular, increased in importance. In 1910 the market was described as 'buoyant' and the birds were said to thrive on nettles, proving that weeds did indeed have a value![12] Even before the outbreak of the First World War, large, specialised production units had appeared. When Pippin Hall Farm, Lidgate (Suffolk), was sold in 1912 it included 'a large modern poultry plant' consisting of incubators, 'foster mothers with lamps', egg baskets and portable fowl houses as well as coops and runs: 150 head of poultry were included in the sale, as well as 100 pigs.[13] Usually, eggs and poultry formed one part of the enterprise, whether on smallholdings or on larger farms. The Fishers, a Norfolk family who farmed first at Letheringsett and later at Gunton in the late nineteenth and early twentieth century, concentrated increasingly on dairying, but eggs and poultry were also significant. Many of the eggs were sent to a London salesman.[14]

The expansion of egg and poultry production continued during the inter-war years. In 1928 R.McG. Carslaw described a Norfolk poultry farm which had been established in 1920 on eighteen acres, using old army huts and 100 breeding hens. The eggs were sold on contract to a large firm of milk producers. In 1925 eight more acres were added and the premises extended. A herd of between eight and ten cows was used to keep the grass down and the number of hens was increased to 3,000. The houses were lit at night to encourage laying and profits were said to be much greater than on an arable farm of equivalent acreage.[15] By 1930 Norfolk Egg Producers had a packing station in King Street in Norwich and thirteen tons of eggs were being processed each week in February. The spring flush meant that by April this had risen to fifteen tons.[16] Intensive egg production could be carried out on a small acreage: no fewer than 5,250 head of 'blood-tested poultry' were kept on the fifteen-acre Highfield poultry farm at Beetley. When the holding was offered for sale in 1932 the premises included two brooder houses for 4,000 chicks, ten laying houses and six colony houses.[17]

The importance of the industry is clearly indicated by the fact that, by the 1920s, special sections on poultry were always included after the general farming notes in the *East Anglian Daily Times* and the *Eastern Daily Press*. Moreover, a separate poultry catalogue was introduced at the Norfolk show from 1914 and a wide range of items relating to poultry production was displayed at both county shows. Egg boxes for transporting eggs by rail appeared from 1910 and from 1918 'intensive' and 'semi-intensive' houses with slatted floors were displayed. In 1927 the Ministry of Food staged an exhibition at the Suffolk show on the marketing of eggs.[18] The inter-war years also saw increased emphasis on intensive production: a three-tier fattening battery for 150 hens was shown at the Suffolk in 1933.[19] By this stage a wide range of equipment was being exhibited, including laying cages, incubators, a 'double breeding pen for 20 birds', and 'improved' batteries for laying hens comprising three tiers of four cages as well as slatted-floor laying houses measuring six feet by five, to accommodate fifty hens.[20] The industry was not an unqualified success, however, and as the general state of the economy deteriorated in the 1930s it perhaps suffered more than most small-scale agricultural enterprises. In 1930 fears were already being expressed about increasing production and falling demand.[21] By 1935 the poultry columns had disappeared from the local papers and the position of the eggs and poultry industry was described as 'disastrous' as a result of increased output and imports.[22]

The production of small fruit was increasing rapidly by the late nineteenth century, particularly in the Fens and in north-east Norfolk, although problems were experienced in getting the crop to market in good condition in hot weather, and attempts to develop cold storage systems proved unsuccessful.[23] The business was a lucrative one: Rider Haggard in 1902, for example, described forty acres of strawberries at Wiggenhall St Germains which 'never returned less that £20 an acre'. In the 1910–12 Inland Revenue Field Books many Fenland farms were described as being largely devoted to fruit growing.[24] In east Norfolk blackcurrants were being cultivated around Potter Heigham on some scale by the 1880s and in the 1890s they began to be marketed collectively, and sent by rail to the Midland markets. In both districts, production increased dramatically in the inter-war years. Fruit growing was sometimes carried out on a large scale, as on the 756-acre fruit-growing estate operated by the Harrison brothers at Wiggenhall St Mary, on which ten farms were run as one.[25] But, for the most part, soft fruit farms were relatively small concerns, sometimes run on a part-time basis, and a number of co-operative organisations developed to assist in marketing and/or to offer help and advice. Norfolk Fruit Growers Ltd was set up in 1913, and by 1926 was marketing seventy-seven tons of fruit, valued at £5,607, per annum, rising by 1929 to 507 tons valued at £17,128.[26] In 1920 the East Norfolk Fruit Growers' Association was formed to promote the interests of local growers. Trips to more traditional fruit-growing areas such as Kent were arranged and *The Eastern Daily Press* described it as a 'very useful group … It is very pleasant having capable gentlemen looking after our interests and advising when to sell and at what price'.[27]

By 1935 there was a total of 16,000 acres under soft fruit in East Anglia as a whole. But, in a direct parallel with the poultry industry, while output was increasing the value of the crop was falling; by the mid-1930s blackcurrant growers, in particular, were suffering from overseas competition and in 1935 Norfolk Fruit Growers were even undecided as to whether it would pay to pick the crop.[28] Nevertheless, it was recognised that the progress of the industry had been 'extra-ordinary' over the previous decade and a half: only the county of Kent now produced more fruit.[29] The success of the industry in Norfolk was attributed by Mosby in 1938 to the skill of a handful of pioneers in the Fens and the north-east of the county; to the need for small farmers to diversify in this period of depression; to the activities of Norfolk County Council's Department of Horticulture, which had research stations at Emneth and Burlingham; to the vigorous advertising campaign mounted by the growers' associations; and to 'the establishment of jam, pulp, and canning factories at Wisbech, Kings Lynn, Thetford, Banham, North Walsham, Yarmouth and Lowestoft'.[30]

Of perhaps greater importance, however – and with a far more durable impact upon the rural landscape – was the phenomenal expansion in orchards producing apples, pears and plums. Small-scale commercial enterprises had been a feature of many farms for centuries in Suffolk and Norfolk, but these old orchards were deemed by the 1930s to be 'small, unimportant, and usually old and neglected'.[31] The new commercial enterprises, in contrast, were an important part of the rural economy, especially in Norfolk. Their development was only in part a response to the depression, for large commercial concerns had begun to appear in the Fens as early as the 1850s. In north-east Norfolk the industry developed slightly

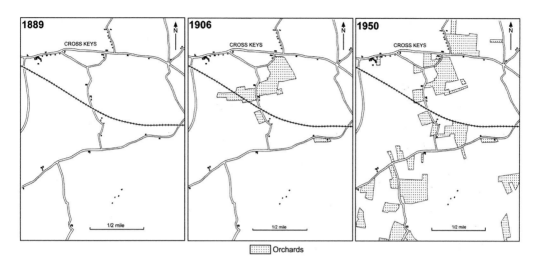

Figure 8. The expansion of orchards in the Norfolk Fens: the area between Walpole St Andrew and Tilney All Saints, 1889–1950, as shown on successive Ordnance Survey maps.

later. The Cubitts of Honing and the Petres of Westwick planted the first commercial orchards in the district in 1898,[32] and four years later Rider Haggard noted the expansion of orchards in the area around Martham. In both districts the industry grew steadily in importance, so that the area devoted to orchards in Norfolk as a whole rose from 6,345 acres in 1914 to 8,414 in 1926, reaching 10,089 in 1936 (Figure 8).[33] In Suffolk orchards were fewer – 3,526 acres in 1926 and 4,484 in 1938 – and more widely dispersed, although with some noticeable concentrations around Ipswich and Sudbury.[34]

The orchards of the silt Fens formed part of a wider fruit growing district which embraced the adjacent areas of Cambridgeshire and Lincolnshire and which was centred on Wisbech:

> This area extends from Upwell in the south to Terrington in the north, being about a mile in width in the south, it widens rapidly in the neighbourhood of Wisbech and exceeds 6 miles in the north at Terrington. The older orchards are to be found near Wisbech and the more recent extensions in the north, but so far the orchard area does not extend more than half a mile north of the Lynn-Sutton Bridge road. East of Terrington the continuity of the orchards is broken by grass and arable land, but there is a big concentration of orchards on both sides of the Great Ouse in the Wiggenhalls...[35]

The Fen orchards mainly produced cooking apples and plums, which were sent to the north of England or used in local jam factories. The orchards in the east of Norfolk were more widely scattered and grew dessert apples such as the Worcestershire Pearmain and Cox's Orange Pippin. Brick Kiln Farm, North Walsham, sold in 1937, was described as 'very suited to high class dessert apples': there were eighteen acres of ten-year-old orchards on the holding.[36] Some orchards in the district supplied apples to the Gaymers' cider factory at Attleborough, which had been set up beside the railway line in 1896.[37]

Market gardening also expanded fast, especially in the inter-war period. Asparagus-growing was, by the late 1930s, concentrated in the area around Fakenham and Thetford.[38] The crop was 'sold in bundles at Covent Garden and in the local markets and part of the crop is sent to soup and canning factories'.[39] Celery was also cultivated on some scale, especially in the Fens. But the greatest growth was in the cultivation of carrots, sprouts and cabbages for human consumption, the acreages of which in Norfolk alone increased, in the ten years between 1926 and 1936, from 212 to 1,610, 185 to 1,832, and 750 to 4,066 acres respectively.[40] Some of these vegetables were grown on large farms as part of normal field rotations, especially in the 'Good Sands' area of north-west Norfolk. At the 1935 British Association for the Advancement of Science meeting in Norwich Mr C.T. Joice of Testerton described how between 500 and 600 acres of his 3,000-acre farm was given over to vegetables, which were sold though a London agent (if prices were poor he fed them to his livestock, thus saving on feed bills),[41] while in 1934 Home Farm, Wiggenhall St Mary (203 acres), was described as 'a capital potato and market gardening farm'.[42] But for the most part vegetables were, like fruit, cultivated on 'small farms and smallholdings in the Flegg and Loam regions, particularly in the immediate neighbourhood of Norwich, Hickling, Stalham and Martham', and to an important extent in the Fens.[43]

In part the prominence of small fruit-growing and market-gardening enterprises in these two areas reflected the suitability of their rich soils for these forms of business. But it was also a function of the fact that these districts had long been characterised by relatively small farms, often in the hands of owner-occupiers, the kinds of enterprise which were now scarcely viable as conventional grain producers, but which were well suited to such small-scale, intensive forms of husbandry. Indeed, many inter-war writers emphasised the greater flexibility and adaptability of such enterprises when compared with large grain farms. 'To cut costs on an arable farm of five hundred acres without letting it go to ruin was very difficult, or to increase production without adding to them. But 50 acres was a much more flexible unit …'.[44]

The new forms of diversification, in other words, offered a lifeline to struggling small farmers. Most, however, depended on the availability of seasonal labour. By 1912 the Wisbech strawberry growers, for example, relied heavily on seasonal pickers from the East End of London and Sheffield. Often whole families would come, and were photographed by the local press.[45] Appropriate facilities had to be provided; when Manor Farm in Walpole St Peter was put on the market in 1933 there were forty-one acres of fruit trees, a brick and timber fruit pickers' cookhouse with twelve brick fireplaces, four ovens and four coppers, and 'timber built and corrugated iron bunks with cubicles six feet by four feet and sliding doors'.[46]

Other forms of diversification developed in East Anglia in the inter-war years, including lavender-growing, which was begun in 1933 at Heacham by Chilvers and Son; the farming of silver foxes, which started in 1927 near Sheringham and which was being carried out on seven separate farms in Norfolk by 1937; and coypu farming, which started on a small scale in the early 1920s.[47] All these were, once again, enterprises which were viable on relatively small acreages. Lastly, flax had long been grown in south Norfolk and Suffolk but seems to have been neglected during the agricultural revolution and high farming years. It now experienced a modest revival. Francis Fairweather of Whatfield sold his flax crop for £173 in 1920[48] and in 1935 the Linen Research Association of Northern Ireland set up a Flax Research Institute at Abbey Farm, Flitcham, in west Norfolk. Some flax was produced regularly in the area, following barley in the crop rotation, and a flax mill was set up on the river Babingly.[49] Production was to become more important during the Second World War.

## IDEALISTS AND COMMUNES

The deepening depression in agriculture saw an increased concern for the fate of small farmers and the rural poor on the part of an educated, largely urban and often not very well-informed elite of intellectuals and commentators. There was a widespread belief that enclosure and the emergence of large capitalist farms during the eighteenth and nineteenth centuries had eroded the character of the English countryman. With a marked reduction in the number of farms, the sturdy yeoman had declined to the status of the mindless Hodge, who was now deserting the countryside for the excitement, better wages and higher living standards of the towns and cities. The larger farmers who remained were increasingly distanced from their workforce: 'When farmers become gentlemen, then labourers become slaves'.[50] But such sentiments were clouded and confused by the increasing idealisation of rural life which developed apace in the Edwardian period. 'Under the influence of a fundamentally anti-entrepreneurial intelligentsia, Edwardian society had turned away from the glorification of industrial enterprise to be captivated by the myth of England as a pre-industrial Garden of Eden.'[51] The farm labourers who came to the towns rarely wanted to return to their old life in the countryside. Instead, it was the comparatively well-to-do who formed the reading public for the ever-increasing volume of books stressing the imagined, often anti-materialist values of country life. Such ideas burgeoned in the inter-war years. The Suffolk small farmer and journalist Adrian Bell contributed a regular column to the *Eastern Daily Press* in which he wrote eloquently on country matters: 'If men could begin to realise the rich physical heritage which they have lost, cheated by industrialism of their birthright, then they would turn and seek first and foremost for a new wholeness.' This could only be found in a life on the land, ideally on a small family farm, with all the stability of family, soil and seasons that this implied.[52] Bell was one of a small but influential group in the 1930s known as the 'ruralists', who believed that the future of agriculture lay not in larger farms and increased mechanisation, but in a return to relatively small, preferably organic, farms, and in the re-creation of a society of small-scale craftsman producing goods locally. This, they believed, would arrest the depression and revitalise and repopulate the countryside.

The 'ruralist' group included the author Henry Williamson, who took on a farm near Stiffkey in north Norfolk in 1937 and attempted to bring it back into profitable production. He believed that a decline in standards of cultivation and a perceived decline in the character of national life went hand in hand.[53] The ruralists argued that if Britain was to recover her soul and be culturally, spiritually and economically awakened, leadership must come not from scientists or civil servants but from the countryside itself, in the form of the established landowning class. To Williamson and Bell, and to others, such as the Dorset landowner Rolf Gardiner, the emphasis placed by modern economists such as C.S. Orwin and Daniel Hall on business efficiency, farm rationalisation and economies of scale were misguided.[54] Most of the leading figures in this loose movement, however, were writers and journalists rather than farmers, including not only Bell but also H.J. Massingham, whose father had begun his journalistic career with the *Eastern Daily Press*.

In this potent mix of ideas, concepts of co-operative organisation and living emanating from such nineteenth-century idealists as William Cobbett and Robert Owen continued to have an appeal. Indeed, some continuous threads of practical experience as well as of intellectual discourse link the 'alternative' approaches to agricultural organisation of the early and of the later nineteenth century. John Gurdon, who owned much of the parish of Assington in South Suffolk, established a farming co-operative in 1830 by letting a 100-acre farm to '20 of the better class of labourers'. Each paid £2 as a guarantee on the £400 which Gurdon lent their enterprise. In 1852 two other farms, Knott's Farm and Several's Farm, were let to thirty labourers on similar terms. The initial enterprise survived until 1913, when 'Society Farm' was finally wound up and taken over by its foreman, George Rice: by this time there were twelve members who each received a share of £121 3s 6d. The other two farms kept going until 1918, when they too failed, the shareholders in this case receiving nothing.[55] In its final years the 'Society Farm' was run as a mixed enterprise, producing wheat, barley, oats and turnips, as well as sheep and cattle. Pigs and poultry were also kept, with pigs, butter, milk, chicken and eggs being sold to members.[56]

In the late nineteenth century the majority of co-operatives and communes were associated not with rural labourers and small farmers but with middle-class socialist and anarchist intellectuals. Most such schemes were short-lived, partly because of the lack of practical farming knowledge on the part of the participants, and little is known of them. One of the better-documented examples is the Methwold Fruit Colony in the Norfolk Fens, set up in 1889–90 on two acres of land by R.K. Gooderich. He grew fruit trees on half the plot and sold fruit and eggs directly to contacts in London, thus dispensing with the need for a middleman. By 1900 he had erected a small jam factory behind his house. Following a series of articles in newspapers and vegetarian publications (vegetarian settlers were preferred, although some plots were available for non-vegetarians),[57] other Londoners followed him. Neighbouring fields were bought and divided up and bungalows built. By 1900 there were said to be about fifty settlers on two- and three-acre plots. Each needed about £500 to buy his land, build his house and buy tools, seeds and fruit trees, a figure which would have excluded working-class aspirants. 'At Methwold in Norfolk, a new order of things has been inaugurated. The land there has been taken possession of not by country folk but by clerks and tradesmen from London....'[58] By 1908 the jam factory seems to have disappeared but Gooderich was still there, together with a number of other 'fruit growers' on the 'fruit colony'. No fruit growers are listed in the 1916 Directory,[59] however, although the land continued to be cultivated in small plots with orchards into the 1960s. The settlement, now known as Brookville, remains as an island of late nineteenth-century 'colonists'' houses, interspersed with a number of much newer buildings, in the middle of largely open cereal-growing countryside.

## COMMONS AND COMMONERS

Late nineteenth- and early twentieth-century polemicists had surprisingly little to say about more traditional forms of smallholding – cottagers and part-time farmers living on the margins of subsistence: and in particular, they made few comments on the surviving areas of common land in the two counties, upon which many such people had traditionally depended. As we have seen, vast areas of common had been removed during the period of parliamentary enclosure in the early nineteenth century, but some had survived and, in addition, there were numerous areas of 'poors' allotment', blocks of land set aside for the benefit of the village poor by the various enclosure acts. A minority of these were used, in effect, as small commons, exploited by the local poor for livestock grazing as well as being cut for fuel, animal bedding and other resources. Most, however, were simply fuel allotments, sometimes exploited directly by the poor (especially where deposits of peat existed), sometimes leased out to provide money with which coal could be purchased.[60]

For the most part, the period under consideration here saw a steady reduction in the intensity with which both commons and poors' allotments were exploited. The cutting of bracken for cattle bedding, and of furze and ling for fuel, the extraction of peat, and the mowing of rushes, reeds, sedge and rough hay all declined. This was only in part a consequence of the agricultural depression, being primarily the result of a much broader and largely independent range of social, economic and technological developments which rendered redundant many of the products which had once been cut from such areas of marginal land. This process was already well under way by the end of the nineteenth century, and as early as the 1870s it was reported that the local population had ceased to cut turfs on Whitwell Common because 'the houses and fireplaces of the commoners are unsuitable for the burning of turf.'[61] But it accelerated thereafter: Bird, describing the use of East Ruston 'Common' (really a poors' allotment) in north-east Norfolk in 1909, noted that the cutting of flags, peat and furze for firing had largely ceased, and while fodder cutting was still continued the use of the common for grazing had much declined.[62] Here, as in many other places, 'The poor are too poor to buy a cow'. Indeed, there were insufficient animals to prevent the colonisation of much of the area by gorse. Clarke, in 1918, noted a number of places where traditional forms of cutting and mowing, for peat, reeds, sedge or litter, persisted. The Oxburgh Fuel Allotment, for example, was mown each year on a date fixed by the villagers: 'the man employed puts the litter in heaps and receives about 1sh. for each heap; these are numbered and the ownership for each is settled by drawing lots.'[63] On Marsham Heath and Buxton Heath both *Calluna* and *Erica* were cut 'for besoms or sink brushes'.[64] Even bracken was still mown in some places, as at Congham, North Wooton and Great Bircham.[65] But, in general, traditional uses were in decline: peat, for example, was still dug on a number of the fens, 'though formerly to a much greater degree than at present'.[66] At Boughton turf was still cut, but only 'to a small extent'.[67] At Old Buckenham the 'Poor have right of turf-cutting, never exercised',[68] while at Brunstead, although mowing and grazing continued, no peat had been cut for fuel 'for the past ten years'.[69]

As the local poor ceased to involve themselves in these archaic forms of land use, the rights were sometimes let, or were used informally by local farmers, because (as Bird noted in 1909) 'the grazing would be wasted if those who ought not did not make use of it.'[70] But larger farmers generally had little interest in exploiting the meagre grazing provided by this often unfenced marginal land, especially as the volume of road traffic increased in the course of the twentieth century. Many commons were entirely ungrazed by the inter-war years, or grazed lightly or sporadically, and often by horses or donkeys rather than by sheep or cattle. Changes in grazing regimes themselves led to alterations in the character of the vegetation, as we shall see (below, pp. 135–6). Butcher drew attention in 1941 to the numerous village greens in Suffolk comprising 'poor grassland which includes a lot of scrub and weeds and which is used by the local inhabitants or nomads for a generally miscellaneous lot of animals'.[71] There is some evidence that urban commons, where these existed, were more intensively used, especially for grazing donkeys owned by small delivery businesses. At Fakenham attempts to enclose the common in 1870 met with stiff opposition from the townspeople, many of them local traders: the new fences were taken down and burnt.[72] But for the most part, as traditional uses declined, commons became places for fly tipping, dumping, fires and gypsy camps.[73]

Commons in East Anglia, as in many parts of England, were thus increasingly seen as a problem by local authorities. The Local Government Act of 1894 gave parish councils a range of powers over common land, and the Commons Act of 1899 allowed them to draw up rules for regulating its use.[74] In 1907 Mulbarton Parish Council debated the future management of the local common and listed the various problems from which it currently suffered, including illegal grazing, manure heaps and gypsy vans.[75] Three years later, when East Dereham Urban District Council applied for a scheme to regulate the use of Neatherd Moor, similar difficulties were described: 'At the present time it is a horrible nuisance, the pit full of dead dogs and dead cats, and broken glass bottles, rendering it dangerous to cattle and children which might stray into it.'[76] Few, if any, areas of common and waste were ploughed up during the First World War, although a number of poors' allotments were cultivated, including those at Marsham and Blo Norton. Most continued to slide into dereliction, and by the 1920s cars were becoming an additional problem, churning up the grass and posing a threat to grazing stock.[77] Regeneration to scrub, and eventually to woodland, was the fate of many.

Attempts to tidy up places like Neatherd Moor were associated with a new attitude to the commons, emanating from the major urban conurbations, which saw them primarily as 'green lungs', place for healthy recreation, rather than as part of traditional rural life and a vital resource for the small farmer. It would have been hard for most liberal intellectuals to think of such increasingly derelict areas as part of the plan to restore the English yeomanry. That was to be achieved by new, and radical, measures.

## THE COUNTY SMALLHOLDINGS

From the early nineteenth century a variety of commentators, from a variety of political perspectives, urged that land needed to be found for the rural poor in the form of allotments or smallholdings. In the 1830s John Bright and J.S. Mill had established the Liberal Land Tenure Association, while around the same time the Chartists had attempted to establish a number of land settlements.[78] But serious agitation for smallholdings of between five and fifty acres, and for allotments of under five acres, really began with the onset of the depression in the 1880s. The extension of the franchise as a result of the Reform Act to include farm labourers meant that the Liberal party took up previously marginal issues such as allotments and smallholdings. This development was also part of a wider collection of policies intended to appeal to middle-class liberals, including opposition to primogeniture and to the settlement of landed estates.

The Ipswich MP Jessie Collings, the Birmingham Liberal Joseph Chamberlain and their supporters saw agricultural workers as the degraded remnants of a proud and independent yeomanry and believed that if they could be restored to their former condition they would be a stabilising force in the countryside against radical social upheavals.[79] Chamberlain also thought that a proliferation of rural allotments and smallholdings would be popular with urban workers, as it would discourage rural labourers from moving to the towns. By the terms of the Allotments Extension Act of 1882 and a further act of 1887, where a need could be demonstrated, a public enquiry had been held, and no land was available for sale or rent, a compulsory purchase order could be issued through a Provisional Order of the Board of Agriculture. Originally the land went to the Local Sanitary Authority but in 1894 powers of purchase were transferred to the new Rural District Councils. Initially, land bought was only to provide allotments of less than five acres.[80]

The Norfolk Small Holdings and Allotments Committee, set up in 1889, was one of the earliest in the country. It mainly comprised major landowners, including members of the Boileau, Buxton, Le Strange, Ripenhall, Wodehouse and Colman families. Almost immediately twenty-two applicants called upon the Committee to help them find land in Besthorpe which could either be purchased or rented by the Wayland Sanitary Authority:

after much negotiation suitable land was found.[81] A year later an application was made by twenty labourers in Kelling for a total of seventeen and a quarter acres, and similar requests soon followed from Horsham St Faith, Bawburgh, Litcham, Shipdham, Wells, Southrepps, Erpingham, Clenchwarton and Salthouse. Usually, land could be found by negotiation but the Horsham St Faith request resulted in a public enquiry and a compulsory purchase order.[82] The individual allotments were usually under an acre, and the rent charged was between 30s and £2 an acre per annum.

In 1892 Collings managed to get his Small Holdings Act through parliament. This allowed, but did not oblige, county councils to buy land for smallholdings, as opposed to allotments. The holdings were to be sold by hire purchase to the occupants, with one fifth of the purchase price to be paid as a down-payment and the rest following over a number of years.[83] This put smallholdings out of the reach of most potential applicants, especially as they had also to demonstrate that they possessed sufficient working capital, estimated as £5 per acre, to take on the holding. Government grants and loans at 3.5 per cent were available to local authorities for purchase, and for drawing up schemes, but nationally a total of only 881 acres was acquired under the scheme between 1892 and 1908.[84] During 1895 there were thirty-two representations from Norfolk parishes to the Smallholdings Committee; some were satisfied but twenty-two were still pending at the end of the year. Applicants had to be from the 'labouring population' and requests had to be for less than five acres.[85] In only one case, at Ringland, were powers of compulsory purchase employed.

The Lincolnshire county councillor Richard Winfrey, who later became MP for south-west Norfolk from 1906 to 1923, was a prime mover in the smallholdings movement. He set up, and became chairman of, the Lincolnshire Small Holdings Association in 1894 (the first of its kind in the country), an organisation which rented 650 acres around Spalding from Lord Carrington and sub-let them to 202 separate tenants. The success of this scheme convinced Carrington that *tenancy*, rather than *ownership*, was a more realistic way of reviving smallholdings.[86] These ideas soon spread, and in 1900 the Norfolk Small Holdings Association was set up, with Winfrey as chairman. Farms at Swaffham, Watton and Whissonsett were bought and divided, the latter between eighteen tenants, all of whom lived in the village. No new buildings were erected on any of the three farms, and nearly all the tenants had other paid work. In 1902, 130 labourers in Nordelph asked Winfrey to help them to obtain smallholdings. They petitioned Norfolk County Council for 500 acres and Winfrey bought fifty acres in the parish, but this was only a start and in 1904 the county council purchased a further ninety-one acres at Chapel Farm. Thirty-five holdings of between one and twelve acres were laid out. The tenants included twenty-eight agricultural labourers, a carpenter, a baker, a grocer, and a man who worked as a travelling showman in the summer and in the winter hired his horses to his neighbours to work their fields. The success of the scheme was attributed to the local availability of part-time work and the fertility of the soil.[87]

**Plate 1**

| | |
|---|---|
| ▪ | 45 and over |
| ▪ | 40 - 44 |
| ▪ | 35 - 39 |
| ▪ | 30 - 34 |
| ▪ | 25 - 29 |
| ▪ | 20 - 24 |
| ▪ | 0 - 19 |
| ▪ | No information |
| ▪ | Urban |

**Plates 1–3:** the percentage of land under pasture in East Anglia in 1886, 1906 and 1936.

In 1886 the main pasture-farming areas of East Anglia were found on the grazing marshes in the Norfolk Broads and at various places along the coast; on the clays of central Norfolk; on the heavy soils to the south of Kings Lynn; and in parts of Breckland. By 1906 (**2**) pasture had increased in all these areas, and was also now dominant across much of the claylands of south Norfolk and north east Suffolk. By 1936 (**3**) there had been various changes in detail, in part as a consequence of the localised expansion of sugar beet cultivation and milk production, but the total area under grass was much the same. Source: MAFF Agricultural Returns.

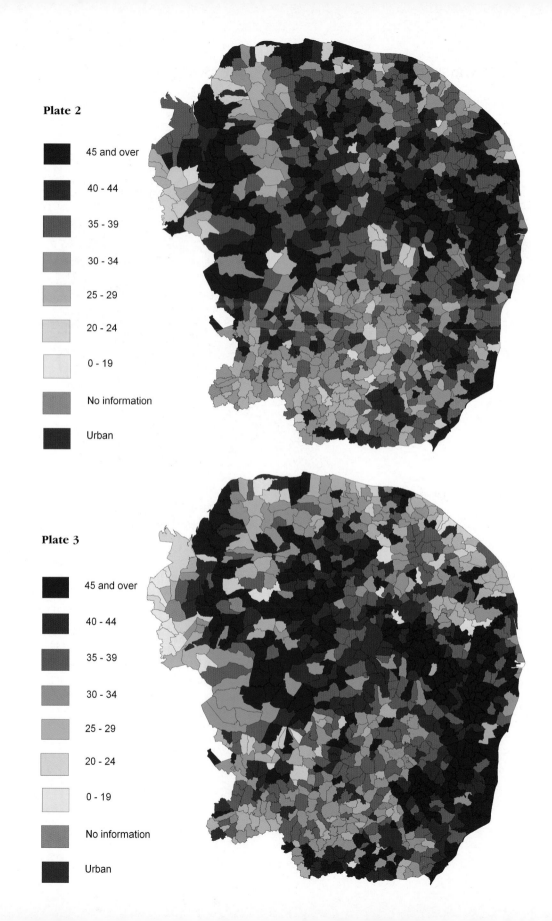

**Plate 2**

- 45 and over
- 40 - 44
- 35 - 39
- 30 - 34
- 25 - 29
- 20 - 24
- 0 - 19
- No information
- Urban

**Plate 3**

- 45 and over
- 40 - 44
- 35 - 39
- 30 - 34
- 25 - 29
- 20 - 24
- 0 - 19
- No information
- Urban

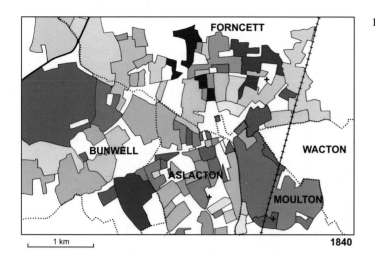

**Plate 4**

1840

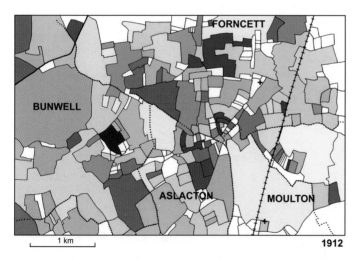

1912

1941

**Plates 4–6**

The changing pattern of farm holdings in sample areas of East Anglia in c.1840, 1912, and 1941. On each map the various colours represent separate units of occupancy. **4**, on the clays of south Norfolk between Bunwell and Wacton; **5**, on the fertile loams of Flegg; **6**, in the silt Fens. Source: Tithe Award Maps, Inland Revenue Land Valuation Surveys, and the 1941 National Farm Survey.

**Plate 5**

**Plate 6**

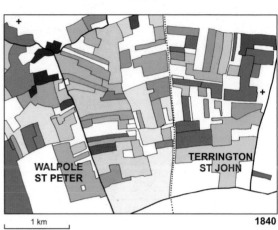

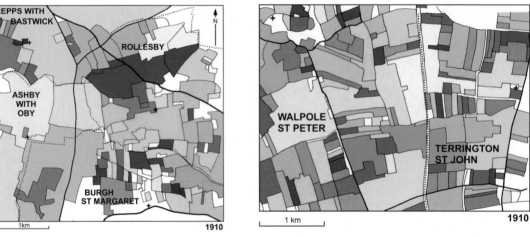

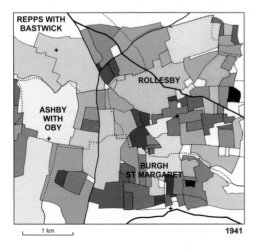

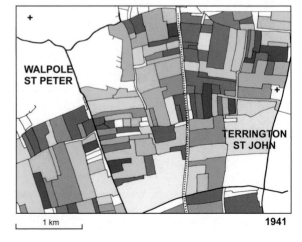

After the 1906 general election the Liberals were back in power and Winfrey became MP for south-west Norfolk. A further Small Holdings and Allotments Act was passed in 1907 and consolidated in 1908.[88] This required every county council to set up a Small Holdings and Allotments Committee; councils could purchase land either for rent or for hire purchase, something which widened considerably the pool of potential applicants. The government was particularly keen on promoting co-operatives and 'colonies' of smallholdings on which tenants could work as a community. Land could be let directly to co-operative associations, and the Board of Agriculture published a series of leaflets on co-operation. Earl Carrington told a National Congress on Rural Development in 1911 that 'What we have to aim for is a peaceful rural revolution.'[89] Between 1908 and 1914 205,103 acres were duly acquired in England and no fewer than 14,045 smallholders settled on the land.[90]

The Norfolk committee was particularly active. It looked for land to buy, and used its powers of compulsory purchase ninety-four times (more than any other county council in England).[91] In addition, compulsory hiring orders were obtained for land in Colkirk, Edgefield, Outwell and Upwell, West Rudham, Thursford, Hindringham, Hunworth, Happisburgh, Inglesthorpe and Wood Dalling, although these were often lifted when suitable alternative land was offered. By 1914 there were 1,295 tenants on 9,083 acres of purchased land and 3,884 of hired land in the county.[92] The purchase costs were borne by the county council and serviced by income from rents. The most extensive holdings were on the fertile loams of east Norfolk, where the Burroughes and Jary estates, taking in nearly all of the parishes of Burlingham St Andrew and St Edmund and covering 3,063 acres, were purchased in 1914. Large areas were also acquired in the west of the county, in the Fens.

There was also much activity to the south of the Waveney, although far fewer records from Suffolk have survived. East Suffolk County Council began buying land in 1909, with the acquisition of 59 acres at Ringshall, 47 acres at Mendlesham, 154 acres at Mutford and 72 acres at Barking. In 1910 46 acres were purchased at Winston, 80 acres at Debenham, 19 acres at Snape, 12 acres at Ilkeshall and 6 acres at Old Newton. By 1914 a further 548 acres had been made available.[93] Nevertheless, the scheme made a slower start in the county than in Norfolk. By 1918, according to a government report, there were 1,350 holdings in Norfolk, but only 83 in east Suffolk and 231 in west Suffolk.[94]

By 1914 government interest in smallholdings was waning. The Liberals regarded the introduction of a minimum wage and the improvement of rural housing as more important issues than the revival of the 'yeomanry', while the Tories believed that protective tariffs would help agriculture and thus the condition of those living and working in the countryside. The outbreak of war had a profound affect on the acquisition of smallholdings. The purchase of land ceased completely and the purchasing committees were disbanded. The end of the war, however, saw renewed interest. In 1919 the Land Settlement (Facilities) Act provided a fund of £20 million to buy and equip smallholdings principally for ex-servicemen, rather than for local labourers, and gave county councils increased powers of compulsory purchase.[95] Alongside this went the Small Holdings Colonies Act, which provided for the establishment of co-operatives on which ex-servicemen could be settled, and a circular letter from the Board of Agriculture urged councils to buy land in sufficiently large blocks for 'colonies' to be established.[96] It also urged that Councils should write to the principal landowners in their respective counties asking for land, and that letters should be sent to all returning ex-servicemen about the scheme. The requirements of local men should be met before applications were accepted from outside the county, and ex-servicemen were to be given priority.[97] Applicants had to have capital equivalent to £20 per acre before they could be considered, and the upper size-limit for holdings was now seventy acres, although most were much smaller.

The timing of the act was unfortunate, however. The county councils bought properties at inflated post-war prices, but by the time the smallholders actually began to farm depression had returned. Indeed, in July 1921, in the middle of the driest summer on record, the Suffolk committee announced that 'in view of the altered circumstances of agriculture, all approved applicants not allotted holdings and those awaiting interview to be asked as to whether they desire their applications to stand.' As a result of this exercise forty-four people were removed from the list, but there were still thirty-three new applications.[98]

In spite of these difficulties, 24,000 ex-servicemen were resettled in the country as a whole in the post-war years, and as a result the number of smallholdings more than doubled. East Anglia played its full part. In 1919 the Norfolk purchasing committee was reinstated and reports came flooding in from the local sub-committees suggesting where the required land could be bought. Between January and October 1919 5,669 acres were purchased at a cost of £101,681 (an average of only £17 an acre). Orders for compulsory purchase were made in Salthouse and Kelling. A report to the committee stated that over 12,000 acres in the county had been inspected and that 3,782 acres, providing for 178 tenants, would be available for occupation in September 1919. Most of the land acquired took the form of relatively small blocks, such as those at Rookery Farm, Reepham (177 acres at £25 per acre), High House Farm, Hindringham (558 acres with buildings and seven cottages), or Hill House Farm and Broad Farm, Hassington (275 acres). The committee judged the purchases carefully and land of poor quality, or that was too far from a major road, was usually rejected. Purchases continued over the following years, including four farms in Hilgay, covering 1,533 acres, acquired by compulsory purchase.[99]

The early 1920s were also busy years in east Suffolk, and by 1925 there were 4,334 acres of smallholdings here, mainly concentrated on the Corton estate near Lowestoft and at Copdock near Ipswich.[100] In west Suffolk applications reached a peak in April 1921, when there were 683 outstanding, 217 of which were from civilians. Between 1919 and 1922 4,738 acres were acquired and 244 tenants (fifty-two of whom were civilians) were settled: by this time there was a total of 318 holdings, with 170 houses and 138 sets of buildings, on 7,499 acres of land.[101]

This post-war period of expansion was short-lived, however, and went into rapid reverse after 1925 when the ex-servicemen's scheme came to an end. The intensity of the inter-war depression meant that land could be a financial burden on the county councils, and there were fewer suitable applicants. Where land had been leased it was frequently given up when the time for renewal came round. By this time, however, Norfolk owned 27,479 acres, making it the county with the largest area of land (1/48th of the area of the county) held for smallholding purposes.[102] Suffolk still lagged markedly behind, but in 1931, when government finance for buying smallholdings finally ended, there were nevertheless 7,449 acres of land in smallholdings in west Suffolk[103] and 5,870 in east Suffolk.[104]

There was, however, yet another burst of interest and activity, when in 1933 the government made money available to buy smallholdings to resettle the long-term unemployed. Between June and September Norfolk County Council acquired a further 1,461 acres in South Walsham, Haddiscoe, Gimingham, Happisburgh and Feltwell and by December forty-five new holdings had been created. Indeed, Norfolk County Council continued to be one of the most enthusiastic promoters of smallholdings. By 1946 it had 1,896 tenants in the county occupying 31,928 acres.[105]

In addition to the schemes run through the county councils, in 1934 the government set up the National Land Settlement Association, partly funded by voluntary bodies.[106] Its aim was to buy up large farms around the country which would then be broken up into small units; tenants for these would be selected from among the unemployed. They had to become members of the farm co-operative and buy and sell through it. A few hundred families, mostly from areas of high unemployment, were settled in this way, but many soon returned home. A 337-acre farm at Newbourne, eight miles east of Ipswich, was purchased in 1936 and divided into forty-eight holdings. All the tenants were provided with bungalows and glasshouses, and fifteen with poultry battery houses. All had piggeries for between four and six pigs and the scheme survived into the 1960s.[107] Many of the bungalows still stand, although the glasshouses are largely derelict.

## THE COUNTY SMALLHOLDINGS IN PRACTICE

Looking back from the standpoint of the early twenty-first century, the most striking aspect of the various smallholding schemes seems their radicalism. Not only was the State prepared to engineer a major change in patterns of rural occupancy and ownership, but, at a local level, the policy was carried out with a ruthless enthusiasm. Although the county committees were largely composed of major landowners, they seem to have been quite happy to compel other major landowners to sell or lease land. In Norfolk in 1910, for example, Lord Stafford was forced to give up thirty-four acres at Bawburgh and Lord Townshend forty-nine acres at South Creake, while in 1911 forty acres in South Creake were compulsorily hired from Lord Leicester.[108] Given the state of agriculture and the level of rents, compulsion was perhaps nominal – landowners do not seem to have been antagonistic to the scheme, on the whole, probably because it provided a further outlet for land sales at times of depressed demand (when one of Lord Stradbrooke's Suffolk farms became vacant in 1918 he advised his agent to 'Write to the secretary of the East Suffolk Small Holding Committee at County Hall, Ipswich. They are often asking for small holdings').[109]

More surprising is the attitude taken by the committees to existing tenants on purchased properties. Cottagers were often given notice to quit because their houses were needed by smallholders – something which must surely have gone against the grain for Agricultural Union members of the committees, such as George Edwards in Norfolk. When the tenants of cottages at Burlingham refused to move when the estate was acquired in 1914 the officers for the sub-committee responsible reported that they had 'utterly exhausted our powers to obtain vacant possession of these last-named cottages, principally because of a lack of alternative accommodation. We are now asking the committee for guidance.' It was reported that the clerk had been instructed to 'take necessary steps to obtain vacant possession of cottages required'.[110] In the post-war period the policy was pursued with perhaps even greater zeal, existing tenants now being uprooted to make way for returning servicemen. Several farmers on the Burlingham estate were said to be suffering from nervous breakdowns because they could not find suitable properties to move to. 'I doubt it is to the national advantage', wrote the farming correspondent of the *Eastern Daily Press*, 'that some of the most practical and skilful farmers in the world should be ejected to make room for the small holder.'[111] The farmer at Manor Farm, Hilgay (229 acres), was typical of many: although a long-standing tenant, he held on only a yearly lease, and was summarily displaced in 1920.[112]

Once the land had been bought, the holdings had to be equipped. The properties purchased usually included at least one farmhouse and associated buildings, and often a number of tied cottages. In some districts, such as the rich loams of east Norfolk, the old buildings were often extensive and well-built, although their very scale sometimes made them difficult to maintain. Large farmhouses might be divided, as at Hall Farm, South Burlingham, in order to provide the multiple occupancy required to serve the new holdings. Conversely, small cottages might be amalgamated to provide suitable accommodation. But as well as utilising existing buildings, right from the start entirely new ones were also erected. By 1918 the Norfolk Committee had acquired 141 houses for its smallholders, but had also built fifty-eight.[113]

A government report of 1913 contained a large section of advice on the design of houses for smallholdings.[114] Three-bedroom dwellings with living room and scullery, and separate dairy and wash room, were recommended. In practice, the economic stringencies of the post-war period ensured that more *ad hoc* accommodation was often provided. In August 1919 fifteen army huts were purchased by Norfolk County Council for conversion to dwellings, and in 1920 a further hundred were bought for use at Burlingham and elsewhere, 'owing to the urgency of equipping the council's purchases'.[115] By 1923 many of the 2,154

Figure 9. An asbestos house on a Norfolk County Council smallholding near Lingwood: a rare survivor of a once-common type.

Norfolk tenants were living in hastily erected bungalows constructed of wood and/or asbestos. Others were occupying lodgings which lay at some distance from their holdings.[116] The problem was highlighted by an article in the *Norfolk Chronicle* in August 1921 entitled 'Ex-servicemen's scandalous grievances', which pointed to the Council's 'shabby and scurvy treatment of those who fought'. The fifty new settlers at Burlingham, nearly all of whom were disabled in some way, were living either in badly subdivided old houses or in new asbestos bungalows which were too hot in summer and freezing in winter. They had no proper stoves or water supplies.[117] In September 1921 108 tenants from Burlingham and the immediate neighbourhood met to complain about the lack of buildings and the poor quality of their housing.[118]

Norfolk County Council had built ninety-three asbestos (trade name 'Poilite') bungalows by 1925, but many rapidly proved very unsatisfactory. The roofs leaked as the rubberoid perished, and the ceilings sagged (Figure 9). The walls rapidly ceased to be weatherproof as the wooden splines shrank, and the fireplaces were unsafe. Limited repairs and improvements were sanctioned in 1925, but the buildings still remained below standard.[119] In some cases, however – in periods when finances allowed – exemplary brick houses were built for smallholders, both on the Burlingham estate in east Norfolk and at Popenhoe and Fern House Farm in the west of the county. Those in the east were of red brick, with long eaves and in a vaguely Tudoresque 'cottage style', while those in the west were square-built grey-brick structures. All had three bedrooms, a parlour and living room, with a scullery and dairy at the back. Baths were provided under a removable work surface in the scullery.[120] The influence of the Council for the Protection of Rural England was already being felt, and the land agent for the Norfolk Committee felt it necessary to justify his building policy in the light of their concerns. He gave his own optimistic opinion in 1926 that the Small Holdings Sub-Committee could 'justifiably claim, with the possible exception of the bungalows, to have maintained the local characteristics where they have erected new, or altered or repaired existing buildings'.[121]

When the 1935 Housing Act came in, reducing the extent of overcrowding, the Norfolk Small Holdings Committee voted to give a good example and set itself even higher targets: 'It is not anticipated that there will be many cases of overcrowding in houses occupied by tenants of the Council.'[122] However, if they were not overcrowded, the committee minutes reveal that many of the smallholders' houses remained in a very poor condition. Three cottages at Kidman's Corner, North Walsham, for example, were reported to be in the same bad state in 1936 as they had been before the war, when they had been let to farm labourers, and were considered 'therefore not at all suitable for the dwellings of small holders'. Three were to be amalgamated into two dwellings, and an additional new house was to be built. New wash houses and dairies were to be erected and the properties in general 'brought up to standard'.[123] The dwellings on the Burlingham estate came in for repeated criticism. The June 1938 quarterly report stated that 'In view of the present trend towards improving housing conditions in rural areas, a good deal of sub-committee building activities are directed towards these ends.'[124] Nevertheless, as late as 1948 tenants in Nordelph and Stow were still living in timber, uralite and asbestos-roofed bungalows which were 'fast becoming uninhabitable'.[125]

The reports make it clear that the provision of outbuildings on smallholdings was considered as important as the condition and location of the dwelling house. Again, the government report of 1913 set exacting standards. While smallholdings engaged in market gardening might need little more than a packing and tool shed with a stable and cartshed alongside, all of wood, rather more was required for a mixed holding of twenty to thirty acres: a fodder and chaff house, a stable for two horses, a cattle shed, a cartshed and a yard with boarded fence. Dairy farms needed a cow house, allowing 800 cubic feet per cow (600 if they were out during the day), a mixing room, stabling for two horses, a cartshed with loft above and three loose boxes opening onto a partially covered yard.[126] As with the dwelling houses, these aspirations were not easily achieved, and successive reports acknowledged the difficulties experienced in finding tenants for poorly equipped holdings, in spite of substantial sums spent on the provision of buildings – no less than £5,993 in 1927 alone.[127] The Milk and Dairies Act of 1926 added further expense as it necessitated major improvements to cow houses, although many holdings were equipped with a 'standard type of cowshed, generally suited to small holders'.[128] By the 1930s most holdings of thirty to forty

Figure 10. Few of the farm buildings erected for the county council smallholdings in the inter-war period still survive. This set, erected in 1927, is at Litcham in Norfolk.

acres came to be provided with an L-shaped wooden and weatherboarded range erected on brick foundations and with pantile roof, featuring open lodges – for pigs, poultry, and so on – a workshop, an implement shed, feed stores and three loose boxes.[129] Some larger holdings had more extensive provision arranged around three sides of a yard (Figure 10), and at Lodge Farm, Burlingham, one was even provided with a covered cattle yard. By the late 1930s newly built farmsteads were likely to include a tractor shed.

The county smallholdings were not evenly distributed across East Anglia (Figure 11). There were marked concentrations in the Fens and on the fen edge: in Suffolk, the parishes of Lakenheath and Mildenhall thus contained nearly 3,000 acres of smallholding land, with a further 309 acres in neighbouring Freckenham, while in Norfolk there were 105 smallholdings in Terrington St Clement and 116 in Welney. There was another marked concentration in east Norfolk, where there were 115 holdings in Burlingham and over twenty in each of the parishes of Ludham, Potter Heigham, Martham and Beighton. Elsewhere they were more thinly scattered, although there were noticeable clusters in Wickhambrook and Stradishall in Suffolk; along the Essex border around Cavendish; in Debenham and Winston; and to the north of Lowestoft. The main concentrations reflect the fact that smallholders were primarily involved in market gardening and fruit-growing, and the suitability of the areas in question (as we have already noted) for enterprises of this kind. Norfolk County Council were particularly keen to encourage fruit production, and eight acres at Burlingham and three and a half at Emneth were let to the Agricultural Education

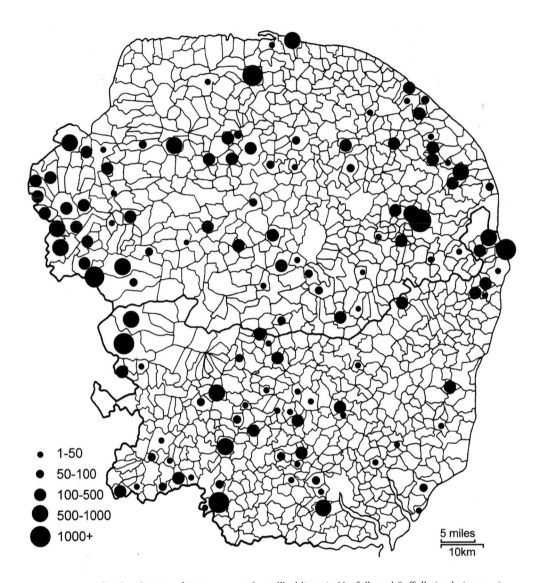

Figure 11. The distribution of county council smallholdings in Norfolk and Suffolk (scale in acres).

Sub-Committee as demonstration plots. From 1920 the Norfolk Committee made grants available for the purchase of fruit trees and by November 1921 200 trees had been provided to tenants on the Chilton estate in Suffolk.[130] In 1926 the Norfolk committee purchased fruit sprayers which were to be kept at Burlingham and made available for hire.

Although most of the holdings were thus horticultural enterprises, some were run as traditional mixed farms, especially in east Norfolk. These were generally the larger holdings, whose tenants were more likely to be full- rather than part-time workers. Some commentators doubted the viability of these miniature mixed farms: 'Too many of the smallholders imitate the methods of the large farmer, instead of going more thoroughly into fruit and vegetable growing, sugar beet, poultry and dairying.'[131] As with other farms in the region, the acreage of sugar beet on smallholdings increased during the 1920s, with 879 acres being grown on Norfolk holdings in 1925 and 1,747 in 1926.[132] By 1934, 22 per cent of all smallholding land in the county was in sugar beet and, as this was often the only way smallholders could pay their rent, the Committee was anxious that the sugar beet subsidy should not be removed.[133] In common with their larger neighbours, many smallholders were putting land down to permanent pasture as the inter-war depression deepened, the seed usually being provided by the committees. In Norfolk, eleven tenants were provided with seed for sixty acres in 1931 and similar help was being given in 1932.[134] In 1933 about 150 acres were reseeded as permanent pasture.[135]

Dairying was a particularly important activity for the county smallholders in the inter-war period, and 119 new dairies and cow sheds were erected on Norfolk holdings alone in the early 1920s, mostly in the eastern half of the county.[136] This sector continued to expand: the reports of the Norfolk smallholding competition, run between 1927 and 1930, show that the number of cows increased steadily, although generally competitors did not have enough stock to merit milk recording. Pig-keeping was also widely practised, especially in Suffolk. Poultry, too, was a major concern, and while in the early 1920s it was thought that 'too large a proportion of them [Norfolk tenants] are still content with the haphazard methods of feeding and management', a few years later it could be said that 'in some cases poultry keeping was undertaken on up-to-date lines', while the competition report for 1930 commented that poultry husbandry had improved as tenants were keeping good laying strains.[137] Like fruit-growing, poultry-keeping was a form of enterprise deemed particularly suitable for smallholdings by the county committees, and in September 1928 a leaflet entitled simply 'Poultry Keeping for Small Holders' was sent to all Norfolk tenants with their rent demand.

## THE FORESTRY COMMISSION SMALLHOLDINGS

The county councils were not the only organisations actively involved in the establishment of smallholdings in East Anglia in the first half of the twentieth century. The Forestry Commission, which (as we shall see) afforested extensive tracts of poor heathy land in the region in the 1920s and 30s, also created a significant number. As well as acquiring large amounts of poor-quality land suitable for planting, largely through the purchase of decaying landed estates, the Commission also obtained some land of reasonable agricultural quality which could be used for smallholdings.[138] This was a sensible policy from the Commission's point of view, as much forest work was seasonal in character:

> Forest holdings are designed to house the forest worker and give him a piece of land of
> about ten acres to keep farm stock and to cultivate. He gets winter work in the forest
> for about 100 days and, for the rest of the year, he can devote himself to the cultivation
> of his holdings.[139]

In some cases, especially in Breckland, the period of work was extended to 150 days.
Tenants were also charged a rent, based on the capital value of the property, and were
committed by the terms of their lease to perform a number of other duties. They had to
keep a watch over and protect Commission property in the vicinity of their holdings, and to
'exterminate and keep exterminated all rabbits hares and vermin', as well as to use their
'utmost endeavours to preserve the game and eggs and young of game from being injured
and destroyed', as the Commission was keen to preserve the income from its game leases.[140]
It was partly for these reasons, but mainly because many were laid out beside houses which
had originally been estate cottages, that the holdings were widely scattered through the
afforested areas, although there were some concentrations, as at Drymere near Swaffham in
Breckland. Here, as in a number of other places, the specially constructed bungalows were
built by direct Commission labour using brick, with roofs of timber and asbestos: many of
the bricks were salvaged from demolished estate buildings, including Santon Downham Hall
in Norfolk.[141]

The history of the Forestry Commission smallholdings is poorly documented in written
archives but local tradition – recorded in the early 1990s – provides additional details. One
interviewee recalled how the smallholders:

> Went into blackcurrants and asparagus, things like that, you know a little bit of corn and
> that, built them a pigsty. What happened with a lot of them was that they had a horse,
> and very often the Forestry Commission would employ that horse, ploughing for
> planting and things like that. I suppose it was a good idea at the time.[142]

By 1926 there were as many as 120 smallholdings in Thetford Forest alone, many growing
small fruit and vegetables suited to these light soils. A co-operative marketing scheme had
been established and poultry, eggs and honey were sent 'direct to the consumers in London
at prices lower than those prevailing there but considerably better than can be obtained
locally'.[143] In the 1930s some of the holdings were used to resettle unemployed people from
depressed areas in northern England. The recruits were given basic training and assistance
with stocking. Local tradition asserts that this part of the scheme, at least, met with little
success: 'I don't think they had the experience, of course, them being miners. They came
out of the cities, or the depressed areas. A local man did best, probably. We've got one or
two who made a go of it.'[144]

## THE SUCCESS OF SMALLHOLDINGS

Nevertheless, the overall success of these various attempts to revive and support the smallholder in East Anglia, and the more general health of smallholders and small farmers as a class in the inter-war period especially, is reasonably clear from the evidence. In the case of the State-sanctioned schemes, it is true, the issue is somewhat complicated by the fact that their strategic aims changed over time. In the initial stages, the objective of arresting the decline of the 'peasantry' by providing local labourers with land was never fully realised: the necessity for applicants to prove that they had enough capital to stock and equip the holdings meant that most were not in fact agricultural labourers at all. In Norfolk only 250 of the 800 tenants in 1911 fell into this category.[145] On the other hand, the schemes do seem to have been relatively successful in resettling returned veterans after the First World War, with Suffolk in fact being one of the few counties to succeed in settling all the ex-servicemen on its list by July 1922.[146] In terms of the economic viability of the new holdings the sources certainly suggest a measure of success. It is true that in the First World War the Agricultural Committee commented on the poor condition of many Norfolk examples, and noted that 'the County Council might generally notify their tenants of the importance of cultivating their holdings in a proper manner.'[147] Nevertheless, in 1916 no fewer than ninety-five holdings in the county were classified as 'very highly satisfactory' by the Committee, while the highest number (534) were deemed 'satisfactory'.[148] The annual inspections carried out by the County Smallholding Committees likewise suggest that, on the whole, the smallholdings were working well. Of the 813 Norfolk tenants in 1913, 108 were categorised as 'very highly satisfactory' while the largest category (296) were 'satisfactory'. Only thirty-nine were either 'not satisfactory' or 'very unsatisfactory'.[149] True, specific farms gave cause for concern. A report on the holdings on a 287-acre farm at Litcham, presented in June 1914, thus described how the land was not being cultivated to its best advantage and, indeed, suggested that the tenants generally failed to understand how best to work this heavy land. It ought to have been cultivated on a four-course system, but some tenants were growing two or more corn crops in succession.[150] But some reported failings were the result of particular, understandable circumstances, which the Committees immediately strove to do something about. In April 1921, for example, the Committee's agent visited a tenant on Brandon Creek Farm at Southery where one field was well farmed on a four-course system, but the other was full of twitch. The tenant explained how he had lost a horse and was unable to plough it. An agreement was reached with a neighbour to lend him a horse, and the field was duly ploughed.[151] It is noteworthy that a government report of 1918 suggests that only 5.7 per cent of holdings in Norfolk actually failed, about average for the counties listed, and an impressive figure.[152] The support and advice provided by the two county committees must have helped many holdings, while strenuous efforts were made, even in peacetime, to maintain standards of husbandry – as in 1921, when notices to quit were given to several Suffolk tenants with 'an intimation that such notice will be withdrawn if an improvement in the cultivation thereof is effected'.[153]

As the inter-war depression deepened the viability of smallholdings began to be challenged. Four Norfolk tenants were in arrears in 1921 and when 'persistent visits from the District Officer had proved fruitless' it was felt that 'some more drastic action should be taken'.[154] In 1922, £197 was owed in rent in west Suffolk, although it was considered that 'there was a fair prospect of recovering the remainder'.[155] For the most part, the county committees displayed a measure of financial flexibility which allowed many hard-pressed tenants to weather the worst years, and only rarely were they asked to quit. Rent rebates were often made. There were rebates of half a year's rent in Norfolk because of the drought of 1921 and the bad growing season and fall in prices in 1922,[156] while in 1922–3 there was a rebate of between 15 and 20 per cent in west Suffolk.[157] In December 1923 the bad debts of thirty-six Norfolk tenants, amounting to £1,227, were written off: the debtors were described variously as 'bankrupt', 'gone away suddenly' and 'in prison', but in one case it was simply recognised that the 'tenant has no money'.[158] As the depression continued into 1925 a need for further reductions was acknowledged,[159] but twenty-nine Norfolk tenants were ordered to quit unless the previous year's rent had been paid by 8 October. Even so, £228 was written off as unrecoverable. Explanations for these bad debts were varied. While one man was described as having 'no means and is one of those who spends his time dodging work', other cases were described with greater sympathy. One man 'was badly gassed during the war, discharged with no pension, lung trouble set in and he has since died'.[160] In January 1926 18 per cent of the annual rent roll was outstanding. Out of a total rent due of £11,172 in the east of Norfolk, a reduction of £446 was recommended, while in the west, where £9,093 was due, a reduction of £1,701 was proposed. Neither of these sums was accepted by the Ministry of Agriculture, however, who had the final say in the matter, and after some negotiation somewhat smaller amounts were settled upon.[161] From 1926 agreements were reached with several defaulting tenants in Norfolk whereby they were allowed to remain as long as the guaranteed income from their sugar beet crop was assigned to the county council.[162] Such forbearance was appreciated. In March 1929, when one Mr Meed finally paid his rent, he wrote in the accompanying letter: 'enclosed, rent due as per demand, thanking you for your patient endurance; hoping to enter into a period of more timely payments before too long'.[163]

The economic situation did not, as we have seen, greatly improve over the following years and in 1930 the Norfolk Committee decided that 'in view of the very serious and continued fall in the prices of cereals, the sub-committee proposes to consider the question of making an abatement off the Michaelmas rents.'[164] In 1931 the West Suffolk Smallholders' Association asked their council for a reduction of rent: 'in view of the continued depression in agriculture and the decline in prices of all kinds of crops, the members of the Association are alarmed at their precarious position.'[165] A rent reduction of 12 per cent was granted by the Norfolk Committee in 1930 and 1931, but it was thought that an 'abatement was no longer possible' in 1932.[166] In that year £649 was written off as bad debt (the average for the past six years had been £381) and in November 25 per cent of the rents due in April were still outstanding. The fact that the number of tenants wanting to leave (twenty-three) was lower than in previous years, however, suggests a measure of optimism about the future – or a lack of alternative forms of employment. The 12 per cent rent rebate was reinstated in 1933 'as prices are still low', and was continued in 1934. Partly because of such measures Norfolk arrears, even in the worst years of the early 1930s, never amounted to more than 15 per cent of the annual rent bill. By the end of 1934 conditions were improving, moreover, with the state of farming generally, and the number of notices to quit (fourteen) was the lowest for several years.[167]

To some extent, then, the success of the county smallholdings was the result of subsidies from local ratepayers. But it is important to emphasise that the majority of smallholdings and small farms below fifty acres in East Anglia were *not* owned by the county councils, and that the number of such holdings, as we have seen, remained remarkably buoyant throughout this period, in marked contrast to the steady contraction which had taken place during the previous three centuries. Indeed, given that government statistics did not concern themselves with holdings of less than five acres – and many smallholdings, both council-owned and otherwise, were smaller than this – the official figures displayed graphically in Figure 7 probably underestimate the comparative success of this sector: a success which was largely the result of the expanding market for vegetables, fruit, eggs and poultry in this period, itself the consequence (as we have already noted) of improvements in transport, the growth of urban populations and improvements in diet. This sector of the farming economy flourished, in essence, because of the increasingly urban character of British society in the late nineteenth and early twentieth centuries: in 1851 half the population of Britain lived in towns and cities, but by 1911 this had risen to 80 per cent.[168] Mosby and Butcher leave no doubt that, on the eve of the Second World War, smallholding, market gardening and fruit-growing were the most vibrant sectors of the East Anglian farming economy.

To many inter-war writers such holdings, together with the many small arable farms which had been obliged to diversify into poultry, egg-production and the rest, represented modernity: not least because of the novel structures which many required and the improved forms of transport on which they generally depended. Adrian Bell, typically, described encountering, on a neighbouring farm, 'A smart young man in drill overalls walking about where not long since had been old labourers with bent bodies but nimble hands, while two laying houses of great length were going up in two ten-acre fields.'[169] These enterprises were, indeed, often associated particularly with the young, and with the inter-war expansion of formal agricultural education. As Bell again explained:

> It was indeed a time for the young and opinionated, for their elders could no longer point to the proven success of traditional procedure. In fact the tables were turned, and in their despair they listened to the young men who brought technicalities of agricultural mass production from their colleges, as to prophets, inspected their hundred-yard-long 'battery brooders' where chickens lived on wire trays from a few days old to killing time without ever seeing the outer world.[170]

## CONCLUSION: THE LANDSCAPE LEGACY

The long-term landscape legacy of all these great changes – the expansion of horticulture and market gardening, the creation of smallholdings by the county councils and the Forestry Commission – was much more limited than their contemporary impact on rural society and the rural environment. The most significant contribution came, perhaps, from the creation of large commercial orchards, for many of these still remain, especially in the silt Fens of west Norfolk, in spite of a decline in the industry over the last three decades. They look like, and are often considered to be, 'traditional' features of the rural scene, and are valued today for their role in maintaining biodiversity in what is otherwise, for the most part, an intensively arable landscape (Figure 12). Conservationists are thus keen to preserve them, and others strive to perpetuate the various 'traditional' varieties of East Anglian apple and pear – in spite of the fact that many of the latter do not, in fact, date back to the remote past but, like the commercial orchards themselves, were developed in the century after 1880. Of the fifty-three varieties identified as important by the Norfolk Apples and Orchards Project, for example, no less than twenty-nine first appeared in the period between 1870 and 1950. Some of these were, as in earlier times, the result of experimentation at (or natural selection arising in) the kitchen gardens of country houses, but many were created by the new commercial nurseries, such as the Emneth Early or Lynn's Pippin, both developed by the Lynn family of Emneth in 1899 and 1942 respectively.[171] In north-east Norfolk, many commercial orchards were surrounded by high 'hedges' of poplars or similar fast-growing trees which made, and in a few cases still make, an important contribution to the landscape.[172]

The creation of smallholdings on a large scale by the county councils, and on a smaller scale by the Forestry Commission, has in general had a more subtle long-term impact on the landscape. Pre-existing farmhouses, cottage and farm buildings were extensively reused, being subdivided or amalgamated as necessary as dwellings for smallholders, as we have seen, and it is their origins, rather than this important later phase of their history, which is most obviously 'read' in the landscape. Moreover, the new houses and buildings erected by the county councils in the early years of the century have not survived well: most of the houses were timber and asbestos structures, and were replaced in the post-war period, or clad in brick. Fifty-one were still in use in 1957 but of these, only thirteen had still not been clad in either brick or cement and only one still survived in 2003 in its original form (at Lingwood in east Norfolk, on what was part of the Burlingham estate). The brick houses which were erected in places during the 1920s and 30s provided rather better accommodation, and more of these remain, although they are not always easily recognised for what they are unless, as in places in the Fens, they are concentrated along particular roads. Many of these better-built structures were also removed, however, when enthusiasm for the smallholding movement ran out after the Second World War and holdings were amalgamated. New brick houses, often with a date stone, were then built to serve what became medium-sized farms. The farm buildings erected for the smallholders have fared

Figure 12. Orchard near Wisbech. Although it looks like a part of the 'traditional' landscape, in common with most others in the Fens this example was only established in the period after 1880.

even less well. A few examples of the characteristic L-shaped ranges of wooden and pantiled farm buildings erected by Norfolk County Council still remain, as at Chamery Hall, South Walsham, and at several places around Burlingham. Examples of the larger U-shaped ranges also survive in Nordelph, Burlingham and Litcham. Most, however, have long since disappeared. Like many other agricultural buildings erected in this period, they were constructed of wood, asbestos and wire netting, and have either collapsed or been replaced. Much the same goes for the buildings associated with other smallholdings, in private hands, which developed in this period.

The impact of the smallholdings on the wider fabric of the landscape is perhaps more interesting. In some places existing fields were subdivided when the new holdings were created, although, to judge from the map evidence, this was not always the case. Many of the holdings were in the silt Fens, where the landscape was already fairly minutely divided by drainage dykes, often arranged in a distinctive strip pattern which had originated when the area was first colonised in the twelfth and thirteenth centuries.[173] The new holdings were simply slotted into this more ancient landscape. However, there are some signs that the presence of these small properties, and their partial survival into the 1950s and 60s, served to preserve the density of drainage dykes as this was, in other areas, reduced wholesale and the ancient field pattern much simplified in the period of agricultural intensification following the Second World War. This tendency is particularly marked in the parishes of Wiggenhall St Germans, Wiggenhall St Martin and Wiggenhall St Mary. Indeed, in a number of other areas the presence of county council smallholdings effectively served to arrest the general 'prairification' of the landscape. In the central Norfolk parish of Brisley, for example, Willow Farm still stands as an island of ancient fields within a drastically simplified landscape.

These are all, however, surprisingly slight traces of such an important, radical phase in the region's agrarian history. It is a sobering thought for the landscape historian that, in the case of the county smallholdings schemes, such scant physical traces are all that remain of a process in which property was acquired and managed on a massive scale (more than a fiftieth of the entire area of the county, in the case of Norfolk) and large numbers of new houses and buildings erected to serve the new holdings. One wonders whether any earlier revolutions in landholding on this scale have left similarly meagre traces in 'our richest historical document'.

CHAPTER 4

# Estate Landscapes

## THE DECLINE OF THE LANDED ESTATE

The break-up of large landed estates looms large in accounts of both the social and the landscape history of England in the period between 1880 and 1950. Landowners were assailed by both declining rental incomes and rising maintenance costs, and also by death duties, which were introduced in 1894, raised to 15 per cent by Lloyd George and, subsequently, in 1919, raised again to 40 per cent on estates valued at more than £200,000.[1] Established landowners were gradually obliged to sell their ancient properties: mansions were demolished, parklands ploughed, and the wider estate land fell into the hands of a new class of owner-occupier – former tenant farmers – with a radically different range of land-use priorities. The demise of the country house and its landscape was not, however, simply the result of agricultural depression, but was also a consequence of broader ideological and cultural changes. The dominating position of the mansion in the Victorian countryside had been a direct reflection of the central place of large landowners in rural life, but this was eroded by legislative changes, especially the Local Government Acts of 1888 and 1894. County affairs were no longer in the hands of county magistrates and justices of the peace who were largely drawn from the ranks of the landed elite; nor were parish affairs now under the control of parish vestries dominated by the local squire. Although landowners continued to play a role in the new county, rural district and parish councils which were established by these acts, they did so as elected members, and in the company of individuals from very different social backgrounds. The passing of the country house represented, to some extent, these new structures of power. It also reflected a more general sense of insecurity amongst the traditional landed classes, encouraged by such things as the proposed land tax of 1909.[2] This led to an 'atmosphere of apprehension' in which 'many landowners began to sell off their estates in whole or part at an increasing pace', something repeated in the early 1930s with Philip Snowden's proposals for a Land Value Tax, and rumours of land nationalisation.[3] It was all these things, as much as the crisis in agriculture *per se*, which led to the sale and break-up of ancient estates and the demolition of their country houses.

Estate accounts and correspondence certainly leave no doubt that, from the 1880s, most East Anglian landowners were faced with declining rent rolls as agriculture grew less and less profitable. In the face of farm bankruptcies and a lack of demand for tenancies they had no alternative, as we have seen, but to reduce rents.[4] The rental income from the Blickling estate in Norfolk, for example, fell from £11,685 in 1877 to £9,893 in 1892, and a major recalculation of rents in 1894 resulted in a further reduction of over a third to £6,018.[5] Similar reductions took place on the Adair estates in north-east Suffolk, where a rental of £18,567 in 1878 had declined to £12,000 by 1885,[6] while on the mid-Norfolk Kimberley estates the half-yearly rents went down from £5,909 in 1880 to £3,144 in 1901.[7] The situation was made worse by the fact that many major landowners already had substantial debts as well as mortgages charged to their properties, obligations which had been acquired at a time when incomes had been high and money easily borrowed to finance family settlements, estate improvements or general extravagance. Whatever their origins, accumulated debts could not easily be serviced in the new economic climate. Janice de Saumarez described in 1895 how the income from the family's Suffolk estates (Shrubland, Livermere and Broke Hall, Nacton) had fallen from between £10,000 and £12,000 in 1882 to virtually nothing. Tenants had been giving in their notice, and 'although we have arrived at the point of having no income, everything indicates a further fall of indefinite and incalculable amount'. She went on to note that 'The estate which cannot now nearly meet its mortgage and charges, in spite of all possible reductions, is Shrubland', adding that the sale of that property might be 'the only way of escape'.[8] Decline in rental incomes continued, albeit at a less dramatic rate, into the early twentieth century: those from the Ickworth properties in west Suffolk, for example, fell from £11,646 in 1903 to £8,764 in 1909.[9] The First World War saw some recovery of agricultural fortunes, incomes and land values, as we have seen, which continued into the immediate post-war years; but this was followed by a rapid slump in the early 1920s. The accounts for Nowton in Suffolk show that the estate was just breaking even between 1913 and 1920, with a surplus of income over expenditure of between £4 and £164 per annum. In 1920–1 this became a deficit of £484, growing to £1,196 in 1921–2.[10]

Landowners initially dealt with the mounting crisis in their finances by making economies or by selling possessions. Famous East Anglian examples include the sale of Lord Amherst's library at Didlington in Norfolk in 1909 (which raised nearly £110,000) and the auction of 565 lots of Maiolica and Limoges enamels in 1884 by the Fountaine family at Narford Hall in the same county.[11] More widespread was the systematic felling of timber. Annual income from timber sales on the Meade estate, in south Norfolk, rose from £100 in 1878 to £800 in 1883.[12] Timber to the value of £1,226 was felled on the Hare Stow Bardolph estate in 1880–1.[13] But by the early years of the twentieth century the deepening depression ensured the necessity for land sales, and over the following seven decades there was a veritable revolution in patterns of ownership in East Anglia. In Suffolk there had been forty-six estates of over 3,000 acres in 1871, which owned between them 359,202 acres (c.42 per cent of the total land area of the county). By 1941, there were thirty-five such properties accounting for around 20 per cent of the land area. In Norfolk seventy estates of over 3,000 acres had been reduced to forty-three by 1941, the share of the county they owned declining from 49 per cent to 28 per cent.

Between 1873 and 1941 the amount of land in the eastern counties in estates of over 2,000 acres declined by a third: 43 per cent of land in eastern England was owner-occupied in 1941, compared with an average of 20 per cent for the years 1887–1922.[14]

## THE CHRONOLOGY OF ESTATE EXTINCTION

Nevertheless, the decline of the great estate in the period after 1880 was more complex than is sometimes assumed, especially by landscape historians.[15] It was neither wholesale nor immediate – not least because most owners had alternative investments or larger and more profitable properties elsewhere. The owner of the Earsham estate in south Norfolk typically noted in 1922 how it was 'very disappointing that the estate does not run itself … it takes so much money from the Irish estate to keep the English estate afloat'.[16] Indeed, in the early phases of the depression some established landed properties actually increased in size, as owners bought up the lands of small freeholders hit by declining agricultural prices: the Ashburnham estate at Barking in Suffolk grew from 3,372 acres in 1871 to 3,902 in 1906; Dalham in the same county from 2,913 in 1871 to 3,475 in 1901.[17] Additions were still being made to the Oakes estates, centred on Nowton in Suffolk, as late as 1913.[18] Many families were, of course, in serious trouble, but the sale of an estate was not necessarily the same as its demise. Properties simply passed undivided and intact to new owners, something which had always gone on, albeit now at a noticeably faster rate. Many of the purchasers had made their money in commerce, industry, the colonies or government administration – but this, again, was a long-established pattern. In Norfolk, the Salle estate was sold in 1888 to Timothy White, whose family had made their money in the pharmacy business; Sennowe Park went to Thomas Albert Cook, heir to the famous travel agency business, in 1898; Hanworth Hall to the banking family, the Barclays, in 1902; and Heacham went to C.E. Stacham, the owner of extensive rubber plantations, in 1904. All thus passed to new owners undiminished in size.[19] In Suffolk the situation was the same. The Dalham estate, owned by the Afflecks since the early eighteenth century, was sold to Cecil Rhodes in 1901: he subsequently sold it on to Sir Laurence Philips, but it remained intact as a property. Little Glemham in east Suffolk, covering just under 3,000 acres in 1871, had been owned since the seventeenth century by the Norths but was sold to the Cobbolds, a brewing family, in 1923 and remains in that family's hands to this day; while High House, Campsey Ashe, was sold by the Sheppards (who had, again, been in possession since the end of the seventeenth century) to the businessman William Lowther in 1883.[20] Hengrave, owned by the Gage family since the sixteenth century, was purchased in 1893 by a Mrs Lysaught and passed subsequently to Sir John Wood, the Glossop cotton manufacturer: it was not broken up until 1952.[21] Similarly, the 17,000-acre Elveden estate in Suffolk was bought from the Maharaja Duleep-Singh in 1893 by the brewing tycoon Cecil Guinness, created Baron Iveagh in 1901 and Earl Iveagh and Viscount Elveden in 1905, while in the same year the Bennet family sold the Rougham estate in the same county to Sir George Agnew, son of the publishing tycoon Sir William

Agnew.[22] In this context it is noticeable that sales catalogues were often clearly phrased with the socially conscious *parvenu* in mind. The Nowton Hall estate, Suffolk, offered for sale in 1889, was typically described as being 'Immediately between the well-known seats of Harwick and Nowton Court in an aristocratic neighbourhood'.[23]

Economically challenged estates often survived in another way. Their owners leased the mansion and grounds, often with the sporting rights, and took up less costly residences elsewhere in Britain or abroad: examples include Bertram, Second Lord Cornwallis, who went to enjoy a life of big-game hunting and farming in Uganda;[24] and Lord Walpole, who, when he inherited Wolterton and Mannington in 1894, immediately moved out of Weybourne Hall on the coast and let it to 'a London tenant'. He chose to live at Mannington, and let the shooting at Wolterton for £300 per annum in the 1890s, a sum rising to £593 by 1901. In 1899 the 'cottage' at Burnham Thorpe – an outlying portion of the main estate on the north Norfolk coast – was renovated, furnished and likewise let: in 1909 it was advertised as a 'moderate-sized and well-furnished shooting box' with 'first-class partridge and wild fowl shooting' over some 6,700 acres. In 1905 Mannington Hall itself, and its shooting, were let for £1,100.[25] The London firm of W. Webster and K. Cauldwell managed many such lets, including Morton (on-the-Hill), Raynham, Beachamwell, West Harling, Methwold, Hockwold, Cockley Cley and Earsham, all in Norfolk; and Fornham, Henham, Sotterley and Euston in Suffolk. Some estates, once let, might then be sub-let. In 1902 Charles Morby leased the mansion house and fourteen acres at Great Saxham in west Suffolk, together with the shooting rights over another 2,526 acres, to Ernest Dresden for £1,100 per annum. In 1910 Dresden was attempting to sub-let all this to Sir John Smiley for £1,350.[26]

Change there certainly was in the ownership and occupancy of East Anglian estates, but for the first four decades or so of the agricultural depression few, if any, were actually broken up. Indeed, when the 8,150-acre Bylaugh estate was put on the market in 1917 as 140 separate lots the fact was remarked upon in the press as unusual.[27] It was only in the period during and after the First World War that large properties actually began to disappear, sometimes after direct heirs had been killed on the battlefields. The immediate aftermath of the war was a period in which the land market was unquestionably feverish: between 1917 and 1921 at least 51,000 acres were sold within Norfolk and at least twelve of the 106 large estates in the county changed hands.[28] Great Barton in Suffolk disappeared in 1915; Acton, also Suffolk, was broken up in 1915. In Norfolk, Bylaugh went in 1917, followed by Stratton Strawless and Costessey in 1918 and Thursford, Burlingham, Elmham and Rackheath in 1919. Livermere, in Suffolk, went in the same year, Rendlesham and Easton, in the same county, in 1922.[29] As the inter-war depression deepened, however, tenants and others became more reluctant to buy, yet landowners often remained desperate to sell. Although some estates continued to be broken up – Weston in Norfolk in 1926, for example – more noticeable in this period were the activities of the Forestry Commission, which purchased a number of entire estates on the poor marginal soils of Breckland in the 1920s, including Downham Hall, Lynford, Weeting, Didlington and Croxton (below, pp. 97–8).

In the years leading up to the Second World War the rate of loss appears to have accelerated again as farming fortunes began to recover and the chances of finding purchasers for lots improved. In Suffolk, Culford was broken up in 1934, Sudbourne in 1935, Tostock and Finborough in 1936, Heveningham in 1937, Assington in 1938 and Nowton in 1939;[30] while, in Norfolk, Honingham disappeared in 1935 and Gissing in 1936. Even then, however, it often proved difficult to shift some of the lots. In 1936, when the Gressenhall House estate was offered for sale, two of the five farms were withdrawn because they did not reach their reserve price.[31] Many of the farms on the 2,670-acre Mildenhall estate were unsold in an auction in 1933 because there were no bids, or because the land failed to reach its reserve price.[32] It was only in the immediate aftermath of the Second World War, as farming boomed, that sales generally proved easier, and it was now that the real avalanche of estate extinctions occurred, with the disappearance of such Suffolk properties as Flixton (1952), Brandeston (1949), Campsea Ashe High House (1949), Ufford (1950) and Hengrave (1952); and the Norfolk estates of Riddlesworth (1946), Ketteringham (1947), Oxburgh (1951), Congham (1956), Langley (1954 and 1957), Colney (1957), Kimberley (1958) and Quidenham (1958).[33]

The precise point at which an estate ceased to exist is not always easy to establish, however. Often disappearance was phased and gradual. Sir Lawrence Jones sold the bulk of the Cranmer estate in north-west Norfolk to its tenants in the 1930s, but the estate only finally disappeared when the last 394 acres were sold in 1946. Financial problems were often initially met by the sale of outlying portions of property, sometimes in several stages, followed by the eventual disposal of the rump – the period between the events being short where two or more family deaths followed in rapid succession, but sometimes extending over several decades. The Assington estate, over 2,800 acres in 1871, thus sold 1,260 acres of outlying land in 1921, with the rest going in 1938.[34] The Ashburnhams of Barking owned 3,372 acres in 1906, divested themselves of 369 acres of outlying farms in 1917, and sold the remainder of the estate, which was then broken up, in 1919.[35] The Rendlesham estate on the Suffolk Sandlings covered around 20,000 acres. The outlying Broxted lands – 2,428 acres – were sold in 1914, and a further 5,832 acres, scattered through the neighbouring parishes, followed later in the year. In 1919, 2,028 acres in Butley were sold. The following year the remaining core areas of the estate were put on the market.[36] Between 1920 and 1922, thirty-two farms amounting to about 6,500 acres were sold by the Nowton estates at prices ranging from £15 to £40 an acre (at least four were sold to sitting tenants and in only one case was it specifically noted that 'the tenant has declined to purchase').[37] But the estate continued to exist into the post-Second World War period. Sometimes such staggered sales were simply a reflection of the poor state of the land market and an inability to find buyers for all the lots. The Easton Park estate, for example, covering some 4,939 acres, was up for sale in 1919 – as 137 lots – but 783 acres (including the mansion and park) remained unsold, and were back on the market in 1922.[38]

The final extinction of an estate as a meaningful entity in social and landscape terms is thus, perhaps, best marked by the demolition of the mansion. True, the break-up of an estate did not always lead to this, for some great houses were found new, institutional uses. Culford Hall thus became a school in 1935, and Rendlesham a sanatorium for alcoholics and people with drug problems in 1925, subsequently becoming a Ministry of Labour Instructional Centre.[39] Indeed, owners seem to have had a genuine reluctance to demolish, and preferred whenever possible to find new uses for the ancestral pile. In 1926 John Wood, agent to the Thornham estate, discussing the Hon. John Henneker's attempts to let Thornham Hall as a school, noted: 'if the worst does come to the worst and you have to pull the house down, you will have the satisfaction in knowing that that you have tried.'[40] But new uses were harder to find in rural East Anglia than in the Home Counties, and final estate break-up was usually followed by demolition.

The chronology of demolitions emphasises, even more than that of sales, the very gradual demise of the great estate. In Suffolk, very few great mansions were actually demolished in the period up to 1939: Barking Hall (1926), Great Barton (burnt down in 1914), Easton Park (1925) and Livermere (1923) more or less complete the list.[41] A much higher number were demolished (or partly demolished) in the immediate aftermath of the Second World War, often after they had been effectively trashed by military occupation: Euston (1950), Flixton (1953), Henham (1952), High House, Campsey Ash (1953), Redgrave (1946), Rendlesham (1949), Rougham (1953), Sudbourne (1953), Tendring (1955), Thorington (1949), Thornham (1945?) and Ufford Place (1953).[42] In Norfolk the pattern was similar. Few mansions were demolished during the period of the agricultural depression – Costessey, Santon Donwham, Weston, North Elmham, Congham, West Harling and Marsham were the principal examples. In the wake of the Second World War, in contrast, there were far more – Boyland, Brook Hall, Burlingham, Bylaugh, Castle Rising, Cranmer, Didlington, Feltwell, Garboldisham, Haveringland, Heacham, Hillington, Honingham, Hunstanton, Morton, Weeting, Woodbastwick, Wretham and Wroxham were all lost between 1945 and 1950.[43] But we should also note that appearances can sometimes be misleading: some large estates survived without a mansion. The Thornham estate still remains in the hands of the Hennekers although the hall itself was demolished in 1937, the family choosing to reside instead at the Home Farm.[44] Tendring Hall was demolished in 1955 but the property of the Rowley family remains extensive. Redgrave Hall, the home of the Holt Wilsons since the eighteenth century, was either let or unoccupied for most of the first half of the twentieth century until finally demolished in 1946. The estate itself, however, survived until it was sold in 1971.

In short, we should neither hurry, nor over-estimate the extent of, the decline of the landed estate in East Anglia. The amount of land owned in blocks of 3,000 acres or more in East Anglia was certainly reduced by around half within the period studied, but this does not mean that half the landed estates actually disappeared. Most estates of over 3,000 acres in 1871 were still substantial properties in 1939, and a significant number survive to this day, many owned by the same families as in the nineteenth century; places like Sotterley in east Suffolk, 6,424 acres in 1871, still in the hands of the Barne family; neighbouring Benacre, still owned by the Gooches; or Tendring, in the south of the county, still in the hands of the Rowley family. But these estates were generally smaller than in the period before the depression, landowners having survived by divesting themselves of some proportion of their land – usually outlying farms, occasionally secondary estates acquired through accidents of inheritance, such as Livermere in Suffolk, acquired by the de Saumarez family of Shrubland Park and leased for many years before being sold in 1919 (the hall was demolished four years later and the estate dismembered). Somerleyton, purchased by the Crossleys in 1863, remains in that family's hands today although large areas have been sold, most notably 804 acres of outlying land in 1919.[45] Shrubland Hall has only recently been sold by the de Saumarez family, although by the 1950s the estate was less than half the size it had been in 1871. The Dukes of Grafton had, similarly, lost around half their 11,000 acres by 1950. Other examples of survival through peripheral sales include Helmingham, Heveningham, Ickworth and Melford Hall, the rump of the last two both finally passing to the National Trust, in lieu of Death Duties, in 1951.

For most of the period 1870–1940 the majority of landed estates thus remained in existence, if somewhat smaller in area than before, and they continued to be a powerful influence on the landscape. The reasons for this are simple. Well into the twentieth century, the kudos attached to the ownership of a large landed property remained strong, so that when established families succumbed to mounting problems there was usually a steady stream of individuals with 'new money' keen to take their place. In addition, most established landed families had investments or properties outside the agricultural sector, and so were not entirely dependent on the fortunes of local agriculture. It was only in the aftermath of the First World War and, in particular, with the arrival of a more general economic recession in the 1930s, that large numbers of owners found themselves completely unable to meet their obligations: while, at the same time, the supply of purchasers from outside the ranks of traditional landed society dried up. Yet even so the depressed state of the land market held many owners back, and it was only after the Second World War (during which many country houses had been occupied, and badly damaged, by the military), in a climate of increasing political hostility in which ostentatious possession of extensive acres seemed unwise, that sales, dismemberments and demolitions came thick and fast.

It is also important to emphasise that the disappearance of landed estates and the demolition of mansions were not spread evenly, or randomly, across East Anglia. Estate extinctions were instead concentrated in particular areas, principally those of the poorest, lightest soils – especially Breckland in the west of the region, the Sandlings of east Suffolk, and the acid heathy soils to the north of Norwich. There were two reasons for this. Firstly, as has already been explained, it was these marginal soils that suffered the greatest fall in agricultural rents. This was particularly poor land, much of it reclaimed in the nineteenth century from heaths, which was only kept in cultivation by substantial inputs of fertiliser and lime: land which became less and less viable to cultivate as prices fell and wage costs rose. As Rider Haggard commented on the northern parts of Breckland in 1902:

> Much of the light soil around Swaffham that in the prosperous days commanded 7/6 an acre, was practically derelict … The landlords were much crippled and many of them, after paying charges, taxes, tithe and repairs, etc., had only their shooting rights on which to live.[46]

Secondly, large estates had (again for reasons already discussed) for centuries been concentrated in these very same marginal areas, especially Breckland, where parks, ornamental plantations and other signs of elite possession dominated the landscape. Not only mansions and immediate grounds but also more extensive canvases of elite display were here particularly vulnerable, and the Acquisition Reports drawn up by the Forestry Commission when estates in Breckland were purchased in the 1920s paint a picture of chronic dereliction and decline. The Downham Hall estate, for example, bought in 1923, was described as a 'wilderness': 'The various land and timber speculators through whose hands these lands have passed during the past 7 years are responsible for the deplorable condition of the estate.' The mansion was in disrepair and much of the timber had been felled:

> In consequence of the timber operations the park, as such, has ceased to exist. An avenue of limes and a few quasi-ornamental trees of little commercial value are all that are left, except in some of the wild belts where a few ragged conifers remain, the best timber having been cut out.[47]

Certain kinds of countryside were thus affected more by the decline of large estates than others, but such geographical patterns are somewhat obscured by the fact that accidents of family and estate history also played a major part in the fate of landed properties. Two or more deaths, and associated duties, in rapid succession could destroy an estate: conversely, possession of property and financial interests outside East Anglia, and/or investments in industry or the colonies, could bolster one which would otherwise, dependent on agricultural rents alone, have been broken up. The Elveden estate occupied some of the worst land in East Anglia but it flourished throughout the first half of the twentieth century thanks to its purchase by the Guinness family in 1893; Benacre, much of which lay on the poor lands of the Suffolk coastal heaths, was sustained by the Gooch family's properties in Birmingham.

## MANSIONS, GARDENS AND PARKS

Historians have generally concentrated on the increasingly derelict and neglected appearance of country houses and their grounds from the 1870s, but there is little doubt that, to judge from the East Anglian evidence, such accounts are exaggerated. Maintenance and improvement were essential, given the importance of keeping up appearances. Rental incomes at Blickling were plummeting in the last decades of the nineteenth century, but annual expenditure on the gardens nevertheless rose from £662 in 1896 to £793 in 1900.[48]

Moreover, the purchase of a property by a new owner usually brought an influx of new money, and often an enthusiasm to make changes. Sales catalogues, diaries and illustrations leave no doubt that most country house grounds were maintained in all their elaborate glory well into the twentieth century. Indeed, the fact that many were being opened to the public for the first time in this period made it imperative that they should be well maintained: for several landowners followed the lead taken by Lady Lothian at Blickling in 1894, and opened their parks and pleasure grounds on a regular basis; these included Culford, Cavenham and Hardwick (from c.1905) and Sandringham (from 1913).[49] New areas of garden continued to be created even after the First World War – as at Earlham in Norfolk, for example, where part of the park was converted into a formal sunken garden at some time between 1910 and 1925. Areas of formal parterres certainly disappeared at many sites in the early twentieth century, including Houghton, Lexham and Ryston, but in part this was a consequence of new fashions, rather than a symptom of impoverishment.

For this was a period in which new modes of garden design continued to emerge, although, for the first time, the stylistic lead was taken not so much by the owners of great estates as by other social groups, especially '… rising middle class suburbanites … whose gardens were their only property'.[50] Although many successful businessmen in the late nineteenth and early twentieth centuries, as we have seen, were keen to buy a full-blown country estate, for many this seemed to bring too many problems and financial responsibilities. A house in the country, rather than a country house, was what many now desired: preferably in a healthy coastal location, of moderate size, designed in the 'arts and crafts' style developed by E.S. Prior, C.F. Voysey and Edward Lutyens, and built using a mixture of local and modern materials; or some smaller Tudor or Stuart manor house, of manageable size but reeking with rural antiquity. Such diminutive residences required grounds in an appropriate style, simpler and less flamboyant – and certainly less labour-intensive – than the vast parterres of bedding plants so popular in the High Victorian era.[51]

The new styles were complex, however, with many elements. In 1870 William Robinson published the first edition of *The Wild Garden*, in which he argued that hardy plants, either native or naturalised (such as bamboo), should be given more prominence in the garden, and that less reliance should be made on the kinds of half-hardy bedding-out plants which had dominated the gardens of High Victorian England.[52] Robinson rebelled against the fashion for formal beds and argued that flowering plants should be widely scattered across the lawns, and through shrubberies and areas of woodland, ideas which he developed further in his *English Flower Garden* of 1883.[53] The most influential voice in garden design in the late nineteenth and early twentieth centuries was, however, Gertrude Jekyll, who worked with the architect Edward Lutyens in designing gardens from 1890, and whose first book, *Wood and Garden*, was published in 1899, followed by *Home and Garden* the following year.[54] It is on the ideas of Jekyll and Lutyens that the character of the 'arts and crafts' garden largely rests. The style involved the combination of strong architectural

Figure 13. Most country houses in East Anglia, and their grounds, were well maintained at least until the outbreak of the First World War. Many, as here at Bylaugh in Norfolk, adopted elements of the latest styles of garden design.

elements with profuse and informal planting – mainly of hardy species, and particularly in wide herbaceous borders. The 'hard landscaping' was designed in the same vaguely vernacular style, and employed the same vaguely vernacular materials, as 'arts and crafts' houses: and there was much of it, with steps, terraces, walls, areas of paving, pergolas and summer houses in 'rustic' style all featuring prominently. These more architectural elements were laid out close to the house: further away there was usually a series of garden compartments, defined by neatly cut hedges (generally of yew or privet). Some of these might be given over to various sports – there was an increasing interest at this time in healthy outdoor pursuits, and tennis, bowls, cricket and croquet were particularly popular (so too was an active involvement in gardening itself, following the lead set by Jekyll). Other compartments might contain fruit gardens or specialised rose gardens. In the more distant areas of the grounds woodland gardens, now planted in a more naturalistic way than those of the High Victorian period, were popular. These were gardens designed for relaxed rural living, appropriate to the *nouveau riches* who increasingly sought their place in the country.

To some extent the new styles could be adopted at existing country houses. Indeed, the comparatively low costs of maintenance may have made them attractive to hard-pressed landowners (Figure 13). The owners of Shrubland Hall in central Suffolk may have been experiencing catastrophically declining rental incomes by the late 1880s, and the vast Italianate gardens here had, according to article in the *Gardeners' Chronicle* in 1888, been 'shorn of much of their former magnificence', but alterations continued to be made. 'One of the finest modern developments at Shrubland is the planting both sides of a ravine with hardy Bamboos intermixed with Dracaenas, Cannas, Maize, Funkias, and other bold and graceful plants';[55] something which the 1890 edition of the *Chronicle* ascribed to the head gardener, Mr Blair, 'at the suggestion of Mr Robinson'.[56] In the early 1890s the pattern of planting in the Balcony Garden, immediately below the house, was transformed along 'arts and crafts' lines. The parterres of sand, boxwork and bedding plants was replaced by more informal beds and borders which featured roses planted around with more transient annuals, including carnations, and with smaller areas of campanulas, pansies, yuccas, chrysanthemum, asters, antirinum and *gladioli anemone*.[57]

At many country houses earlier patterns of beds were maintained, but the new forms of planting were adopted within them. Soon after Hengrave Hall was purchased by Sir John Woods in 1897, for example, the pattern of paths and beds which had been laid out to the west of the hall in the 1850s and grassed over in the 1890s was recut, but now planted 'using a mixture of bedding and roses in a display of modern taste'.[58] Elsewhere, more extensive modifications were made. Around the turn of the century Edwin Johnstone at Rougham Hall in Suffolk worked closely with his head gardener, Mr Henley, to alter the gardens in the modern style. Typically, their design featured prominent architectural elements near the house (simple flower beds cut into lawns, gravel terraces, etc.), and further away, a series of compartments including a rose garden, flower garden, walled kitchen garden and woodland walks.[59] More impressively fashionable were the gardens at Boulge Hall in Suffolk, transformed in the 1890s following the purchase of the estate by the White family.[60] In 1893 the architect Gambier Parry was paid the immense sum of £1,299 for 'Garden and terraces'.[61] The old formal beds were removed and the terrace now looked out over an area of lawns and specimen trees sweeping down to a newly constructed lake.[62] Family diaries refer in 1896 to a Dutch garden, an arborvitae walk, a flower-bed lawn, a poplar border and a 'wilderness'. There was a nut walk with rolled paths, rhododendron beds and a summer house. The same year two new tennis courts were constructed and a new herbaceous border, with box edging, begun.[63] These were extreme examples, perhaps, but in the gardens of most country houses modifications in line with the new fashions, rather than neglect and dereliction, were the order of the day, at least for the first four decades of the depression.

Landscape parks generally survived intact, and continued to develop, well into the twentieth century. A comparison of the first edition OS 6-inch maps, surveyed in the 1880s and early 90s, with the second edition of 1905–10 reveals few places (around 6 per cent) in East Anglia where the area denoted as parkland actually decreased. In contrast, in around 30 per cent of cases parks apparently grew in size. Sometimes the expansion involved only the addition of small fields on the margins of the park but in nearly half the cases growth was in the order of 25 per cent or more, as at Ryston in west Norfolk where the parkland area increased by around 40 per cent between 1888 and 1906; by 1929 the main addition, in the south of the park, had been planted up as an arboretum. It is possible that in some cases change is more apparent than real, reflecting differences in cartographic perceptions and conventions adopted by successive surveys, but on the whole the documentary evidence suggests otherwise. At Bayfield – a small but elegant landscape park in north Norfolk – the expansion of the parkland to the south-west is recorded in the diary of the owner, Alfred Jodrell: 'four new clumps of trees planted opposite the side of water which has been put down with permanent grass to make it park' (Figure 14).[64] Jodrell had outside business interests – cotton factories in the north of England – which allowed him to throw significant amounts of money at the landscape: the lake was cleaned, partially lined with tiles and provided with a bypass channel to reduce silting. But this was not the only lake to receive attention in this period. That at Rackheath was extended some time between 1886 and 1919, and an entirely new nine-acre lake was created at Sennowe around 1900 by damming and diverting the river Wensum.[65]

Letters, diaries and sales catalogues reveal that the old aesthetic attitudes towards landscape parks, which had developed during the previous two centuries, were strongly maintained. Particular parks were praised for their 'undulating character' or for being 'well timbered'; Bylaugh Hall was noted for occupying a 'very fine position on a sheltered knoll and commanding Beautiful and Distant views over the finely timbered slopes of the park'.[66] Privacy was also still of paramount importance, and public access through part of Earsham Park was actually curtailed in 1887 using the long-established procedure of the Quarter Sessions Road Order. The closure of four lanes met with violent opposition – fences and gates were broken down, and ten local people were fined – but it was ultimately successful, and considered something 'of great benefit to the Earsham Hall property' which had 'considerably increased its value as a residential and shooting estate'.[67]

The area of park woodland – belts and clumps – often increased, with the growth of perimeter belts across adjacent areas of arable land, and existing areas of woodland were often replanted. Estate accounts and diaries show that conifers – Scots pine, larch and spruce – formed a major part of these plantings, although hardwoods were by no means neglected. Some estates spent considerable amounts of money on such forestry campaigns – no less than £1,650 between 1880 and 1884 at Earsham, for example – and while planting activity was not restricted to the core areas of the estate it was for the most part, as in earlier centuries, concentrated there.[68] There are, once again, signs that activity was greatest where estates were acquired by new owners, or where owners had access to outside sources of income. The Gooch family were able to use income from their Birmingham properties to more than weather the storm of depression and, following the accession of the tenth Bart, Thomas Vere Sherlock, in 1899, a range of improvements was carried out which included the construction of a massive water tower to serve the hall, the addition of new drives and, above all, a sustained planting campaign in and around the park. Between 1908 and 1911 the

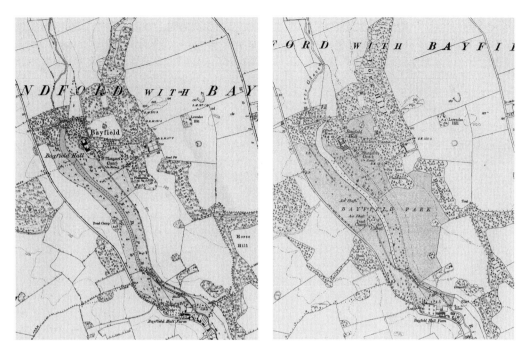

Figure 14. The growth of Bayfield Park in north Norfolk, as depicted on the 6-inch Ordnance Survey maps of 1891 and 1907.

park clumps, planted in the early nineteenth century and now grown gappy, were restocked with sycamore, ash and elm, and the belts were augmented and underplanted with snowberry. New areas of park woodland were created, the accounts referring to the 2,170 hazels, 70 walnuts, over 1,000 sycamores and 1,000 horse chestnuts planted in the 'New Plantation Front Park' between 1903 and 1905, and to the 300 hazels and 229 ash used to establish the 'New Plantation Ice-House Park' in 1907.[69] Bayfield in Norfolk similarly saw a sustained forestry campaign which began with the estate's purchase by Alfred Jodrell in 1882 and continued until his death in 1929, all funded largely with income from his Lancashire cotton mills. Existing woods were restocked and linked with new planting, so that the park was increasingly enclosed by woodland to the north and east, with outlying plantations framing or closing the more distant views from the house. The prominence of box and rhododendron in the planting, here as on other estates, shows that one of the main intentions was to provide cover for game. Rhododendron had been introduced into England in the eighteenth century but, to judge from the available evidence, was only widely planted in estate woodlands in East Anglia from c.1860. In part the expansion of woodland, albeit integrated into the design of the country house landscape, was a reflection of the contemporary obsession with shooting, discussed in more detail below; and in part it represented a form of economic diversification, and a fashionable interest in forestry.

Figure 15. Benacre, Suffolk. The south drive, planted with sycamore in the first decade of the twentieth century.

Planting of free-standing timber in parks also occurred on some scale, and once again especially where owners had access to outside sources of income. At Benacre the existing north and south drives were fenced from the park and lined with sycamores and rhododendron bushes soon after 1900; and, between 1907 and 1912, large numbers of new trees were added to the open parkland, including more than 118 horse chestnuts and a large number of limes (Figure 15).[70] Today these trees – now with girths of 2–3 m – visually dominate the parkland. The nineteenth century had seen an increasing interest in the use of lime, sycamore and chestnut as parkland planting but the early twentieth century seems to have seen an intensification of this trend wherever large schemes of planting were undertaken.

The embellishment of the main drives at Benacre has many parallels: tree-lined approaches and avenues, which had enjoyed a revived popularity since the 1830s, continued to be created (notable examples include 'King Edward's Ride' at Quidenham). Again, lime, sycamore and horse chestnut were the species most favoured for the purpose. One particularly noticeable feature of the period was the changes made to the arrangement of access drives, something which was at least in part related to the increasing importance of the motor car; and lodges continued to proliferate well into the twentieth century, with new examples appearing at many places in the period up to the First World War, including the

Norfolk estates of Bayfield, Raveningham, Ryston, Weston, Earlham, Sennowe, Rougham and Earsham.[71] Changes to drives and entrances continued to be made at some places well into the 1930s, in spite of the worsening economic situation. All these and similar developments have ensured that many landscape parks in East Anglia, as we experience them today, are so heavily influenced by late nineteenth- and early twentieth-century alterations and additions that they are, in effect, as much products of this period as they are of earlier phases of history.

Parks had always been used for recreation, and their importance as game reserves if anything increased during this period. But other forms of entertainment also began to make a mark, in an age in which healthy outdoor pursuits were increasingly valued. By the turn of the century cricket grounds were features of many parks, including Elmham, Lexham, Quidenham, Rackheath, Bayfield, Benacre and Houghton. When Lexham was put on the market in 1911 the catalogue boasted that 'in the park is a first class cricket ground said to be one of the best in the country.'[72] Cricket matches between the 'house' and the 'village' were a familiar feature of the rural calendar, subtle forms of social control in which – to quote Leo Colston in *The Go-Between*, set in the fictional Norfolk estate of Brandham Hall – 'class distinction melted away'.[73] The third Earl of Leicester at Holkham (1848–1941) reportedly said to his librarian that it was most important 'in presenting [ecclesiastical] livings to ensure that parsons are keen cricketers'.[74]

As the more general economic recession began to bite in the later 1920s and 30s gardens and pleasure grounds were often neglected, reduced in scale and managed less intensively, their borders and beds grassed over. But parks almost invariably survived with only minor changes. Indeed, in one sense the agricultural depression offered them a measure of protection, because the low prices of grain meant that there was little incentive to clear them of trees and plough them up. Even where mansions were demolished their parks sometimes remained intact, as at Gawdy in Norfolk, although they often slowly deteriorated. Mosby in 1938 described how 'Weston [Longville] House has been demolished … the finest trees in the park, many of them 150 years old, have been cut down. The park is poor pastureland, very sandy: parts are already reverting to heath.'[75]

## NEW COUNTRY HOUSES

The continuing vitality of the country house as an institution well into the twentieth century is clearly indicated by the fact that a number of examples were extended, remodelled, or even entirely rebuilt in this period, usually but not invariably when purchased by new owners. Lord Iveagh thus greatly enlarged Eleveden Hall between 1899 and 1903 to vaguely Italianate designs by the architect William Young, and a substantial formal terrace was constructed on its southern front.[76] Culford Hall was rebuilt and massively extended for the Earl Cadogan in the years around 1900, again to designs by Young in an Italianate style, but here featuring a prominent asymmetrical tower. A new staircase was also added, and the gardens transformed: the rather informal pleasure grounds to the south of the hall, separated from the park by a ha ha and a low wire fence, were replaced with a much more architectural setting comprising a substantial Italianate terrace overlooking the park.[77] Hengrave Hall was also extensively altered following its acquisition by Sir John Woods in 1897: the north-east wing was built, the Great Gallery created on the ground floor, and (as we have seen) the gardens much altered.[78]

Some existing country houses were not merely remodelled or extended, but largely or completely rebuilt in this period. Haughley Plashwood, near Stowmarket in Suffolk, was rebuilt on a new site, 100 m to the south-west of the old, in the 1890s, and new gardens, including an 'embroidered parterre' of gravel and box, were laid out around it.[79] Sennowe in mid-Norfolk was acquired by Thomas Cook, as mentioned above, in 1898, and was largely rebuilt and considerably extended by the Norwich architect George Skipper around 1906. The result was a house with a principal elevation of seventeen bays and extensive terraced gardens (Figure 16).[80] Once again the chosen style was a robust Italianate, but some builders of country houses went for other alternatives. Pickenham Hall, a Neoclassical house of the early nineteenth century in west Norfolk, was virtually rebuilt in Neo-Georgian style by the architect R.W. Weir Schultz in 1902–5, and the grounds laid out in 'arts and crafts' mode, with a terrace of stone and brick, yew hedges, a sunken garden and a Chinese garden.[81] Broadly similar was Cavenham Hall, rebuilt to designs by the arts and crafts architect A.N. Prentice between 1898 and 1899 and provided with gardens laid out in appropriate style under the direction of the London-based designer H.E. Milner.[82] Riddlesworth Hall, in contrast, overlooking the river Waveney in south Norfolk, was rebuilt by its owners – the Norwich banking family the Champions – in 1899, following a disastrous fire, in a somewhat traditional classical style – with a pediment supported on Corinthian columns – yet with the main elevation arranged, somewhat curiously, in an asymmetrical manner around it.[83]

As already noted, one of the most distinctive features of the late nineteenth century was the tendency for individuals who had made their money in commerce, industry or the professions to purchase, rather than a large country house and its attached estate, some small Tudor or Stuart manor house which had long before declined in status to a small working farm. This they would restore, adapting surviving gardens in the modern style and sometimes laying out a small park at the expense of the surrounding fields. East Anglia had a large number of picturesque manor houses of this kind and, with agriculture in a state of depression, several were up for sale at a reasonable price. The wealthy Leicester architect Arthur Wakerley bought Gedding Hall Farm in Suffolk in 1897, carefully restored the building and laid out a suitably compartmentalised garden around it: several of the pasture fields around were thrown together to make a small park.[84] The early Tudor manor house of Giffords Hall near Sudbury, with its walled gardens, was bought by J.W. Brittain in 1888. At this date the hall was surrounded by a landscape of hedged fields but by 1903, according to the second edition OS 6-inch map, a sparsely timbered park of c.100 acres (around 40 ha) had been created.

Figure 16. Many country houses in East Anglia were rebuilt or extended, often on a grand scale, in the late nineteenth or early twentieth century. Sennowe in Norfolk was massively expanded between 1906 and 1909 to designs by the Norwich architect George Skipper. The great terraced Italianate gardens are also by him.

More dramatic was the transformation of Stutton Hall, overlooking the estuary of the river Orwell in the far south of the region. This had been an important residence in the sixteenth century but by the early eighteenth had declined in status to a tenanted farm.[85] It was purchased by James Oliver Fison, the Suffolk agricultural chemical manufacturer, in 1887. He restored and extended the house, repaired the old walled garden, and laid out fine new gardens in a vaguely arts and crafts style to the south of the house – an area of lawn with lines of topiaried yews (some Irish), and with a number of distinct compartments defined by neat yew hedges. Particularly striking, however, was the new parkland which Fison created around the hall. The first edition OS map of 1884 shows a landscape of fields and farmland; by 1905, a park of some 45 ha had appeared. This contained a number of old oaks retained from the earlier hedgerows, but was mainly planted up in lively fashion with a mixture of oak, horse chestnut, sweet chestnut, Wellingtonia and (most striking of all) cedars – Cedar of Lebanon, Deodar cedar, and a number of examples of Atlas *glauca*, paired in several places with horse chestnut – an unusual but effective combination. Belts ran, and still run, along the northern edge of the parkland, planted with Corsican pine, Scots pine, chestnut and oak.[86]

Some entirely new houses, on entirely new sites, also appeared. The most striking is perhaps Bawdsey Manor, on the Suffolk coast some nine miles south-east of Woodbridge, the creation of Sir Cuthbert Quilter, founder of the National Telephone Company. It began life in the 1880s as a small holiday home, conveniently located at no great distance from the family's principal residence at Hintlesham Hall, to the west of Ipswich. In the 1890s Quilter decided to make Bawdsey the main family residence, and the house was extended, piecemeal, in a number of stages to create a curious building in a mixture of styles – gothic, Elizabethan, Jacobean and unclassifiable. Quilter acquired around 8,000 areas of land in the vicinity, as well as the title of Lord of the Manor of Bawdsey – allowing him to rename the house Bawdsey Manor. New farm buildings were constructed, and a number of new farmworkers' cottages.[87] Most striking of all were the elaborate gardens laid out around the house in a medley of styles. Immediately below the house, on its south-western side, was (and is) a series of Italianate terraces, featuring an elaborate tea house with boat house below. On the north-eastern side was a circular sunken garden, originally a rose garden, formed 'on the exact site of an old coastguard station [in fact, an early nineteenth-century Martello tower], which he first had to blow up with explosives'.[88] This was linked to other parts of the grounds by grotto-like underground tunnels, partly constructed with materials from the demolished tower, one of which led – and still leads – to the most striking part of the gardens: the 'rockery wall' or artificial cliff. This feature, which is 50 m high and extends along the shore for some 400 m, is constructed of cement generously embedded with artificial 'Pulhamite' stone and local crag. A precipitous path still leads along the side of the cliff, several metres below its summit, threading in and out of alcoves and cave-like recesses. Other features of the grounds included a Pergola Garden, an extensive kitchen garden with classically detailed orangery, and 150 acres of parkland occupied by grass lawns and plantations featuring, in particular, pines, holm oak, sweet chestnut and sycamore.[89]

Bawdsey was the most impressive new country house with extensive grounds to be erected in this period. But there were other places in East Anglian where entirely new mansions were built, with new parks laid out around them. Bentley Park in Suffolk, for example, did not exist when the First Edition OS 6-inch map was surveyed in 1884: a small farmhouse occupied its site, and the land around was divided into arable fields. By 1905, however, 'Bentley Lodge' had been built, a medium-sized Edwardian house of brick with a

Figure 17. Cars, garages and chauffeurs at Ampton Hall in Suffolk, shortly before the First World War. Motor cars rapidly became a central feature of country house life: stables, drives and entrances were modified accordingly.

slate roof, surrounded by a simple park of around 30 ha. A perhaps more noticeable development was the proliferation, especially in the period before the First World War, of new houses close to the coast which lacked extensive grounds – they had gardens rather than parks – and were designed in a broadly arts and crafts style. Some were retirement homes, others holiday retreats; they were usually built for wealthy businessmen but sometimes (as with Happisburgh in north Norfolk) for landed families living elsewhere in East Anglia. Notable examples include Kelling Hall in Norfolk, built in 1912–13 to designs by Sir Edward Mauf for Sir Henri Deterding, Chairman of the Royal Dutch Shell oil company; Overstrand Hall, built in 1899 by Edward Lutyens for Lord Hillington, a partner in the bankers Glynn Mills; Felixstowe Lodge in south-east Suffolk, designed for the brewer Felix Cobbold by Robert Schulz Weir; and the striking Happisburgh Manor in north-east Norfolk, designed by Detmar Blow for Albemarle Cator and built in 1900.[90] All made extensive use of local materials and boasted a variety of vernacular details. Their design was closely integrated with that of the surrounding gardens and they often displayed novel features in their plans and elevations: both Happisburgh and Kelling, together with Home Place, Holt (1904–5 by E.S. Prior), thus made use of the 'butterfly' plan, allowing the rooms within to have maximum exposure to the sunlight. All were well provided with garaging for cars, something which proliferated at wealthy residences of all kinds in the early years of the twentieth century, often through the conversion of existing stables (Figure 17).

## SHOOTING AND GAME PRESERVATION

Game shooting had long been a prominent feature of country life in East Anglia, as elsewhere, but it unquestionably became more important in the period after 1880, and the numbers of game shot on most estates increased steadily in the period up until the First World War. On the Holkham estate the annual 'bag' rose from 3,252 partridges and 1,443 pheasants in 1853–4 to 4,599 partridges and 4,149 pheasants in 1900–1; at Kentwell in Suffolk it increased from 2,018 in 1853 to 5,099 in 1887.[91] At Stowlangtoft in Suffolk average bags of around 2,700 in the 1850s rose to an astonishing 13,296 in 1897–8 (although a visit by the Prince of Wales and Earl Haig may have ensured that all the stops were pulled out, and this bumper year was followed by more modest, but nevertheless impressive, figures of around 10,000 per annum).[92] At Hengrave in Suffolk the total bag was 4,923 in 1898 and 4,692 in 1899; it then rose, gradually if erratically, to reach 5,886 in 1906 and 8,572 in 1914.[93] At Blicking in Norfolk the total number of birds and animals shot rose from 1,196 in 1887 to a peak of 4,390 in 1901, although it then declined again, to 2,617 in 1903; while at Felbrigg numbers rose fairly steadily from the early 1890s, when the bag had varied between 1,266 and 2,341, to a peak of 5,462 in 1899, thereafter remaining at levels of around 3,000 until the First World War.[94]

The war years saw a marked decline as the shortage of labour reduced the intensity of gamekeeping. At Felbrigg, the total bag thus dropped from 3,908 in 1913/14 to 2,133 in 1914/15, and to 1,111 the following year. On the Broxted estate in Suffolk, an outlying part of the larger Rendlesham estate, total bags of 3,922 in 1912 and 3,590 in 1913 were followed by 2,818 in the first year of the war, while at Rendlesham itself the figures fell from 15,651 in 1913 to 8,458 in 1914 and 11,586 in 1915.[95] At Earsham the average bag between 1890 and 1900 had been around 3,600; in the period up to the outbreak of the First World War it was usually around 4,600; but during the war and immediately afterwards (in the years up to 1920) it fell back to 3,000.[96] The 1919 sales catalogue for Livermere boasted of the numbers of birds taken between 1916 and 1918 in spite of the fact that both active preservation and rearing had been abandoned.[97] Everywhere, however, the numbers of game killed soared again in the post-war period: at Beechamwell, for example, the number of pheasants shot rose from 783 in 1922 to 3,036 in 1929. True, there were fluctuations year by year, but figures for the same years show similar increases on other estates (Euston: 1,967 to 2,338; Sotterley: 2,065 to 3,009; West Harling: 943 to 1,774; Henham: 4,162 to 5,725).[98]

The increasing interest in shooting in the late nineteenth and early twentieth centuries was part of a more general enthusiasm for outdoor rural pursuits shared by wealthy businessmen and traditional landowners alike. But it was also inspired more directly by the fashion set by the Prince of Wales at Sandringham in west Norfolk, where game preservation was seen as more important than farming, the gamekeeper was said to 'treat every farmer as a poacher', and cottages for underkeepers took precedence over the needs of farm labourers.[99] It was also a function of the fact that cultivating the poorest, lightest soils no longer made good economic sense – game preservation was, in effect, a form of agricultural

Figure 18. Pheasant pens at Elveden, Suffolk, in the late nineteenth century. Elveden was one of the great shooting estates of Breckland.

diversification (Figure 18). As already noted, during the winter months most of the Breckland estates in Norfolk and Suffolk were abandoned by their owners to incomers from industrial or commercial backgrounds who took over their houses to enjoy the shooting. Lord Walsingham, owner of the Merton estate on the edge of the Breckland, commented to Rider Haggard that local owners were able to 'muddle along' by letting the shooting.[100] Some outsiders, such as the civil engineer, Edward Mackenzie of Fawley Court, Henley-on-Thames, could afford to buy up such shooting estates. As well as the 3,737-acre Croxton estate in the Norfolk and Suffolk Breckland, he owned 6,364 acres in Kirkcudbright and 2,962 in Dumfries.[101] On the poorest soils, individual farms were sometimes let to men more interested in shooting than farming, especially in the Suffolk Sandlings.[102] All this added to the problems of hard-pressed farmers, for the success of gamekeepers in eradicating foxes led to an explosion in the numbers of hares and, in particular, rabbits. They battoned freely on the crops and farmers were often prevented from controlling them. As Michael Home described:

If a farmer set foot after rabbits in the woods that hemmed in his land he was guilty of
trespass in pursuit, for woods were ground hallowed for the safe laying of pheasants'
eggs and the roosting of the grown birds.[103]

The leasing of estates to outsiders exacerbated these problems. The Suffolk land agent
William Biddell thus complained that 'The shooting tenant frequently does not regard the
interests of the farmer', and tenants in west Suffolk maintained that while they did not object
to the preservation of game for the landlord and his friends, 'we do care very much about
having strangers shooting who care nothing for our interests. We object to the land being let
to make two rents.'[104]

Yet the impact of all this on levels of cultivation and on the extent of dereliction were
actually rather complex, for where farms were let simply or primarily for the shooting, fields
which might otherwise have been abandoned might be ploughed and planted for feed or
cover. Game preservation might in fact encourage the cultivation of marginal land more
generally for, as Butcher explained in 1941:

> … among the things deemed necessary, are arable fields left long in stubble crops such
> as buckwheat and mixed corn which can be used direct as food for game. Consequently
> the question as to whether the yield of a crop repays the labour involved is not always
> the one taken into consideration and some land in this district may have been
> maintained as arable even though the yield has been low.[105]

Shooting had other effects, less complex and more direct, on the landscape. Landowners
continued to plant woods for game cover, as they had throughout the nineteenth century,
and on light land, especially, thin strips of conifer plantation were widely established along
field margins. In Breckland, the single lines of pines – originally managed as hedges –
bordering the fields were increasingly augmented with further planting to create the strips
of pines so characteristic of the district. Even on the heavier and more fertile land the
number of small woods, mainly intended for game cover, increased. Nicholson in 1913 noted
that 'The occasional planting of pure coniferous woods on heavy land, naturally adapted to
oak and ash, is probably due to the need of raising fresh cover for game in the shortest time
possible.'[106] Planting was not, of course, entirely motivated by an interest in shooting:
forestry had long been an activity peculiarly associated with large estates, and was carried
out for a range of aesthetic, economic and ideological reasons.[107] But much of the estate
planting in this period took forms which clearly indicates its primary role as game cover:
small blocks, clumps and narrow strips predominated, as on the Sennowe estate in mid-
Norfolk where, in the 1920s, Thomas Cook 'added a large number of plantations to his
estate, mainly 'roundabouts' in the centre of large fields, narrow belts on the sides, and
triangular woods on the corners'.[108] Landowners, as we shall see in the next chapter, did
undertake some purely commercial planting – it represented another form of diversification
– but many believed that too great an emphasis on commercial forestry could actually
interfere with game conservation and it was, indeed, true that a change of owner, from one

with great interests in forestry to one whose main concern was shooting, might have a significant impact on the landscape. On the Brandon estate in west Suffolk, for example, the extensive plantings made by the Bliss family in the nineteenth century, and by Almeric Paget after 1903, were neglected by subsequent owners Sir John Bird (1917) and Lewis Wigan (1923).

> Mr Wigan's interest, like that of Sir John Bird, was centred solely on game, and everything was sacrificed to it ... deer were encouraged by the provision of racks for feeding, and some of the natural regeneration was either heavily thinned or mutilated in order to provide more cover for the increased stock of game. Broom and gorse were introduced to make more cover, and fear of fires resulted in indiscriminate cutting of rides which caused, apparently, more beetle damage than the war-time felling. The rotted heaps of poles remain in places.[109]

## CONCLUSION

The influence of large landed estates on the development of the East Anglian landscape did not come to an abrupt end as farming fortunes declined from the 1870s. For the first four decades of the depression few large estates were actually broken up. Many changed hands, it is true, but the advent of new owners often led to the rebuilding of mansions and the enhancement of gardens and parks. In the wider countryside, the burgeoning obsession with game shooting probably had a greater impact, especially on wildlife, than ever before. Only from the mid-1920s did landed estates begin to disappear on a significant scale, and even then the greatest losses were concentrated in areas of especially poor land. In the countryside as a whole the majority of large landed properties survived, although they were often much reduced in area. Their impact on the wider countryside steadily diminished, especially (as we shall see) in terms of the built environment: the construction of estate housing was rare after the First World War. Yet in terms of fields and farms, parklands and, above all, game coverts, the influence of squire and aristocrat on the landscape was probably much less diminished in Norfolk and Suffolk on the eve of the Second World War than we sometimes assume.

# CHAPTER 5

# New Landscapes

## INTRODUCTION

The history of the rural landscape in the period between 1880 and 1950 is usually viewed in essentially negative terms – as a time of decline, decay and dereliction. Yet, as we have seen, this is an oversimplification. Most of the landscape continued to be farmed; country houses and parks were usually maintained and, on occasions, improved and expanded; entirely new agricultural enterprises, in the form of smallholdings, appeared. This last innovation was not, moreover, the only novel addition to the countryside in this period. The agricultural depression, coupled with the growing intervention of the State in rural life and a range of wider social and economic changes, encouraged the development of other new forms of land use, many of which continue to have a major impact on the East Anglian countryside.

## AFFORESTATION

The greatest change to the rural landscape of the region in the first half of the twentieth century was unquestionably the establishment of extensive conifer plantations in areas of poor heathy soils, principally in Breckland and the Suffolk Sandlings. This development was a direct consequence of central government policy. For many decades there had been mounting concern in government circles about the limited area and poor condition of the nation's woodlands. In 1916 the Prime Minister, H.H. Asquith, appointed the Forestry Sub-Committee of the Ministry of Reconstruction 'To consider and report upon the best means of conserving and developing the woodland and forestry resources of the United Kingdom, having regard to the experience gained during the War',[1] a period when curtailment of imports had more forcibly drawn attention to the limited extent of the nation's timber reserves. The committee proposed that, over the following eighty years, no less than 1,770,000 acres (c.72,000 ha) of land should be planted with trees. One and half million acres of this should be acquired by direct state purchase and planting, the rest through private enterprise or by joint public/private schemes. The committee's recommendations were accepted by the cabinet. In 1918 an interim Forestry Authority was established and in 1919 the Forestry Act authorised the appointment of eight Forestry Commissioners, who were empowered to acquire land.[2] Some 50,000 acres (c.20,000 ha) were bought before the deepening post-war recession caused the Commission's general authority to purchase land to be rescinded.[3] The Geddes Committee, appointed to find appropriate cuts in state expenditure, recommended that the whole policy should be scrapped, but the threat was fought off and in 1922 the Treasury agreed to reinstate the Commission's general authority to purchase, although it advised that the maximum price paid for land should not exceed £3 per acre – an instruction changed in November 1922, when the upper limit was set at £4 per acre; annual purchases were not to exceed 20,000 acres (c.8,100 ha).[4]

Concern for strategic timber reserves, especially of softwoods, was the main reason for the establishment of the Forestry Commission. But, as John Sheail has recently emphasised, right from the start the government had other motives. The new forests were to be concentrated in areas of low agricultural productivity but also of low employment, especially in the north and west of Britain.[5]

In 1922 the Commission made its first land purchases in East Anglia, beginning with a small area near Swaffham, followed soon afterwards by the purchase of 3,149 acres (1,275 ha) of the Elveden estate (Figure 19). This marked the start of a sustained policy of land acquisition in Breckland: Downham Hall (4,944 acres) was bought in 1923; Lynford (6,208 acres, c.2,500 ha) and part of Beechamwell (822 acres, c.330 ha) in the following year.[6] In 1925 the Cockley Cley estate, and parts of the Croxton and Didlington estates, were acquired; in 1926 the Weeting estate; in 1927 further portions of the Didlington and Croxton estates; in 1928 4,299 ha of the Croxton Hall estate (much of it already leased by the Commission); and in 1930 the West Harling estate (3,077 acres, 1,245 ha), together with a further portion of Lynford and 2,025 acres (820 ha) of the Hockham Hall estate.[7] After this there was a lull in acquisitions. In 1931, in the face of mounting economic crisis, the Commission's budget was again reduced, land purchases were concentrated elsewhere in the country, and only small quantities of land (such as a property of 176 acres at Feltwell, acquired in 1933) were purchased in the area.[8] Not all the land planted by the Commission in the 1920s and early 30s was purchased freehold, however. Some was leased for periods of between 120 (enough time to obtain two successive crops of timber) and 999 years.

Most of the land bought by the Forestry Commission in Breckland thus came in large blocks. Owners of estates on this poor land were eager to sell, given the impoverished state of their finances. And the sums paid for the land were low, almost invariably below the £4 per acre stipulated in 1922, with £2 4s 8d per acre being paid for the Downham Hall estate, £3 10s for Weeting in 1926, and just over £3 per acre for Croxton in 1929.[9] Such prices reflected the derelict or semi-derelict condition of many properties in this most agriculturally marginal of areas, something which is very clear in the various acquisition reports drawn up prior to purchase. That for Croxton Park, for example, made in 1929, described the estate as 'partly heath and partly low grade light arable or pasture land which has passed, or is about to pass, out of cultivation'. Feltwell Hall was found to consist almost entirely of heath land, divided here and there by narrow belts of Scots pine which had formerly sheltered arable fields.[10] Not that such properties completely lacked assets – a

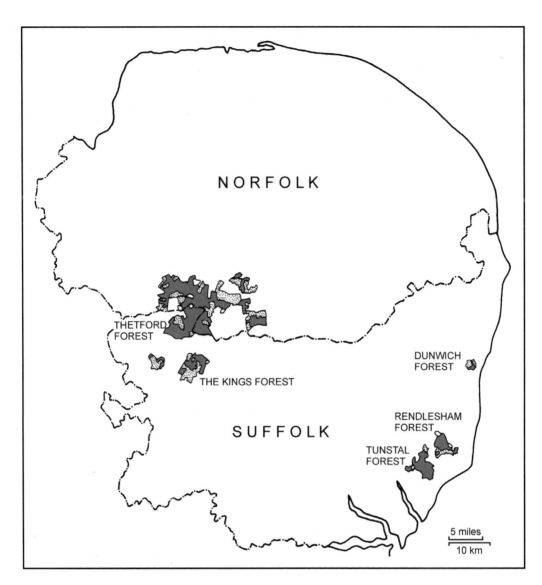

Figure 19. The location of the main Forestry Commission plantations in East Anglia on the eve of the Second World War (after Butcher 1941) (stippled areas represent land acquired by the Commission but not yet planted).

former employee of the Commission, interviewed in the 1990s, recalled the time when he met Sir William Taylor (chairman of the Commission) on a tour of the West Harling estate:

> 'Do you know Steel', he said, 'the timber that came off Fifty Acre Plantation bought the whole estate'. And he laughed and said: 'Whoever was agent for the Nugent estate really fell down there'.[11]

By 1934 the Commission's financial position had once again improved and land purchases in Breckland resumed, with attention now turning to the area to the south of Thetford and to the acquisition of the area which was to become King's Forest. This began with the purchase of the bulk of the Culford Estate in 1934. The Commission valued the estate – 6,900 acres (2,550 ha) of land, the timber, the sporting rights and all the estate buildings – at £30,088, or around £4 7s per acre. They offered the vendor £28,200.[12] Next, later in the year, the Mildenhall estate was bought from J.W. Norton, an acquisition followed two years later by the purchase of the Brandon estate, to the west of Thetford.[13] This was the last substantial addition to the Thetford forests, although there were further minor purchases which brought the Commission's holdings to 59,000 acres (23,000 ha) by 1939, of which over three-quarters was owned freehold and the rest leased.[14]

The Commission's activities in Breckland were mirrored, albeit on a smaller scale, in the Suffolk Sandlings, where three main areas of forest were established: Rendlesham, Tunstall and Dunwich, the last always the smallest of the three. The story of Rendlesham Forest effectively began in 1920 with the purchase of 1,878 acres (760 ha) from Lord Rendlesham,[15] followed by the acquisition of part of the Sutton Hoo estate and further purchases from the Rendlesham estate in 1926: this amounted in all to around 5,000 acres (1,742 ha). After this, purchases in the area tended to be on a smaller scale than in Breckland, with individual acquisitions generally covering less than 40 ha and usually comprising areas of existing estate woodland, such as Culpho Wood and Ufford Thicks.

Tunstall Forest was built up more gradually. The Commission's first purchase was of 437 acres (177 ha) from the Sudbourne estate in 1920. In 1929, a further 906 acres (367 ha) was acquired from the Campsea Ashe estate. By 1938 more than 3,800 acres (1,538 ha) had been acquired, although, once again, after this only relatively small portions of land were added. Rendlesham and Tunstall were initially managed as a single unit called Rendlesham Forest.[16]

The rather smaller Dunwich Forest began life later than the others, with the acquisition of 343 acres (139 ha) from the Dunwich estate in 1925 followed by the purchase of 840 acres (340 ha) from the Westleton estate in 1929. There were fewer acquisitions here until after the Second World War, and these again were mainly small blocks of land, many being less than 40 ha in size. As in Breckland, most of the land acquired by the Commission in the Sandlings was bought cheaply, generally for between £3 and £6 an acre. The vast majority consisted of either heathland or derelict arable, as at Walk Farm in Tunstall, acquired in 1931:

> Fine grasses with gorse and bracken are the principal features on the heath while the derelict arable fields carry the typical weeds of the locality and some bracken here and there ... Only some 35 acres [out of 431] are now cultivated and the farm has for some time been kept in hand for the sake of the sporting.[17]

In both Breckland and the Sandlings the Commission acquired not only land suitable for afforestation but also all the usual components of great estate landscapes – mansion houses, standing timber, parkland, farms and cottages. Sometimes farms and cottages were sold off, but often they were retained as housing for forest workers and to create smallholdings. Some of the mansions were sold, while others, such as Downham Hall, were demolished. Here the whole building was systematically cannibalised with timber, slates, bricks, doors and windows being salvaged for future use by the Commission.[18]

The dismemberment of great estates was only the start of a veritable revolution in the landscape of both districts. With remarkable speed arable and heath gave way to conifer plantation. The average planting rate in Breckland during the period 1922–1960 was around 1,300 acres (c.525 ha) per year, but the majority of the forest was established within the first twenty years, and the bulk of this in the first decade. The numbers of trees planted grew steadily through the 1920s, peaking in 1927, when no fewer than eight million trees were planted on 3,700 acres in the main area of Breckland, with a further 700 acres being planted up around Swaffham. Between 1924 and 1929 an average of 2,226 acres (909 ha) of plantation was established annually. Only in the period after 1931 was there a gradual decline in planting, as the number of new land acquisitions dwindled and the available acreage was planted up.[19] In the Sandlings the planting rate was similarly impressive. By 1926 2,302 acres (932 ha) of Rendlesham/Tunstall had been planted, rising to 3,501 acres (1,417 ha) by 1930. By 1935 4,790 acres (1,938 ha) had been afforested, reaching 4,905 acres (1,985 ha) by 1938.[20]

When planting began in the 1920s the Commission's initial choice as the main forest tree in East Anglia was the Scots pine, a species which had a proven track record in local plantations and as a hedging plant.[21] It was never the only species used, however, and Corsican pine, in particular, was employed in certain locations from the early 1920s, although seeds were harder to obtain and the tree more difficult to establish, especially in open situations. Douglas fir and European larch were also planted in places in the 1920s, but these were soon found to be less tolerant of local conditions than the pines. The same was true of other softwoods, such as Serbian spruce, silver fir, western red cedar, western hemlock, maritime and lodgepole pines, all of which were tried on a small scale.[22] What is perhaps more surprising is that a substantial number of indigenous hardwood trees – principally oak and beech – were also planted, far more than the present make-up of the East Anglian forests would suggest. In 1935, 1,186 acres (480 ha) of conifers were planted in Breckland, but as many as 428 acres (150 ha) of hardwood trees also went in. The main problem with both oak and beech was their vulnerability to spring frosts and browsing deer. They also grew more slowly than pines, and the numbers of both species being planted declined markedly after 1935.[23]

There was, however, a more significant change in planting policy during the 1930s, with more emphasis on Corsican as opposed to Scots pine. Although the latter was easier to establish in these hostile environments, the former produced a higher volume of timber per acre, had a better stem form, a greater tolerance of the thinner soils, and a better resistance to fungal diseases and insect pests. By the 1950s Scots pine was being planted only on the very best soils, or in pronounced frost hollows where Corsican would fail. Nevertheless, as the first fellings commenced in the 1960s the East Anglian forests were still overwhelmingly composed of Scots pine: more than 54 per cent of the seventy square miles in Breckland was

Figure 20. Labourers
planting young trees in
Thetford Forest in the
1930s. Most of the
planting of the great
East Anglian pine forests
was carried out by hand.

occupied by Scots pine and only 21 per cent by Corsican (together with 2 per cent of
Douglas fir, 8 per cent of other conifers, 4 per cent of mixed conifers and broadleaves and
11 per cent of broadleaves alone, mostly in roadside belts).[24]

Planting these vast areas was poorly paid, arduous work. The area to be afforested was
first securely fenced against attacks from rabbits, and all rabbits within it killed or driven out
– a task carried out by gangs of warreners employed directly by the Commission. It was then
ploughed, initially using horses, but with tractors gradually taking over during the 1930s. At
first a single mouldboard plough was used to make furrows spaced at intervals of four and a
half feet. Later, in the 1930s, a specialised form of plough was adopted which cut two parallel
furrows spaced at the correct planting distance. Labourers walked down the furrows, placing
the young trees in small spade-dug holes, also at intervals of four and a half feet, giving an
overall planting density of about 2,100 trees per acre (5,189 per ha) (Figure 20).[25] Such dense
planting was intended to ensure the rapid upward growth of the trees but also to provide a
canopy thick enough to kill off competing vegetation. When first planted, however, the
plantations had to be kept clear of bracken and other plants using reap hooks and sickles,
and any trees which had died were replaced – a particularly important activity because gaps
would lead to uneven and deformed growth in the adjacent trees. Low labour costs allowed

all this to be carried out remarkably cheaply: the entire cost of planting in the 1920s was usually no more than £4 10s per acre.[26] As noted, state forestry had always been seen in part as a means of reducing rural unemployment; conversely, the availability of cheap and under-utilised labour, in Breckland especially, was seen as a positive advantage when planting was first mooted. The Acquisition Report for the Santon estate, for example, noted that there were between 600 and 700 unemployed men in the area.

As we have seen, some of the labour needed to establish the forests was provided by smallholders, who were established on pockets of better agricultural land within the generally poor and heathy soils of Breckland and the Sandlings. As the depression deepened in the 1930s some of the holdings were also used to resettle unemployed workers from depressed areas in the north. More radical was the use of the forests as the location for camps run by the Ministry of Labour. These were first established in 1928 and were originally designed to train men for overseas colonial settlement, providing instruction in land-clearance, drainage, fencing, and so on. But within a year they had been given a simpler role. The overseas training element was dropped, and they were now expressly intended for:

> A class of men to whom our existing training schemes do not apply. I refer to those, especially among the younger men, who through prolonged unemployment have become so 'soft' and temporarily demoralised [that they are a] danger to the morale of the ordinary training centres … and … cannot be considered for transfer until they are hardened.[27]

By 1938 there were twenty-one camps in Britain, and a further ten which were used only during the summer months, scattered through the nation's infant forests. These housed, in all, nearly 6,000 men.[28] Four of these institutions were in Breckland: at West Tofts, High Lodge, Cranwich and Weeting. The Weeting camp made use of the redundant Weeting Hall; the others were purpose-built collections of huts, rather like army camps. All were run on strict disciplinarian lines and men generally attended for a maximum of twelve weeks. To begin with the camps only took those for whom subsequent employment or further training could be arranged. But later, as the depression deepened, jobs were given only to the more conscientious trainees, and used in effect as a tool to maintain camp discipline. From 1934, anyone claiming National Insurance had to attend a camp if required to do so, or lose their benefits. The 'trainees' retained only 4s of their benefit, reduced to 1s in 1934, the rest being taken for board and lodging. There was some compensation in the form of free boots, overall, oilskins, and so on, which could be retained by the minority of individuals who stayed the full three months.[29]

The camps did provide some rudimentary education in gardening, joinery and other skills, but they mainly supplied cheap labour for the Commission:

> The course of instruction takes the form of giving the trainees work such as road-making, scrub-clearing, etc., which will ultimately prove useful in working the forests but would not normally be undertaken for some years to come. There is consequently no displacement of local labour.[30]

Figure 21. Only from the air is it really possible to appreciate the vast scale of the Breckland plantations established by the Forestry Commission in the inter-war years.

The great plantings of the 1920s and 30s were thus dependent on poorly paid and – in part – conscript labour. Yet they were a phenomenal achievement, especially when it is remembered that the work was largely undertaken by hand and in the absence of effective forms of chemical weed control (Figure 21). Planting, moreover, was followed by a series of further tasks. Firstly, when the trees were about twenty feet high and the canopy had closed the plantations were *brashed* – that is, all side branches up to a height of around six feet were removed in order to improve shape and upward growth, and to make access to the plantations easier. Next, when the trees were between eighteen and twenty years old, the plantations were thinned, usually by removing between 200 and 300 trees per acre (500–740 per ha). Thinning began on a relatively small scale during the Second World War, under the auspices of the Timber Production Department, but it was only after the war ended that it began in earnest.[31] The Commission was fortunate in having a ready-made market for the thinned poles: they were purchased by the National Coal Board for use as pit props, there being a national shortage of material suitable for this purpose because of the intensive wartime exploitation of Britain's reserves of woodland. The thinner poles and the tops of the larger ones were made into fencing posts or sold for use as scaffolding. The smallest ones were converted into pea-sticks, for use in gardens, or into netting-stakes for the local rabbit warrens. The curved poles and irregularly shaped cuttings were simply sold as firewood.[32] The quantity of thinnings produced rose rapidly and, by 1950, 46,000 tons of wood were being extracted each year from the Breckland forests alone, more than the Coal Board required, and the Commission were constantly seeking new outlets for this material: for only by selling it could the income be generated to cover the costs of further thinning.[33]

The new East Anglian forests were, in essence, sudden and unnatural impositions upon the landscape, and were vulnerable to a wide range of threats. In particular, conifer plantations are much more combustible than deciduous woods, and in East Anglia this problem was exacerbated by climatic factors – exceptionally low rainfall – and geological ones – the absence, over wide areas of the former heathland, of any surface water.[34] Fire was a hazard even when the pines were very young, because the clearance of weeds created piles of dry, highly combustible vegetation. But the greatest risk came during the 'thicket' stage, after five to ten years' of growth, when the trees formed a low, dense, bushy mass. There were a number of fires in the late 1920s, and 1933 was a particularly bad year. Not only did the thick growth of vegetation provide a mass of combustible material, but it also made it harder to gain access to burning areas.[35]

One fire-prevention practice, adopted from the earliest days of the forest, was to plant belts of less combustible hardwood trees, particularly along roadsides.[36] Today these strips of beech, lime, oak, chestnut and other trees form a particularly distinctive and attractive element of the local landscape, and it is often assumed that they were originally established for aesthetic reasons, to mitigate public criticism of large-scale afforestation. Although amenity considerations were of some importance, the deciduous strips were mainly intended as a fire-prevention measure, not least because most fires originated on the public roads running through the forest – started by matches or cigarettes dropped by passers-by, or by sparks from steam-powered vehicles. Additional protection for the young forests was provided by leaving unplanted strips between these perimeter belts and the main body of the plantation; these were generally around 20 m wide and contained a 6 m band which was ploughed, or burnt under controlled conditions, to keep it free of vegetation. Other fire breaks were placed at other strategic points within the plantations and, in particular, beside the railway lines running through the forests.

As the trees grew higher the likelihood of fires decreased, but at the same time it became progressively more difficult to obtain wide views across the terrain, and thus harder to spot fires in their early stages. By the end of the 1930s watch towers began to be erected at strategic points. Accidental fires continued to be a problem through the 1940s, however, with one particularly serious outbreak in 1946, when 225 acres (c.90 ha) in Thetford forest were entirely destroyed.[37]

In addition to fire, deer, rabbits, and the Pine Shoot Moth all caused repeated problems, but the greatest threat to the maturing forest was the fungus *Fomes annosus* or, as it is now known, *Heterobasidion annosum*. *Fomes* first became a problem when the forests began to be thinned;[38] the airborne spores of the fungus took hold in the stumps of felled trees, then spread through the root system to infect the roots of adjacent, standing trees. The fungus soon produced ever-widening circles of dead and dying timber.[39] Methods of treatment, involving the inoculation of stumps with another fungus and the systematic removal of stumps in the areas of more calcareous soils where the pines were most prone to *Fomes*, were soon developed. *Fomes* remains a problem to this day, especially in Breckland, but one which can be dealt with through careful management.

The great plantings brought about radical changes in the appearance and ecology of the heathland districts of East Anglia, changes which were regularly bemoaned by naturalists and others, as we shall see. But it is important to note that much of the planted land was not virgin heathland, as is often supposed, but redundant arable, reclaimed during the 'agricultural revolution' and 'high farming' periods and now derelict or laid to grass because of the depression. Most of the land on which the plantations were established was thus already subdivided by boundaries, tracks and roads. Indeed, from a landscape historian's point of view one of the most interesting features of the forests, especially in Breckland, is the way that their layout and configuration – the boundaries between different compartments, and the pattern of access tracks – has perpetuated in broad terms the disposition of the roads and field boundaries which existed in the previous landscape (Figure 22). The smaller subdivisions of the planting blocks were themselves influenced by this framework, so that the whole layout of the new landscape 'ghosts', to a surprising extent, the configuration of the old.

It was thus in Breckland and the Sandlings that commercial forestry made its greatest mark in the first half of the twentieth century. But other areas were also affected. The Commission undertook extensive plantings on the outwash gravels to the north of Norwich, and in the area around Swanton Novers in central Norfolk, in the 1920s. From 1921, and especially from 1923, they also encouraged private owners to plant areas of woodland through a system of non-repeatable grants, with £2 per acre for conifers and £4 for hardwoods.[40] A number of East Anglian landowners took advantage: on the Quidenham estate in Norfolk, for example, 5,500 Scots pine, 3,000 larch, and 3,000 oak were planted under the scheme.[41] Indeed, with or without state aid a number of landowners continued, as they had long done, to take a keen interest in forestry, partly for aesthetic reasons, partly for game conservation, but also because tree-planting represented a useful form of diversification in these difficult times. Sales catalogues suggest that in the middle of the century many estates had areas of 'young' plantations. But most new planting, as we have seen, was concentrated in and around parkland, and took the form of relatively small blocks

Figure 22. These three maps, of an area near Hockwold in Norfolk, show the typical pattern of landscape development in Breckland in the late nineteenth and early twentieth centuries. By 1840 much of the heathland in the area had been reclaimed and ploughed, and a number of shelter belts established. Much of the reclaimed land reverted to heath around the end of the century and, with the expansion of interest in shooting, a number of additional belts and coverts were planted. By 1950 the area had been largely planted up by the Forestry Commission. Yet in spite of all these changes, the main pattern of tracks and boundaries displays a high degree of continuity, and the layout of the subdivisions within the afforested areas was strongly influenced by the earlier disposition of roads and boundaries.

designed primarily as game cover. Butcher, in 1941, thought that on the majority of Suffolk estates 'most of the woodlands are of old standing and recent plantings are rare.' He considered that only 3,320 acres had been privately planted in the county since 1905.[42] Most private owners, in spite of the differential payments offered by the Commission, and in contrast to their eighteenth and nineteenth-century predecessors, clearly concentrated their attention (like the Commission itself) on relatively fast-growing species. Butcher thus contrasted the twentieth-century plantations on Suffolk estates, which were 'mostly spruce, Douglas fir, Scots pine, and very mixed plantings with conifers in the majority', with the 'older woods', which were mainly of 'Scots pine, elm, poplar, beech … chestnut and oak'.[43]

One novel development in forestry practice had an important impact, albeit one that was limited and transient, on the East Anglian landscape. In the early years of the century, inspired in part by an article in the *Journal of the Royal Agricultural Society*, large numbers of 'cricket bat willows' (*Salix alba* 'Coerulea') were planted, especially in central and southern Suffolk, either in lines around field margins or as small plantations. Butcher drew attention to the 'cricket bat willow plantations' in the south-west of the county: 'These are situated chiefly along the water meadows of the River Stour and there are in addition long rows of such trees around the fields and along the lanes.'[44] A few still survive, now over-mature. A survey in 1927 noted that most of these fast-growing trees were already approaching maturity, but warned that few had any real commercial value: 30.5 per cent were the 'wrong type of willow or otherwise faulty set'; 31 per cent had been planted too close to produce good bat timber; most of the rest suffered from a range of diseases; and only 5 per cent were judged likely 'to make good quality bats'.[45] The failure of the willows to come up to scratch became something of a local joke, Lilias Rider Haggard, for example, consoling herself over the loss of some willow sets with the thought: 'My only consolation is that when it comes to the point no willow is ever found to be *quite* the right sort to make bats!'[46]

A key theme in the landscape history of early twentieth-century East Anglia is thus the phenomenal expansion of the area under various kinds of woodland. This was not, however, a period in which all aspects of forestry flourished. Traditional forms of management were systematically neglected, and some areas of woodland were destroyed altogether. On the outwash gravels to the west of Norwich the extensive plantations established by the Costessey estate in the course of the nineteenth century, mainly consisting of beech, chestnut, oak and larch, were largely felled following the sale of the estate in 1918: 'The despoliation of these woods was carried out without any thought for the future, and in consequence, the greater part of the area is now coppice or a thicket of high shoots which have grown from the old stumps of the stately trees which once adorned the landscape.'[47] Woods composed almost entirely of these outgrown pseudo-coppices are still a striking feature of the landscape of the area. Large-scale and indiscriminate fellings frequently followed the sale of landed estates: even before this, landowners often cut down timber before it was ready in an attempt to bolster estate finances. There was, moreover, general agreement that the small farmers who normally acquired land when estates were broken up had little interest in forestry and, at best, managed existing woods and plantations on desultory lines. Butcher believed that the average farmer in Suffolk 'rarely looks after the timber or plants a single tree'.[48]

## THE WASH RECLAMATIONS

Perhaps the most surprising new landscape to emerge in these years was that beside the Wash in Norfolk where, in spite of the depth of the agricultural depression, extensive areas of new land were reclaimed from the sea. As Mosby explained in 1938, 'Under favourable conditions small areas of about 200 to 400 acres have been enclosed by high banks, and thus protected from inundation by spring tides.'[49] The banks were around twenty-four feet high and had sluices through which surplus water drained away at low tide. Following enclosure, the marsh was grazed by sheep for two or three years, by the end of which time 'the marine grasses have been displaced by land grasses and clover'.[50] Reclamation of saltmarsh had continued on and off in west Norfolk since the Middle Ages, but a new spurt of activity, directed more towards the mudflats than the saltings, commenced with the establishment in 1839 of the Norfolk Estuary Company, a body with ambitious aims: the creation of an entire new county called Victoria, which would extend over an area of more than 200,000 acres, by channelling all the main rivers flowing into the Wash into a single embanked river and constructing embankments across its mouth.[51] The actual achievements of the Company were rather less than this, but remain impressive nevertheless.

In 1846 an act was passed which authorised the reclamation of 32,000 acres of saltmarsh on the margins of the Wash, in two sections: a northern, running from near Snettisham to as far north as Wooton; and a southern, in the vicinity of King's Lynn.[52] The latter involved the construction of a new channel to carry the river Great Ouse out to the sea, the former changes to the course of the rather smaller Babingley River. Further acts were passed in 1849, 1853 and 1857 which, among other things, laid out the compensation due to the Crown in lieu of its loss of foreshore rights, and to the 'frontagers', those whose land had formerly formed part of the coast.[53] The works were directed by the great engineer John Rennie and by 1851 it was reported that 600 men and about 200 horses were employed on the scheme, and were moving around 5,000 cubic metres of earth daily, figures shortly rising to 800 men, 300 horses and 7,000 cubic yards.[54] The northern reclamations were in four blocks, two of which were completed in 1858 and the others in 1861 and 1866; the southern, in the vicinity of Lynn, were in two blocks, completed in 1865 and 1881.[55] Most of the reclaimed land was leased, rather than sold, to local farmers and estates.

It might be thought that with the onset of the agricultural depression this work would have come to an abrupt end. Instead, at a meeting held in 1900, it was declared that the reclamations were still in their infancy, and the potential for further reclamations was discussed.[56] A new embankment was to be constructed, parallel to the existing line of reclamations, which was to be called the Century Bank: seven new blocks of enclosed marsh would be made in its lee (Figure 23). The required money was raised from mortgages secured on the value of two of the blocks of land already reclaimed. By 1904 the first of the new enclosures, covering 571 acres, had been completed at a cost of £6,799.[57] When, in 1906, most of the existing enclosures were sold off – mainly to large landowners, some of whom

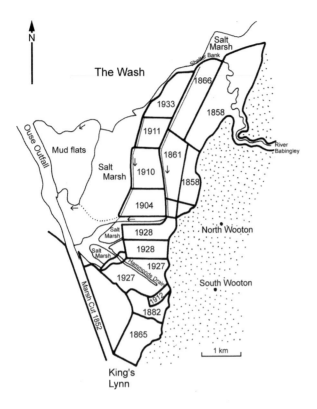

Figure 23. The Wash reclamations, showing the dates of the main blocks of new land (after Mosby 1938). In spite of the depressed state of agriculture, extensive tracts of saltmarsh and mudflats on the margins of the Wash continued to be reclaimed right through the late nineteenth and early twentieth centuries.

were members of the Board – the sales raised sufficient cash to clear the mortgages and to leave £4,697 to invest in further reclamation work.[58]

In 1908 it was estimated that the rest of the proposed new enclosures in the lee of the Century Bank could be completed at a cost of £1,045. The bank itself had now been standing so long that it was partly derelict, and a replacement was needed to complete the scheme. Further large blocks of land, to the north of the 1904 reclamations, were completed in 1910 and 1911, and another small area just to the north of Lynn – 'Enclosure number 10' – was reclaimed in 1914.[59] There was then a hiatus in activity, which continued through the First World War and into the 1920s (although some maintenance work was carried out on the banks during the war, using German prisoners of war).[60] The Company continued to operate, selling land and mooting further proposals, but only in 1923 did work on embanking recommence, now in the area between the 1904 enclosures and the land reclaimed in 1882, to the north of Lynn. In August 1927 the main sea wall around this second batch of enclosures was closed and the water excluded from 300 acres. In 1928, the work was completed and two new enclosures made.[61]

At this time the government proposed taking over the assets and liabilities of the company through the Ouse Drainage Bill, but the plan came to nothing and embanking continued. A further 175 acres (Enclosure number 14, at the northern end of the reclamations, and abutting on the block enclosed in 1911) was completed in 1933; the new land was valued at £5,250. But no further intakes from the marshes were made, in part because of fears that the Great Ouse Catchment Board would make a claim on the Company under the terms of the Drainage Act on the grounds that the land reclaimed had largely accreted as a result of the work which the Board had itself carried out in changing the character of the river outfalls. The Second World War ended further work, and only after the war had ended were further reclamations begun, with three further blocks being enclosed from the saltings in 1949. The Company was taken over by the Crown Estate under the Norfolk Estuary Act of 1964, and some further reclamations were made into the late 1960s.[62]

During a period in which some areas of land a few miles away in Breckland were actually going out of cultivation, the continuing success of marshland reclamation in west Norfolk is striking and superficially perplexing. The explanation, however, is relatively simple. The value of the rich siltlands was considerable and, as already noted, the costs of reclamation relatively low. The fortunes of the company were greatly favoured by natural processes. The levels of mudflat and saltmarsh were rising fast, especially near the outfalls of the major rivers, and this process could be accelerated at little cost by 'blocking up smaller arms of the creeks and using other devices'.[63] Reclamation was also assisted, as earlier ones had been, by the speed with which the poor saltmarsh vegetation changed following embanking. Petch, in the 1940s, noted that:

> The most striking feature of these lands is the rapidity with which the salt marsh species disappear. Within a year or two of the exclusion of salt water, they have been replaced by the common pasture grasses, and the docks, nettles, thistles, buttercups and daisies of arable fields.[64]

The reclamations still survive, albeit now – since the 1940s – almost entirely under arable cultivation. On the ground they appear little different from the more ancient reclamations which border them to the south and east. Only in plan does the markedly rectilinear layout of banks and boundaries, reminiscent of the Dutch polderlands, proclaim their modernity.

## LEISURE AND TOURISM

The new landscapes developing in this period of depression were not all agricultural or arboricultual in character. Another influence on the appearance of the countryside, fuelled in part by the need to diversify the rural economy but mainly by improvements in transport and higher levels of disposable income among the middle classes, and subsequently the upper levels of the working classes, was the expansion of the tourist industry. Coastal resorts in Norfolk and Suffolk had attracted visitors since at least the eighteenth century, but it was only from the middle decades of the nineteenth that the industry began to have a major impact on the landscape. Almost invariably, the distribution of development was closely linked to the rail network.

In 1867 the King's Lynn–Hunstanton branch line was opened and immediately Hamon le Strange, owner of the Hunstanton estate, began to develop New Hunstanton, a mile from the existing village (which itself became known as 'Old' Hunstanton), as a holiday resort. The potential of the place, with a good beach and fine scenery, was obvious. A new parish church was erected in 1865 and by the 1890s the town – with its tall boarding houses and hotels built of the distinctive local carrstone and laid out around a grid of streets – could boast a pier some 800 feet long, as well as a golf course, town hall and theatre.[65] By 1900 its population had risen to nearly 2,000. Cromer, on the north coast of Norfolk, had likewise attracted visitors since the eighteenth century and could boast a bath house by 1814. Between 1800 and 1845 its population doubled, in spite of a disastrous flood of 1837 which destroyed many of its facilities. It continued to develop, but with particular rapidity after the arrival of the railway in 1877.[66] 'Hotels of a size and magnificence that makes the dwellings on the cliff seem humble in comparison adorn perhaps too well, the unpretentious coastline, like jewels on the dress of a simple village maid.'[67] The Royal Links Hotel was built in 1887, at a time when golf was only just moving south from Scotland. The Grand and Metropole Hotels were opened in 1890 and the Hotel de Paris, which had originally been constructed in 1840, was rebuilt in the same year.

> Quietness and freedom from excitement, together with the charm of the town and the beauty of its surroundings, are the prevailing characteristics of Cromer; but for visitors who require attractions beyond those of sea and sand, woodland and down, there is ample provision. Bathing may be enjoyed on the firm sands under pleasant conditions. The golfer, the cricketer, the lover of bowls, and tennis will all find occupation.[68]

Today, although the core of the old fishing village, with cottages of beach pebbles clustered around the church, is still very evident, the seafront is dominated by nineteenth-century hotels and guest houses, while late Victorian red-brick residences line streets extending to the west and south-east. In the 1880s and 90s additional rail lines opened up nearby Sheringham and Mundesley, further east along the coast, the latter described as 'a rural retreat where the cornfields, the fair country lanes, and the trees are close to the sea'.[69] Both received their share of large hotels and both experienced huge increases in population in the last twenty years of the nineteenth century. Between Mundesley and Cromer, the coastal villages of Overstrand, Sidestrand and Trimingham owed much of their popularity to the poem *Poppy-land*, written in the 1880s by Clement Scott:[70] Overstrand was known in the tourist literature as 'The Gate of Poppyland'.

At Great Yarmouth, too, an existing holiday centre greatly expanded with the arrival of the railway. Lacking the scenery and quietness that attracted a genteel clientele to the north coast, late nineteenth-century Yarmouth was valued more for its excitement, and especially for the fun-fair which developed along the long sandy beach facing out from the medieval town.

> The Yarmouth sands and piers are as unlike those of Cromer as could well be imagined and Yarmouth holidays are organized in a way not understood elsewhere along the Norfolk coast, but Yarmouth sands in August are a complete refutation of the charge that we take our pleasures sadly, and no one seeking to understand the Englishman's attitude to his leisure can afford to neglect Yarmouth.[71]

The Yarmouth seafront is still dominated by the large hotels and villas of the pre- or early railway age, while terraced boarding houses in the streets between the seafront and the old town housed the majority of the late nineteenth-century holidaymakers.

Further south, in Suffolk, the story was much the same. The small fishing community of Southwold grew dramatically following the arrival in 1879 of the railways, in the form of the narrow-gauge branch line from Halesworth, run by an independent company, which itself became something of a tourist attraction. In 1889 the Cliff Hotel was constructed by the brewers Adnams, followed by the Marlborough in 1900 and the Grand in 1901.[72] In 1900 the town acquired a pier, one of the last to be built in the country and – like those constructed at Lowestoft and Felixstowe – the work of the Coast Development Company, founded in 1898. It carried a small pavilion but served principally as a place to land passengers brought by steamers from London.[73] Felixstowe also flourished, following the construction of the new railway line from Ipswich. As well as new docks, two new hotels were built, the Pier and the Manor House. West Carnie, writing in 1898, remarked how 'the houses are scattered about here, there and everywhere, over a huge area'.[74] In 1902 the Felixstowe and Walton Improvement Act gave the Council the authority to acquire land along the seafront and to construct a sea wall with two miles of promenade.[75] Railways did not always lead to development on quite this scale, however. A branch line was constructed from Saxmundham to Aldeburgh in 1860: primarily intended to serve Garrett's engineering works at Leiston and the small fishing industry at Aldeburgh itself, it stimulated the local tourist trade, and in the late 1870s work began on building a pier in the town, part of the mania for these things that swept England after the passing of the General Pier and Harbour Act of 1861 made it easier for consortia of businessmen and local authorities to undertake their construction.[76] The Aldeburgh pier was only ever half-finished, however, and was eventually abandoned altogether and demolished: Aldeburgh remained, and remains, a comparatively small resort.

The late nineteenth century thus saw the growth of coastal towns and villages into holiday resorts wherever railways allowed easy access from major population centres in the North, London or the Midlands. The twentieth century, in contrast, saw a more generalised sprawl of holiday accommodation in many coastal areas, as hard-pressed farmers sold off available land for low-grade holiday development and as the growth in car ownership provided greater mobility. The minutes of the rural district councils make it clear that in the 1920s and 30s, in places like Hemsby in east Norfolk, most requests for planning permission concerned bungalows, rather than two-storey houses.[77] Much holiday accommodation, however, comprised little more than shacks. Indeed, a great deal consisted of untidy and insanitary summer camp-sites featuring tents and makeshift huts. The east Norfolk coast to the north of Yarmouth was particularly affected by such development: the organised, extensive caravan parks which now characterise this area were largely a post-war development (the Seabreeze Caravan Park at Hemsby, which opened in 1950, was one of the earliest). In 1938 Mosby described:

> The increasing popularity of Yarmouth and the enormous crowds of holiday-makers which flock annually in ever-increasing numbers to this popular seaside resort, to the broads and to the innumerable huts and bungalows which are clustered almost the whole length of the Flegg coast have brought additional sources of revenue to this region.[78]

Similar developments occurred along the southern section of the Suffolk coast, especially around Shingle Street, Butcher describing how: '... Recently, as the result of easier accessibility by the motor-car, land, other than that around the large resorts, has been acquired for the erection of permanent dwellings or temporary dwellings often called "camps".'[79] There was much contemporary criticism of 'assemblages of caravans and converted buses which have littered and spoilt many a charming stretch of coast line',[80] for the problem was not confined to East Anglia, but extended along much of coast of England, especially in the south and east.[81] In the words of the Council for the Protection of Rural England in 1936, the period following the end of the First World War had witnessed 'a national movement seawards'.[82] One more organised aspect of this phenomenon was the establishment of the holiday camp at Mundesley in 1933, the second in the country (the first being on the Isle of Wight). Its layout, with wings running out from a central hub, was intended to reflect the pattern of the sails of a nearby windmill, although to some it may have seemed more reminiscent of a workhouse. There were 172 chalets which catered for up to 360 holidaymakers.[83]

It is important to emphasise, however, that not all areas of the coast were equally affected by holiday development. Suffolk, on the whole, saw less than Norfolk, in part because of the configuration of the coastline:

> The county contains some of the quietest rural country to be found anywhere and a coast which, owing to its unusual formation cannot be opened up from North and South with a single road, and a continuous ribbon of seaside shacks.[84]

In Norfolk, the north coast saw much less development than the east or west, in large measure because the land here was mainly owned by large landed estates, especially Holkham, whose owners regarded shacks and caravans with a horror not shared by smaller proprietors suffering the affects of the depression in agriculture.

The impact of tourism was not, however, restricted to the coast. The Broadland rivers and lakes in east Norfolk and north-east Suffolk also saw much development. The area had been used by the local inhabitants for recreation and entertainment for centuries – by the late eighteenth century many Norfolk landowners had their own pleasure craft, kept in boat houses on the rivers and broads – and with the arrival of the railways in Norfolk in the 1840s people began to be attracted from further afield. But it was only in the last two decades of the nineteenth century that the area began to develop as a major holiday destination. By the 1880s Norwich could be reached from London in less than four hours,[85] and the popularity of the Broads was encouraged by a spate of publications, including G. Christopher Davies'

*The Handbook to the Rivers and Broads of Norfolk and Suffolk* (1882) and *Norfolk Broads and Rivers, or the Waterways, Lagoons, and Decoys of East Anglia* (1885); and E.R. Suffling's *Land of the Broads* (1885). Davies described how 'To persons of a certain bent of mind, there is an engrossing charm in the lakes and rivers of East Anglia'. It was the 'wildness' and the 'solitude ... so dear to the naturalist and sportsman' that attracted him and no doubt many visitors.[86] Bygott emphasised how the marshes were 'silent with a vast agricultural and industrial silence, they speak to the man who has leisure, temporary or permanent, to study Nature and the little subjects of her kingdom'.[87]

The expansion of the Broadland holiday industry in the last two decades of the century was dramatic. John Loynes was the only boatbuilder listed as offering boats for hire in the first edition of Davies' *Handbook* of 1882. By the time the 1891 edition appeared, there were no less than thirty-seven companies offering boats, ranging in size from three to seventeen tons, many of which were converted wherries (the traditional trading vessels of the east Norfolk waterways). New forms of specially designed pleasure craft soon followed, and by 1900 steam launches were also becoming available. Agencies devoted to finding boats for prospective customers had begun as early as 1895 under Ernest Suffling, but they really became important with the establishment of Blakes from 1907 (Hoseasons, the other principal agency, was not established until the late 1940s).[88] The inter-war years saw further growth. By the early 1920s the first motor launches, powered by internal combustion engines, were being hired out (initially by Alfred Ward, whose boatyard was at Thorpe).[89] The number of boats for hire increased inexorably: in 1920 there were around 165, of which only four were motor cruisers. By 1949 there were 547, of which 301 were motor cruisers.

The impact of tourism on this remote wetland area was profound, and not entirely welcomed by elite observers.[90] Miller described, in 1935, how

> Each year they had seen the crowds growing and the holiday season lengthening, until it seemed that the beautiful waterways would be turned into a Blackpool or a Brighton ... great fleets of tripper-boats ... hired yachts, floating ice-cream vendors, bum-boats and craft of every description, largely in the hands of people who had not the slightest knowledge of how to manage them.[91]

But the new industry provided alternative sources of employment at a time when agriculture was in depression, and river transport, along with associated boatyards and riverside public houses, was in decline as a consequence of the expansion of the railways, and subsequently because of improvements in road transport. As on the coast, tourism initially had its greatest impact on the landscape where railway stations existed in close proximity, especially in the upper valleys of the Bure and Yare, which were anyway generally considered the most picturesque parts of the Broads. The villages of Wroxham, Horning, Hoveton, Brundall and – to a lesser extent – Potter Heigham all experienced significant development, as did Oulton Broad, with its fine, extensive area of water located only a short distance from the expanding seaside resort of Lowestoft. As early as 1903 Dutt thought that 'the red-brick villas and castellated houses which have sprung up on this side of the Broad have ... robbed Oulton of what little beauty it once possessed.' Wroxham, too, was being ruined by 'by the erection of unsightly modern houses for the accommodation of visitors'.[92]

In the course of the twentieth century, and especially in the inter-war years, large numbers of small bungalows, cheaply constructed in various pseudo-vernacular styles, were erected along the rivers – most notably along the Thurne above Potter Heigham, where they still run in a continuous line for nearly a kilometre, and in more patchy fashion even further. Many were built by the Norwich firm of Boulton and Paul, but smaller local builders were also involved, like Donald Curson of Wroxham.[93] They were constructed of light wood or iron framing, covered with weatherboarding or painted corrugated iron, and provided with low pitched roofs of wooden shingle tiles, corrugated iron or thatch, decorated with ornamental finials. Most had verandas facing the river. Conservationists regarded them with horror: one commentator described them simply as a 'disgusting spoilation of Broadland scenery'.[94]

In other contexts, and in other forms, the pseudo-vernacular 'Tudoresque' style displayed by the majority of such buildings met with less hostility. One of the most interesting holiday developments to emerge in East Anglia in the inter-war years was Thorpeness, on the east Suffolk coast just to the north of Aldeburgh. In 1898 Thorpe, in the parish of Aldringham, was described as 'a quaint little hamlet on the Suffolk coast. If ever a place gave the impression of being dropped from the clouds, that place is Thorpe ... There is no street and only one shop.'[95] But Glencairn Stuart Ogilvie, a successful barrister and playwright, inherited the 600-acre Sizewell Hall estate in 1908, which included seven miles of coast between Dunwich and Thorpe, and in 1910 the place – suitably renamed – began to be developed as a holiday village, catering for the wealthy middle classes. Ogilvie was something of a philanthropist who wished to bring economic revival to this depressed area of Suffolk. He was also influenced by contemporary ideas about the importance of fresh air and healthy exercise, including the *plein-air* movement inspired by the French realist painter, Jules Bastien-Lepage. His plan was to create a settlement which would be 'an expression of Art as well as an effort of Science'.[96] He personally oversaw, and always retained a personal interest in, the development, although day-to-day running was in the hands of a commercial company called Seaside Bungalows Ltd. The new settlement's central feature was a 25-ha lake developed from the natural mere which had formed behind a coastal spit (Figure 24). Around this were scattered neat houses in a range of eclectic styles – some in medieval mode, decorated with timber-framing and weatherboarding; others Jacobean in inspiration. The result is a kind of idealised suburbia, magically transported to the seaside. Two architects, William Gilmore Wilson and Frederick Forbes-Glennie, were employed, but Ogilvie appears to have designed many of the buildings himself. In 1914 a new station was opened to serve the resort on the Saxmundham–Aldeburgh line and, while development was interrupted by the outbreak of the First World War, it resumed soon after its close.[97] There was a theatre, extensive gardens and tennis courts. Curiosities of the village include an early nineteenth-century post mill which was moved here from nearby Aldringham and

Figure 24. Thorpeness, Suffolk. General view of Glencairn Stuart Ogilvie's holiday village, clustered around the 'Meare', with the 'House in the Clouds' in the distance.

used to pump water into an unusual water tower, the 'House in the Clouds', in which the water tank itself, perched on top of the tall weatherboarded tower, was disguised as a house.

A booklet, published in 1912 and probably written by Ogilvie himself, describes the philosophy behind the creation of the new village, and also emphasises the market at which the enterprise was aimed, stating, for example, that control of the beach would be 'an important and powerful weapon of defence against the invasion of trippers and other "undesirables"…'.[98] The design of the village harked back to a more stable past, '… an England of a happier day'.[99] It was in part inspired by the Garden City ideas of Ebenezer Howard, and Ogilvie's book refers to the movement for building new urban centres which could 'as far as possible preserve the Natural Beauties and Healthy Conditions of Country Life', describing how 'Letchworth, Port Sunlight, Golden Green, Whiteleys Village and other Garden Suburbs are tentative endeavours to effect this purpose.'[100] The design of the houses also, to some extent, echoed the ideas of the 'arts and crafts' movement and William Morris, although their mode of construction – in some cases, of concrete – would not have found much favour in that quarter. The pioneer town planner Patrick Abercrombie was not entirely complimentary in 1934, considering that Thorpeness was 'without perhaps a sufficient grip upon a logical plan' and had an emphasis on 'too miscellaneous a picturesqueness of architecture': it was, nevertheless, 'a delightful contrast to the usual seaside place'.[101]

Thorpeness is indeed unusual – a one-off, idiosyncratic development. But much about its design was palely echoed in those of smaller, more piecemeal developments elsewhere, even many of the shack-like bungalows erected in Broadland and on the coast in the inter-war years. For these, too, albeit in a less sophisticated way, often drew their inspiration from a romanticised view of the rural past. Whatever the design, many contemporaries – especially those who had themselves moved relatively recently to the region – regarded holiday developments with horror, not least because they paid little heed to the real local styles of vernacular architecture.

But middle- and, subsequently, working-class enjoyment of the countryside did not necessarily lead to significant landscape change. Bed and breakfast accommodation was increasingly offered by local farms, a useful form of diversification. As early as 1895 *The Eastern Daily Press* was urging farmers to take in paying guests to bolster declining incomes and was suggesting that the railway companies could advertise the availability of such accommodation: 'The teeming populations of the large towns could be glad to spend a week or two in the beautiful villages of the country.'[102] In the later nineteenth century rambling clubs began to make their way out from major towns and cities into the countryside for a day's healthy walking, and East Anglia, although it lacked large urban populations, was to some extent affected by this trend. In July 1891 The Vegetarian Rambling Club set out by train from London to Ely and from there made their way to Stoke Ferry in west Norfolk to visit, after an hour's walk, the fruit colony at Methwold. Here they were shown round by the colonists, and 'The points which came up for discussion proved so engrossing, that little time was left to reach Stoke Ferry Station, so we had to step out, and the genial afternoon caused us to be in a delightful glow when we took our seats in the train.'[103]

By the 1930s improved transport meant that access was easier, and the countryside was increasingly enjoyed by working-class ramblers, hikers and cyclists. The Youth Hostel Association was set up in 1930 and the Ramblers' Association in 1935. Adrian Bell described in 1935 how:

> Bank Holiday would be unnoticed in the country here, were it not for townsfolk friends and relations that give the little station four miles distant the bustle of a suburban one on the following Tuesday between eight and nine. The labourer works as usual, but the people from the neighbouring towns, employed and unemployed, go walking, cycling or coaching by.[104]

Accommodation might be provided by tents, often pulled in small hand carts or behind bicycles. By the 1930s troops of Boy Scouts were also coming out from the towns and, having perhaps first introduced themselves to the local vicar, would ask permission to camp in some farmer's field. Campers were not always so considerate. Having complained about those who pitched tents without permission, left gates open and dropped litter, a correspondent to the *Eastern Daily Press* went on to say 'I am confident that any Norfolk farmer would accede to any reasonable request which would promote the enjoyment of holiday-makers, but it is not fair to expect us to suffer fools gladly.'[105] Most visitors took advantage of the established network of railways and the expanding network of bus routes, but the more affluent explored the region by car, armed with the appropriate guide books – such as Arthur Mee's Norfolk and Suffolk volumes in the *King's England* series, described on the back cover as 'The indispensable companion of the Motor Age' – and the 1-inch Ordnance Survey maps, without which 'A holiday in any part of Great Britain is incomplete'.

Farming may have been in depression and, in part at least as a consequence, the influence of large landowners on the countryside was slowly waning. But the rural landscape of East Anglia was being shaped by new forces. In the planting of the great pine forests, as much as in the widespread establishment of smallholdings discussed in Chapter 3, we can see the effects of new forms of political power and political organisation reaching deep into this comparatively remote region. And in the expansion of resorts – as much, once again, as in the expansion of smallholdings – we see reflected the increasingly urban character of British society and the successive revolutions in transport which broke down distance and allowed the easy movement of both people and commodities.

CHAPTER 6

# The Changing Countryside

In the view of almost all environmental historians the twentieth century was, in terms of the rural landscape, 'a game of two halves'.

> Whilst farming was generally depressed, the countryside of the first half of the century was typically diverse, beautiful and rich in wildlife. Farming boomed in the second half of the century, as those concerned with the conservation of amenity and wildlife … came close to despair.[1]

While such a picture may adequately capture the relationship between farming and the rural environment in some parts of Britain, in East Anglia it is at best an oversimplification. The depression did not necessarily lessen the intensity with which land was managed and exploited; and habitats continued to be destroyed or degraded, although not, primarily, as a direct consequence of agricultural developments.

## DERELICTION

Many writers have suggested or implied that the most important change in the landscape during the agricultural depression, in East Anglia as elsewhere, was the spread of derelict land, as abandoned arable tumbled down to weeds and as pastures were colonised by scrub, radically changing both the appearance of the countryside and the kinds of habitats available for wildlife.[2] This impression is largely founded on the polemical writings of men like Rider Haggard or Henry Williamson: 'the dereliction, the mud, the weeds, the dilapidated buildings, swarms of rats, broken tiles, rotting floors … swampy meadows, cracked bridges, flat gates and overgrown hedges'.[3] More sober commentators, and especially government surveys and estate records, portray a less dramatic picture. In essence, dereliction was largely restricted to particular districts of very poor soil, especially Breckland; and, even here, it was rather less extensive than has often been assumed.

For the most part, as we have already noted, unprofitable arable land was simply laid to pasture. Henry Rew thus noted in 1895 that between 1881 and 1894 the area under the plough in Norfolk had decreased by 35,843 acres: but while 30,887 of this had gone to grass only 4,956 had passed out of cultivation altogether.[4] William Fox, reporting on the state of Suffolk agriculture in the same year, described how 'On the clay and very light soils the land is frequently very foul, being choked with charlock, weeds and thistles'; but only around 5,000 acres in the county had actually been abandoned, and almost all of this was on the poorest, lightest land, in Breckland or on the coastal heaths of the Sandlings – less than 0.5 per cent of the total agricultural area of the county.[5] Clare Sewell Read, similarly, noted in 1905 that there were some farms on the heavier clays 'where the land, left entirely to itself, has grown nothing but couch grass and weeds': but the most severe problems were restricted to Breckland, where 'Thousands of acres … are now derelict'.[6]

As already noted, the crisis years of the First World War saw a short-term abatement of the agricultural depression, and some abandoned or degraded land in the region was ploughed up. Most of these reversals proved temporary, as farming returned to slump in the 1920s. Inter-war commentators seem unanimous, however, that large-scale dereliction was restricted to Breckland, and to a lesser extent the Sandlings. Mosby thus described in 1938 how, in the former district, 'many acres have gone out of cultivation following the phenomenal decline in prices' between 1919 and the early 1930s. 'This type of land has practically no grazing value, and may be described as derelict arable, capable of being cropped again when prices of grain rise to a sufficiently high level.'[7] Indeed, by this time the district had become a byword for dereliction, Michael Home eloquently describing how:

> Scattered about the great heaths are ruins that once were buildings and the homes of labourers, but they are hard to find or even to discern when almost found. The bracken covers them, and canker-wed, and the endless burrows of rabbits have made what were once their gardens an indistinguishable part of the open heath.[8]

Yet there are good grounds for believing that Breckland's very status as an icon of agricultural decline ensured a measure of exaggeration; and that some observers mistook some of the surviving areas of virgin heathland in the district for abandoned farmland. The maps produced by the Land Utilisation Survey in the 1930s do not, unfortunately, distinguish between these two categories of land, recording both simply as 'heathland or rough grazing', but it is nevertheless possible to estimate the relative proportions of each by looking at how the areas so defined are depicted on the first edition 6-inch Ordnance Survey maps of the 1880s. Taking the core of Breckland – essentially, the district bounded by Mundford to the north, Larling to the east, Culford in the south and Lakenheath in the west – around 70 km² of heathland/rough grazing appear to fall into the first category, of virgin heath; but only 50 km², at most, seem to have comprised abandoned farmland. Moreover, both these categories were dwarfed by a vast area of land simply categorised as 'pasture' – grassland of at least reasonable quality – which extended through the northern part of the district, embracing a number of large parks (at Elveden, Buckenham Tofts and West Tofts), some warrens or former warrens, and much former arable land. Even in Breckland, in other words, the depression had mainly witnessed the expansion of pasture at the expense of ploughland, not outright dereliction.

It might be argued that the degeneration of 50 km² of former farmland to rough grazing represents a major change in the agricultural landscape. But the real status of much of the land so categorised by the Land Utilisation surveyors is, in fact, unclear. Butcher, in the Suffolk volume, described the normal succession of vegetation on abandoned arable land:

> For the first year or so after cultivation these fields are a mass of wild plants of all kinds, some of which are, in England, confined to this district … Later, on the better land, a turf forms of the three common heathland grasses and … [sand] sedge … *At this stage the land is often ploughed up again*. If allowed to degenerate further, bracken, heather, and various under-shrubs appear, and the land becomes to all intents and purposes heath. [my italics][9]

Long fallows of seven to ten years had always been a feature of farming on the worst soils of the district: some of the 'derelict' arable fields may thus simply have been outfield 'brecks' given a longer period than usual in which to lie fallow. This gradual lengthening of the traditional breck fallow was, indeed, noted in passing by a number of writers: Clarke, for example, described how land on Rushford Heath, ploughed in 1904, 'had been fallow for about 20 years'.[10] Such deviations from normal patterns of arable husbandry, as Butcher emphasised, could be difficult to classify.[11] In addition, questions of definition were complicated in Breckland by the diversification of estates (especially in the early stages of the depression) into shooting. Some fields, instead of being abandoned altogether, were cultivated on a desultory basis for game feed or cover. It is also worth noting that both here in Breckland and on the heaths of eastern Suffolk the pattern of land use was not static, but changed over time. In addition to the arable expansion of the First World War, there were other phases during which areas of heath were reclaimed in response to changes in technology, slight fluctuations in prices, or the energy or optimism of particular landowners or farmers. Clarke noted in 1908 how

> Within the past decade big areas of heath and derelict 'breck' – notably on Rushford, Knettishall, Snarehill, Melford, Roudham, and West Tofts heaths, Brettenham Drove, and on the Elveden estate – have been brought under cultivation by the steam plough.[12]

Similarly, Butcher noted that around 250 acres of poor, sandy land in east Suffolk had been brought back into cultivation between 1932 and 1939 'as a result of Oldershaw and Garner's demonstration of the efficiency of chalk dressings'.[13]

The Land Utilisation Survey reports drew attention to other districts of East Anglia where the abandonment of land was noticeable, but seldom extensive. Butcher noted that only around 0.4 per cent of the heavy land in northern and central Suffolk comprised derelict arable, and although in the south-west of the county there was rather more land of this kind it nevertheless amounted to only 3 per cent of the total area.[14] He also noted a scatter of places where pastures were becoming invaded by scrub, but the impression given is that these were relatively few and far between. On the clays of south and central Norfolk the quantity of derelict land was so small that Mosby, in 1938, didn't even bother to discuss it: indeed, the *total* area of agriculturally unproductive land in these areas, including commons which had never been cultivated, was only around 1.5 per cent.[15] Dereliction, where it occurred on the clay soils, was usually the consequence of particular factors which just tipped the balance against the profitable cultivation of particular farms or fields: tithe charges, distance from well-made roads or railways, the neglect or death of a particular tenant.[16]

There were a few other areas where marginal land, reclaimed in the late eighteenth or nineteenth centuries, fell out of use in the depression, although they were scarcely mentioned by Butcher or Mosby. In particular, many of the peat marshes in the Norfolk Broads, enclosed and improved in the decades around 1800, were now abandoned once more, often after some natural disaster had severely damaged the drainage works, so that the owner was simply unable or unwilling to pay for the necessary repairs. Thus Strumpshaw marsh was abandoned for grazing following the great flood of 1912, which wrecked the drainage windmills and sluices.[17] Today Strumpshaw 'Fen', as it is now known, is a swampy morass of reeds and rushes. A number of the valley fens in the district, in spite of their wild and primeval appearance, have a similar history. The ruined brick drainage mills in the middle of Catfield Fen, or to the south of Hickling Broad, attest to the fact that these apparently wild areas, seemingly untouched by human exploitation, had once been drained for grazing land.[18]

While some poor land, or land which required expensive maintenance, was certainly abandoned during the depression, contemporary writers seem thus to have over-emphasised its extent, concentrating their attention on those areas of particularly poor soil, especially Breckland, where the tide of profitable cultivation had always ebbed and flowed. Even here they seem to have exaggerated their case, often to make wider political points about the extent and depth of the depression and about the degraded condition of rural society more generally.

## WOODS AND HEDGES

If the agricultural depression rarely led, in East Anglia at least, to widespread dereliction of land, some recent commentators have assumed that it had a more pervasive, if more diffuse, effect on the fabric of the countryside. In particular, falling farm incomes led to a neglect of hedges and boundaries after a century or more of particularly intensive management and sustained change. Certainly, there is no doubt that during the agricultural revolution and high-farming periods hedges were well maintained and field boundaries frequently altered or removed, especially in the anciently enclosed districts.[19] This process was evidently continuing into the 1880s. In 1887 Augustus Jessopp, vicar of Scarning in Norfolk, bemoaned how:

> The small fields that used to be so picturesque and wasteful are gone or are going; the
> tall hedges, the high banks, the scrub or the bottoms where a fox or weasel might hope
> to find a night's lodging ... all these things have vanished.[20]

Some have argued that the depression years simply witnessed a reversal of all this, and that hedge removal, in particular, came to an end. In Oliver Rackham's words, 'From 1870 until 1945 there was very little change in hedges', which were often poorly managed so that they grew tall, and saplings within them were allowed to develop into mature trees.[21] Indeed, Rackham has compared (for the country as a whole) the numbers of trees shown on the first edition OS 6-inch maps of the 1880s with the 1951 Forestry Commission's estimates of the density of farmland timber to argue that the number of hedgerow trees in England as a whole increased from around 23 million to some 60 million:

> The period 1750–1870 was, on the whole, an age of agricultural prosperity in which hedgerow timber almost certainly decreased. The period 1870–1951 was, on the whole, an age of agricultural adversity, in which there was less money to spend on either maintaining or destroying hedges. Neglect gave innumerable saplings an opportunity to grow into trees.[22]

In East Anglia, at least, there are major problems with these hypotheses. To begin with, on *a priori* grounds it seems unlikely that the fellings of timber in plantations which accompanied the financial embarrassment of large landowners and the break-up or contraction of large estates, or which occurred during the First World War, would have passed hedgerows by, and, indeed, many contemporaries commented on the decline in the number of trees in the countryside. In 1902, for example, Rider Haggard noted the large-scale felling of hedgerow oaks in the area between Whissonsett and Wendling in Norfolk, commenting: 'I think that 'ere long this timber will be scarce in England.'[23] Lilias Rider Haggard similarly described in the 1930s how 'the wholesale cutting of timber all over the country is a sad sight, but often the owner's last desperate bid to enable him to cling to the family acres …', noting elsewhere: 'The other day, going past a well-known and well-loved place, I was hit like a blow in the face by a scene of complete desolation – every tree gone.'[24]

The purchase of estate farms by former tenants was, likewise, frequently accompanied by wholesale felling to help recoup the purchase price. But there was another reason why the density of hedgerow timber is more likely to have decreased than increased in this period. Timber was the landowner's property, not the tenant's, and in these changed times, when there were often problems in finding tenants for farms, landlords were more sensitive than they had formerly been to complaints concerning the shade which mature trees cast over the adjacent fields. Lilias Rider Haggard typically described:

> A consultation about the always difficult question of tree cutting on the farm. This particularly affects the arable fields, where the farming tenant has cause for some complaint. Decided somewhat sadly that some dozen small oaks must come out before the sap rises, or next autumn when the crops are off.[25]

There is, moreover, little evidence that this was a period in which young hedgerow trees had the opportunity to grow unheeded to maturity. Indeed, the problem – then as now – was rather the opposite one, of persuading those responsible for maintaining hedges to spare promising saplings. As Lilias Rider Haggard again described:

> It is often difficult to get the hedgers to remember to leave oak and ash saplings unless they have gained sufficient height to be obvious. Down the hedge goes the sickle,

taking in its deadly sweep many a hopeful little tree which would have graced the property in twenty years' time....[26]

Elsewhere she bemoaned 'the unthinking sweep of the billhook [which] destroys many a sapling which might have grown into a valuable tree.'[27]

In theory it should be possible to throw some quantitative light on this question by comparing the numbers of hedgerow trees shown on the OS 6-inch maps, surveyed in the 1880s and 90s, with those appearing on the RAF vertical air photographs of 1946.[28] But in practice such a procedure is fraught with difficulties. The Ordnance Survey did not record every farmland tree – partly because the scale of the maps precluded the depiction of more than one specimen per fifteen metres or so of hedge line, and partly because the instructions given to the surveyors meant that trees with girths of less than 0.6 metres were omitted anyway. And even when the quality of the RAF photographs is sufficient to the task, it is not easy to accurately count trees in densely packed hedgerows, or to ascertain the size of the smaller trees shown. Nevertheless, when used with sensible caution these two source can provide some indication, at the very least, of whether the number of farmland trees increased, or decreased, in this period: and by roughly what percentage.

In the 1880s the density of farmland trees across East Anglia displayed much variation, largely as a consequence of earlier landscape history. The greatest densities were to be found on the level clay plateau of north-east Suffolk and central and southern Norfolk, which was characterised by poorly draining Beccles Association soils. Here numbers of farmland trees recorded by the OS per km$^2$ invariably reached 250, were often over 300, and in some places totalled more than 400; these were found mostly, but not exclusively, in hedgerows. This was in spite of the fact that these soils also carried significant amounts of ancient woodland (reducing the area occupied by farmland, and thus the average hedge length). This was an area of small, anciently enclosed fields, in which pasture farming rather than arable had always, at least in the period up to the early nineteenth century, played a major part in the economy. Away from the very heaviest clays, the density of farmland trees was generally lower. Where the clay plateau was more dissected, especially in west Suffolk; and on the more fertile loams, as in north-east Norfolk, there were normally between 200 and 250 trees per km$^2$. These were again, for the most part, districts of early enclosure, with many small proprietors, but here arable farming had always been of more significance than cattle rearing or dairying, and thus the tolerance of hedge timber over the centuries had presumably been less.

The lowest densities of farmland trees were to be found on the lighter soils, which were generally enclosed from open fields and heaths in the later eighteenth and early nineteenth centuries. This was partly because there were fewer trees in the hedges, but partly because, as the fields produced by late enclosures were generally larger than those in areas anciently enclosed, there were fewer hedges anyway. The lowest densities per km$^2$ were on the very poorest of these soils – on the former heaths to the north of Norwich, and in Breckland. The figures from these areas are to some extent misleading because the numerous plantations and shelter belts established by large estates in the wake of enclosure in the nineteenth centuries were planted at the expense of earlier field boundaries, but they also were low on the better, more calcareous soils of the Breck edge, and in northern and north-west Norfolk, where there were generally between 100 and 200 trees per km². What is perhaps most surprising is the situation in the Fens of west Norfolk, now a largely treeless landscape, and already fairly denuded of trees by 1946. Although the OS maps show that the peat fens, relatively recently enclosed, were fairly poorly treed in the later nineteenth century, the same was not true of the northern silt fens, which had been reclaimed and farmed since medieval times. Indeed, the density of farmland trees here was in many places well in excess of 250 per km². Most specimens grew beside the drainage dykes, but some small areas of densely treed pasture could also be found.

In spite of difficulties of interpretation and comparison, the 1946 aerial photographs confirm the impression of contemporary commentators. Rather than increasing, the density of farmland trees, principally growing in hedgerows, declined considerably during the depression period, although with marked variations from district to district. On the claylands, the decrease varied in sample kilometre squares from 5 per cent to as much as 50 per cent, and averaged around 30 per cent. On the light lands the average was about the same, but there was more variation from place to place, with some areas experiencing virtually no change in the number of trees, while others saw a decline of more than 70 per cent: as far as the evidence goes, the loss appears to have been less in areas where large estates remained intact. On the more fertile loams, especially in the north-east and east of Norfolk, the density fell from anything between 25 per cent and 70 per cent, with the average being around 50 per cent. The most striking reductions, however, were in the northern Fens, which by 1946 had already gained their present, rather treeless, appearance. In one grid square, to the west of the village of Wiggenhall St Mary Magdalene, 441 trees are shown on the OS 6-inch map of 1884: by 1946 there were around fifty. There is, it must be emphasised, a fair degree of subjectivity behind these figures, and the scale of loss may to some extent be exaggerated. There is no doubt, however, that in East Anglia, if not elsewhere in the country, the density of farmland trees declined, rather than increased, in the period under consideration. In most areas this was for the reasons already outlined, but in particular districts other explanations may apply. The drastic reduction in the numbers of Fenland trees was thus probably in part the consequence of wider environmental changes. The trees depicted on the 1880s Ordnance Survey maps were mostly willows, to judge from the small number of survivors, which had probably been planted in the seventeenth and eighteenth centuries, at a time when most of the area was under grass and used for grazing livestock. Improvements in drainage technology after 1800, especially the adoption of large steam pumps, allowed the water table to be lowered, and most of the land was then cultivated as arable: by the 1880s probably three-quarters or more was in tilth. Many of the trees growing beside drainage dykes will not have been replaced after the adjacent land was ploughed up. But more importantly, loss of willows may have been accelerated by the lowering of the water table, leaving many with their root systems well above the level of the waterlogged soil. Both here, however, and in north-east Norfolk, catastrophic levels of tree loss was also probably a consequence of the fact that these were areas in which small farms and smallholdings flourished, and in which little land was in the hands of large estates.

The available evidence also suggests that even in the depths of the depression East Anglian hedges were not, for the most part, allowed to grow tall and unmanaged. True, where farms were left untenanted for any length of time, usually on particularly light or particularly heavy land, the hedges might grow out of control – Henry Williamson described, although perhaps with some exaggeration, how he had to 'cut hedges as high as a cottage roof' when he took over his farm in north Norfolk in 1937.[29] But in many cases what outside observers noted as tall outgrown hedges may, in reality, have been ones managed under the traditional regime of East Anglia – coppicing on a long rotation of ten to fifteen years. Julian Tennyson in 1939 thus described the 'overblown and unruly' hedges of east Suffolk: 'They spread outwards, they spread upwards, they loom majestically ... beyond the reach of man. Nobody bothers to control them.' But he was also well aware that this was merely a phase, a part of a cycle: 'And suddenly some infuriated hedger-and-ditcher ... will leap upon them, not to clip them into delicate, topiary orderliness, but to raze them almost to the ground', the whole process being repeated again after a few years:[30]

> I do not mind when the hedges are suddenly cut down, for in Suffolk it is a most spacious and unusual feeling to find yourself walking for a mile or two between cornfields that come sweeping down to the very edge of the lane.[31]

Observers were not always so sanguine. Lilias Rider Haggard described her 'secret sorrow' at seeing a hedge coppiced back, because it had provided a sheltered spot for sitting and was 'at all seasons beautiful, as old hedges are', although acknowledging that this was necessary as it was 'a formidable tangle of briar and thorn some eight feet through and twelve feet high, stealing the sun from the arable field beyond, and forming an almost impenetrable dwelling place for numerous rabbits.'[32] Even in an age of depression, hedgerow maintenance was essential in arable country, for these two good reasons, if for no others. True, where farms were laid to pasture there were noticeable changes in the way that hedges were managed. Bell described in 1932 how, on his Suffolk farm:

> The gnarled stumps of hedges, close-chopped every year and writhing in all ways as if in an agonised attempt to escape the knife, were allowed to grow ... and were close-knit into paddock walls by a gentler art than that which merely kept them down so that they should not shade the corn at harvest.[33]

But where arable land use continued, and especially in areas where smallholders were dominant, hedges seem to have been cut back, if anything, with greater regularity than before, in part perhaps because of the explosion in rabbit numbers. Tennyson himself described how:

> In west Suffolk there are many long stretches with literally no hedges at all, or at the best hedges that are kept to, and often below, their proper size. And as the fields are larger – they are very large in some places – and the country is flat, there is often nothing to break the view.[34]

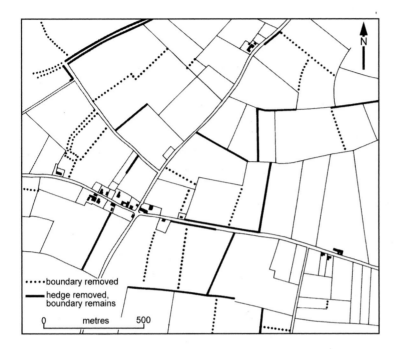

Figure 25 Boundary change in Filby, north-east Norfolk, between 1905 and 1946 (source: second edition OS 6-inch map and 1946 RAF vertical aerial photographs).

He drew particular attention to a 'high, flat belt of land running through the centre [of the county] that lacks both hedges and trees in any number'.[35] Adrian Bell, likewise, described how in west Suffolk 'The hedges were cut to the ground between the cornfields to allow sun and wind to dry the crops at harvest. This gave the higher ground an open aspect.' Butcher, in 1941, noted how south-west Suffolk was a district of 'low hedges and ditches, a high proportion of large arable fields'.[36] He, however, described similar conditions across the Suffolk claylands as a whole:

> Hedges around the fields, because of the shade they throw, are considered detrimental to good arable cultivation and so are kept as low as possible or even rooted out. Consequently one characteristic of the district is the hedgeless or almost hedgeless fields surrounded by deep ditches.[37]

These, he noted, contrasted markedly with the high hedges which were to be seen 'around the meadows, the farm boundaries, and the precincts of the farm dwellings'. A comparison of sample 6-inch OS maps of the 1880s and 90s with the 1946 RAF vertical aerial photographs suggest that the amalgamation of fields had indeed continued in many areas, albeit on a reduced scale, during the depression period. Even more common, however – in southern and eastern Norfolk as much as on the Suffolk clays – was the removal of hedges, leaving only a ditch as a field boundary. While many of these changes may have been effected during the War years, this is unlikely to have been true of most examples (Figure 25). In some areas, as Butcher noted in 1941, such changes were encouraged by the adoption of tractors in place of horses.[38] Certainly, the changing character of the region's fieldscape in

Figure 26. The inter-war landscape in west Suffolk. A single tree remains after hedgerows have been removed to create a vast new field. The prairification of East Anglia was already under way.

the inter-war years was a matter of concern to naturalists like George Bird, who gave a lecture on the subject of 'The Ornithological Life in Suffolk' in 1935, 'throughout which the devastation of the countryside by loss of timber and hedge-shelter was persistently deplored' (Figure 26).[39]

Indeed, not only hedge cutting but also many other routine agricultural tasks – especially those carried out in the winter – seem to have been kept up assiduously during the depression years. In many places under-drainage was probably addressed with more enthusiasm than is often supposed: even small farmers like John Baxter of Grange Farm in Pulham Market were, as we have seen, prepared to invest in this on some scale, at least in the early years of the depression (above, p. 15).[40] The impression of a relatively well-managed countryside is supported by the evidence of photographs taken in the first four decades of the twentieth century which give little indication of a landscape in which hedges were growing tall and unkempt or were crowded with unwanted, adventitious timber. On the contrary: they suggest a rather manicured and tidy countryside (Figures 27 and 28). All this should occasion no surprise. The maintenance of boundaries was winter work, carried out when other tasks on the farm were less pressing. It was comparatively inexpensive work, yet was particularly necessary in a landscape which was, as we shall see, badly overrun with rabbits (which found a ready home in tall, outgrown hedges); in an economic climate in which farmers must have been acutely aware of the effects of shading on crop yields; and at a time when, in some districts at least, tractors were gradually coming into general use. The principal exception to all this does, indeed, prove the rule: for the only evidence for large-scale, systematic neglect of hedges comes in fact from Breckland.

Figure 27. Harvesting at Marjoram's Farm, South Walsham, Norfolk, in the early twentieth century. Note the low-cut, sparsely timbered hedges in the background.

Figure 28. Hall Farm, Fornham St Martin, Suffolk. This undated photograph shows the kind of well-maintained countryside which was typical of East Anglia in the early twentieth century.

Hedges of Scots pine were widely planted in Breckland in the early nineteenth century, when the heaths and remaining open fields here were enclosed. Pines were presumably chosen because they will tolerate the dry, sandy soils of the district better than hawthorn, and rapidly provide shelter for crops and game. The few examples still managed as hedges show that, with an effort, pines can be made to provide a low, dense, stockproof barrier. But a very short period of neglect allows the plants to 'get away', and once they have grown into trees it is impossible to return them once more to bushes. As early as 1908 W.G. Clarke noted the start of a decline in regular management, describing how 'These hedges are made of ordinary trees kept stunted by constant trimming, and many of the lines of fir trees now bordering plantations were originally hedges, but have ceased to be trimmed.'[41] In 1925 he implied that many were still being regularly cut, noting how pines were 'still the characteristic tree of the district, planted either in rows known as 'belts', or artificially dwarfed as hedges'.[42] By the 1930s, however, large numbers were no longer being managed, and Butcher described how 'the rows of trees are in all stages of development and degeneration: there are some very fine hedges along the Barton Mills–Elveden road and some very neglected ones around Cavenham and Icklingham which no longer fulfill their primary purpose.'[43] In most cases management ceased altogether during the Second World War, when manpower was in short supply. The trees grew tall, with a slight twist; lines of such pines bordering field margins are now a characteristic feature of the Breckland landscape, and of parts of the Suffolk Sandlings (especially around Ramsholt and Butley). Indeed, they are considered a quintessential feature of the 'traditional' landscape of the former region, in particular.

This exception aside, hedges seem, on the whole, to have been managed with some intensity during the depression years. But the same does not appear to have been true of the other main semi-natural environment of the farmed landscape – ancient, semi-natural woodland. Such woods in East Anglia were almost all, in the middle years of the nineteenth century, managed on a regular basis as coppice-with-standards. The majority of timber trees were oak; the composition of the coppice varied considerably from area to area, but usually included substantial quantities of ash, hazel, maple and (more locally) hornbeam. Even in the first half of the nineteenth century there were comments about the poor condition of some of the coppice understorey, and the tithe files of the late 1830s, in particular, suggest that its growth was being restricted by an increasing emphasis on timber trees, the canopy of which served to shade out the underwood beneath. At Congham in Norfolk the coppice was typically said to be 'much injured by the timber',[44] while at Fulmodestone it was noted that the coppice would be 'much better if timber was thinner'.[45] Not only was the economic value of timber rising in relation to that of underwood in the first half of the nineteenth century, but the expanding tanning industry required large quantities of bark which in East Anglia, where there was little oak coppice, was best supplied by timber trees, or by young trees thinned from plantations.

Nevertheless, coppicing was still going strong in the middle and later decades of the century. In 1881 Henry Wood, agent for the Merton estate in Norfolk, described in some detail the management of a seventy-acre wood (almost certainly Wayland, near Watton) and listed the varied uses which were made of the coppice poles, principally ash and hazel. Everything was either sold or utilised on the estate: larger poles were used to make hurdles, fencing or bins for storing hay or straw on the home farm; splints, about 2 m in length, were used for building work; smaller material went for thatching broaches and sways, or for pea-sticks; the smaller brush faggots were 'sold to bakers and cottagers for oven wood'; while the off-cuts of all products were sold for cottage firing.[46] On the Hare estate around Stow Bardolph in west Norfolk the coppiced woods were evidently still being regularly exploited in the 1880s, wood sales bringing in around £1,000 per annum, much of which was from coppices.[47] Timber accounts from elsewhere suggest a similar picture, as at Earsham in south Norfolk, where sales of underwood regularly brought in between £200 and £400 per annum in the 1860s and 70s.[48]

The intensity with which traditional woodland was managed declined steadily in the course of the twentieth century, however, and commentators leave no doubt that coppicing in particular was neglected. Much of the timber in ancient woods was cut out during, and immediately after, the First World War, and little restocking seems to have taken place. Butcher, writing about the Suffolk claylands in 1941, described how the woods here were 'entirely neglected except for an occasional coppicing when the undergrowth becomes too thick or the owner runs short of hazel sticks or faggots'.[49] To the south, on the mixed Eocene soils beside the Stour valley, the 4,000 acres of woodland were 'as usual … very much neglected from the forestry point of view'.[50] In part, the decline in management may reflect the fact that, as estates were broken up, many woods came to be owned not by large landowners, but by 'farmers who know little and care less for forestry'.[51] But even where landed estates remained intact traditional woodlands were managed with declining enthusiasm. True, on some of the larger estates – such as Wolterton in north Norfolk – coppicing continued on some scale into the 1940s.[52] But usually it declined in regularity and intensity with each passing decade. On the Ickworth estate in Suffolk, for example, detailed accounts describe the income from wood sales from 1915 to 1952. The material mainly took the form of faggots, billets, hurdles, firewood, posts, pea-sticks and stakes from coppices, but also included some larger beech, ash, elm, oak, spruce and larch sold by the foot, which mainly came from plantations rather than woods *sensu stricto*. During the First World War the income was in the range £300–£500 per annum, with the highest level – £1,415 – reached in 1919. But this declined fairly steadily thereafter, to a mere £125 in 1952.[53]

As already noted, the economic importance of coppice wood had been declining even before the start of the agricultural depression. The availability of alternative materials for fencing, tools and the rest, together with the fact that cheap transport costs ensured that even wood for turning could be imported from distant areas, led to a slow but steady contraction in demand. The penetration of the railways into East Anglia, as into other parts of England, meant that coal was available at relatively low cost, and household grates and ranges were adapted accordingly. Yet this decline in the market for coppice products, while inexorable, was nevertheless gradual. Wood-burning may have become less common, even in the countryside, but it did not cease entirely. Moreover, even into the inter-war period some local industries provided a market for coppice wood. As late as 1923 ash hurdles and wattles were being made at Melton Constable.[54] Fishermen's rollers, for the bottoms of shrimp nets, were made in King's Lynn, while a turnery in the same town made ninepins for skittle-alleys, pump-buckets and bottom-boxes (the top and bottom of well shafts), and plough handles.[55] Brush manufacturers continued to consume substantial quantities. Well into the 1920s a small turnery at Wortham Ling, near Diss, was supplying a one-man brush works in the same village.[56] But by the inter-war years such uses, except brush manufacture, were rare survivals: and even brush-making was increasingly concentrated in large units of production which were less tied to local sources for their raw materials. In 1880 the large factory of S.D. Page and Son, later to become the Briton Brush Company, and subsequently Hamilton Acorn Ltd, was formed, and soon afterwards moved to Wymondham, a town which had long had a reputation as a centre for turnery. The Co-operative brush factory was also located at Wymondham. Both companies used coppiced wood from a wide variety of locations in the county, as well as birch cleared from heathland in north Norfolk. But, increasingly, in the inter-war period, they made use of imported beech from Belgium and France, and even birch from Norway.[57]

Changes in demand were not the only factor encouraging the decline of traditional forms of management. The advent of the Forestry Commission, and of its advisory service in particular, saw the final triumph of 'plantation' silviculture, and many landowners seem thereafter to have viewed coppicing as an old-fashioned practice. Examination of existing woods suggests many examples, such as Hockering in Norfolk, where the coppice understorey (in this case, of small-leaved lime (*Tilia cordata*)) has been 'singled', some time in the first half of the twentieth century, so that it developed into high forest. Woods had always been valued to some extent as game coverts: in many areas this now became their main purpose, although increasingly for yeomen farmers rather than the gentry.[58]

Yet if the character of East Anglia's ancient woods changed in this period, there is little evidence that woods were actually removed on a significant scale. Even the rapid, large-scale fellings of the First World War did not lead to their actual destruction, for even when they were not restocked, timber trees often regenerated from the coppice understorey, often thereby converting a wood of oak timber into one dominated by ash or, across much of south Norfolk and north-east Suffolk, hornbeam. A few woods were destroyed during the Second World War to make way for airfields, as at Thorpe Abbotts in Norfolk, but it was only in the period after c.1950 that large-scale conversion of East Anglia's ancient woods to farmland, or to conifer plantations, began in earnest. Nearly half of the ancient woods in Norfolk, for example, were grubbed up or coniferised between 1945 and 1971.[59]

## HEATHS AND COMMONS

Although vast areas of rough land in Norfolk and Suffolk were enclosed and improved, especially in Norfolk, in the eighteenth and early nineteenth centuries, a surprising amount remained at the end of the nineteenth century. Some, mainly residual areas of common grazing, was located on the heavy clays (such as Wacton Common in Norfolk, or the commons of South Elmham in Suffolk); and some comprised peaty ground on river floodplains, especially in the valleys of the Broadland rivers. But most was on poor light land – areas of leached, acid sands and gravels. Much of this, as already noted, was to be found in Breckland and the Sandlings, but large areas also survived on the Greensand ridge running north from King's Lynn, beside the Wash, and on the various tracts of glacial gravel in the area running northwards from Norwich to the sea. Pockets could also be found more widely scattered across almost all the soil types found within East Anglia – localised accidents of glacial or pre-glacial geology. Such areas generally carried heath or heath-like vegetation.[60]

Some of these areas were private property, but a significant proportion were commons or 'poors' allotments' – land allotted at the time of enclosure either to be used directly by the poor, for fuel cutting or grazing, or leased to raise money for coals.[61] Precise definitions were in fact complex. As the Norfolk naturalist W.G. Clarke put it in 1910:

> After a lengthy experience of seeking to elicit information, I am reluctantly compelled
> to conclude that the only way to obtain a perfectly accurate list of the commons of
> Norfolk would be to hold a judicial investigation in each village, with power to examine
> witnesses, and inspect manorial deeds, Inclosure Acts, award maps, and other essential
> documents.[62]

Nevertheless, he estimated that 'land accessible to the public, and in some way owned by them', was to be found in 157 of the 802 parishes in Norfolk, and totalled in all some 11,324 acres; and to this, as noted, we have to add the many thousands of acres of private heath and other rough grazing. In Suffolk there was less land of this kind, and it was mostly concentrated in Breckland and the Sandlings.

Whatever its precise legal status, and whatever its precise environmental character, all this uncultivated land was crucial for conservation: far more important for preserving biodiversity, and in many districts for the scenic qualities of landscape, than the more productive farmland of cultivated fields, woods and hedges which we have just discussed. As W.G. Clarke put it in 1910:

> Having never been cultivated and in many cases rarely subject to alteration by man,
> these commons are among the most interesting parts of the county to the naturalist, for
> on them to a much greater degree than elsewhere there has been an almost
> undisturbed succession of flora and fauna from post-glacial times.[63]

Heaths had long been one of East Anglia's most distinctive semi-natural environments. Most were dominated by heather, with gorse, bracken and other plants present as subsidiary elements (National Vegetation Classification scheme *H1 – Calluna vulgaris – Festuca ovina* heath).[64] Areas of grass heath could also be found, however, in which grasses like sheep's fescue were dominant and the various undershrubs constituted subsidiary elements. These usually occurred where thin sandy deposits overlay chalk. Heaths of this kind (mainly NVC U1) would have been extensive in north-west Norfolk before the great reclamations of the eighteenth century, and remained common in parts of Breckland.[65] Whatever the precise date at which the East Anglian heaths first came into existence, they owed their distinctive character to continuous, systematic exploitation. This, in particular, prevented their gradual colonisation by scrub, and ultimate regeneration of the birch–oak woodland which was the climax vegetation on these light, acid soils. In addition to intensive grazing by livestock, especially sheep, heaths had traditionally been cut for a variety of products. Heather was used as fuel and occasionally as thatch; bracken was cut for bedding and to some extent for fuel; while furze or gorse was used for both fencing and fuel, especially for ovens.[66] In addition, the turf and matted roots of heather had traditionally been cut from many heaths and used for firing by the poor.

At the start of the twentieth century naturalists rightly considered the heaths to be of considerable ecological interest, and Breckland in particular to be one of the greatest habitats and landscapes of East Anglia, if not of southern Britain. This was in part because its distinctive vegetation included a variety of rare steppe species (such as *Silene conica* and *Medicago falcate*) and in part because of the presence of a distinctive range of bird species.[67] The great bustard had long gone from the East Anglian heaths, having been effectively extinct in the region since the middle decades of the nineteenth century. But the ringed plover, the stone curlew and a number of other species remained abundant. Moreover, the sheer scale of this apparently 'natural' landscape was of perennial appeal, even to those whose knowledge of botany, zoology or ornithology was weak. It was therefore a matter of concern to many conservationists that the character of heaths and similar dry commons changed dramatically in the period under discussion here. There were two main reasons for this: they were being grazed, and cut, with declining intensity; and many were gradually planted up as conifer plantations.

The intensity with which East Anglian heaths were grazed had begun to decline even before the start of the agricultural depression, partly because the new 'improved' breeds of sheep widely adopted in the region in the course of the nineteenth century were less well adapted to the rough grazing provided by heather and other heathland plants than the old traditional variety, the Norfolk Horn. But decline continued more rapidly from the 1880s. When arable farms in these light soils areas were abandoned, the associated heathland would no longer be grazed. But even where land remained in occupation increased wage costs and the difficulty of obtaining shepherds, coupled with alternative ways in which land could be now kept in heart (other than by intensive folding) and the low prices for lamb, all encouraged a decline in size of the flocks kept on the open heaths. To this was added, in the inter-war years, an increasing emphasis on cattle as opposed to sheep on many farms, especially in the Suffolk Sandlings, a change which was itself associated in part with the adoption of sugar beet as a major crop.[68] The decline in the number of poor cottagers and smallholders using areas of common heath for grazing compounded the problem (above, pp. 53–4).

White, discussing the Suffolk coastal heaths in 1885, described how they were:

> Covered with a short velvety herbage of grass or moss and studded more or less with furze bushes. In other places they are completely covered with ling or heather. Sheep readily browse the young shoots of the furze and eat the early grass, but if either gets beyond a few inches in length, neither the one nor the other is usable for sheep's feed.[69]

Reduction in the intensity of grazing thus led to a steady growth in the height of the heathland vegetation. Where rabbits were numerous, especially in Breckland, they kept this process in check to some extent. But they were selective grazers, avoiding older plants and bracken and preferring heather to gorse,[70] and even in rabbit-infested Breckland their impact was often limited. By 1908, to judge from Clarke's account of the ecology of the district, some of the heather was as much as eighteen inches (c.0.5 m) in height – very different from the close-grazed sward of earlier periods.[71] These changes were, moreover, compounded by a decline in the cutting and mowing of heather, gorse and bracken, and the digging of 'flag', on commons and poors' allotments. As we have seen, such practices had more or less disappeared by the end of the First World War.

One almost immediate consequence of these developments was that bracken, no longer kept in check by a combination of regular cutting and the trampling of the young plants by livestock, increased in significance. Clarke described in 1908 how it was 'certainly the dominant plant of the "breck" district, and on several heaths has usurped the position which heather occupied some 20 years ago. Bracken lacks its former economic importance.'[72] By 1918 it was said to be the principal plant on the heaths in other areas of Norfolk.[73] Michael Home described hamlets in parts of Breckland as 'oases … fighting a losing battle against the insidious onslaughts of both rabbits and bracken'.[74] Gorse, or furze, also seems to have become a more important component of the heathland vegetation. Bird reported in 1909 how, on East Ruston Common in north-east Norfolk, 'The best parts of the common for grazing purposes are now being much encroached upon by the spreading of furze … there are not enough Donkeys to nibble down the gorse bushes';[75] while on Barnham Common, near Thetford, Clarke noted in 1918 that 'the original steppe flora has been greatly reduced by the encroachments of furze.'[76] Indeed, many commons – especially those on the glacial sands and gravels to the north of Norwich, and along the north coast – were by the early twentieth century coming to be characterised by scrub, in which gorse was the 'most characteristic member'; or by a scrub association 'dominated by whitethorn, blackthorn, furze, and *rubus*'.[77] Birch and pine, and sometimes oak, were also invading by this stage: their seedlings were 'common on many heaths',[78] often coming in from neighbouring plantations established by local landowners. Some commons and poors' allotments began to be managed by burning, a practice unrecorded in earlier times.[79] By the 1920s and 30s, to judge from the reports compiled by the Forestry Commission when estates were being purchased in Breckland or the Sandlings, many areas of heathland were in a very rough condition, much invaded by scrub and trees. That drawn up when Iken Heath in the Sandlings was purchased in 1920, for example, refers to the 'very strong growths of heather, bracken etc with gorse and thorn bushes and a number of pine groups in scattered form'.[80]

The acquisition reports signal the arrival of the force which dealt the death blow to many of the most extensive areas of open heath. We have discussed the new pine forests created in the inter-war period in the previous chapter in essentially neutral terms, as interesting twentieth-century additions to the landscape, and in the long term they have unquestionably been environmentally beneficial. But most contemporary commentators regarded the new plantations, especially in Breckland, with horror. This was not only because of the damage they did to a range of unusual plants and to the abundant wildlife of the heaths. It was also because the conversion of the area into a 'shoddy coniferous forest'[81] radically changed the appearance of a much-loved landscape characterised by wide, empty prospects – even if some of its apparent wildness was in reality the consequence of relatively recent changes, the spread of dereliction since the 1880s. As H.J. Massingham put it:

> With the exception of Breckland, an area of 400 square miles, all, or nearly all, our wildernesses are pools, not lakes or inland seas of apartness. I once went for a walk on the Brecks with [W.G] Clarke … the Brecks that day gave me an inkling of what it meant to wander forty years in the desert…[82]

Julian Tennyson was equally enthusiastic: 'This country has to be seen to be believed; it is … quite unlike any other country that I have yet discovered.' Hardly surprising, then, that the steady acquisition of this land by the Forestry Commission was regarded with considerable apprehension by conservationists. In Tennyson's words:

> The Commission has worked its way steadily through the centre of Breckland, buying and leasing estates, removing boundary after boundary, until now there is scarcely a couple of miles of ground left unplanted between Lakenheath Warren and Elveden in Suffolk and the road from Methwold to West Wretham in Norfolk. It has swept everything before it: the heaths and brecks in its paths have disappeared for ever. Small wonder that those who loved the old spirit of Breckland should complain that they can now scarcely even recognise their own country.[83]

The situation was made worse by the fact that, from the outset, the Forestry Commission seems to have gone out of its way to give virtually no quarter, and made no compromises on the extent of its activities. A representative actually addressed the Norfolk and Norwich Naturalists' Society in 1928. He explained that he had 'the same love for trees that you have for your wild birds', and sympathised with his audience's 'anxiety to maintain a portion, at least, of your beautiful Breckland'.[84] He emphasised the variety of the proposed plantations – which, as noted elsewhere, were originally intended to include a significant proportion of beech and oak – and foresaw a time when even the mature pines would be appreciated for their aesthetic qualities. But in the short term he agreed that the afforested areas would be visually unattractive, and even in the long term environmentally impoverished: 'Wild life will, I am afraid, suffer from lack of food and sun, and I doubt if these forests of the future will hold as much wild life as your breck lands do today.'[85] But he urged the necessity, and the inevitability, of afforestation. On both economic and strategic grounds, it was imperative to establish a national timber reserve. 'Afforestation has come to stay and the only brake that will be applied is that of cost.' The only hope for nature conservation lay in the preservation of 'small and isolated areas of Breckland', and he urged that the Society should seek to do this.[86] The suggestion that some part of the remaining open heaths should be kept as a nature reserve was widely repeated. In 1935 one Suffolk naturalist, in a letter to the *Times* concerning the Commission's plans to plant up a further 1,200 acres in Icklingham, commented:

> Surely the Commission can see their way to leave this part unspoilt, so as to preserve
> unbroken this fine expanse which includes Wordwell, Berners and Cavenham heaths. It
> is not too much to hope that, before it is too late, an area will be acquired on trust for
> the nation; and I appeal whether something cannot be done to save a portion of the
> Breck for the use of those life-forms for which Nature has made it a home, and for the
> folk who can appreciate its charm and significance.[87]

In the early 1930s the Norfolk Naturalists' Trust attempted to persuade the Commission to sell them 1,200 acres of the 6,000 acre Culford estate which they had recently acquired, but were refused: 'there would seem to be no limit to their activities in the district'.[88] The planting of the 2000-acre Lakenheath Warren was, however, prevented by a different expedient. The Trust simply acquired neighbouring properties with common rights over the heath, rights which would be violated by large-scale afforestation.[89] Other Breckland heaths were, however, preserved by simple acquisition in advance of afforestation – Wretham Heath was purchased by the Norfolk Naturalists' Trust in 1938; and Weeting was acquired in 1942.[90] Nevertheless, by 1944 there was said to be very little typical heath or breck remaining in the district, and in the previous year the President of the Norfolk and Norwich Naturalists' Society, E.C. Keith, accepted afforestation as a *fait accompli*, arguing now principally for a more imaginative and integrated approach to the practice of forestry. A vast unbroken expanse of pine, he thought, was both unnecessary and unsightly. 'Hard woods or even larch would relieve the monotony and add immensely to the beauty of the landscape as well as serving their purpose industrially'.[91] The Commission had in fact made some concessions in this direction from the very start of planting: the belts of broadleaf trees planted, in particular, on roadsides, although mainly established to serve as fire breaks, were in part intended to break up the visual monotony of the pines.[92] And some relics of the heathland vegetation could still be found (as today) in the forest rides. But over much of Breckland the impact of the pines in this period was profound and negative. The stone curlew nested with some success in young plantations, and lapwings nested on the rides between them, but neither for very long: Cadman reported that the former deserted the forests within three or four years of planting, and the latter after around seven years. A range of other species, less rare but nevertheless characteristic of the heaths, likewise decreased: these included skylark, meadow pipit, stonechat and whinchat, and although the ringed plover took to nesting on areas of arable land for a while, it too soon largely deserted the afforested areas.[93]

On the heaths of east Suffolk the plantations were not so vast or continuous, but the changes they brought were nevertheless regarded with hostility by many local people. Indeed, opposition here may have been greater than in Breckland because of worries about the potential impact of afforestation on the local holiday industry, as in other parts of Britain at this time.[94] At an informal meeting concerning recent and potential acquisitions of land by the Commission, held at the request of the Regional Controller of the Ministry of Town and Country Planning in 1949, the clerk of the East Suffolk County Council

> Suggested that as the total suitable areas in East Suffolk were small in relation to Forestry Commission requirements as a whole, could not the Commission acquire all the land they want in one block say in a county such as Northumberland and leave the comparatively small areas of heathland remaining in Suffolk to be enjoyed in their natural state by the public? He felt that once the areas were planted up with regimented lines of conifers the general populace would lose all interest in the district.[95]

It is easy to blame the demise of so many of the East Anglian heaths on afforestation, but in reality their fate was already sealed by changes in land management. Even where the heaths were not acquired and planted by the Commission, many were tumbling down to scrub or secondary woodland by the start of the Second World War. The small number of clayland commons which had survived the enclosure period, such as Wacton or Fritton in Norfolk, continued to be grazed with some intensity, although even these, to judge from contemporary accounts, were often increasingly neglected and overgrown.

## WETLANDS

The changes affecting heaths were paralleled in the wetlands of East Anglia: the various valley-floor fens scattered throughout the region, the small pockets of residual unreclaimed Fenland in the west and, above all, the Norfolk Broads. The most important force for change was, once again, not so much the agricultural depression *per se* as the gradual decline of traditional forms of exploitation brought about by wider social, economic and technological changes. Most low-lying areas of fen ground, especially in the Broadland valleys, had been managed as common land before enclosure by parliamentary act in the early decades of the nineteenth century.[96] Some had then been reclaimed and converted to improved grazing marsh, but many had continued to be managed along traditional lines, whether as private ground or as poors' allotments. Large areas of fen and fen meadow were mown for rough hay or bedding, and extensive areas were cut for reed and sedge, mainly for use as thatching. In addition, peat was still regularly dug for fuel at the start of the period under consideration here, especially in the valleys of the Broadland rivers. W.A. Dutt could describe, as late as 1903, how it was 'a good and cheap substitute for coal in the hearths of the marshmen's cottage homes'. He was able to portray a landscape of managed reed beds, of river banks 'almost covered' with reed stacks in the early spring, and of rafts fully laden with reeds or sedge being 'constantly rowed or quanted down the dykes'.[97] There is more than a possibility of some artistic license and nostalgia in such descriptions, and certainly Bird's more analytical account of the management of East Ruston 'Common' (actually a poors' allotment) in 1909 suggests that here at least peat was no longer being cut on a serious basis.[98] Nevertheless, at the turn of the twentieth century there is no doubt that extensive areas of low-lying wetland, in Broadland and more widely across East Anglia, were still being cut and mown, as well as being sporadically grazed in the dry summer months. The first edition OS 6-inch maps show wide expanses of managed reed beds and fen meadows, while P.H. Emmerson's idealised photographs of Broadland life, taken in the 1890s, depict extensive panoramas of open fen (Figure 37; below, p. 187).

Traditional forms of management seem to have gone into rapid decline during the First World War. Turner was already – in 1922 – able to describe how the impact of the War, and the decline in the market for chaff in London, were dramatically changing the appearance of the valley fens in Broadland. Areas of fen, once mown and grazed by cattle, were now replaced by extensive reed beds, and the fen meadows had 'reverted and their rough herbage is stronger and coarser than ever'.[99] Decline continued over the following decades, and T. Boardman described in 1939 how:

> A great change has taken place over a large portion of the river valleys about here. Thirty years ago all the large acreage of rough marsh covered with sedge rush and grass was mown for what was called marsh litter. The best was made into hay, or chaffed and used for feed locally or sent to London for bus horses and cows, while the rougher stuff was put into the bullock yards to be trodden into manure. Now, since acres upon acres of this material remain uncut and the vegetation gets into such a terrible tangle, the marshes have to be burned. Alders, birch and sallows are taking possession … When the marshes were mown regularly all the young trees were kept under…[100]

The change, thought Boardman, had serious implications for the local flora and fauna, and was the consequence of a wide range of factors: 'motor cars displacing horses, large dealers in milk taking the place of the small cowkeepers in the London district, and cold storage reducing the head of home fed bullocks'.[101] By the 1930s, many of the commercial reed beds were also being abandoned as the local demand for thatching materials declined, and they too often regenerated to scrub and then woodland.

Developments of this kind were mirrored elsewhere in East Anglia. The residual pockets of undrained fen in west Norfolk, for example, were described in 1947 as 'now only a source of rough grazing, the cutting of sedge having been largely given up, and the digging of peat which was in vogue at the beginning of the century, abandoned'. Most of these areas were residual commons or poors' allotments, but 'their usefulness must have declined in recent years'. Sugar Fen, in the valley of the Gaywood River, was said to be 'much invaded by birch and alder'; while Marham East Fen was 'not now grazed and is much overgrown'.[102]

The effects of changes in wetland management on bird life were described in 1922 by E.L. Turner. In areas where marsh had reverted to reed bed and fen, the numbers of lapwings, redshank, snipe and ruff declined and the yellow wagtail virtually disappeared. On the other hand, warblers, reed buntings and meadow pipits abounded in the ranker, reed-dominated vegetation, as did the short-eared owl, until the next stage of regeneration – the spread of alder and willow – led to the development of full secondary woodland, characterised by a more limited range of species, those typical of woods and hedges.[103] More serious were the effects of woodland regeneration on plant life, for many of the most important species only flourished in areas which were regularly mown, declining as these bushed over and disappearing entirely as woodland regenerated. Driscoll and Parmenter's study of Honing Common, where a detailed vegetation survey was made by Robert Gurney in 1908, noted that by 1946 all the lower parts of the common had become wooded, and scrub was invading most of the rest.[104] Gurney recorded a range of important plants on the common, including marsh helleborine (*Epipactis palustris*) and grass of Parnassus (*Parnassia palustris*), but, interestingly, gave 'no indication that he regarded these species as being of particular interest. It must be assumed that their occurrence was then not thought of as being unusual, whereas today they would be considered to be of very great importance.'[105] Driscoll and Parmenter noted that by 1993 none of these species was present on the densely wooded common 'and there appear to be no habitats suitable for them'. Given the evidence for the expansion of woodland across the area by the time of the Second World War, it is more than likely that these plants had already disappeared from the place by then.

The 1940s brought further changes. The Chilean Coypu (*Myocastor coypus*) had been introduced into East Anglia in the 1920s and kept on specialised fur farms. An article in the *Transactions of the Norfolk and Norwich Naturalists' Society* for 1931 noted, ominously, the importance of keeping the creatures securely fenced in, 'since the damage they might do to trees, dams, canals, river banks and so forth might be very serious'.[106] By the mid 1940s they had not only escaped, but were widely established in the wild, particularly in Broadland, where they were described in 1947 as being 'at large in the Yare valley' and busily consuming a wide range of plants, including greater spearwort, great hairy willowherb, cowbane and yellow flag. By the 1950s the coypu 'rat', naturalised in large numbers throughout the Broadland basin and also scattered in other East Anglian wetlands, was a real problem, everywhere causing considerable damage to sedge fens, reed beds and even areas of wet woodland. The animals had some beneficial effects, most notably in arresting the steady encroachment onto the broads themselves of reeds and carr, but nevertheless 'in places their depredations are so intense that they are now considered a serious pest'.[107] Large areas were denuded of water lilies, bulrushes, reed-mace and cowbane, and 'hundreds of acres of saw-sedge were laid low.'[108]

The depredations of the coypu aside, the main changes affecting the character of East Anglian wetlands, especially in the valleys of the Broadland rivers, were unquestionably the collapse of traditional management systems and the consequent spread of scrub and wet woodland. It is therefore noteworthy that throughout the first half of the twentieth century the most serious threat to these environments, and especially to the Broads, was almost universally held to be the steady expansion of the tourist industry, something which – as noted in the previous chapter – had continued inexorably since the later nineteenth century. By 1947 Eric Fowler was urging on his audience at the Norfolk and Norwich Naturalists' Society the need to compromise with the inevitable:

> I prefer to face the fact that the Broads are bound to be 'developed'. They are in fact being 'developed', pretty badly, under our very eyes. In some places they are getting more and more like a seaside boating lake, with mechanical boats and mechanical noises on the water, and urban amusements on shore. In others they are fringed by ramshackle bungalow estates…[109]

This was a situation which, he felt, would only get worse as levels of disposable income increased in the post-war years. Such attitudes were widely shared by naturalists: nature and the holiday industry made poor bedfellows. The impact of increased visitor numbers on coastal wetlands – saltings and marshes – was similarly bemoaned. Gay in 1944 described how, in the aftermath of the First World War, improvements in transport and the advent of the small car had led to:

> The ever-increasing popularity of Norfolk as a holiday resort. Hitherto summer visitors were mainly confined to the Broads and the coastal towns, but now every village became accessible, and the beaches and quiet sea-shore, up to this time known to the comparatively few people interested in the bird-life there, were invaded by holiday-makers.[110]

Yet in reality development on this scale was relatively localised, especially in Broadland. Indeed, what is curious is that observers like Fowler made fewer comments about the more insidious changes taking place in wetland environments, with the steady regeneration of secondary woodland across abandoned and derelict fen and reed bed and, to some extent, the changes in water quality resulting from increased pollution from new methods of sewage disposal, especially in the valley of the river Yare, and from the run-off of agricultural chemicals. It is hard to avoid the conclusion that the reactions of middle-class observers to the expansion of the holiday industry had more to do with class prejudice than a rational evaluation of its environmental impact.

## BIODIVERSITY

Contemporaries, and certainly the educated middle-class enthusiasts who constituted the membership of the county naturalists' societies, were keenly aware of the effects that agricultural intensification in the century or so before the start of the depression had had upon what we would now call 'biodiversity'. The Pasque flower (*Anemone pulsatilla*), for example, was recorded at a number of places in Norfolk in the early nineteenth century – the name of the Tulip Hills near Lexham, where the plant was abundant, was probably derived from it – but had disappeared from the county by the 1880s, and had already gone from Suffolk.[111] Most of the losses were flowers of pasture or meadow, presumably adversely affected by the expansion of the area under tilth during the first half of the century; but a few, like the violet horn-poppy (*Roemeria hybrida*), were arable weeds.[112] More noticeable were the changes in the character of wild bird populations in the course of the nineteenth century. 'The general enclosure of commons and waste lands, the thinning of hedgerows, together with various other farming operations resulting from modern improvements in the system of agriculture, have each, in turn, affected particular classes of birds', as White's *Directory* noted in 1885.[113] Bird-watchers (and game shooters) in the 1870s and 80s looked back nostalgically to the days when upwards of a thousand teal could be taken each year on the east coast decoys. In 1871 Thomas Southwell bemoaned the fact that 'during a period of 150 years, two species only have ceased to breed in Norfolk, but in the fifty years which have since elapsed, no less than six species have entirely deserted us during the breeding season', while a further five had 'virtually ceased to breed here'.[114] Upcher voiced similar sentiments in 1884, commenting that 'The "trips" of Dotterell [*Eudromias morinellus*], formerly so regular in their appearance, are now scarcely ever seen in our fen country'.[115] He thought that both ruff and reeve were extinct in Norfolk. Upcher believed that 'the increase in drainage' was a major factor in the decline of many birds, while the bittern, thought Stevenson in 1885, was 'another of the birds which drainage and enclosure has driven from their old haunts'.[116] Agricultural intensification of the high-farming years had also taken its toll on mammals like the badger, which in 1869 was considered to be 'nearly extinct in Norfolk'.[117] The black rat was 'extremely rare, if not quite extinct', while even the fox was becoming uncommon.[118]

But the greatest loss, widely mourned by contemporaries, was the great bustard, its disappearance universally attributed to changes in landscape and land use. Its numbers dwindled during the first four decades of the century and by the 1840s it was declared extinct. The bird had once been common in Breckland, where it made its nests in the fields of broadcast-sown rye. But following enclosure and improvement wheat was more widely grown, sown in drills and weeded by gangs of labourers: few nests survived. In addition, the landscape was increasingly subdivided by hawthorn hedges, pine rows, and tree belts, 'Not only entirely changing its aspect but rendering it entirely unsuitable to the wary habits of the bustard, which soon learned to become as jealous as any strategist of what might afford an enemy harbour'.[119] There were occasional visits from bustards which flew in from abroad – in 1876 one appeared in Hockwold fen, the first since 1838, and another was shot (and eaten) in 1891[120] – but the species never again bred in the region.

Nevertheless, the effects of the agricultural revolution and high farming on the region's flora and fauna should not be exaggerated. In the late nineteenth century the East Anglian countryside still seems to have positively teemed with wildlife. Henry Stevenson, writing about the kingfisher in 1885, thus described how he was 'informed that at least fifty of these beautiful birds were shot this autumn in the Yarmouth district'.[121] In 1876 short eared owls were so abundant in October that 'some thirty specimens, at least, were brought in from various localities to our Norwich bird stuffers'.[122] The hobby was still nesting sporadically, as in Foxley Wood in 1881; nightingales were commonly recorded. The otter was still widespread in the two counties: its tracks were 'frequently to be seen in the snows in winter on the banks of rivers'. Even the polecat could be 'generally met with', although it was 'by no means common'.[123]

What is striking is that the onset of the agricultural depression did not lead to any reversal of the losses of the high-farming years. Indeed, a number of plants which were already in severe decline in the late nineteenth century continued to disappear from the countryside. Some had always been rare, such as spotted cat's ear (*Hypochoeris maculata*), last seen in Norfolk in 1904 (although surviving in one place in west Suffolk as late as 1980); or the Dutch rush *Equisetum hyemale*, last recorded at Ditchingham in Norfolk in 1888 and extinct in both counties by the mid-twentieth century.[124] But others, while restricted in their distribution, had been more abundant: the Fir club-moss, last seen in the Holt area in 1903, was extinct in East Anglia by mid-century; the meadow saffron *Colchicum autumnale*, and the violet helleborine *Epipactis purpurata*, both relatively common in the late nineteenth century, were by the 1950s restricted to single reserves. The awl-shaped pearlwort, considered to be locally common as late as 1914, seems to have disappeared completely by the middle decades of the century.[125] Most of the losses were, as in the previous century, pasture or meadow plants, but some arable weeds also disappeared, including branched broom-rape and greater broom-rape, last recorded in 1914 and 1920 respectively in Norfolk; the latter survived only at a single site in Suffolk by the 1960s.[126] Sixteen records of Field cow-wheat (*Melampyrum arvense*) are found in the 1914 *Flora of Norfolk*, but there are no subsequent sightings in the county: sharp-fruited Lamb's lettuce (*Vallerianella rimosa*), rare in 1914, is likewise not certainly recorded in any subsequent surveys.[127] The fortunes of birds, mammals and reptiles in the course of the depression years were perhaps better, but there were further disappearances of species, including the pole cat, and the actual *numbers* of many, especially the fox, continued to decline.

Contemporary explanations for these continued reductions in biodiversity were often piecemeal and particularistic. A decline in house martins in Norfolk in the 1880s was thus attributed to improved drainage in urban areas and its effects upon insect populations, although contributory factors were thought to be changes in building materials and architectural styles, coupled with the fact that 'people are more particular now than formerly as to their house fronts'.[128] On the whole habitat change was not cited as a major factor, even in the case of birds. Turner even argued in 1922 against the idea that the ruff had become extinct as a breeding species in Norfolk because of the drainage of the fens over previous decades:

> In Holland where drainage is universal the ruff still abounds, and, like the black tern –
> another extinct British breeding species – has adapted itself to new surroundings. Our own
> British stock need not have become extinct. It was ruthlessly slaughtered for the table, and
> as its numbers diminished, the few remaining birds fell victim to the collector.[129]

Most naturalists in the late nineteenth and early twentieth centuries believed, in fact, that egg and plume collectors, sportsmen and gamekeepers were the main culprits in the decline in the numbers of birds and, to some extent, mammals. Collectors were regarded with particular opprobrium, and the various Wild Bird Protection Acts, which were largely intended to curtail their activities (as well as to give special protection to rare birds from sportsmen), were widely welcomed, a number of Wild Bird Protection Societies being formed locally to ensure that the new laws were observed.[130] The attitude of the county naturalists' societies to game shooting was ambiguous and complex, however, partly because so many of their prominent members were keen sportsmen or the owners of large sporting estates. Indeed, much of the ornithological information in the *Transactions of the Norfolk and Norwich Naturalists' Society* appears to have come from specimens that had been shot. Nevertheless, the activities of gamekeepers were increasingly seen as a threat to wildlife. Norgate, in 1876, thought that barn owls were attacked by keepers in the 'mistaken belief' that they took young pheasants: 'they seize every opportunity of destroying almost every wild bird, beast and reptile that is not game'. He described how the heronry at Herringfleet had recently been destroyed, the keeper having 'shot the Herons from their nests and hung them up to produce maggots to feed the pheasants on'.[131] The president of the Norfolk and Norwich Naturalists' Society, welcoming Lord Kimberley as a new member in 1870, urged him and other landowners to give 'peremptory orders to their game-keepers to spare the occasional visitors to their woods and waters'.[132]

There are good grounds for believing that conservationists' worries about the impact of game preservation on wildlife were not misplaced, especially given the fact that the importance of shooting in rural life increased steadily as the depression deepened. Ravens, crows, magpies, jays, hawks, harriers and buzzards, as well as owls, were, indeed, indiscriminately slaughtered, although, as far as the evidence goes, the rate of attack abated during the inter-war years.[133] More strenuous attempts at game preservation almost certainly led to the final disappearance of the pole cat from East Anglia, prevented a resurgence of badger populations, even though land was going out of cultivation in certain districts, and led to a further decrease in the numbers of foxes, except in those few areas where fox hunting, rather than game shooting, was the preferred sport. Lilias Rider Haggard described in 1943 how she: 'Saw a fox on the road last night, near the meadow where stand in range the farm hen-houses, fortunately shut at dusk. A fox is rare with us, as south Norfolk with its big shoots has nearly exterminated them.'[134]

Yet equally important for the region's ecology were the positive effects of game preservation on some mammal populations. The destruction of foxes, stoats, hawks and other predators 'so that game birds may survive in abundance',[135] coupled with the spread of derelict arable land in some areas and the increasingly scrubby nature of many commons, led in particular to an explosion in the numbers of rabbits. These had long been a problem to farmers, but were most troublesome in areas of heathland where warrens formed a major part of the economy – the estimated damage caused by rabbits on Sturston Hall and Stanford Home farms in Breckland in 1885 was £335.[136] By the 1920s they were abundant almost everywhere, a serious irritant and a major contributor to the decline in farming fortunes. Norfolk was particularly badly affected – it was a 'rabbit-infested country', in Lilias Rider Haggard's words. The increase in numbers, besides having an economic impact which would repay further research, also had complex effects on the region's flora. Rabbits helped reduce the speed with which neglected heaths and commons bushed over but, as we have seen, they also tended to encourage bracken and to some extent gorse at the expense of heather and grasses. They also caused widespread damage to young trees and woodlands: Nicholson noted in 1913 that they had 'a noteworthy selective influence on vegetation – seedling trees are suppressed and woodland fails to regenerate itself unless protected by netting'.[137] A similar combination of factors – game preservation and habitat change in marginal areas – also led to a steady increase in the numbers of deer in East Anglia, and in particular of fallow deer. Lists of wild mammals published in the *Transactions of the Norfolk and Norwich Naturalists' Society* for 1879 and 1884 do not list deer at all: they were restricted to the various landscape parks of the region, including Holkham, Houghton, Kimberley, Ampton and Didlington, and were regarded as semi-domesticated.[138] Their numbers took off in the wild mainly as a result of the large-scale afforestation in Breckland and the Suffolk Sandlings, although also as a consequence of deliberate encouragement for shooting. By the 1940s they were causing serious damage to young trees across a wide area of East Anglia, although they had not yet reached their current levels.

Habitat change may have contributed to the marked increase in the numbers of rabbits and, to a lesser extent, deer, but for the most part it was associated with a *decline* in species numbers, and certainly with a reduction in biodiversity. This was particularly the case with plant life; most of the rarer species of plant in the region were associated with non-arable land – with ancient woods, heaths and wetlands – and many of these suffered simply because these habitats were no longer being managed in intensive, traditional ways. The slender spike rush *Eleocharis acicularis*, rare in 1914 but apparently extinct in East Anglia by the middle decades of the twentieth century,[139] was a plant of damp heaths and almost certainly disappeared as such areas became increasingly infested with bracken and scrub. Wood cranesbill (*Geranium sylvaticum*) died out in the region completely during the early twentieth century, probably due to the gradual cessation of coppicing in many ancient woods, and the resultant increases in canopy shade.[140] The fen violet, *Viola stagnina*, already in decline at the end of the nineteenth century and last seen by J.E. Lousley in West Dereham Fen in 1936 (although it hung on in Suffolk at a single site until 1968), and Marsh Fleabane (*Senecio palustris*), largely restricted to the valleys of the Broadland rivers in 1914 but not recorded thereafter, probably disappeared because of the increasingly overgrown and derelict condition of valley-floor fens in the course of the twentieth century.[141]

Changes in the character of East Anglia's flora and fauna in the period between 1870 and 1940 were thus primarily a consequence of a decline in traditional management practices in areas of marginal land, coupled with the increasing importance of game shooting, although such things as changes in sewage management and the growth of some urban centres, especially Norwich and Ipswich, may have played their part. It might be thought that the negative effects of these changes would, to some extent, have been offset by the fact that in an era of agricultural depression land was generally being farmed less intensively. Indeed, as we have noted, some historical ecologists have characterised the period under discussion as one in which wildlife flourished as hedges were maintained less assiduously, as drainage was neglected, and as inputs of lime and fertiliser on arable land declined. But, as we have also seen, away from those particularly marginal areas where some farmland was abandoned to dereliction, there is little evidence that there was any very marked reduction in the intensity with which land was farmed. In some districts, and especially where smallholdings and horticulture flourished, land was probably farmed *more* intensively. In this context it is noteworthy that in the Norfolk Broads there appears to have been a significant deterioration in water quality between the late nineteenth and the mid-twentieth century, signalled by changes in the character of water plants, even in catchments little affected by increased sewage discharge, such as those of the Ant and upper Thurne.[142] Continuing nutrient enrichment suggests that lime and fertiliser inputs on the adjacent arable land must at the very least have been maintained at 'high farming' levels. The decline of plants like the meadow saffron and the violet helleborine, both of which were characteristic of damp clayland pastures, may, similarly, be an indication that drainage on the heavier soils was not neglected in this period to the extent that is often assumed.

## CONCLUSION

The environmental history of the East Anglian rural landscape in the period 1870–1940 was thus complex, but two features stand out above all others. The first is that the agricultural depression *per se* probably had limited effects on the fortunes of wildlife, semi-natural habitats and biodiversity, although its *indirect* effects, especially in terms of the expansion of game shooting, may well have been significant. Most land continued to be farmed with a fair degree of intensity; hedges and field boundaries were maintained with some enthusiasm. The second is that, as with farming practices and patterns of landholding, the greatest changes occurred in the areas of poorest land; but these changes were not solely the consequence of the downturn of the agricultural economy, but rather had wider and more complex causes. Heaths and commons, fens and reed beds, tumbled down to scrub and woodland as traditional forms of exploitation came to an end; the sandy expanses of Breckland were converted to vast conifer plantations.

Most contemporaries were well aware that the majority of these marginal landscapes were of particular environmental importance, even if they often under-estimated or misunderstood the changes that they were undergoing: in part, perhaps, because they failed to realise the extent to which they had been created and sustained by particular forms of *human* activity. It was in these places, rather than in the farmed countryside on soils of good or medium quality, that the rarest plants and animals were to be found. The logical response was thus to turn some of these areas into reserves, within which these various important forms of wildlife could be afforded appropriate protection. As early as 1893 the Norfolk and Norwich Naturalists' Society lobbied parliament over the terms of the proposed Wild Bird Protection Act, advocating the principle of protection by specified areas rather than by named species.[143] Although the Society for the Promotion of Nature Reserves was founded in 1912,[144] and the first nature reserve in Britain – Wicken Fen in Cambridgeshire – had been established (by the newly formed National Trust) as early as 1899, it was not until 1912 that the first reserve in East Anglia proper, the 1,335 acres of saltmarsh at Blakeney Point, was purchased by public subscription and handed over to the National Trust, with the 1,821 acres of Scolt Head being added in 1923. In the same year the first wildlife trust in Britain, the Norfolk Naturalists' Trust (now the Norfolk Wildlife Trust), was established to save the Cley marshes from being drained for agriculture. Further reserves were established by the Trust over the following decades: Martham in 1928, Alderfen Broad in 1930, Wretham Heath in 1938 and Weeting in 1942.[145]

Already, however, campaigners were urging that larger tracts of land in certain areas of Britain should be afforded particular protection; this was part of a growing belief in the importance of, and necessity for, large-scale land-use planning which, as we shall see, was developing apace in the inter-war years. The Council for the Protection of Rural England argued for the creation of National Parks almost from its inception in 1926, and persuaded the government to accept the idea in principle in 1931. Nothing was done in practice, however, largely because of financial constraints, but pressure continued, particularly from John Dower, whose pamphlet *The Case for National Parks in Great Britain* was published in 1938.[146]

Yet the recognition that particular sites or areas were worthy of special protection carried with it the implication that areas outside these reserves, the 'normal' working countryside, were less important in this respect. Such a philosophy made some sense, given the prevailing conditions. The fields, hedges, woods and meadows in which most wildlife found refuge were not yet being destroyed or neglected on any serious scale, although in certain areas there were already portents of the changes to come. But by the 1940s this had changed: the agricultural depression was over. As E.C. Keith put it in an article in the *Transactions of the Norfolk and Norwich Naturalists' Society* in 1942: 'At the present time we see a great drive being made to bring into cultivation many more [marginal] lands, some of which are probably part of original England, and, if the war should continue for long, I imagine that a great drainage scheme will be instituted which will eventually dry up many of the existing sanctuaries for wild life'.[147] As we shall see, a more general onslaught on the fabric of the countryside mounted steadily in the post-war years, as ploughing, hedge removal, land drainage and field amalgamation continued on an unprecedented scale throughout the 1950s, 60s and 70s. The 'reserve mentality' which developed in the first half of the twentieth century was poorly equipped to deal with this more generalised environmental threat.

# CHAPTER 7

# Change in the Village

If a complex range of influences – many only tangentially connected with the depressed state of farming – shaped the 'natural' environment of rural East Anglia in the late nineteenth and early twentieth centuries, the same was perhaps even more true of the built environment. Agricultural depression and a declining demand for agricultural labour undoubtedly had an important effect on village life and village landscapes. But so too did shifts in the balance of local power, as great landowners and the local gentry were denied their pre-eminent position in county and village life by the Local Government Acts of 1888 and 1894, the growing involvement of the State in the details of rural life, and a whole raft of cultural and technological developments, including the arrival of 'modernity' in the form of improved communications and facilities.

## THE EXODUS FROM THE COUNTRYSIDE

Most East Anglian villages are today dominated by housing which either pre-dates 1880 or post-dates the end of the Second World War. With some notable exceptions, including small groups of council houses erected in many rural settlements, comparatively little building activity seems to have occurred in the period covered by this book. This impression is confirmed by a comparison of the OS maps made in the 1880s, the 1920s and the 1950s, which show little expansion in the built-up area of East Anglian villages, although there is also little sign of the settlement shrinkage described by some early twentieth-century writers such as P.H. Ditchfield.[1] Analysis of the census returns quickly reveals the principal reason why: most parishes in Norfolk and Suffolk lost population between 1851 and 1951 (Figure 29). The main explanation for this is the agricultural depression, but it is worth noting that there were some signs of demographic decline before this began. The number of agricultural labourers in England and Wales as a whole fell from around 1.3 million in 1851 to around 870,000 in 1881: the overall rural population continued to increase, but at a slower rate than that in urban and industrial areas.[2] Workers, and especially the young, were increasingly drawn to the better housing and amenities, as well as better wages, offered in the towns or in the colonies, their aspirations perhaps raised higher than those of the previous generation by improvements in education. In 1881 there were said to be nearly 58,000 Norfolk-born

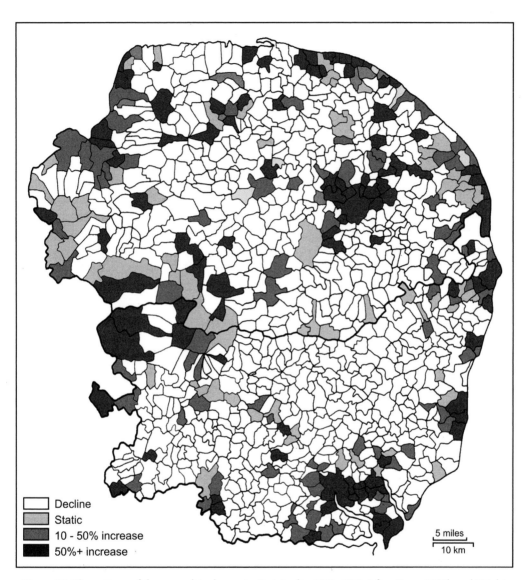

Figure 29. The pattern of demographic change in East Anglia, 1851–1951 (after Grace 1999b and Wright 1993). Although in most parishes the population fell between these two dates, there were some places in which it remained static, or increased – often to a significant extent. The most important of these were villages in the vicinity of the major cities, especially Norwich and Ipswich; along the coast, where the holiday industry continued to expand; and in north-east Norfolk, the Fens, and other areas where smallholdings, market gardens and orchards were all flourishing (compare Figure 11).

women living in London and its hinterland.[3] The depression, however, unquestionably increased this exodus from the countryside. A shift from arable to pasture and less intensive cultivation of the arable led to a decline in the demand for labour.

In general the East Anglian census figures suggest that in most villages the number of labourers involved in agriculture fell by between 15 per cent and 30 per cent in the two decades from 1881, although there was much local variation. On some farms the numbers of men employed actually rose. George Gladden, who farmed at Eastfield Farm and Sutton Hall, Hickling, as well as at Mill Farm, Ingham, employed seven men in 1889 but thirteen in 1897. By 1901 he was employing fourteen, although this fell back to twelve by 1910 and to ten on the eve of the First World War.[4] In most cases, however, such increases can be explained by a change in the character or size of the farming enterprise: Devas Everington thus employed twenty men in 1896 on his 700-acre Castle Acre farm and there were twenty-two on the pay roll in 1944, but the farm was unquestionably bigger by then.[5] Many farms continued, rather, to shed labour through the first decades of the twentieth century. Typical were the Fisher family of Dairy Farm, Gunton, who employed three men in 1908, two during the War and one, accompanied by a part-time worker, in the 1930s.[6] Overall, the available evidence suggests that the industry shed labour fast in the early stages of the depression, but more slowly thereafter, as farmers diversified into new modes of production.

Low demand for labour led to low agricultural wages, although poor pay and conditions also reflected the difficulties involved in organising effective campaigns for better conditions (especially in comparison with industrial workers, and following the breaking of Joseph Arch's National Agricultural Labourers Union in 1874), as well as the fact that with agriculture in the doldrums, smaller farmers at least were simply in no position to offer a reasonable wage. Nevertheless, the impact of the depression on wages seems, in East Anglia at least, to have been gradual. Ten shillings for a full week's work was the average Norfolk wage in 1870.[7] It was the lowest rate that Fox came across in Suffolk in 1881, while Rew gave it as the 'general rate' in Norfolk at the time. Allowing for loss through wet weather, but an enhanced income during August from harvest money, Fox reckoned an average weekly income would be 10s 5d.[8] In 1882 George Gladden was paying his workers between 13s and 14s 6d a week. By the end of the decade this had fallen to between 8s and 12s 6d,[9] but the 1890s saw a slight rise, to a figure sometimes as high as 15s.[10] On the Home Farm at Kimberley in mid-Norfolk daily wage rates remained remarkably stable, at between 2s 2d and 2s 7d, from 1872 until 1901.[11] These figures, such as they are, perhaps suggest that rural incomes declined only gradually in the early stages of the depression, for the period between 1870 and the late 1890s was one in which the cost of most essentials was stable or declining.[12]

On the face of it, agricultural wages held up reasonable well in the early twentieth century. The Fisher family – mentioned above – who farmed at Riverside Farm at Letheringsett before moving in 1905 to Gunton, paid between 11s and 12s per week in 1897, rising to 13s in 1901, 14s in 1905 and 15s in 1913;[13] while on Henry Overman's Kipton and Uphouse Farms on the Holkham estate rates of between 10s and 12s a week in 1895 had increased to between 15s and 18s by 1914.[14] In 1913 the highest earners on Gladden's farm were receiving 16s 6d, a figure that can be paralleled on other medium-sized farms in East Anglia during this period, such as Francis Fairweather's Farneaux Farm at Whatfield.[15] In both Suffolk and Norfolk the average wage in 1914 was said to be around 14s a week,[16] although in that year most Norfolk farmers agreed to pay a weekly wage of 15s a week.[17] Taken at face value, such figures suggest that agricultural wages in East Anglia were rising in the period between 1890 and the outbreak of the First World War: but they need to be seen in the context of a general increase in the cost of living over the same period of around 20 per cent. In real terms, rural wages were falling.[18] On the other hand, it should be noted that the conclusions of the 1913 Rural Land Enquiry (which claimed that, nationally, 60 per cent of agricultural labourers earned less than 18s for a sixty-hour week) were challenged on the grounds that houses, albeit generally of a low standard, were often let to labourers at subsidised rents, and many were provided with large gardens for growing vegetables or keeping a pig and a few chickens.[19] Harvest wages and shepherds' bonuses boosted annual incomes, while farm produce might also be given to workers, or sold to them at a reduced rate. On Gladden's farm the harvest bonus was as much as £6 15s in the 1880s, although this had fallen back slightly to £6 10s by the end of the decade; in 1893 a Christmas box of either one or two chickens was given to ten of the men.[20]

The outbreak of war resulted in the introduction of Wages Boards and a significant rise in workers' wages. By 1917 Gladden was paying his men between 23s and 25s 6d per week, and harvest wages were £11 per man.[21] By 1921 he was paying no less than 42s 6d. The weekly rate paid by the Fishers similarly rose, to 19s in 1915 and 28s in 1917: in 1921 it reached 46s 6d to 54s.[22] Devas Everington, on his large farm at Castle Acre, was paying 37s in 1919 and 48s in 1921, bringing his annual wages bill to £3,837.[23] Average weekly wages in the two counties had reached 46s by 1920, an increase in Suffolk of 229 per cent, and in Norfolk of 221 per cent, over 1914 rates. This is an impressive rise, even though in the same period the cost of food more than doubled, even bread prices increasing by 45 per cent.[24] With the end of the Wages Boards, however, farmers attempted to push wages down again as cereal prices collapsed, and a fall to 25s per week in 1923 resulted in widespread strike action in Norfolk. In 1924 the reconstituted Central Wages Board suggested a rate of 28s for a 48-hour week in the winter, and 29s for fifty hours in the summer, which was more or less what the Fishers were paying at Gunton, although with overtime payments this sometimes rose to 33 or 34s. By 1930 they were regularly paying between 30 and 35s a week, although the workforce had been reduced to a single man who, by 1932, was receiving 36s 3d a week, and by 1939 39s 8d (an additional part-time employee had also been hired at 18s 10d a week).[25] On Devas Everington's farm weekly wages similarly rose from 30s per week in 1922-23 to 41s 6d at the outbreak of the Second World War.[26] The relative position of East Anglian agricultural wages also changed in this period, from among the lowest in England in 1920 to among the highest by 1937.[27]

These variations in wages – falling in real terms until 1914, rising during the war years, and up until 1921, then falling dramatically through the mid 1920s before increasing steadily once more – need to be seen in relation to urban pay rates. Between 1914 and 1919 the index for agricultural wages rose by 91 per cent nationally: but wages in general increased by

103 per cent.[28] In spite of the fact that wages and conditions improved considerably during the later 1920s and 30s, they could still not compare with those offered by most forms of urban and industrial employment.[29] Moreover, agricultural labourers also had to contend with a lack of regular or secure work. Although George Gladden, for example, employed up to ten men in the 1890s, they often received less than a full week's pay.[30]

Many contemporaries believed that village populations were not only falling fast, but also ageing rapidly, especially at the start of the depression. It was the enterprising young who were most keen to leave. Augustus Jessopp, rector of Scarning, described in 1881 how thirty-one young men had left the parish in the previous thirty years to join the police force.[31] By the 1890s, applicants from villages for work either in the police or on the railways – where wages could be as high as 21s a week – were increasing.[32] The rector of the small clayland parish of Welborne, in Norfolk, told Rider Haggard in 1899 that only two of the fifty-six pupils who had attended the school in 1881 still lived in the parish.[33] A common complaint of the time, articulated by C.S. Read and the well-to-do Holkham tenant Henry Overman, amongst others, was that there were not enough young labourers left to work the land;[34] and Haggard gave examples of farms where the workers were mostly over fifty years of age.[35] This perception of an ageing labour force is not, however, entirely borne out by the census figures, which suggest that the decline in the number of younger workers was in the same proportion as that for older ones.[36] Indeed, in many parishes the largest category of labourers by 1901 were in the twenty to thirty age range.[37]

Yet the reduction in village populations was not *only* the consequence of the exit of agricultural labourers. It was also the result of a decline in local trades, crafts and services, largely resulting from improved transport and a consequent centralisation of some livelihoods in market towns and cities, coupled with technological changes in production and, perhaps, a fall in local demand, as the disposable income of farmers and labourers declined.[38] The disappearance of trades and services should not be exaggerated. Horse-related craftsmen, such as farriers, saddlers, wheelwrights and harness-makers, remained until the demise of the cart horse in the 1950s, and while shoppers increasingly preferred to go to the local towns for clothing, grocers and butchers remained in many villages until after the Second World War. In 1943 the male working population in the comparatively small north Norfolk village of Binham consisted of ninety-one agricultural labourers, alongside whom were blacksmiths, carpenters, builders, lorry drivers, barbers, cycle dealers, shop and inn keepers and road men, bringing the labour force up to 123.[39] But the decline of boot-makers, basket-weavers, thatchers, straw-hat makers and coopers was in general only partially compensated for by new trades, including cycle agents and motor and wireless engineers. There are, moreover, some signs that shops and trades were tending to cluster in the larger villages. In the small village of Hollesley in the Suffolk Sandlings, for example, both the number of tradesmen listed in directories and the variety of trades represented declined by around half between 1881 and 1901, although the overall population in this case dropped only from 603 to 575 over the same period.[40] In most East Anglian villages, however, the numbers of people employed in agricultural and non-agricultural occupations across this period fell at roughly the same rate. Either way, agriculture generally remained the single most important occupation. In villages as different as Rollesby and Drayton in Norfolk, and the South Elmhams, Wickhambrook and Hollesley in Suffolk, the proportion of those who worked as agricultural labourers across the last two decades of the nineteenth century remained fairly steady at just under half, with the next largest category of employment being those in domestic service.[41] Although subsequent census information remains unpublished, it seems likely that this would have been true into the 1920s or even 30s. Places which bucked this trend were often ones where the rural economy was undergoing a more profound transformation. In Tottington in the Breckland, for example, there were fifty-eight agricultural labourers and twenty-six individuals in non-agricultural employment in 1881; by 1901 there were only twenty-five of the former but forty-five of the latter, mainly gamekeepers and servants – a clear reflection of the decline in agriculture and the increasing importance of shooting on these poor soils.

## EXCEPTIONS TO STAGNATION

It is important to emphasise, however, that this general pattern of rural decay and depopulation has a number of important exceptions which become strikingly evident when changes in population in the two counties over the period 1851–1951 are mapped (Figure 29). These exceptions fall into three main categories. The first comprises villages in the vicinity of the principal towns and cities in the region (Ipswich, Lowestoft, King's Lynn, Norwich and Yarmouth): for these major urban centres, together with many of the smaller market towns, continued to grow in size, and this had a knock-on effect upon neighbouring settlements. The population of Norwich, for example, rose from 444,974 in 1881 to 504,940 in 1931: the nearby village of Costessey contained 960 people in 1881, but no less than 2,368 by 1931.[42] Mosby in 1938 described how

> During the past twenty years thousands of acres of good farm land have been acquired for building purposes in Norwich and the villages surrounding it, and within this period Norwich has changed from a compact city of small acreage with isolated villages about 2 or 3 miles from its centre into one big conurbation.[43]

Settlements further away from the city also expanded. Up until the 1920s, most such places were on railway lines: Brundall and Cantley, for example, thus saw particularly steep population increases. In the inter-war period, however, the growth of rural bus services led to more generalised growth in satellite villages. South-east Suffolk was similarly affected by the expansion of Ipswich. Abercrombie noted in 1935 'a few regrettable examples of recent building' in the area, such as 'straggling ribbon development along some of the main roads'.[44] According to Mosby, these developing suburbs housed not only urban workers but also some farm labourers, who preferred 'to live in the new buildings on the outskirts of the villages and towns, and cycle daily to their work in the fields'.[45]

All this, of course, was part of a wider, national pattern. Between 1919 and 1939 862,500 houses were built in rural districts in England: yet these were not primarily for rural workers, but for urban commuters.[46] Such remarkable growth might seem surprising at a time of general economic gloom, but the economic depression of the inter-war years mostly affected the old heavy industrial areas of the north and west. The South East, and parts of the Midlands, generally saw much economic growth in the 1920s and 30s, based on new technology, light industry and the expansion of services.[47] The most striking consequence, in landscape terms, was the expansion of suburbs, especially around London but also on the margins of many provincial towns and cities. This development – which arguably included aspects of the 'counter-urbanisation' process usually discussed by geographers only in a post-1950s context[48] – had much less impact in East Anglia, for the economy here remained more resolutely agricultural in character. In 1935 Abercrombie described how east Suffolk had experienced 'some satellite offspring from the metropolis', but emphasised how for the most part it was 'one of those counties which do not show as many signs of change as other parts of this island … There are advantages today in a little remoteness.'[49] Nevertheless, the expansion of villages and small market towns in the hinterland of large urban centres is quite clear from Figure 29, and also on the ground today, in the form of clusters of nineteenth-century houses close to railway stations and some early and mid-twentieth-century developments beside the principal access roads.

The second kind of growth area evident on Figure 29 is perhaps unsurprising, given the discussion in Chapter 4. Many coastal parishes, and especially those on or close to a railway line, grew considerably in size. Aldeburgh, Southwold, Felixstowe and the adjacent parishes all stand out on the map as places which witnessed extraordinary expansion; the same is true of most parishes along the Norfolk coast between Yarmouth and Kelling, and on the west coast from King's Lynn to Hunstanton. The holiday industry brought employment, and workers needed to be housed. But, in addition, second-homers and wealthy commuters, as well as retired businessmen, settled by the sea in some numbers, often in new houses but sometimes in old (in 1942 Scott was able to describe how Norfolk tied cottages were already being sold on some scale to town dwellers: they were 'bought because of their picturesque character and brought up-to-date with all modern conveniences').[50]

The third kind of area in which the population grew in this period is at first sight harder to explain. In parishes across much of north-east Norfolk, well inland from the coast, populations remained buoyant. To some extent this can be explained as a consequence of the growth of the Broads as a holiday destination, and the combined influence of Yarmouth and Norwich. But the situation on the other side of the region, in the Fens – where many parishes experienced growth of 50 per cent or more in the century after 1851 – suggests another explanation. These were the areas in which the new labour-intensive modes of agriculture – fruit production, market gardening and various forms of smallholding – grew steadily in importance from the late nineteenth century. Not only were there larger numbers of individual farmers in such localities, and a greater demand for agricultural workers, but this in turn seems to have acted as a stimulus to the wider economy of services and small industries. In the Fenland village of Terrington St Clement, for example, twenty-six categories of tradesmen and small industries are listed in Kelly's *Directory* of 1880, but by 1933 there were forty-two categories – a striking contrast to the usual pattern of contraction and decline.

In short, demographic developments in East Anglia in the period under discussion were related, fairly directly, to patterns of communication and to the character of the local economy. In the immediate hinterland of large towns, in places where the holiday industry expanded, and in areas where small farms, smallholdings and market gardening thrived, the rural population remained static or grew. Where – as was more usually the case – traditional arable agriculture remained dominant, or where (mainly on the heavier soils of the claylands) livestock husbandry expanded, the population generally fell.

## VILLAGE HOUSING

The migration from villages was only in part a consequence of poor wages and conditions. It was also the result of the increasing gap between standards of housing and amenities in town and country in the later nineteenth and early twentieth centuries, and of the fact that this was becoming more obvious to country people as transport improved and mobility increased. Many contemporary commentators, like later historians, were obsessed with the impact of urban and suburban expansion on public health and public morals, and social reformers often contrasted the wholesome countryside with the degraded cities.[51] But, continuing a tradition which had originated in the early nineteenth century, the housing conditions of the rural poor also exercised many educated minds, and in the late nineteenth century a number of surveys were commissioned into the subject. These suggest that workers' housing was on the whole better on large estates than in areas dominated by small proprietors. Following the Union Chargeability Act of 1865 more serious attempts had been made by landowners to provide workers' accommodation and thus reduce the levels of chronic overcrowding that existed in many parishes. More importantly, as tenant farmers became more difficult to attract as the depression began to bite, good cottages were increasingly regarded as important because of the belief that out-migration reduced the quality of the workforce: 'Landlords have to provide good cottages in order to get tenants who say without good cottages it is impossible to get good labourers.'[52] The largest estates, not surprisingly, embarked on the most extensive building campaigns. In Suffolk, the best rural housing was thus reported to be in the vicinity of Helmingham and around Ickworth and Culford.[53] In Norfolk there were reported to be 521 cottages on the Holkham estate in 1866: by 1895, the number had risen to 730. Expenditure on housing here in the years 1870–1880 was, at £3,657, more than double that of the previous decade. In the two estate villages of Weasenham St Peter and Weasenham All Saints there were thirty cottage tenants in 1820, forty-six in 1860, seventy-three by 1880 and eighty-seven in 1890.[54] The Royal Commission on the Housing of the Working Class was told that conditions in the west of

Norfolk were on the whole better than elsewhere in the county because of the example set by both the Earl of Leicester at Holkham and the Marquis of Cholmondeley at Houghton.[55] Lord Leicester's cottages were said to have 'modern sanitary requirements and good gardens': they cost £300 to put up and were rented for between £3 and £5 a year.[56] Work was also under way on the Prince of Wales' newly acquired Sandringham estate, where estate villages little different from those erected by large landowners earlier in the century were created at West Newton, Flitcham and Shernborne. Such places were intended to cement the paternal relationship between landlord and labourer in a very visible way: villages like this remained very firmly under the control of their owners. Often, as earlier in the century, standard colour schemes were employed on estate housing. In 1901 Lord Walpole of Wolterton thus noted that 'All the cottages were painted an ochre colour', adding: 'I don't think they had been painted in the memory of man.'[57] One source of funding for new cottages were the loans from the Land Improvement Companies, and in the 1880s Lord Stafford borrowed £12,000 for cottages on his Costessey estates, while smaller sums went to the Raveningham and Weston Longville estates, all in Norfolk.[58]

In areas in which large estates were less prominent, such as southern, central and eastern Norfolk and north Suffolk, official reports from the 1880s and 90s generally describe poorer conditions.[59] Many cottages were built of the somewhat inferior materials traditional in these areas – timber framing or clay lump – and were often converted farmhouses of sixteenth-, seventeenth- or eighteenth-century date, in contrast to the carrstone, brick or flint of estate cottages to be found in many estate-dominated areas on the light soils. Yet the distinction between estate and non-estate areas was not as stark as some contemporary commentators liked to suggest, and surveys make it clear that that on some of the large estates housing conditions remained poor. The cottages at Ixworth in Suffolk were notoriously bad, with insufficient sleeping room, roofs and walls which were not watertight, and inadequate or insanitary water supplies.[60] A report on nearly 100 cottages on the West Acre estate in Norfolk made for the Rural District Council in 1897 described leaking roofs, defective ceilings and floors, cracked gable ends, defective privies and well water which was unfit to drink. One cottage in East Walton had a roof which was 'liable to fall at any time'.[61]

Some landed estates continued to erect housing for labourers on a grand scale into the 1890s and beyond. Indeed, there are probably more examples of 'model villages' dating from the late nineteenth and early twentieth century in the two counties than from earlier periods – another clear indication of the way that the demise of the 'great estate' should not be hurried. Elaborate new cottages with tall Tudoresque chimneys were built at Holkham Staithe in the 1890s, while the model village to the south of Holkham Park was completely rebuilt as late as 1921. New owners, with money from commerce or industry and perhaps keen to demonstrate their credentials as the benevolent squire, often built lavishly and ostentatiously. What is now Elveden village in the middle of Breckland, opposite the gates to the hall, did not exist before Lord Iveagh built it between 1899 and 1903; at Guist, Thomas Cook erected several groups of cottages clustered around a green (featuring a clock tower) in

Figure 30. Guist, Norfolk. Estate houses erected by Thomas Albert Cook in the late 1920s, their Dutch gables vaguely referencing local vernacular styles of architecture. Some large landowners continued to build workers' housing on their estates into the inter-war years.

1928, their Dutch gables vaguely referencing local styles of vernacular architecture (Figure 30). However, such projects became rarer in the inter-war years: as the economic circumstances of landed estates deteriorated, they were less and less willing or able to provide workers' housing on a significant scale. Instead, the State increasingly stepped into the breach. So far we have discussed change in the village largely in terms of economics and demography, but the late nineteenth and early twentieth century witnessed, as we have seen, major changes in political organisation and political culture at both national and local levels, and these soon began to have an affect on the provision of rural housing.

The creation of county councils in 1888 was closely followed in 1890 by the Housing of the Working Class Act. Although this was principally intended to cope with urban issues, it also allowed local authorities (after 1894, rural district councils (RDCs) through their county councils) to apply for central government funding to erect houses. This right was rarely taken up, and obtaining the authorisation for building could be a long and painful business. Complaints about the conditions of housing in the Suffolk Union of Thringhoe, for example,

Figure 31. These council houses, at Ixworth in west Suffolk, erected in 1891, are among the earliest examples in East Anglia. Their design, however – a semi-detached pair with gabled ends and central stack – remained standard in the region until after the Second World War.

had been made to the Sanitary Authority for several years before 1890: a disused limekiln was being used as a dwelling and numerous cottages were unfit for habitation. When owners refused to make repairs closure orders were issued, but, in the absence of alternative accommodation, the inhabitants simply refused to move out, and were fined. In February 1891 the Ixworth Labourers' Association wrote to the Sanitary Authority asking them to provide housing under the 1890 Act, and an application was made to the county council for permission to initiate an enquiry into conditions in the village. After many delays an enquiry took place in October, but it was not until April 1893 that the Council agreed that new accommodation was needed in the parish. Four pairs of three-bedroomed semi-detached cottages were duly erected the following year, each with a quarter of an acre of garden (Figure 31).[62] An amendment to the Act made in 1900 allowed any parish council which had been unable to get support from their RDC to go straight to the county council to ask it to apply for government funding: again, this was seldom invoked in East Anglia.[63]

In the early decades of the twentieth century local authorities became steadily more concerned with the issue of rural housing. By this time, the provision of housing had become one of the roles of the new RDCs, who appointed Medical Officers of Health empowered to issue closure notices on cottages which they considered unfit for habitation, and to provide reports on local housing conditions. In 1909 central government began to put more pressure on rural authorities over housing provision, insisting that they should carry out surveys of working-class housing in their areas and set up separate housing committees to deal with the work. Most authorities complained that they were too short-staffed to undertake this task in detail, but a number of reports were prepared. Blofield and Flegg RDC in east Norfolk, for example, recorded that forty-two houses in their area were 'unfit', although their response to the problem was limited: two pairs of new houses were built in Acle in 1914 and six in Reedham in 1916.[64] A report on Great Witchingham, carried out for St Faiths RDC in 1903, described how the 'need for accommodation was obvious and urgent': overcrowding and dilapidation, coupled with a lack of decent drains and proper water supplies, ensured that most of the seventy cottages inspected were well below acceptable standards. Eighteen houses, the report suggested, should be:

> ... absolutely condemned as unfit for human habitation. But there is no accommodation available for displaced persons ... The bulk of the houses are clustered together in the main village street. The houses here are so oddly stuck down at angles and so cramped in together as to appear more like an urban slum than a rural village.

An application was made by the district council under the 1890 Act to erect new cottages in the parish, but most of the ratepayers were farmers who put in a formal objection, pointing out that many of the cottages were inhabited by people working outside the parish, and that twenty were occupied by railwaymen whose employer should have been providing accommodation. As a result the council did nothing, although a few cottages were erected by the neighbouring landowners, and the new owner of the Great Witchingham estate spent £212 on house repairs.[65]

The Rural Land Enquiry of 1913 established that housing conditions in the countryside were on the whole disgraceful, but could suggest no obvious solutions other than that wages should be raised to the point where labourers could pay an 'economic rent', and that rural district councils should be cajoled into undertaking more building.[66] The situation did not improve during the war years. In June 1919 Mitford and Launditch RDC in Norfolk sent out questionnaires to its parish councils concerning the state of housing. North Elmham replied that 75 per cent of the cottages within the parish required repair, although there was no family in need of accommodation.[67] But the root cause of the rural housing problem – low agricultural wages, and thus failure to obtain economic rents – was now more widely recognised. As the case of Great Witchingham demonstrated, local ratepayers would often strongly resist attempts to provide housing under the 1890 Act. A major change was, however, brought about by the 1919 Addison Act, which made it obligatory for councils to build houses; and under the 'Homes fit for Heroes' policy of the coaltion government, money was made available for their construction. Councils were expected to put a penny on the rates to fund housing provision but the shortfall, after account had been taken of income from rents, would be made up by central government. There was obvious room for disagreement over the level of rents, as rural councils maintained that tenants could not afford as much as urban dwellers, and much negotiation between local and national government ensued.[68] At the same time, some stimulus was given to private provision, with grants or loans being made available for house building.[69]

East Anglian RDCs were quick to take advantage of the Addison Act, and some parishes (especially in the vicinity of the major towns and cities, where the population was increasing) saw major buildings schemes. Eighty-six new houses were thus erected in Horsham St Faiths, to the north of Norwich; in Forehoe RDC almost all the houses erected, well into the 1920s, were either in Costessey (fast becoming a suburb of Norwich) or in the market town of Wymondham.[70] In more rural areas levels of provision were rather lower. Depwade RDC, in south Norfolk, for example, put forward a scheme to build only 300 houses, ninety-eight of which were being erected by 1920.[71] In the same year North Elmham Parish Council petitioned the RDC for twenty new houses to be built 'as the need is very great',[72] although it was to be another ten years before any were actually erected there. Nevertheless, even in these more remote areas RDCs displayed increasing concern over housing in the immediate post-war years. In 1920 Wayland RDC wrote to other Norfolk councils asking for their support in a request to central government that 'in consequence of the serious shortage of housing, powers be given to RDCs to commandeer, with reasons, all empty cottages'.[73] Unfortunately, the high standards of building set by the Addison Act meant that the costs of erection were high – between £900 and £1,000 per dwelling, to judge from RDC records[74] – and the rents were therefore higher than most farm labourers could afford. Moreover, as the national economy went into a general depression in 1921, government funding came to an abrupt end and so, after only two years, the 'Homes fit for Heroes' initiative was dropped.

After a gap of two years, however, attempts were again made to address the problem. The Housing Acts of 1923 and 1924 resulted in a government subsidy being paid on every house built, whether by local authorities or by private landowners (in 1927 Lord Walpole recorded that he had built two cottages in Weybourne 'for which I can claim £97 ten shillings each').[75] The 1924 Act acknowledged, for the first time, the particular difficulties faced in rural areas, where the need to transport materials long distances made the cost of building greater than that in towns, and where low wages meant that significantly lower rents had to be charged. For the first time special subsidies were made available for new houses built in such areas. Problems remained, however, not only in the numbers but also with the standard of new dwellings. Council houses were still being built without fixed baths in places where water supply or drainage was inadequate[76] and in 1924 Mitford and Launditch RDC in Norfolk applied to the Ministry of Health for exemption from the rule that all new houses eligible for a subsidy must have a fixed bathroom 'as there is not enough water for this'.[77] Moreover, even with the help of grants many of the new houses were still too expensive for farm workers to rent. In an attempt to remedy this, the Rural Workers' Act of 1926 provided that grants should be available for reconditioning cottages and converting other buildings for housing purposes. The grants do not seem to have been widely taken up.[78] In Norfolk, 478 cottages benefited from these grants over the following ten years, and in Suffolk 823:

> In East Suffolk, existing coach houses, stables and barns have been converted into dwellings, whilst on the Suffolk coast there can be seen, in the place of an old dilapidated cowshed, a five-roomed bungalow which makes an ideal home for a rural worker, being much superior in design and accommodation to many now being erected on new seaside estates.[79]

Barn conversions may have moved up the price and social ladder, but they are certainly not a new idea.

Further Housing Acts, in 1930, 1935 and 1938, encouraged further provision in rural areas, including special bungalows for older inhabitants (in 1936 thirty-one of the 101 dwellings completed or in the course of being erected by Forehoe and Henstead RDC were of this type). It remains unclear precisely how many council houses were erected in East Anglia in the period before the Second World War, although the numbers were certainly significant – it has been suggested that Norfolk may have built more than any other county.[80] Unlike the often ornate and distinctive estate cottages which had preceded them, the new local authority houses were plain, sometimes almost severe, in design, with symmetrical doors and windows. Most were semi-detached, with gabled roofs. Although, in order to obtain a grant from central government, councils had to accept the lowest tender, Addison's Act laid down minimum room size and ceiling height, and most houses had three bedrooms and two living rooms: the need for a bath was also now generally accepted. A report in the *Eastern Daily Press* for 1937 described examples in Sculthorpe, in Walsingham RDC, which had running water and electricity and 'wardrobes and plate racks above the scullery sinks': 'the site has been planted with trees and shrubs and presents a most pleasing appearance.'[81] The use of local materials had been recommended by the Act, but national requisitioning meant that the bricks were often obtained from the London Brick Company, resulting in a lack of local character (both Forehoe and Depwade RDCs considered, but rejected, the use of clay lump).[82] Rendered flettons were sometimes used, however, leading to a degree of variety in style and finish. Most houses were provided with tiled roofs but some, as at Smallburgh in Norfolk, were thatched. The majority were placed in groups, often in a straight line along an existing road leading into a village: so located, they remain a striking feature of the rural landscape. The councils seem to have had little difficulty obtaining land in appropriate locations. It was usually purchased, but occasionally donated by large landowners, as at Tottington in 1925 (Colonel de Grey) or Melton Constable in 1920 (Lord Hastings).[83] The question of how many houses should be built per acre exercised the mind of many councils. While six houses to the acre was usual, there were those who argued for only four. 'The countryman is, or ought or be a man who can make good use of the land, and besides growing vegetables, wants to keep poultry and perhaps a pig. For such domestic husbandry a quarter of an acre is certainly not too much.'[84]

In addition to encouraging the provision of new houses, legal changes in the early twentieth century made it easier to clear away sub-standard accommodation. District councils made a few closure orders under the 1890 Act, but usually failed to compel owners to put cottages in proper repair. But with the passing of the 1930 Housing Act major programmes of demolition and rebuilding were initiated, and the appearance of rural settlements was thus changed not only by the erection of new council housing but also by large-scale demolition of older cottages, those deemed insanitary or uninhabitable. Schemes in Lakenheath in west Suffolk, for example, involved the demolition of ten houses in Dumpling Bridge Lane and twenty-one in Anchor Lane; in Barton Mills eight were demolished, and no less than forty-four in the various hamlets of Mildenhall.[85] A further 139 houses in Mildenhall RDC were registered as 'unfit', although it is unclear how many were actually knocked down.[86] By 1937, sixty-three new houses had been built in the District and all the 234 people displaced had been rehoused.[87] In Depwade, on the claylands of south Norfolk, over 100 properties were put forward for demolition in 1934 alone, although action in some cases was delayed and in others a programme of repairs was agreed with the owners so, again, it is not clear how many were actually pulled down. Nevertheless, the south Norfolk villages of Ashwellthorpe, Fundenhall, Tacolneston, Aslacton, Moulton, Bunwell, Carleton Rode, Forncett St Mary and St Peter, Hapton, Hempnall, Fritton, Stratton St Mary and St Michael, Tasburgh and Thurton all saw significant numbers of demolitions.[88] Many of these condemned dwellings were doubtless 'clay lump' dwellings of the kind cheaply erected on a large scale in this part of East Anglia in the late eighteenth and early nineteenth centuries.

Further legislative changes were made in the late 1930s: from 1935 subsidies were made available to reduce overcrowding, and in 1936 county councils were given the power (subject to the approval of the Ministry of Health) to make grants to the RDCs for houses erected.[89] But the problem of housing in the countryside remained acute at the outbreak of the Second World War. In 1938, almost 50,000 rural houses in England as a whole were deemed unfit for human habitation, while a survey of 1936 reported that 42,000 working-class dwellings in the countryside were grossly overcrowded. Local evidence suggests that East Anglian housing conformed to this pattern. A sale catalogue of 1939 for an estate in Great Whelnetham in Suffolk, for example, describes some brick and tiled cottages with two living rooms and three bedrooms, but also many clay lump and stud and plaster two-bedroom houses with only a scullery and living room downstairs.[90] A White Paper published in 1944 estimated that up to 30 per cent of the rural population of England and Wales had no mains water and that earth, bucket and chemical toilets abounded, and recommended that £21 million should be spent over five years to bring piped water and decent sanitation to rural Britain.[91] The 1933 Local Government Act had enhanced the powers of RDCs to provide basic infrastructure, but improvements had mainly been directed towards the larger rural settlements. Again, East Anglia was typical, with most rural settlements still lacking proper running water and sanitation even in the 1940s. In 1943 a proposal was put to Loddon and Clavering RDC that 'no more houses be built until all houses, old and new were equipped with proper water and sewerage'.[92] 'For the majority of rural workers a bathroom is a real luxury.'[93] Many villages and smaller hamlets in East Anglia, and most outlying farms, lacked mains electricity when war broke out in 1939. Only in the post-war period did the extension of the electricity grid, improvements in water supply and sanitation, and more extensive schemes of council house building, really address problems of rural deprivation in the region.

## CHURCHES, CHAPELS AND SCHOOLS

If the majority of rural houses in East Anglia were built outside the period studied in this book, the same could not be said for the various public buildings to be found in villages: places of worship, schools and village halls. In these, the late nineteenth and early twentieth centuries have left a more important mark on the village landscape. By the 1870s the main period of parish church restoration was over, although some major refurbishments continued, as at Tottington in the Breckland in 1885–6.[94] A handful of new 'mission churches' were built in those few areas where the rural population continued to grow – as at Stowbridge in the west Norfolk Fens – and a very small number of parish churches were comprehensively rebuilt at the whim of particular landowners or incumbents, often of an eccentric nature: one striking example is Booton (Norfolk), which was completely refaced, the tower rebuilt, and numerous embellishments made to the design of the rector and amateur architect, the Rev. Whitwell Elwin, between 1875 and 1891. But if the great age of Anglican church building was over, the various nonconformist groups continued to build on some scale in rural areas.

Nonconformity had been strong in Norfolk and Suffolk since the later seventeenth century. In the eighteenth and early nineteenth centuries 'New Dissent', represented by the various Methodist splinter groups, had also been highly successful. But it was the latecomers, the Primitive Methodists – who first established congregations in the region in the 1820s – who were the most numerically significant group by the middle of the nineteenth century. The 1860s and 70s saw a phenomenal burst of chapel-building activity, and while the rate of construction then fell back, even in the 1890s it was probably higher than it had been in any decade up to 1840. Moreover, even where chapels had their origins in the seventeenth or eighteenth centuries they were often comprehensively rebuilt or refronted in this period, so that the rural legacy of nonconformist chapels is to a significant extent a late nineteenth- and early twentieth-century one.[95] As a result of this activity, more than 300 villages in Norfolk and over 190 in Suffolk had some alternative to the established church by the time of the First World War.[96] Not all nonconformist groups displayed the same degree of vitality during the period studied here, however. A systematic survey of Norfolk chapels has shown that while the older dissenting groups – Baptists, Presbyterians, Congregationalists, Quakers and Unitarians – managed to build or comprehensively rebuild only six chapels in the 1880s and 90s, and the Methodist groups only ten in the 1880s and eleven in the 1890s, the Primitive Methodists managed more than twenty in each of these decades.[97] They had at least 192 chapels in the county by 1914. In Suffolk, a county in which 'Old Dissent' had always been stronger than in Norfolk, the 'Prims' made a later and lesser impact. The county had only about fifty-three Primitive Methodist chapels by 1914, but at least ninety Baptist and Congregationalist ones, some of which were very large, compared with Norfolk's forty-four. That at Horham, built in 1857, could seat 900, while several others could accommodate over 600.[98] Nevertheless, here too it seems that it was the 'Prims' who built the majority of new chapels in the late nineteenth and early twentieth centuries.

The rate of chapel construction fell away markedly in the aftermath of the First World War: only a scatter of new examples seem to have been erected in the East Anglian countryside in the 1920s and 30s, mainly by Primitive Methodists (such as Brooke in 1924, or East Ruston in 1928), although the Free Methodists (Frettenham 1929) and Methodists (Great Cressingham 1932, Langham 1935) were also active (all in Norfolk). Some existing buildings were expanded, often by the addition of a schoolroom: but on the whole activity slowed. This may in part reflect the fact that sufficient buildings existed for the needs of congregations – especially as the size of some must have been declining.[99] But an absence of money, especially on the part of the small and medium-sized farmers who had been major contributors to earlier building campaigns, was also a factor, and some dissenting congregations continued to make do with makeshift accommodation, such as the cottage in which the United Methodists at Plumstead, near Holt in north Norfolk, were still meeting in 1925.[100]

The architectural style of nonconformist buildings changed in the later nineteenth century. The vast majority of chapels erected in East Anglian villages in the years between 1820 and 1870 were brick-built rectangular gabled buildings in a loosely classical style, with simple pilasters, string courses, fan lights and pediments. The gable end usually faced the road and formed the main façade, with a single central door flanked by two long windows. Above was a decorative pediment, often carrying a date stone, which also usually stated the denomination of the chapel. While such buildings continued to be constructed in the 1880s and 90s gothic detailing – often combined with polychrome brickwork – increased in popularity and by the first decade of the twentieth century nearly half the chapels being erected were in a clear gothic style.[101] Even some very small congregations, such as those at Great Witchingham (1905) and Postwick (1901) in Norfolk, erected buildings with fine traceried windows in the main façade. For the less affluent congregations the building of a 'tin tabernacle' was an alternative. These could be locally supplied by the Norwich firm of Boulton and Paul, who advertised both iron and wooden varieties in their 1902 catalogue.[102]

The location and setting of meeting houses and chapels had changed significantly by the start of the period studied here, a reflection of the greater acceptance of dissent among the population at large as well as the numerical superiority of dissenting congregations in many villages. Up until the first decades of the nineteenth century the overwhelming majority of chapels had been in remote, isolated or hidden locations – in the midst of fields, on the edges of villages, or – if in one of the market towns – set back from the street, behind other buildings, and reached by an alley. The proportion of new buildings erected in such hidden or marginal locations declined steadily through the early nineteenth century, falling to around 10 per cent by the 1840s. By the time of the building boom of the 1860s and 70s, such locations were extremely rare: most new chapels were much more publicly positioned.[103]

The other noticeable legacy of the late nineteenth and early twentieth centuries in East Anglian villages are the schools, a high proportion of which are – like chapels – now redundant and converted to residential, retail or industrial use. Rural schools in East Anglia had been increasing in number during the nineteenth century; they were built by the Church of England's National Society for Promoting the Education of the Poor in the Principles of the Established Church (with support of local landowners) or, more rarely, by the nonconformist British and Foreign School Society. But even so, only around a quarter of villages in Norfolk and Suffolk possessed one in 1870. Calls for universal compulsory education had been increasing since the mid-nineteenth century, but the clash of views between those who wanted a secular and those who wanted a religious-based system had hindered progress. A compromise act was passed in 1870 – the Elementary Education Act, brought in by the Gladstone government – which was designed to 'complete the present voluntary system, to fill up gaps' while 'not destroying the existing system in introducing a new one'.[104] The country was divided into School Districts, each of which consisted of a group of parishes which were responsible for ensuring that there was sufficient school accommodation for the population. Where there was insufficient provision from the voluntary sector, School Boards were to be set up and empowered to levy a rate to build a school. They were also permitted to make attendance compulsory, although they were not compelled to do so until a further act of 1886.[105] Local School Boards remained responsible for elementary education until 1902, when their duties were taken over by county councils. Over time, the 'voluntary' schools were increasingly dependent on public money, and an increasing number were placed in the hands of the counties.[106] Schools of both types had to follow the syllabus set down by successive Education Acts, which was broadened beyond the religious instruction and basic skills in reading and numeracy which had generally been provided in the period before 1870.

While the population of most villages was declining, school provision steadily increased. There were at least 196 village schools in Norfolk and 138 in Suffolk in 1870: over the next ten years about 120 more were added, some by the voluntary societies and some by the School Boards. Over the next thirty years, however, numbers more than doubled, and numerous schools were extended, some several times.[107] Only in the inter-war period does there appear to have been some retrenchment; smaller schools were amalgamated, especially in Norfolk, where the number of head teachers seems to have fallen slightly from 536 in 1919 to 409 in 1932.[108] In spite of these improvements, educational provision remained poorer than in the towns: there were higher proportions of uncertified teachers, and teachers were worse paid.[109]

Figure 32. Village school at Gunthorpe, Norfolk, built in 1868. The gothic architecture is typical of schools sponsored by the established church.

Schools erected before 1870, mostly by the Church of England, were normally in a simple gothic style, single-storey and with steep roofs and high arched windows set well above eye level. Built, in many cases, largely of flint, they were not dissimilar in architectural terms to the parish churches with which they were closely associated (Figure 32). The same was true of the majority built after 1870 under the aegis of the established church. A number of writers urged that Gothic exteriors made for unsatisfactory interiors, for the high-pitched roofs produced draughts and an inconvenient echo, while the high windows meant that the room was often dark and gloomy.[110] The new Board schools, such as that erected at Langham in north Norfolk, were more likely to be built of brick and, while sometimes likewise boasting gothic details, were generally more functional in appearance, although they too had tall windows with sills high enough to prevent children being able to look out and thus be distracted from their studies.[111] Schools of both types were often provided with separate entrances and play areas for boys and girls. A few were very small buildings with only a single room, although these were often closed and amalgamated with neighbouring schools in the course of the inter-war period; the majority had two rooms, or one large room divided by a partition.[112]

After 1902 Local Education Authorities were empowered to provide some sort of higher education and a few secondary schools were built in villages across Norfolk and Suffolk. A

'High Standard School' was opened at Briston in Norfolk in 1913, with four classrooms and provisions for handicrafts and cookery. A secondary school was built in Walsingham in 1912 and another, which was enlarged in 1912, at Leiston in Suffolk in 1908.[113] For the most part, however, secondary schools were confined to the market towns and major urban centres.

## VILLAGE HALLS, READING ROOMS AND MEMORIALS

From the end of the nineteenth century social commentators identified a lack of leisure opportunities as a major reason for the migration of workers from the country to the towns. The young, in particular, were leaving for the excitement of urban life as much as for higher wages. At the same time, temperance campaigners were critical of a situation in which public houses were the only focus for community life, while philanthropic and paternalistic landowners and clergymen were keen to promote opportunities for self-improvement within venues over which they could exercise some influence.

During the late nineteenth century there was a slow but steady growth in the number of parish libraries, reading rooms and working men's clubs. These were built by a wide range of well-meaning people in an effort to 'reform leisure activities' and promote 'social harmony in small communities'.[114] As the landowner W. Bulmer put it at the opening of the Cawston Reading Room in 1863, 'They [the villagers] will be enabled to pass some of their evenings rationally and profitably, without being driven to the bar or the tap room as the only place of resort.'[115] Reading rooms were small buildings in which local and national newspapers were made available, as well as a library. Some also had billiard tables and provided a meeting place for village and working men's clubs, as well as for mechanics' institutes. Many were provided by local landowners as an act of philanthropy, like that built by Lord Cadogan at Culford in 1915. Others were erected by incumbents, or by members of their families, such as that at Dalham, built as a memorial to the rector by his wife in 1896. The parish room at Bradfield St George was described in the Directory as being 'connected to the rectory', a fairly typical arrangement. A few, however, were built by public subscription, like those at Belton (1885) and Combs (1887). However they were funded, reading rooms, village libraries and similar institutions remained in relatively short supply. In Norfolk, for example, there were probably only around eighty by 1900.[116] A few examples of rather larger public rooms, true village halls, were also erected in East Anglia in this period. Some were built by the various friendly societies, such as those constructed by the Odd Fellows in South Creake and Litcham (which included a stage as well as a retiring room), and by the Foresters' in Walton in 1886 and Mendlesham in 1889. Most, however, were again provided by private landowners. These too remained rare before 1900, with perhaps no more than twenty examples scattered across the two counties.

There was a steady increase in the numbers of village halls and rooms in the early years of the twentieth century (Figure 33), and a number were erected in the immediate aftermath of the First World War. Parish meetings were held throughout East Anglia in 1919 to consider the

Figure 33. The village hall at Hindringham, opened in 1911.

most appropriate way for commemorating the war dead: suggestions ranged from a simple tablet or cross to clocks, drinking fountains, recreation grounds and almshouses, but at least twenty villages in Norfolk and thirteen in Suffolk saw 'memorial' halls as a particularly fitting tribute. At Binham there was to be 'a life-size portrait of each fallen hero' in the proposed reading room (these now hang in the new village hall).[117] The architect W.R. Lethaby, writing in *The Builder*, expressed the widely held view that a hall, as well as providing a memorial to the dead, also helped the living, 'starved for a lack of means of civilisation'.[118] Much has been made of 'memorial halls', and in some rural areas a desire to commemorate the fallen was clearly a major stimulus to provision. But in East Anglia at least the number of village halls had in fact been increasing rapidly before the war, with – to judge from the *Directories* – forty examples being built in Norfolk, and twenty in Suffolk, between 1900 and 1914.

Some village halls were cheap and impermanent structures, as at North Elmham in Norfolk where, in the aftermath of the war, surplus army huts were used.[119] But most were more substantial structures, especially where local landowners contributed generously to the fund. They came in a bewildering variety of styles, but in general became more functional in appearance, with fewer gothic/vernacular details, as the century progressed. Weaver, who wrote the standard work on the subject in 1920, argued that halls should be large, adequately ventilated and furnished with a suitable stage 'for the lecturer with his magic lantern, concerts and amusements'. They would be used by groups as varied as boy scouts and adult school classes, and for events such as dances and glee parties.[120] He published a plan and photographs of a substantial example in Brantham, Suffolk, in 1914. It was architect-designed, erected at the expense of a local dignitary, well-lit and provided with a stage. Under the windows were bench seats which lifted up to 'form lockers in which can be kept chess boards, draughts and other games'.[121]

The proliferation of village halls, and the continuing growth in the number of reading rooms, was part of a wider revival of community life in rural areas which included the establishment of societies such as the British Legion (1919), the Young Farmers' Clubs (1921), the Village Clubs Association (1919) and the Women's Institutes (1915). As Weaver wrote, 'Village life has to be renewed and the provision of a common meeting ground is one of the ways to do it.'[122] The establishment of village halls was largely the work of a grass-roots movement, rather than a direct consequence of government policy, and this was particularly true in East Anglia. In many counties halls were part-funded with the help of Rural Community Councils, the first of which was set up in Oxfordshire in 1920. These could draw finance from the National Council for Social Service and the Carnegie Trust. But there was no such support in East Anglia, for the RCC in Suffolk was not founded until 1937 and that in Norfolk only after the Second World War.[123] The movement was, in fact, a sign of a new assertiveness on the part of country dwellers, filling a gap in rural life left, in many cases, by the retreat from village affairs of local landowners and by the declining influence of both the established Church and the nonconformist chapels. For the new halls differed from earlier examples in that they were mainly run by independent committees, free of outside interference. Indeed, Weaver thought that previous efforts to create village clubs and halls had often been unsuccessful because they had not been the 'outcome of the people's own desire', but of the goodwill of others who wished 'to lead the village in their own way'.[124] This independence was often secured after a fight, however. In Wells, for example, the vicar and his supporters tried hard to enshrine in the constitution of the new hall a condition that a Sunday school should be held in it every week, a proposal finally defeated by the committee.[125]

Village halls were not the only form of practical memorial raised to the dead of the First World War. North Walsham cottage hospital was built as a memorial, with several villages contributing to the cost. At Bodham the vicar came to a meeting called to discuss ways of commemorating the fallen well prepared with architect's costings, and managed to persuade those present to agree to the restoration of the church tower.[126] More usually, the war dead were remembered simply with a memorial, which listed all the men of the parish who had died and also usually those who had served. These still survive in considerable numbers, poignant details in the rural landscape.

The concept of remembering and honouring a group of men who were united not by class or social standing but by a common place of residence was new, and arose in large part from the fact that more people had been involved in this than in any previous war: and a fifth of them had not returned. Memorials provided a site for mourning and remembrance, but also expressed local pride which, in some regions, was reflected in the conscious choice of local materials, as in Surrey, where Grieves has found that great efforts were made to employ local stone.[127] No such concerns have been noted in East Anglia, although Arthur Mee, when describing the memorial screen in Great Ryburgh church, was keen to emphasise that it was made by 'Norfolk craftsmen'.[128] Even before the war had ended discussions were taking place about memorials, and a meeting was held in June 1918 at the Royal Academy to establish guidelines for 'suitable' designs; the following year there was an exhibition of memorials at the Victoria and Albert Museum. A War Graves Commission was set up, with Sir Edward Lutyens, Herbert Baker, Reginald Bloomfield, Rudyard Kipling and Adrian Hill as members, and this had a strong influence upon the architecture and language of remembrance in the post-war countryside.[129] A cross or tablet was the usual choice, but there were often arguments about where it should be erected. The churchyard might appear the obvious place but, in a region in which nonconformity was strong, this could be seen as sectarian: in Carleton Rode the problem was solved by putting a tablet in both church and chapel.[130] More usually, the monument was placed in a prominent roadside position. The most striking example in East Anglia must surely be the great Corinthian stone column erected by Lord Iveagh on what is now the A11, at the point where the Suffolk parishes of Elveden, Eriswell and Icklingham meet, as a memorial to the fallen, their names inscribed on tablets set to face the parishes from which they came. The importance which memorials soon assumed in the landscape is reflected in the frequency with which they are described in inter-war guide books, such as Arthur Mee's volumes in the *King's England* series. At Ditchingham, for instance, Mee drew attention to the sculpture in the church, depicting in bronze a soldier 'lying in his trench coat, his head on his haversack and his helmet close by, on a tomb as if asleep'.[131]

## COMMUNICATIONS

Railways, as we have already noted, had penetrated deep into the East Anglian countryside by the 1870s. Indeed, nineteenth-century *Directories* frequently locate settlements in terms of their distance from the nearest railway station: by 1900 most villages were within 8 km of one. But the late nineteenth century also saw a steady increase in the number of steam-driven road vehicles – traction engines pulling heavy loads, and steam lorries – and this began to put serious pressure on rural roads. Responsibility for road maintenance went through a number of important changes in the late nineteenth century. Under the terms of the Highways and Locomotive (Amendment) Act of 1878 all turnpike roads, as well as those dis-turnpiked since 1870 and a number of other major routes, were classed as 'main roads', and Highways Committees were set up by the Courts of Quarter Sessions to maintain them. Counties were to contribute half of the maintenance costs, the rest coming from central government. Other roads continued to be the responsibility, as they had long been, of local (parish) Highway Boards. When the county councils were created in 1888 they immediately took on the duties of the Highways Committees, and one of their first tasks was to appointment a County Road Surveyor.[132] By a further Act, in 1898, county councils were made responsible for registering and licensing locomotives, and attempts were made to prevent them from using certain narrow roads, and also to limit the size of the loads that they pulled, as well as to insist that all vehicles should put skids on their wheels when going downhill[133] – restrictions which had to be withdrawn under pressure from the owners of the engines. Throughout the 1890s the County Highways Committees continued their work of improving the major roads, principally by surfacing them with granite and flint. Steam rollers were purchased and payments made for the 'raising and breaking of stones'. Bridges were built or rebuilt, like the cast-iron ribbed girder bridge twelve feet wide erected by East Suffolk County Council between Wiston and Worlingford in 1891.[134]

The responsibility for minor roads passed from parish Highway Boards to rural and urban district councils when these were established in 1894.[135] The districts were divided into sub-districts. In Depwade, for example, there were six, each responsible for about forty miles of road. Each was under the control of a district surveyor whose work involved constant travelling to inspect the roads, so that frequently a bicycle allowance was provided by the council (in 1904 the surveyor for Clare in Suffolk claimed to have cycled 8,300 miles in eighteen months: his bicycle was worn out and he was granted a motorised tricycle to replace it).[136] Besides maintaining the road surface, the RDCs provided signposts, railed in dangerous ponds and sorted out blocked drains.[137] Material for repairs was provided by the parishes in the form of picked stones and gravel, which was delivered to the roadsides in the summer months; road mending was generally carried out in the winter, allowing the RDCs to fulfil their statutory duty of providing work for the unemployed at a time when there was less agricultural work available.

Steam engines, and especially railways, had done much to break down rural isolation, but it was the motor bus and motor car which really began to transform rural life in East Anglia. The first decade of the twentieth century saw a slow but significant expansion in the number of private cars on the region's roads, and the establishment of the first public bus services. All this put further pressures on rural roads, eroding the surface and producing great clouds of dust, but new technology offered a solution. Tarmac was patented as a road surfacing material in 1902 and the firm of Tarmac Ltd was established in 1903.[138] As early as 1901 a short stretch of road in Trimley in east Suffolk was coated with tar 'with a view to alleviating the dust problem'. The county surveyor was not impressed by its capabilities in this respect, 'but as a road preservative, it is very good indeed'.[139] At Copdock and Stratford St Mary 'Hahuite' – a compound of tar and oil – was used with some success,[140] and 'tar paving' was carried out at Clare in 1904.[141] The use of these materials presumably increased over the following years (especially following the Development and Road Improvement Act of 1909, which provided grant aid for road surfacing) for a report made in 1911 by the Road Tarring Joint (East and West Norfolk) Committee recommended that ninety-one miles of road in the county should be tarred, including twenty-two miles 'not previously treated'.[142] The lengths involved were relatively short, however – anything between three and fourteen miles – and usually where significant roads passed through towns or major villages.

In 1910 a Central Roads Board was established at Whitehall, and was empowered to use funds from vehicle licences, and from a newly introduced petrol tax, to improve the most important national roads. But most maintenance continued to be financed by the county councils and RDCs, and work on improvements continued slowly but steadily through the early years of the century as roads were widened and dangerous bends removed.[143] Particular attention was paid to bridges – a report in 1911 showed that Suffolk County Council was responsible for 112 of them.[144] Many were strengthened (such as Dumpling Bridge, Lakenheath in 1904,[145] and (in Norfolk) those at Gressenhall, Fransham and West Lexham in 1914). Some entirely new ones were erected, mainly in iron (North Elmham, 1906; Lyng, 1909) but occasionally of ferro-concrete. River crossings on unclassified roads were the responsibility of the RDCs, and many fords were now replaced by bridges: that at Shotesham in south Norfolk, for example, in 1914.[146] The movement of military traffic during the First World War placed extra pressure on the region's main roads, and central government agreed to contribute 50 per cent towards further surface tarring on the Newmarket Road through Thetford 'whilst it was subject to military traffic'.[147] But it was the immediate post-war period that witnessed the real expansion in the number of motor vehicles using the region's roads.

Bus services had been 'uncommon' in East Anglia before 1914,[148] but expanded rapidly during and after the war. By 1916 Ernest Moyes and Herbert Moyes were operating a service between Debenham and Ipswich, in competition with another provider, Richard Sage.[149] E.B. Hutchison soon became the largest company in the region, and as early as 1919 was running a number of services, including one between Norwich and Aylsham which continued on to the seaside town of Cromer in the summer months. Hutchison's United Automobile Service gradually expanded its network of routes throughout eastern England, including Lincolnshire.[150] Smaller local providers also flourished – in 1919 the Eastern Counties Road Car Company was formed to operate buses out of Ipswich – and daily buses soon connected all the principal villages and market towns to Yarmouth, Norwich, King's Lynn and Ipswich. By 1925 five buses a day operated between Norwich and Bungay, for example, with extra services on Tuesdays and Saturdays.[151] Further piecemeal expansion in provision took place through the later 1920s, and by 1934 east Suffolk was said to be 'well-served by bus routes which run along all A roads, the majority of B roads and a large proportion of minor roads'.[152] The Road Traffic Act of 1930 regulated bus companies, creating the regional monopolies that existed until the 1980s.[153]

There was increasing concern during the inter-war years on the part of local authorities about the impact of this expansion of public transport on country roads, although all new services had, in fact, to be formally approved by the relevant county council. In December

1919 a conference was held at Ipswich to discuss the issue, with representatives attending from Essex, Norfolk and east and west Suffolk. Buses were said to be travelling at between 25 and 30 mph and were the 'most damaging traffic on our roads today'. Further growth in services, it was argued, would lead to escalating road maintenance costs, and the conference agreed to try and recoup some of the cost from the bus companies themselves. An appeal was made to central government, stating that 'the question of reconstruction and adaptation of roads, particularly main roads, to the needs of modern traffic grows in urgency and should be dealt with as a matter of national importance.'[154]

The inter-war period also, and more significantly, saw a steady increase in the number of private cars.[155] In 1920 200,000 private cars were registered in Britain: ten years later the number was nearly a million.[156] Even in rural East Anglia, the rate of increase was extraordinary. A Norfolk's County Surveyor's report of 1925 pointed out that a scheme for reconstructing the main roads in the county, adopted in 1923, was already inadequate as there had been a 60 per cent growth in traffic since that date. An average of 174.48 tons of traffic per day had passed a survey point on the Cromer–Hunstanton road in 1912: now the figure was 2,326.68 tons.[157] In 1927 it was estimated that the volume of traffic had doubled in Norfolk over the previous five years.[158] All this put phenomenal pressure not only on the main roads of the region but increasingly on the minor ones as well, and there were frequent requests for 10 mph speed limits through villages, although these were seldom granted. Costs rose inexorably. Depwade RDC in Norfolk, for example, spent £2,334 on local road maintenance in 1895–6[159] and £2,897 in 1903–4.[160] By 1914 this had risen to £3,903 3s 8d,[161] and by 1924 it had reached £6,632.[162] Although the RDCs sometimes received grants from central government to put the unemployed to work on the roads,[163] these were still substantial sums. The RDCs also claimed, on occasions, that the failure of the county councils to adequately maintain major routes placed added pressure on the minor roads under their own control. In 1924, for example, Loddon and Clavering RDC complained that the poor state of the Norwich–Bungay road meant that more traffic used the neighbouring minor roads: 200 loads of stone were needed to mend the road running through Bedingham, Seething and Brooke 'in consequence of the heavy traffic now passing on the road, such traffic being diverted from the County Council road on account of the poor condition thereof'.[164]

In spite of the increasing amounts of money spent on maintenance, by the mid-1920s complaints about the state of unclassified roads in the region were more frequent than ever. In 1924 those in the mid-Norfolk village of Swanton Morley, for example, were described as 'deplorable'. Mitford and Launditch RDC believed that 'great mileages of these roads … are worn out, but it is not possible, with the present Highway Rate, to make any attempt to resurface them.'[165] In May 1924 a letter was sent by the council to members of the government stating that because of the distress in rural districts, rates could not be increased and therefore roads could not be adequately maintained. The council 'would accept no responsibility for the deterioration in the condition of important highways in consequence of an inability to shoulder the additional financial burden of more improved methods of construction which are now considered essential if such highways are to be maintained in a suitable condition for present-day traffic'.[166] Similar requests were sent from other RDCs in the region, including Mildenhall in Suffolk, which described in a letter to Whitehall how it viewed 'with much concern the serious deterioration of roads under their control owing to the continuous growth of heavy and fast-moving traffic and notwithstanding that they are spending more each year on maintenance'.[167]

The RDCs made some improvements to minor roads using the new, 'more improved methods of construction', grant-aided in some instances by the new Ministry of Transport. In Norfolk, for example, Loddon and Clavering District Council tarred 11,880 square yards of road in 1924, the work being carried out by Bristows Tarvia Ltd of London at a cost of nearly £1 per 100 yards.[168] In Suffolk there were discussions between Blything RDC and the county surveyor over the relative merits of refined hot tar and cold bitumen, while Hartismere RDC intended filling holes with tarmac and then treating the whole road with tar and local grit or shingle.[169] But a Norfolk County Council report of 1927 nevertheless acknowledged that the condition of local roads remained 'poor' and pressed for urgent action: 'Many unclassified roads will be completely impassable in a short time.' It was proposed to upgrade thirty-five miles of unclassified roads each year using granite, tarred slag, Macadam and stone chips, although applied in a 'somewhat lighter' manner than to the main roads: the total cost would be £1,447,000.[170] This proposal was rapidly revised upwards, however, and seventy-one miles of improved surfacing was scheduled for 1927–8.[171]

This increasing involvement in the maintenance of minor roads culminated, in 1930, in the county councils taking full responsibility for the network, and a sustained period of improvement followed (Figure 34). In Norfolk, well over 100 miles of minor road each year were provided with a modern surface throughout the 1930s; many roads were widened and dangerous corners removed. But such improvements never really kept pace with the volume of traffic, which in 1935 was estimated to be four times what it had been eleven years before.[172] Vehicles were also driving faster, leading to further deterioration in the condition of roads. Although, on the eve of the Second World War, a significant proportion of even the minor roads in the two counties had been surfaced with tarmac, they remained for the most part quite inadequate for the volume of traffic they were supposed to bear.

Increasing road traffic meant that there was a need for more signage, and county councils were responsible for both direction and warning signs, another escalating cost. In 1919 the East Suffolk Committee 'expressed the opinion that the multiplication of signs was undesirable',[173] but by the 1930s signs were becoming a familiar feature of the rural landscape, with 319 new posts being erected in East Suffolk in 1938 alone, and a further 500 ordered in 1939. 'This has resulted in a marked improvement in the sign-posting of roads, though much remains to be done.' By this time 30 mph speed limits had been introduced through most villages.[174] The rise in car ownership had other effects on the landscape: petrol

Figure 34. Road mending at Fornham St Genevieve, Suffolk, in the 1930s.

stations and repair garages proliferated, a significant proportion developing directly from village blacksmiths, and the number of applications made to RDCs for licenses to keep petrol increased year by year through the 1920s and 30s.[175] And, as we have seen, it greatly increased the number of tourists visiting beauty spots and the coast, and dispersed them more widely through the countryside.

## CONCLUSION

The appearance of East Anglian villages did change, more than we sometimes acknowledge, in the period between 1870 and 1939. Some new houses were built – estate cottages in the early part of the period, council housing in the inter-war years – and the latter, in particular, still make a strong visual impact on many rural settlements. A range of new public buildings appeared, and the archaeological contrast between the periods before and after the First World War is again noticeable: in the former, nonconformist chapels, reading rooms financed by the established Church and the gentry, and church-sponsored schools with strong gothic, indeed ecclesiastical, detailing; in the latter, village halls and other public amenities often paid for by public subscription, and schools increasingly functional in appearance. The pre-1914 village world looked back to the old days of the Victorian countryside, dominated in many cases by the squire and established Church, or by nonconformist congregations. The simple modernity of the village council-house rows looked forward to a newer, braver world.

This distinction should not, however, be too sharply drawn, for in the development of settlement, as in so many other aspects of rural life, the influence of the very largest landowners, in East Anglia at least, waned slowly. Indeed, although the old distinction between 'open' and 'close' parishes ought to have dwindled to some extent with changes in the funding of poor relief during the nineteenth century, villages clustering at the gates of the largest landowners often continued to be visually different from their neighbours, the lives of their inhabitants still controlled, to varying degrees, by wealthy landlords.[176] Such places were rarely provided with shops, and rarely boasted public houses. Some landowners declined to have council houses built there. The housing in the parishes of Holkham, Quarles and Egmere was not inspected by Walsingham RDC's Housing Committee in 1919 'because it was known that cottages in these parishes were in a superior condition, and Lord Leicester had intimated his intention of building what further cottages were required'.[177]

The greatest change in the life of the village was perhaps the progressive breakdown in isolation as the proliferation of private cars and, in particular, bus services ensured that rural settlements were much less inward-looking, far more connected to the wider world. Yet, in spite of the strenuous efforts of local communities and the county and district councils to improve amenities, rural areas in 1939 still lagged behind their urban counterparts: most East Anglian villages lacked a supply of running water or mains sewage and many minor roads remained poorly surfaced, while most villages continued to stagnate demographically.

# CHAPTER 8

# Imagining the Countryside

## THE THREE COUNTRYSIDES

The East Anglian countryside in the period of the Great Depression was not, we have argued, a scene of unremitting gloom, decay and dereliction. This may have been a period in which some farmers made a poor living; it was certainly one in which rural wages lagged significantly behind those of urban and industrial areas, and in which the amenities of the countryside compared poorly with those available in the towns. But in landscape terms this was a time of continued change, rather than of stasis or decline. Not all districts lost population. New houses, and new forms of public building, continued to appear in many villages. Most of the old landscape – country houses, parks, woods and arable farmland – remained intact, and new landscapes – of smallholdings, vast conifer plantations, holiday resorts – emerged in many areas. In broad terms, this appraisal is in line with recent interpretations of rural society in the inter-war years by historians like Jeremy Burchardt, Paul Brassley and Alun Howkins, who have all in their different ways interpreted this as a period of revival and renewal.[1] But our emphasis differs slightly, from that of Howkins in particular. This is in part because our research focus has been the landscape – the physical environment – over a rather longer period of time. But it is mainly because, as in earlier periods of history, there was much variation in the experiences of different regions.

In particular, Alun Howkins has emphasised the fact that in the inter-war years a distinctively rural way of life began to be seriously eroded by urban expansion and by suburbanisation: 'Somewhere around 1930 rural history, in the way we have hitherto understood it – as cows and ploughs, as landlord, farmer and labourer, as cottage and castle – comes to an end.'[2] Such a view, while doubtless correct for much of south-eastern England and parts of the Midlands, makes rather less sense in a region like East Anglia. There were massive social and institutional changes here: a decline in the authority of church and squire, an increasing assertiveness on the part of local communities, above all the growing involvement of local and national governments, elected by the people, in the running of the countryside. But whether in village or in farm, on smallholding or landed estate, relative geographical isolation and a paucity of employment opportunities ensured that a distinctly rural way of life was maintained at least until the outbreak of the Second World War. Suburbanisation was limited in scale, and many of the main eruptions of the non-agrarian world into the countryside were associated with the holiday industry.

It might be more useful, in terms of both the real and the imagined landscape, to conceptualise East Anglia in the period of the Great Depression, and perhaps especially in the inter-war years, as comprising three basic types of countryside. These were not necessarily spatially discrete or static: in general they were interpenetrating, and the prominence and extent of each changed over time. And they were not identified with unitary social groups or single lifestyles. Those people associated with each kind of countryside were, to some extent, distinct from and in opposition to those inhabiting the other varieties; yet each was nevertheless fractured, by class interests, by different ideas about the future of the countryside, and by different interpretations of the past and the present.

First and foremost there was what we might call the 'traditional' countryside of East Anglia, although this was in reality a world, and a landscape, which had been moulded by relatively recent social, economic and agrarian changes – by developments in the later eighteenth and nineteenth centuries. This was the countryside of large or medium-sized arable or mixed farms, whether held by tenants or owner-occupied; of landed estates, with their parks and pleasure grounds and mansions; of vernacular houses, but also of estate villages; of ancient parish churches, but also of not-so-ancient nonconformist chapels. This world was in partial and ordered retreat in the face of massive economic, social and political change, but it was not in outright decline, nor yet was it unchanging and stable. Most of its inhabitants continued to adapt to new conditions; and their ranks were constantly being replenished by individuals moving in from outside the region and buying wholesale into its established patterns of rural life, whether farmers migrating from elsewhere in England, or from Scotland, or new landowners, men who had made their money in commerce or industry or the colonies, and who now wished to adopt the lifestyle of the country squire. Some elements of the traditional landscape were, it is true, changing out of all recognition. Areas of common land were bushing over and becoming disused, and in districts where extensive areas of marginal land had been reclaimed during the previous century there were signs of dereliction. But the former areas should perhaps be seen as survivals from a still more ancient peasant countryside, which the world of estates and capitalist farms had replaced in the course of the previous centuries; while the extent of dereliction in the latter areas has, as we have repeatedly emphasised, been exaggerated.

A second kind of countryside was emerging almost everywhere in East Anglia, and was becoming dominant in certain limited areas. We might call it the landscape of rural modernity. We have just traced, in the previous chapter, its increasing manifestation in the built environment of rural settlements, in new forms of public buildings and council housing, and in the improved roads and transport systems which linked the region's villages. It was a world which shunned, for the most part, the architectural styles of the traditional countryside in favour of the modern and the functional. For this and for much else it was viewed with hostility by the controlling elements, at least, of the traditional world, who evidently saw its outward signs as direct products of outside influences, and especially of the growing power of a centralising state over the localities. Yet it was not, of course, simply an unwelcome intrusion from elsewhere. The fictional Suffolk agricultural union worker in Doreen Wallace's *The Noble Savage* was not the only indigenous inhabitant of the region who dreamed in the 1930s and 40s of the day when the countryside would be 'dotted profusely with new cottages of villa type and netted all over with wires carrying electricity. The landmarks were water towers and village halls…'.[3] In most areas these two worlds co-existed. Indeed, signs of modernity could be found to some extent everywhere, as small farms were obliged to diversify into new kinds of enterprise. Adrian Bell described how 'more and more the fields came to resemble factory sites, with these long, low poultry-sheds in the middle of them'. But this was, above all, the world of the smallholder – of orchards, horticulture, market gardens and small dairying enterprises – made most manifest, as we have seen, in the east of Norfolk and the Fens. And it was, in contrast to the 'traditional' countryside, a world of relative economic and, in particular, demographic buoyancy. To some extent it was also more mechanised, for tractors seem to have been more widely adopted on market gardens and small vegetable farms, especially in the Fens, than on the farms of the 'traditional' countryside (above, p. 35). This landscape and this society were strikingly new, yet they did not emerge from nowhere, and their particular association with the north-east of Norfolk and the Fens shows that they had deeper roots, for these areas had long been characterised by small farms, and to a significant extent by a high density of owner-occupiers.[4]

In environmental terms the 'traditional' world was characterised by areas of managed woodland, well-maintained hedges and an abundance of hedgerow timber. In contrast, we have already noted how the greatest decline in the numbers of hedgerow trees occurred in the Fens and in north-east Norfolk; and that loss of trees, and the grubbing-up of hedges, was in general most characteristic of small owner-occupied farms and smallholdings. Adrian Bell described in 1931 how the woods around Benfield in Suffolk were 'cherished for their sporting value by the yeomen', but added: 'The few smallholders were the only real enemies of trees.'[5] Mosby described in 1938 this emerging landscape in north-east Norfolk:

> The fields are of medium size – 20 to 30 acres, but there is a tendency in some areas to enlarge the fields by removing the intervening hedge. Where this has been done the farmers, particularly those who use a tractor plough, have reduced their labour costs.[6]

This was a more functional, less picturesque world than that of the 'traditional' countryside, a place for producing food rather than an arena for recreation. It was also, perhaps, a world whose creators had a shorter timescale, in which buildings were built to last for a generation, not for posterity, and in which the long-term investment represented by hedgerow timber was an economic irrelevance. Visually, it was often a world of wood and wire, asbestos and corrugated iron. Those dwelling within it, moreover, especially those cultivating market gardens or orchards, were often viewed as something distinctly 'other' by the inhabitants of the traditional countryside. To Bell, the smallholder was 'the importunate widow of the agricultural world'.[7] One of his characters described how smallholders 'always work like the devil and they've never a shilling to bless themselves with. They'd be better off by half if they went to work for somebody.'[8] They had little time or inclination for shooting

Figure 35. The Alley brothers, who farmed a vast territory in the area around South Creake in Norfolk in the early 1930s, were pioneers of mechanised agribusiness farming.

or the other 'traditional' amusements of the traditional yeoman farmer: 'These men had a stubborn and narrow existence, earning no more than day labourers yet lacking their irresponsibility, nor allowing themselves the diversions of farmers. They bartered the pleasures of life for an illusory independence.'[9]

Readers might wish to place some of the other emerging East Anglian landscapes in this 'modern' category, for although they were less closely associated with the new breed of small agricultural producer they too contrasted visibly with, and were in some sense in direct opposition to, the 'traditional' rural world: the new prairie farms emerging in parts of north-west Norfolk or, above all, the vast pine plantations in the Suffolk Sandlings and Breckland (Figure 35). The latter, in particular, were a direct manifestation of state power and a truly alien eruption in the countryside. Almost symbolically, they replaced quintessential estate landscapes and were planted indiscriminately across the derelict remains of country houses, parks and large tenanted farms.

Our third kind of countryside was, in a sense, a manifestation of the progressive suburbanisation of England in the inter-war period, although also with aspects of the 'counter-urbanisation' usually discussed by geographers as a post-war phenomenon.[10] It was the landscape of non-agricultural incomers. Although, as we have seen, there was a measure of commuter settlement on the margins of the larger East Anglian towns and cities, and in satellite villages, in both counties this was on a limited scale. More striking in both visual and social terms was the marked growth of coastal resorts, and of some Broadland settlements, the consequence both of the expanding holiday trade and of incomers settling permanently in these areas, often following retirement. This was the most internally fractured and contested countryside of the three, as we shall see, with certain 'kinds' of visitor or settler resenting the environmental impact made by others. It was also, perhaps, the most varied in its visual manifestations. At one extreme, incomers attempted to merge visually with the 'traditional' countryside which they had come to enjoy, preferably by buying some existing farmhouse or cottage. As early as 1927 Bensusan, writing about Norfolk, described how:

> The young man and still younger girl are going from the beauty of the countryside to the ugliness of the slums because there is no room for them in the village of their birth, but we may pass within a mile of their respective homes at least half a dozen charming cottages ... all in the occupation of folk from the town.[11]

Where new developments took place their architectural style often consciously echoed the kinds of houses erected by large landed estates, with gothic or picturesque details, rather than the local vernacular. Places like Thorpeness are not entirely dissimilar, for example, to model estate villages like Somerleyton. At the other extreme, however, were developments which made no concessions to the 'traditional' world – ranks of red-brick villas, sprawling settlements of bungalows and shacks. Lilias Rider Haggard was in 'daily dread that the rest of this so far untouched and lovely line of coast [of north Norfolk] will fall a victim to the builder', and went on to say:

> It is not that we are unmindful that the town dwellers want (and are entitled to) their share of this country of ours, but it is the method of their acquisition which is so painful, resulting often in a ghastly huddle of cheap and squalid dwellings, without design or plan in their placing – built of materials so foreign to our soil that they cry aloud in their incongruity.[12]

These three countrysides co-existed in East Anglia in the first half of the twentieth century, but they were not all equally represented in the texts and images produced in the period.

## REPRESENTING EAST ANGLIA

Descriptions of the East Anglian countryside in the late nineteenth and early twentieth century can be divided into two main groups. Firstly, there are those written by people most closely associated with the 'traditional' countryside – autobiographical and biographical works which described the experiences of people attempting to make a living in what is usually depicted as a difficult world: most notable among these, perhaps, are Henry Williamson's *Norfolk Farm*; the various works by Adrian Bell; George Baldry's *The Rabbit Skin Cap*; and Michael Home's books describing his early life in Breckland.[13] Merging with writings of this kind are those which are essentially polemics about life in rural England, but which in passing describe the physical face of the countryside; these were written by people ranging from Augustus Jessopp to Henry Massingham.[14] The ways in which the rural landscape is represented by these writers varies greatly, but in many of their works we see decline and dereliction. The 'traditional countryside' had been betrayed by modernity, and was in need of salvation:

> Black thistles and the frost-wreckage of nettles lay everywhere on the grass, rotten sticks and branches lay under the trees, the lane or road leading to the buildings was all water, and the yard we looked into seemed nearly three feet deep in mud.[15]

Indeed, it is largely from the writings of this group that the myth of extreme rural decline in this period is derived. Others writers, more positively, contrasted the dignity and stability of the traditional countryside with the superficiality of the new urban and suburban world. This is the East Anglia described by Betjeman in his poem *Death of King George*, inhabited by 'old men in country houses'

> … who never cheated, never doubted
> Communicated monthly, sit and stare
> At the new suburb stretched beyond the run-way.[16]

Secondly, and perhaps most importantly, is a range of travel guides and topographic works written essentially for outsiders. Some were also written *by* outsiders, like the East Anglian volumes in Arthur Mee's famous series *The King's England*. But many were the work of people who were (or who had recently become) residents, and who invariably seem to have been eager to announce this fact. W.A. Dutt's *Norfolk* (1900), typically, opens with the words: 'We Norfolk folk'.[17] These writers, too, were mainly concerned with aspects of the 'traditional' landscape, although inevitably, given their target audience, they had also to engage with aspects of the landscape of tourism.

Although written from different viewpoints and for different purposes, these various texts display a number of common themes. The first, not surprisingly, is that East Anglia is invariably depicted as a resolutely rural region. Not only was it in reality remarkably untouched by industrialisation and urbanisation, but, in addition, these characteristics became, in relative terms, more marked with the passing decades, as major conurbations in the south of England and the Midlands expanded inexorably and as – with improvements in transport – the countryside in these regions became progressively suburbanised. Even if such regions were not much *physically* changed, that is, their hamlets and villages were nevertheless becoming occupied by people whose work and lifestyle were more urban than rural in character. In the words of Professor Dennison, a member of the Scott committee who produced his own minority report in 1942, 'There are many areas in which the countryside has become essentially suburban though retaining much of its traditional appearance.'[18] Urban and suburban growth, and this kind of 'counter-urbanisation', were largely concentrated in a 'central coffin-shaped area between south Lancashire and the Home Counties'.[19] When people came to visit or settle in Norfolk and Suffolk , in contrast, they expected to find the *real* countryside, and they wanted to keep it like that.

The importance of such genuinely rural regions increased in the national psyche during the later nineteenth century as a greater and greater proportion of the population came to dwell in towns.[20] As Sheail has emphasised, 'The evolving social structures, political economy and cultural ferment of those years of industrial and urban growth could not have created a more conducive climate for nostalgia towards the countryside.'[21] But as well as being seen as a source of moral and physical health, the countryside was becoming associated with – was becoming a way of defining – Englishness.[22] The traces of the past in the physical environment and the associations of places with past events in national history were used to create a sense of pride and belonging at a time when more and more of the nation's inhabitants were living in urban and suburban worlds which lacked any real time-depth or obvious historical associations. Moreover, the wider countryside itself came to epitomise the distinctive character of the 'island nation', and the lifestyle of its inhabitants was widely seen as a living version of a common past. Nationhood, history and the rural became conflated: for only the countryside appeared permanent and traditional, a shared and stable inheritance in a rapidly changing world. Hence places like East Anglia, almost by definition, held a peculiar fascination for outside visitors. And yet, as David Matless has emphasised, a sense of Englishness was also created in this period 'through relations with elsewhere and through internal differentiation':[23] and this, coupled with increased personal mobility for a substantial section of the population, ensured that there was a greater awareness than ever before of regional variation in the character of rural lives and landscapes. East Anglia was thus perceived as having its own distinctive identity, different from that of other remote rural areas. Yet understandings of that identity changed markedly over time.

During the agricultural revolution and high-farming periods the two counties, although Norfolk especially, had mainly been renowned for their progressive, scientific agriculture – for their role as Britain's breadbasket. This was the land of 'Turnip' Townshend, of Coke of Holkham, of Trollope's great industrial farmer Mr Cheesacre, proudly showing off his immense muck heap and boasting of Norfolk's ability to feed a third of the nation.[24] But as the mid-nineteenth-century boom years of high farming gave way to depression, the East Anglian countryside was increasingly presented as a gloomy world, one of hard toil by brutalised labourers in muddy fields, of 'gangs' of women working in the wide Fenlands, themselves and their children doped on opium. The land depicted by the Norfolk novelist and farmer's wife Mary Mann in the 1880s and 90s is one of an alien workforce, quaint or brutalised by turns. While we learn little of the landscape in which they live, scattered references to their cottages and vegetable gardens, often standing in lonely, isolated locations, make it clear that this was not a happy countryside:

> In a tumble-down cottage at one extreme end of the parish of Dulditch Wolf-Charlie lives. It is one of couple of cottages in such bad condition that they are held past repairing. Year by year Sir Thomas threatens to pull them down, and year by year, merciful man that he is, holds his hand.[25]

Yet, at the same time, the two counties could also be seen as places of particular rural beauty, unsullied by industry, commerce and modernity. It is noteworthy that the reputation of John Constable grew steadily during the later nineteenth century, and by the 1890s tours of what was already being described as 'Constable Country' were being organised by Thomas Cook.[26] These twin images of the region – remote and unspoilt, yet archaic and brutalised – continued to be presented into the twentieth century, and reflected a genuine ambivalence on the part of a predominantly urban and suburban population about the countryside and about the past.

In addition, different parts of the region could be presented as more or less remote and strange than others. Representations of English regional landscapes in the first half of the twentieth century have, Dennis Cosgrove has suggested, a recurrent structure – a kind of essential mythical geography. London, civilised and familiar, lay at the nation's centre; outside were the 'heartlands' of the English landscape, an amalgam of the Home Counties, the Cotswolds and the familiar images of 'Constable Country'. Beyond this comfortable zone were the north and west, partly comprising the wild, picturesque and distant landscapes of the Lake District, Cornwall and Devon, and partly the less inviting industrial areas of northern England and south Wales.[27] East Anglia, however, fits somewhat awkwardly into this *schema*. Parts of Suffolk have a gently rolling topography, with villages of thatched cottages clustered in picturesque fashion around village greens. These areas were a recognisable part of the 'heartlands', and in the first half of the twentieth century villages like Great Bardfield were repeatedly painted, and the landscape of Constable's Stour valley was once again evoked in paintings by John Nash, who settled there in 1929.[28] Artists were also drawn to the picturesque coastal villages of Suffolk, and to ports like Blythburgh and Southwold.[29] Indeed, from the 1880s there was 'an almost tidal influx' of young painters and etchers, including Phillip Wilson Steer and Edward Stott, into the village of Walberswick; many of them were involved in the New English Art Club, established in 1886.[30] But many parts of Suffolk and Norfolk were different, or at least were represented in a very different fashion. They were less conventionally picturesque. They were ruder and more remote. 'I don't know any part of England where you feel so off the map as on the by-roads of Norfolk', commented Bertram Wooster, shortly before his car broke down: 'And there we were, somewhere in Norfolk, with darkness coming on and a cold wind that smelled of guano and dead mangel-wurzels playing searchingly about the spinal column.'[31] Moreover, physical remoteness and temporal distance were effectively conflated by some writers. By the middle decades of the twentieth century, in a world dominated by educated, liberal, urban opinion, going to Norfolk or parts of Suffolk was like going back in time, to a district of selfish squires, Victorian shooting parties and impoverished tenant farmers. In L.P. Hartley's *The Go-Between*, the mythical Brandham Hall in Norfolk is physically remote for the younger Leo, but distant and alien in another sense for the older: 'The past is a foreign country: they do things differently there.'[32]

Many writers throughout the period thus emphasised the essential otherness of the East Anglian landscape. At the end of the nineteenth century the Suffolk coast, with its long lonely beaches and curious mixture of heaths and wetlands, formed the evocative setting for several of the ghost stories of M.R. James, which often dwelt on the dangers of disturbing the dark forces lying dormant in barrows and the like, and this was a period in which the rather undramatic prehistoric monuments of East Anglia, set in their heathland landscapes, were first given particular attention by writers. In Breckland, the high tide of Victorian farming had now receded and writers like W.G. Clarke waxed lyrical about the area's ancient monuments and primeval beauty, conveniently forgetting that much of what they saw was the consequence of quite recent abandonment and recession.[33] Indeed, it is noteworthy that Breckland was effectively invented in this period by Clarke. The term does not seem to have been used as a regional label before, only being used to describe particular fields under periodic cultivation. Other writers, like H.J. Massingham in the 1920s, emphasised the vast, lonely scale of the great heathlands.[34] This was clearly not a part of the English 'heartlands', but a far less cosy world.

The paradox is that this recognition of much of the region as remote, rural and archaic was associated with improvements in transport which made it more accessible, and thus broke down its isolation. By the 1880s, as we have seen, Norwich could be reached by London in less than four hours. G. Christopher Davies' *The Handbook to the Rivers and Broads of Norfolk and Suffolk* of 1882, and his *Norfolk Broads and Rivers* of 1885, were followed by numerous other volumes, most notably those of E.R. Suffling and John Payne Jennings (Figure 36).[35] Indeed, by 1897 one reviewer was able to comment wryly that:

> Surely no spot in the British Isles has been so 'be-guided' as the Norfolk Broads … hardly a magazine exists which has not opened its pages to the flood of contributions on this apparently fascinating subject; and the whole has culminated in a shower of guide-books which enlivens the railway bookstalls with their gay exteriors.[36]

No less than thirty-three books on the Broads were received by the British Museum Library between 1880 and 1900.[37] Around the same time the beauties of the north Norfolk coast were being extolled by the journalist Clement Scott, whose *Poppy-land* (1883) described a landscape more gentle, less raw than that of James' Sandlings, but one nevertheless strangely remote and distant:

> Had I been cast on a desert island I could not have been more alone. Not a human being on the cliff, not a footfall on the beach … and mile after mile of virgin sand, unsoiled by stone or pebble.[38]

## IN SEARCH OF HISTORY

The 'traditional' East Anglian landscape which urban visitors and settlers were searching for thus embraced a range of landscapes, from domestic pastoral to the lonely and the remote. Moreover, the image of the happy cottager always existed beside that of the oppressive squire and the brutalised peasant. This was because the whole point of the countryside, and

# Rivers and Broads
## of Norfolk and Suffolk

### G. CHRISTOPHER DAVIES

Figure 36. The cover of the 50th edition of Christopher Davies' best-selling *Rivers and Broads of Norfolk and Suffolk*.

especially such 'real', remote, unsuburbanised countryside, was that it allowed visitors to escape backwards in time, and the past could be threatening as well as comforting. For again and again we encounter, in topographic writings in particular, the notion that in this remote countryside elements of the past, and often the distant past, still survived, and could be rediscovered through exploration, on foot, by bicycle and, increasingly, by car. 'Motoring became styled as a modern practice in pursuit of an older England …'[39] Yet two distinct layers of the past are generally presented in topographical writings. The contemporary East Anglian countryside was quaint, unspoilt and backward compared with the towns and suburbs. Its inhabitants spoke with an accent which was presented as idiosyncratic, archaic and comical by turns, but which many writers – even in the nineteenth century – believed was under threat of contamination by urban forms of speech, especially Cockney. P.H. Emerson's striking but carefully posed photographs of Broadland labourers, taken in the 1890s, seldom show any machinery – no steam-ploughs or threshing machines (Figure 37).[40] His subjects are equipped with simple hand-tools which would not have been out of place centuries earlier. But in addition, the countryside contained abundant traces of a more distant past, traces which in most urban areas had been erased by development. In Jessopp's words:

> In the great hives of industry which have come into existence during the present century … the men never seem to care about the *past*.... the mechanic of the town is a Sadducee. He saw every house in his street built from basement to roof. *There* there are no old closets, dim passages, and cranky holes and corners....[41]

Figure 37. P.H. Emmerson's carefully staged photographs from the 1890s deliberately emphasise the archaic, unchanging character of Broadland labourers, and of the landscape in which they live.

M.R. James' Suffolk is haunted by the ghosts of the past, and often the primaeval past: and many contemporary descriptions of the landscape are suffused with a strange nostalgia for faded glories. Norfolk and Suffolk presented many opportunities for these kinds of musings, littered as they were with vast isolated churches which told, not altogether misleadingly, of a decline from medieval greatness. The elemental force of the sea, the stories of erosion and coastal retreat, were also appealing to those in the right mood, and, combining the two, many commentators focused on the site of Dunwich, the medieval city in east Suffolk lost to the waves (Figure 38):

> And so we came to Dunwich, across the wild stretches of gorse-covered heath, weirdly impressive in the strange sunset glow peculiar to flat countries where marshlands abound. Dunwich the desolate, the city of the dead; once the most populous, the most important seaport of these shores … now a heap of ruins, a handful of crumbling grey stones …[42]

More strangely, the indigenous inhabitants of this landscape could themselves be seen as a direct link with the remote past. They were genetic relics, who preserved something of the character of the long-lost races out of which the nation had been forged. In Dutt's words:

Figure 38. 'Dunwich and Desolation', from Vincent's *Through East Anglia in a Motor Car* (1907).
For many topographic writers, East Anglia's decline from medieval greatness was epitomised by the lost
city of Dunwich on the Suffolk coast.

Taken as a whole, the farm hands, of whom the greater proportion of the rural
population consists, are good-natured folk, markedly lethargic, but generally willing to
put themselves to a good deal of trouble on behalf of strangers. Some of them, in whom
traces of Nordic descent are still evident, are sturdy handsome fellows, whose massive
forms, fair hair, and clear blue eyes make them look like Vikings.[43]

Elsewhere he described the 'typical marsh farmer' of the Norfolk Broads as 'a tall, fair-
haired, blue-eyed, ruddy-cheeked giant, who might have stepped out of the pages of the
*Saga of Burnt Njal'*.[44] In reality, the population of this particular part of East Anglia, at least,
were already a fairly cosmopolitan bunch: Arthur Patterson, in his book on the Broads,
published as early as 1909, describes one African or Afro-Caribbean waterman, while one of
his Breydon punt-gunners was a German.[45] Such variety was usually suppressed. For the
links with the nation's childhood to be maintained, the extent to which new people had
come to Norfolk and Suffolk had to be down-played, and continuities – of families, and of
ways of life – exaggerated. Addison, describing Grimes Graves, the Neolithic flint mines in
Breckland, passed immediately from the knappers of ancient times to the gunflint industry
which still at that time continued at nearby Brandon, but which had only begun in the area
in the late seventeenth century. No break between the modern and prehistoric working
could be contemplated: flint had been worked 'in the same place, and practically by the
same method, ever since'.[46]

## LANDSCAPE AND PLACE

It is noteworthy that contemporary travel writers, with a few notable exceptions, made relatively few comments about the general appearance of the countryside, beyond vague asides regarding the extent to which it was wooded or undulating. They concentrated instead on individual places, especially villages and historic buildings like churches and country houses, rather than on the spaces between them. In this respect, the serious visitor was well served with learned antiquarian books, as well as by the publications of the county archaeological societies.[47] Some of these covered not only the largest and finest architecture but also smaller farmhouses and cottages.[48] Yet the landscape context of these buildings and monuments – the character and disposition of woods and fields and settlement – received little attention in this pre-Hoskins world. The Broads (the upper river valleys at least) were, it is true, valued for their scenery, which was described at some length, and many writers praised and described the region's 'wild heathlands', especially in Breckland before the Forestry Commission obliterated them. But 'ordinary' countryside was not considered very interesting. Dutt, for example, could dismiss the whole twenty miles between Wymondham and Thetford in the following terms:

> Save for a more or less ruined church here and there, or old country house of no unusual interest, the journey is rather a barren one from the tourist's point of view, and you may prefer to make it by train.[49]

Similarly, although the scenery between Norwich and Aylsham was 'generally pleasing, and some charming "bits" are often met with, there is not much to delay you'.[50] This tendency is, perhaps, less marked in visual representations – in paintings, photographs, even postcards – but even here the focus tends to be on villages, cottages and villages, or on coastal scenes. Indeed, the most celebrated East Anglian artists of the period, such as Alfred Munnings and John Arnesby Brown, generally included landscapes only as backgrounds to scenes of rural life. The main exception, perhaps, is Edward Seago, who painted a number of notable landscapes, although these were often the same Broadland scenes that delighted the topographic writers.

The concentration of travel writers, in particular, on *places* rather than on *landscapes* was to some extent bound up with wider ideas about the nature of locality and nation. A sense of belonging and nationhood depended fundamentally on an appreciation of a shared, glorious history, and this was best conveyed to the generality of the population through association. Places were important because great men had lived there or great events had taken place there. It was thus that the local was nailed to the grander narratives of the national. When Dutt stressed in 1900 the variety of the Norfolk landscape, and argued that it was, contrary to popular belief, far more than a succession of cornfields, he emphasised not the diverse character of its topography or land use but the fact that it was full of monuments with national associations, such as 'a church containing some memorials associating the place with a great historical event or world-famous personage'.[51] This tradition continued unabated into the inter-war years, and books like William Addison's *Suffolk* or Arthur Mee's *The King's England* volumes for Norfolk and Suffolk present a succession of descriptions of churches, great houses and quaint villages, all where possible with stories connecting them with national history. Indeed, the very title of Mee's series emphasises this essential connectedness of the local and the national. In Mee's volume for Suffolk Ampton is singled out as the birthplace of Admiral Fitzroy, one of Darwin's companions on the *Beagle*; Barsham as the home of Nelson's mother; while the main claim to fame of the church at Beccles was that 'within these walls one of the most thrilling chapters of English history may be said to have begun' – with the marriage of Nelson's parents.[52] Indeed, the deeds of Nelson – 'The Norfolk hero' – loom large in many accounts of both counties. Dutt's treatment of Yarmouth in 1900, for example, is dominated by the Nelson connection, although other associations are also noted – the house where Louis XVIII stayed, and the inns where Charles II and George IV lodged.[53]

The quaint and peaceful character of rural villages and market towns was frequently contrasted with their glorious role in national history. Thornhill thus described how Bungay was a 'sleepy little place today', but it 'has passed through stirring times, and the history of England can be verified by the history of the little town'.[54] Moral lessons were to learnt as much as national pride celebrated: at Barsham, near Bungay, 'there is an "atmosphere", especially around the Church and the Old Hall. Great people have lived at Barsham, people who had ideals and were willing to suffer for them.'[55] Thornhill insisted, typically although rather unconvincingly, that 'There have been some famous people connected with Geldeston', an obscure village in the Waveney valley.[56] But places were also important for their archaeological sites, for these connected them with the past migrations and folk movements out of which the English nation had supposedly been forged. Again and again a place's association with ancient 'races' and 'invaders' is singled out for attention, even if there were, in fact, few surviving physical remains of remote antiquity. Geldeston was deemed to have been an excellent landing place in the past, and 'there was much coming and going by the different invaders, who all left traces'.[57] As we have seen, such connections with the distant racial past were also made by identifying particular characteristics in the form and physiognomy of the countryfolk. Topographers created or repeated a wide range of archaeological misinformation, some of it merely reflecting the relative infancy of archaeology as a discipline, but some motivated by a concern to identify particular monuments with suitably ancient groups – Celts, Romans, Saxons, Danes. Particularly noticeable is the tendency to attribute, wherever possible, pre-medieval origins to earthworks which most archaeologists had long accepted were of medieval origin, especially castle earthworks.

## THE THREAT FROM OUTSIDERS

To find the unspoilt and the unchanged – to discover the places where the past continued – required exploration, for the tentacles of the 'octopus' of modernity, even in remote East Anglia, were beginning to erode isolation. Dutt described in 1900 how:

> In some districts 'main road' is only another spelling of monotony: it too often means
> a straight level highway bordered by a wearisome succession of telegraph poles, and
> with an inn at fairly regular intervals. Along such routes the seeker of the interesting and
> the picturesque often journeys in vain, while all the while, not far away, down the
> winding and leafy lanes, there are charming scenes[58]

– where there was the sound of 'bird songs instead of bicycle bells'. At the start of the
twentieth century car journeys along major routes could be described almost as epic feats of
exploration.[59] But the volume of traffic and visitors increased in the inter-war years, and main
roads in particular became safer and more dependable. The growth of motoring and the
'discovery' of East Anglia went hand in hand. As one commentator observed in 1939, 'It is
only through the growth of motoring as a national pastime that the natural charm and
archaeological wealth of Norfolk have been thrown open.'[60] But at the same time, the
searcher for the 'unspoilt' was urged to travel deeper and deeper into the distant recesses
of the countryside, to avoid not simply modernity in a general sense but also the disruption
brought by fellow travellers.

For middle-class commentators (and visitors) in search of an archaic, unspoilt world
always feared that this was on the point of destruction by an influx of outsiders, often
including people of lower social status. There is an obvious paradox here, in that the books
they were writing of necessity encouraged further visitors to come to the region. Scott's
*Poppy-land*, while praising the unspoilt beauties of the north Norfolk coast and the quaint
ways of its inhabitants, did much to stimulate the burgeoning holiday industry in the area
around Cromer and Sheringham. The 'honest miller' Alfred Jermy and his family became
celebrities. China, postcards and much else liberally decorated with poppies were produced
in quantities in the locality. The frontispiece of Scott's book included a timetable for trains
from Liverpool Street Station. Over half a century later Addison's book *Suffolk*, published in
1950, assumes throughout that the visitor will travel by car: yet that does not prevent him
from complaining about the dismal impact of road traffic on the countryside. Clare in
Suffolk, for example, is praised on the grounds that 'there is none of that confused traffic
common to places on main roads, which so distracts attention from the buildings'.[61]

The problem was compounded by the fact that not all visitors could be expected to behave
in the correct ways, modes of behaviour which writers of travel books assumed were shared
by their own readers. The 'hordes' made too much noise, erected unsightly accommodation,
and instead of paying the correct attention to the great antiquities of the landscape ignored or
even vandalised them. Dutt thus bemoaned the fate of the great fifteenth-century castle at
Caister in Norfolk: 'like many other ruins, those of the castle are seen at their best by
moonlight, which fails to show the traces of the vandalism so conspicuous in the daytime.'[62]
The Broads were a particular focus for such prejudices and, as Matless has noted:

> Considerations of the 'right' and the 'wrong' reasons to visit the Broads, of the character
> of the place and the social and architectural conduct of the people within it … have

been central to definitions of Broadland since the area was appropriated for commercial activities in the late nineteenth century.[63]

Christopher Davies' popular book on the Broads was sponsored by Great Eastern Railway, but he was keen to criticise the visitors which the company had helped attract to the district. He was woken at 7 a.m. one morning while moored on Wroxham Broad by the occupants of a neighbouring boat loudly playing the piano.[64] Successive writers made similar complaints.[65] Miller described in 1935 how:

> Each year they had seen the crowds growing and the holiday season lengthening, until it seemed that the beautiful waterways would be turned into a Blackpool or a Brighton … great fleets of tripper-boats … hired yachts, floating ice-cream vendors, bum-boats and craft of every description, largely in the hands of people who had not the slightest knowledge of how to manage them.[66]

For the connoisseur of the countryside, such honeypots could only really be visited in the winter months. There were, in effect, two parallel worlds, that of the visitor and that of the indigenous inhabitants. Dutt described how by October:

> The cruising yachts which have lingered late on the rivers disappear as if by magic, and at Oulton, Wroxham and Potter Heigham the fleets of white-winged craft are rapidly dismantled, drawn up on to the 'hard' or hauled in to the boat sheds … For the next eight months the wherrymen, reed-cutters, and eel-catchers will have the rivers and Broads to themselves.[67]

## PRESERVING THE COUNTRYSIDE

The countryside of tourism – our third variety of countryside – was thus internally fractured and contested, and to some extent this was reflected in the kinds of architecture associated with different incoming social groups and the extent to which they could be visually assimilated into the 'traditional' landscape. In landscape terms, the influx of those insufficiently sensitive to appreciate the East Anglian countryside was thus manifest in the shacks and bungalows which, as we have seen, began to appear in some numbers in the inter-war years not only in Broadland but also more widely along the coast, one of the manifestations of the 'octopus' of modernity which exercised members of the Council for the Protection of Rural England from its foundation in 1926:

> There is a curiously gimcrack look about the larger waterside places on the Broads – so many new-looking wooden shanties, tottery bungalows all made of boards just clapped together, little sheds where fizzy coloured drinks and sun-spoilt sweets are sold, nothing dignified, nothing old …[68]

When issues of landscape conservation were raised in the first half of the twentieth century, it was often where the 'traditional' landscape came into conflict with the landscape of tourism. But the world of rural modernity could also, of course, be seen as a threat. A typical note in the CPRE files for 1929 reads 'The old Roman roads are being replaced by a race track, banks and hedges gone, with needless destruction of wayside beauty. A deep curb holds all the dirt, and the path is made of sticky material to which papers adhere.'[69] A Norfolk supporter of the CPRE wrote to their London Office in 1927 complaining that the 'picturesque' old bridge in Wiggenhall St Germans was to be handed over to the County Council and that a 'new ferro-concrete bridge with high arches … will be a monstrosity'.[70] In 1927 objections were raised to the use of railway carriages as dwellings on the Norwich road across Freckenham Heath while in 1936 Mr Bristow of Hunstanton wrote to the London office of the CPRE complaining about the development along the King's Lynn road, which was 'being destroyed of its charm by the continual erection of the commonist type of bungalow'. Letters commented on 'the work of destruction being carried out by the firm of Dutch Sugar Beet growers', which included a threat (never in fact carried out) to demolish the great sixteenth-century barn at Paston in north-east Norfolk.[71]

Yet, as Matlass has argued, the CPRE and those associated with it were not straightforward defenders of the 'traditional' landscape.[72] Many inter-war conservationists were motivated less by simple, reactionary nostalgia for a passing rural idyll, by a love for the traditional countryside, than by an essentially modernist agenda which prioritised the importance of state planning against the *laissez-faire* attitudes of the Victorian past – asserting, in effect, the public over the private interest. Indeed, the aims of the new society, as stated in 1926, were to 'preserve all things of true value and beauty', yet also to ensure 'the scientific and orderly development of all local resources'.[73] Significant members of the movement, such as Clough Williams-Ellis or Patrick Abercrombie, embraced the modern world to such an extent that they could even condone large-scale hedge removal on the grounds that it opened up sweeping vistas of productive corn fields.[74] It was the unplanned, scruffy sprawl of the inter-war years that filled such men with horror – the suburbs, road signs, adverts, holiday shacks and petrol stations which formed, to use the title of Williams-Ellis's famous book, 'The Octopus' that was strangling rural England.[75] Clean lines of modernity, in contrast – such as electricity pylons – were not in themselves necessarily a blot on the landscape, in the right context. The vision of the countryside shared by such men was not one which harked back mindlessly to the 'traditional' world of squires, country houses and village greens, but was also forward-looking, embracing the world of village halls, Women's Institutes, improved roads and rural housing – what we have defined here as the landscape of rural modernity. However imagined and defined, the countryside needed to be protected not only against the minor intrusions of signage, advertisements and hoardings, but also from the expansion of extractive industries, suburbs and airfields (Stamp calculated that between 1927 and 1939 nearly 800,000 acres in England and Wales had been taken out of agriculture by these things).[76]

The concept of land-use planning developed gradually during the first half of the twentieth century. The 1909 Housing and Town Planning Act provided for urban or rural district councils to formulate planning schemes for 'land in the course of development, or likely to be used for building purposes'.[77] Town and country planning, in the sense of schemes which fixed areas which might be used for industry, residences, businesses and open spaces, and laid down densities for houses, were being drawn up in many parts of Britain by the 1930s, usually those undergoing rapid development. In 1932 the Town and Country Planning Act encouraged local authorities to produce workable plans for development and to control the standard of building within their areas,[78] and urged the production of regional planning schemes. The leading town planner and president of the CPRE, Patrick Abercrombie, was employed by East Suffolk County Council, and the rural and urban district councils within the county, to produce a Regional Planning Scheme which was presented in 1934. Although east Suffolk was seen as remote and rural, there was still a need for planning so that 'Architectural seemliness could be insisted upon'. Ribbon development 'of the bungalow type' was condemned, while petrol stations often introduced a 'discordant note'.[79] But this did not mean that new developments should display a 'pedantic affectation of old-worldliness'. Instead, 'straightforward and honest building' was what was required.[80]

## MISSING MODERNITY

In the writings of Bell, Williamson and the rest the vibrant and economically buoyant world of rural modernity – of the smallholders, village halls, the electric grid and council houses – is largely absent. Its eruptions when mentioned are regarded with hostility or with resignation. When Williamson took over his Norfolk farm power lines had already been laid across one of the fields: 'It was too late to stop the concrete posts and thick black wires across the barley field; anyway, it would bring fresh power and clean light to the old and dark cottages and buildings of the countryside.'[81]

And in the writings of the topographers the modern world is almost invisible. The countryfolk are of necessity quaint and with limited horizons. Doreen Wallace is virtually alone in describing East Anglian farm workers who dreamt of a world where 'they all made enough money to buy Baby Austins, carpets and wireless sets'.[82] The reasons for such systematic omission are straightforward. A visit to the countryside was supposed to be a trip back in time: the importance of the rural lay largely in its direct connections with the nation's past. To Dutt or Thornhill contemporary agricultural or economic conditions were, by definition, of little interest: and so the depressed state of agriculture is scarcely mentioned, beyond a few vague references to the difficulties of farming 'in these hard times'. Only in the works of the 'ruralists' is a different twist given to this. For Bell or Williamson the *present* countryside does indeed represent the nation, but in moral and political decline. And in these writings we duly get some glimpse, usually greatly exaggerated, of spreading hedges, dilapidated buildings and weedy fields. In most descriptions of rural East Anglia, in contrast, the landscape *per se* hardly appears, except as the space to be crossed between places.

This, in turn, has a further implication. This attitude to the cultural landscape mirrored those to the natural environment shared by most naturalists in the inter-war years. Importance attached to particular sites and places, rather than to wider areas and territories. Blickling Hall and its estate were granted to the National Trust by Lord Lothian in 1912, but only the hall and its grounds were on show to the public. As with nature conservation, attitudes in this respect were starting to change by the 1940s, with Arthur Mee in 1941, for example, advocating that Breckland should be scheduled as a National Park, as much on cultural and aesthetic as on nature conservation grounds.[83] But for the most part, sites and places were what mattered, not the spaces between them: quaint villages, historic houses and ancient churches. Such an attitude left those concerned with the preservation of the wider historic landscape poorly prepared for the destruction which was to be wrought by agricultural intensification in the years following the end of the Second World War, as the landscape of 'rural modernity', now drawn on a scale larger than ever before, triumphed almost everywhere.

# CHAPTER 9

# Postscript: The Second World War and its Aftermath

## THE IMPACT OF MILITARY OCCUPATION

The Second World War had profound effects on the East Anglian countryside. The region was not only, as we shall see, expected to produce more food, but was also a first line of defence against attack from across the North Sea. A wide variety of sources, but perhaps most clearly the vertical air photos produced by the RAF in the immediate aftermath of the war, testify to the extent to which the area was militarised. Never before had military struggle had such an all-pervasive effect on the countryside.

Coastal defences had been constructed on some scale during the First World War but they have left little trace in the landscape: trenches were dug and pillboxes erected wherever it was thought practical for an enemy to land, with secondary lines of defence running along the Ant valley in Norfolk.[1] However, all this was minor compared with the huge efforts made during the course of the Second World War. Some coastal defences were erected soon after the outbreak of hostilities – two anti-aircraft artillery practice camps were established at Stiffkey and Weybourne in north Norfolk, for example, and a battery at Yarmouth, in 1939. But with the fall of France in 1940 activity intensified, a scarcity of resources after Dunkirk ensuring that emphasis was placed on Britain's first line of defence – its beaches.[2] The works were planned by the Royal Engineers but constructed, for the most part, by local contractors. By late 1940 there was an almost continuous band of anti-invasion defences running from King's Lynn in west Norfolk to Landguard Point in south Suffolk, which included pillboxes, gun batteries and emplacements, concrete anti-tank blocks, anti-tank and anti-glider ditches, minefields, lengths of scaffolding on the beaches, and mile upon mile of barbed wire. Defence was concentrated on the more inviting beaches and around the mouths of the principal estuaries. By 1943 there were fourteen coastal batteries in Norfolk and nineteen in Suffolk.[3] Many trenches were dug across farmland under powers granted by Defence Regulation 50, which allowed the military to enter and construct any works necessary. The damage to agriculture was particularly serious within five miles of the coast, where, according to J.B. Priestley, 'the most flourishing crop seemed to be barbed wire.'[4]

Most of these defences were removed at the end of the war – some had gone even before then – but large numbers of pillboxes remain (Figure 39). The majority are hexagonal in plan

Figure 39. Second World War pillbox at Bawdsey, Suffolk.

(DFW3/22 and 3/24 types) but there is also a scatter of square and octagonal forms, and many idiosyncratic variants also exist. Numerous examples of the concrete blocks designed to stop enemy tanks can also still be found. Other remains are rather less obvious, like the anti-glider trenches which can still be traced in a number of surprising places, as beside the Anglo-Saxon burial mounds at Sutton Hoo in south-east Suffolk. Bases for spigot gun mortars also sporadically survive. On a number of coastal marshes – as at Barthorp's Creek in Hollesley – existing drainage dykes were widened to provide anti-tank defences,[5] while the entire area of drained marshland to the south of Walberswick was deliberately flooded in order to slow down an enemy advance, and was never again reclaimed.

Not all defence was concentrated near the coast. There are also internal lines of fortification, most notably the 'Eastern Command Line' and the 'GHQ Line' which ran diagonally across Essex and Suffolk and on into Norfolk and Cambridgeshire.[6] Both are marked by pillboxes and anti-tank defences positioned beside roads and railways, especially where these cross significant rivers. Some pillboxes were made by adapting earlier structures, such as the nineteenth-century drainage mill near Ludham Bridge on the Norfolk Broads.

But it was East Anglia's role as Britain's airfield that has left the greatest mark. In 1934 there were only four active air bases in the region. By 1939, as a consequence of the 'expansion' initiative, there were fifteen, and five satellite landing grounds. But with the outbreak of hostilities construction escalated and, in all, no fewer than sixty-seven airfields, used by fighters and bombers of both the RAF and the USAF, were built in Norfolk and Suffolk during the war. They occupied some 333,259 acres: more than 1 per cent of Suffolk's agricultural area and around 7.5 per cent of Norfolk's.[7] Some of this land was of poor agricultural potential – for example, that in Breckland and the Sandlings – but land quality seems to have been a minor consideration when sites were chosen. The main requirement was for a relatively level site and many airfields were thus to be found on clay plateaux, which were moderately good farmland in most cases. The airfields were, in effect, self-contained townships, with a wide range of buildings. Land was levelled, hedges were bulldozed and woods felled on an awesome scale: even today the sites of former airfields announce their presence by the featureless emptiness of the landscape (Figure 40). A handful remain as airports, either military (Marham, Lakenheath, Mildenhall, Swanton Morley, Wattisham and, until very recently, Coltishall) or civilian (Beccles and Norwich). But most survive as relict features of the landscape. In some cases buildings and structures remain, although these are fewer with every passing year: officers' messes, aircrew quarters (mainly comprised of Nissen huts), and sometimes control towers, low two-storey features like those surviving at Langham or Lavenham. More striking are the water towers, very necessary in a flat countryside where most surrounding villages lacked piped water; and, above all, the hangers. These come in a variety of forms: 'J' and 'K' Type, with their curved quarter-inch steel-plate roofs (as at Swanton Morley); the small 'Blister' hangers, with curved roofs sweeping to the ground, now very rare; the Bellman and various 'T' types, with gabled roofs (like those at Methwold).[8]

Even when all these have gone, the pattern of the runways often remains. The main runway generally ran in the direction of the prevailing wind, roughly south-west to north-east, and was usually around 2,000 m long and 50 m wide. Two subsidiary runways formed a triangular pattern and a perimeter track gave access to numerous 'dispersal pans', where the aircraft could be concealed from attack. There are numerous variations relating to particular uses. Woodbridge in Suffolk, for example, which was opened in 1942 to accommodate returning aircraft which were badly damaged, low on fuel or otherwise in need of an emergency landing place, was equipped with a particularly large runway 3,000 yards long and 250 wide, the construction of which necessitated the felling of more than a million young trees planted in the previous decade by the Forestry Commission.[9] The runways were normally removed when the bases were abandoned, but not always. At Hethel the runway pattern forms the basis for the test track for Lotus Cars, at Snetterton for a racing circuit (the Type T hangars still stand on the opposite side of the A11). Even when they were removed, the hard core beneath often made for such poor agricultural land that they were planted up as shelter belts. Many were used to provide bases for chicken houses, their layout being strikingly 'ghosted' in this way at Longham or Weston Longville in Norfolk.

Figure 40. Weston Longville, Norfolk. This vertical air photograph, taken by the RAF in the immediate aftermath of the war, shows the immense impact made by wartime airfields on the landscape of East Anglia.

Wartime airfields also impacted on the wider countryside in a variety of ways. Footpaths and roads were closed on a scale that paralleled the great changes made in the late eighteenth and nineteenth centuries when landscape parks were created. Few of these rights of way were reinstated at the end of hostilities. Air bases occasionally had associated installations and depots: ancient woodlands made eminently suitable places for off-site bomb storage, and the small-leaved lime wood at Hockering in Norfolk was filled with Nissen huts and bomb storage bays which survive today as low sub-rectangular earthworks scattered along the edge of the old woodland rides, which were themselves provided with a hard concrete surface. The archaeology of the Second World War is so ubiquitous, and still so close to us in time, that we scarcely notice much of it, and have only recently begun to value it.

Perhaps the most dramatic and long-lived impact of the war on the rural landscape of East Anglia was the creation of the Stanford Battle Training Area in 1942. Unlike the airfields, this was intentionally located in the agriculturally marginal area of Breckland, partly to avoid the loss of productive farmland but also because the district was fairly sparsely populated. Nevertheless, three Breckland villages – West Tofts, Tottington and Stanford – together with the remaining farms in the long-depopulated parishes of Langford, Sturston and Buckenham Tofts, were absorbed into its area:[10]

> There is little you will want to hear in the way of sympathy and the last thing anyone wants to do is turn Englishmen from their homes [but] … it is essential that certain areas be reserved wholly for military purposes and therefore entirely evacuated by the civilian population.[11]

The residents – 750 in all – were promised that they could return at the end of the war but the area is still today occupied by the military, some of the villages having been converted into battle-training 'scenarios'. But, by a strange twist of fate, in terms of wildlife conservation this is now one of the most important areas in East Anglia, managed sensitively and largely unscathed by the agricultural intensification which devastated so much of the local countryside in the post-war years.[12]

The end of hostilities in 1945 did not see a complete or dramatic reduction of the military presence in East Anglia. From 1948, as the Cold War intensified, new contingents of the USAF arrived to occupy bases in the region. Improved facilities, both for the RAF and USAF personnel, and the need for longer runways as larger aircraft – especially the B-29 bombers – came into use, led to further expansion of many airfields, and the associated closure and diversion of public rights of way. The most striking and enduring impact of the Cold War on the landscape, however, was in south-east Suffolk, where the long, lonely promontory of Orford Ness was developed as a testing ground for the Atomic Weapons Research Establishment and the Royal Aircraft Establishment. The archaeology of the Cold War that distinguishes the site includes the 'Pagodas', with their huge concrete roofs designed to absorb accidental explosions – not from a nuclear bomb, but from the conventional charge associated with the delivery device.[13] This bleak and lonely place, vacated by the government in the 1990s, is now in the care of the National Trust, its grim remains now, somewhat bizarrely, firmly on the tourist map of the region.

## FEEDING THE NATION

Important though the region was as one of Britain's 'front lines', it was as the nation's bread basket that East Anglia contributed most to the war effort. The outbreak of hostilities in 1939 saw the country better prepared to increase food production than it had been in 1914: indeed, its readiness in this field was probably better than in any other area of war economics,[14] despite the fact that it was still dependent on imports for 88 per cent of its wheat.[15] Although, as we have seen, the East Anglian countryside in the 1930s was by no means a scene of decay and dereliction, many contemporaries believed that the fabric of farming – land, buildings and equipment – was deteriorating: 'inadequate capital, on the part of both farmers and landowners, is a major factor in bringing about the indifferent farming that is to be seen today.'[16] A survey of farms in Suffolk, carried out immediately before the war by the Suffolk branch of the NFU, suggested that field drainage could be improved (105,344 acres were in need of attention in this respect) and that 22,800 acres could be brought into cultivation from pasture or dereliction. The assertion that 1,232 sets of farm buildings were in need of repair should be treated with more scepticism, however, given the nature of the source, and while 15,853 acres in the county were reported to be derelict this in fact represented little over 2 per cent of its total agricultural area.[17] More reliable, perhaps, are the surveys carried out immediately after the outbreak of the war by the District Committees of the War Agricultural Executive Committee, using standard forms which still survive.[18] These included spaces for comment on the condition of the land and buildings on particular farms, and on the standard of farming practised, which was graded from A to C. These suggest that there was little derelict land in either Suffolk or Norfolk, and that it was mainly restricted to the poor, leached and acidic soils of Breckland and the Sandlings. Conditions in the former district were particularly bad. In Tottington and Sturston, for example, all the nine farms were infested with weeds and rabbits and only Mortimers Farm in Tottington was managed satisfactorily. Waterloo Farm in Sturston was run on very extensive lines, chiefly for game; Westmere Farm in Tottington was in hand but suffered from bad management, presumably, again, because game was seen as more important than agriculture.[19]

There were also negative comments about many clayland farms, but these need to be seen in the context of the urgent need to convert land from pasture to arable. Thick hedges, poor drainage and muddy access roads were part of the normal way of things on a small pasture farm, but constituted serious obstacles to cereal production, and criticism of farmers in these districts should, at least in part, be viewed in this light. It has also been plausibly suggested that the reporters favoured large holdings over small, and the claylands were characterised by small farms, often owner-occupied.[20] Of the six farmers in South Elmham St Cross, for example, four received a B grade, three for 'minor reasons' and one because of old age. The bad management of the nine-acre Grange Farm meant that the farmer was graded C and at the 782-acre Elms Farm the B-grade occupier lacked 'the average farmer's ability'.[21] Some sexism is apparent in comments about Park Farm, which was run, unusually, by a female farmer. 'She employs two or three men, but cannot manage the farm. I should say she is rather difficult.'[22] On the heavy claylands around Hempnall in south Norfolk the land had last been bush-drained, and then badly, as much as fifty years previously. Hedges had grown wide, and many ditches had been filled in. Such comments were typical, yet the farms in these districts were not simply 'dog and stick' enterprises: many, for example, were equipped with milking machines.[23] It is also noteworthy that the arable on clayland farms was in many cases described as 'good', even when the pastures were only 'fair', or infested with weeds and thistles. The farms on the heavy lands, in short, were being judged by people who believed in the urgent necessity for the creation of large-scale arable enterprises. These same biases may also explain why, while most of the land on the fertile loams of north-east Norfolk was said to be well and intensively farmed, there were exceptions among the grazing farms on the marshes, which were often described as badly managed, and among the numerous county council smallholdings in the area, many of which were deemed to suffer from 'faulty management'.[24]

But for the most part, away from the very heavy and very light land – on soils of high or medium quality – the state of farms recorded by the survey was generally good. In the intensively farmed Fenland parishes of Wiggenhall St Mary, West Walton, Terrington St John, Marshland St James and Walpole St Peter, for example, nearly all farmers were graded 'A', although a few part-timers were not spending enough time on their farms (one at Terrington St John 'puts in much of his time at an observation post'). Even the county council smallholdings in this district were found to be decently equipped and their tenants were judged to farm well, although a number of small owner-occupiers had buildings that were in a poor state, and lacked capital, and there were some criticisms of the state of drainage ditches.[25]

Other sources – such as the Land Utilisation Surveys, discussed in Chapter 2 (above, pp. 37–8) – support this general picture. There was some derelict land on the more agriculturally marginal soils and the details of hedge and ditch maintenance had been neglected on heavier land, although usually where farms were dominated by pasture; but, overall, farming was in reasonable heart. Indeed, other commentators at the outbreak of war considered that farming prospects were improving. Land prices had been rising from the mid-1930s and to some extent agriculture was already adjusting to a post-depression situation.[26] Nevertheless, much remained to be done to meet the challenge of the German blockade.

## EXPANDING PRODUCTION

The *Farmers' Weekly*, in its edition immediately following the declaration of war, stated proudly that 'British farming is mobilized up and down the country.'[27] The County War Agricultural Executive Committees (WAECs) immediately came into existence with, under them, the District Committees (DCs). These powerful bodies could order the ploughing-up of pasture for crops and even dispossess inefficient farmers and work land directly. Ploughing-up targets were laid down and in Norfolk alone 25,000 acres of grass and derelict land were to be returned to arable.[28] There were carrots as well as sticks: the Agricultural Development Act of May 1939 offered farmers a grant of £2 an acre to plough up old grass land.[29] Advertisements urged farmers to plough night and day, and the slogan 'Plough Now' regularly appeared in the local newspapers: 'Every acre brought under cultivation is a nail in Hitler's coffin.' Prices for the main agricultural products were fixed. Tractors began to appear in far greater numbers and tractor sheds became a standard building type. A wet and cold winter made work difficult, but by Easter 1940 Norfolk's 25,000 acres were nearly ploughed and, by June, this had been exceeded by 12,150 acres. Numerous commons were ploughed up with the support of the Committees – Ridlington by Mr Cargill, Thwaite by Mr Scott – 'drainage and the removal of trees resulted in wonderful crops of oats.'[30] Ranworth Common, Roughton Heath and Wacton Common were also taken on by WAEC itself and partly ploughed by the end of the war.

There was, however, some opposition to this sudden expansion of arable, as there had been during the First World War. Most farmers still relied to some extent on livestock as a source both of profit and of fertility. When in 1940 the Norfolk WAEC proposed that a further 18,000 acres should be brought into tilth during the following year, many expressed the view that the large-scale ploughing of grazing marshes and other long-established pasture which this would entail was misguided (although some, it should be noted, argued that it might improve poor, overgrazed pastures, when these were eventually reseeded at the end of hostilities).[31] In practice, the extent to which the arable acreage expanded across East Anglia during the war varied considerably from district to district, depending on how much land was already in cultivation. The Farm Surveys show, for example, that on the fertile loams of north-east Norfolk only small parcels of pasture existed which could be brought into tilth, like the ten acres on Clarke's Farm, Rollesby, which was ploughed for approved crops, or the eighteen acres in Martham, seeded with wheat.[32] In the Fens, similarly, there was very little pasture and therefore little scope for further expansion of tillage. In Breckland, in contrast, large areas of abandoned land or heath could be reclaimed: in Sturston and Tottington, for example, in 1939–40, fifty-seven acres of Eastmere Farm were ploughed up for rye and twenty-six acres for oats; ten acres at Church Farm, Tottington were planted with sugar beet; while the 96-acre Grange Farm was taken over by the WAEC to farm themselves.[33] On the heaths of east Suffolk, similarly, extensive areas of derelict arable and virgin heath were ploughed; and throughout the region isolated pockets of rough grazing were reclaimed, such as the 500 acres of Massingham Heath brought into cultivation by Weasenham Farms. As Upcher notes: 'Many other bracken-covered lands were ploughed up and have grown good crops.'[34]

The most significant and successful expansion of the cultivated acreage, however, was on the heavy clays. At Wacton in south Norfolk, for example, the WAEC gave orders in 1941 for the planting of nine acres of wheat, twenty-three acres of oats, twenty-three acres of barley, ten acres of wheat and a small quantity of peas.[35] At Hall Farm, Bawdeswell, in mid-Norfolk they ordered the ploughing-up of thirty-two acres for wheat, oats, sugar beet, oats and grass crops; a further fifty-eight acres in the parish were ploughed for wheat, oats and linseed.[36] In neighbouring Bylaugh almost the whole (325 acres) of Park Farm was ploughed in 1940 for oats, flax and sugar beet, with a further fifty acres cultivated for barley and sugar beet the following year, in spite of the poor state of field drainage.[37] In nearby Billingford the breaking-up of pasture resulted in the planting of an additional forty-three acres of oats, thirty acres of wheat and two and a half acres of potatoes in 1941.[38]

This expansion of tillage involved a range of tasks, depending on the type and condition of the land in question: whether it was light land or heavy, whether it was pasture, neglected pasture, heathland or marsh. Kelsale Lodge Farm at Saxmundham in east Suffolk was taken over by the WAEC in 1940. It covered 267 acres of heavy land, of which ninety-four were derelict pasture. No corn had been harvested on the holding for several years. Bushes were cleared and the stumps pulled up; then the land was drained using mole drains, and ditches dug out. Some of the fields were bare-fallowed to kill the weeds and improve soil texture before being cropped, and much of the land was treated with phosphates. The resultant yields were said to be good.[39] On land like this attention to drainage was crucial, not only where pastures were being ploughed but also on existing arable. In the nine years following 1939 5,052,879 acres in England and Wales benefited from improved field ditches, 371,142 acres from tile draining and 486,579 from mole draining.[40] Fifty per cent drainage grants were available: schemes were approved by WAEC and drawn up by the drainage sub-committee. No less than 8.2 per cent of the heavy land in south Norfolk and 18.8 per cent in Suffolk was scheduled for mole draining in 1940 alone.[41] In all, over 15 per cent (161,000) of Norfolk's farmland was redrained during the war.[42] The figure for Suffolk was probably similar and work carried out on the Stradbroke estates was no doubt typical: in 1941 the drainage officer had a machine available and wanted to start work on the 'Valley Farm scheme'. The fields near Blyford Wood were ditched and mole-drained, and later in the year drainage at Dooley Farm was said to be 'well ahead'. Partly as a result of all this activity the agent was able to report to Lord Stradbroke that 'Your property is in a very much better state than it was a few years ago.'[43]

Drainage was also a major consideration where wetlands were being improved or reclaimed. In the southern peat fens some areas had become waterlogged and derelict during the depression years and needed to be brought back into cultivation. Most famously, an area of no less than 1,500 acres of Feltwell and Methwold Fens was now reclaimed, new buildings erected and cereals and potatoes grown using the Land Army and labour from POW camps. 'Once they were names of desolation. They now speak for some of the most highly productive areas in Britain.'[44] Oxborough and Eastmoor Fens were also reclaimed by District Committees, and fens at nearby Wretton, Stoke Ferry and Whittington by private enterprise. Some coastal grazing marshes were likewise brought into cultivation, especially in west Norfolk. Pumping engines were erected on the Dersingham Marshes, ditches were straightened and a concrete road built: a similar scheme was undertaken on Snettisham Marsh.[45] The marshes in North Wooton and Sandringham were also ploughed, and by the end of the war almost all the Wash reclamations were in tilth. On the east Norfolk and Suffolk marshes there was less expansion of the cultivated area, although some land was ploughed, such as that between the New Cut and Hickling, 'where reeds grew to six foot high'.[46]

On poor, acid land, especially in Breckland and the Sandlings, a different range of techniques was required. A survey made of the latter district in 1941 noted that while some land only needed ploughing, fertilising and sowing with a crop of oats to bring it back into cultivation, where there was more heather, gorse, bracken and brambles treatment with a gyrotiller was required, together with heavy applications of lime.[47] Crops of rye and lupins were planted, followed in some instances by turnips, which were fed off by sheep. In some places the yields of cereal or potatoes were said to be 'excellent', but some of this land was so poor that it scarcely repaid cultivation even in these difficult times. About 116 acres of Levington Heath near Ipswich was treated in this way and, although the crops were not heavy, 'some food was produced where none grew previously'.[48]

On light land like this lime and chemical fertilisers, rather than improvements to drainage and hedges, were the key requirements, and the Agricultural Development Act provided a subsidy on lime and basic slag. Before this, the annual use of lime in the country as a whole was probably not more than 400,000 tons per annum. By 1944 this had risen to over 4 million tons.[49] Use of nitrogenous fertilisers similarly increased, by as much as 64 per cent between 1939/40 and 1940/41.[50] Of course, increased applications of lime and fertilisers and improvements in drainage were not made only where land was being brought back into cultivation. They were more generally applied also to existing arable, and it was probably largely because of such subsidised improvements that wheat yields increased in Norfolk from 17.5 cwt per acre in both 1940 and 1941 to 20.2 cwt per acre in 1942.[51]

It must be emphasised, however, that the expansion of tillage was not all directed towards an increase in the wheat crop. Where the land was particularly poor, the cultivation of oats rather than wheat was often ordered by the WAECs, as, for example, on various farms on the heavy clays in the South Elmhams in north Suffolk.[52] But it was the increase in the acreage under potatoes, a crop which had previously been mainly confined to the Fens, which was most dramatic. The acreage across Norfolk and Suffolk more than doubled from 26,689 in 1935 to 56,221 ten years later.[53] Sugar beet cultivation was also encouraged, hardly surprising given that alternative sources of sugar were now denied by the blockade. War-time conditions also resulted in new crops being planted, especially flax. In 1940 Ransomes was selling machines for dressing flax seed to a company at Glemsford Mill in Suffolk, and to His Majesty's Norfolk Flax Company at Flitcham Abbey Farm on the Sandringham estate.[54] Neither of these companies survived for long after the war.

Although the area under grass contracted markedly in the two counties, not all forms of livestock husbandry were neglected. Dairy farming continued to be promoted and new dairies were built on many farms. Cooling houses were now becoming standard and milking machines were fast replacing hand milking. Tuthill Farm, Stanfield (Suffolk), was described in 1943 as having 'two capital modern cowhouses with Alva Laval milking equipment'.[55] Even a much smaller holding, like the 46-acre Town Farm at Attleborough, where only thirty cows were kept, had 'model farm premises with good dairy accommodation from which a retail milk round is supplied' in 1944.[56]

By 1944, across England as a whole, there had been an increase of 90 per cent in the production of wheat, 87 per cent in potatoes, 65 per cent in vegetables and 10 per cent in sugar beet. Neither potatoes nor wheat needed to be rationed. True, there was some fall in livestock numbers, and perhaps a decline in the quality of some of the commodities produced, especially grain: but the achievement was impressive nevertheless.[57] And, on average, farmers' real incomes trebled during the war, as prices for farm produce doubled. East Anglian grain and potato producers gained disproportionately, especially those cultivating a large acreage: men who were best suited to benefit from government help to mechanise, drain and fertilise land. The smaller livestock farmers in the region, on the other hand, often lost out. Even when they did plough up land it was often less suited to cereal cultivation, and so yields were low. At the same time, they were obliged to contract their livestock operations due to a shortage of animal feed and grazing.

Nationally, the arable acreage rose by 5 million acres between 1939 and 1945.[58] Of course, the scope for ploughing up more land was less in East Anglia than in most regions because it was already intensely arable. True, some 83,000 acres in Norfolk and 29,957 in Suffolk were converted from pasture to tillage, but in percentage terms this only increased the arable acreage from around 75 per cent to around 80 per cent of the farmed landscape.[59] Nevertheless, the visual effects could be dramatic. As the *Eastern Daily Press* put it at the start of the ploughing campaign in 1941:

> Even the general pattern of the English scene has altered, with more frequent splashes or ploughland breaking up the green of permanent pasture. It is remarkable that an addition of little more than 10 per cent to our arable land should make such a difference to the look of the countryside.[60]

Moreover, the impact of the war on the farming landscape was not limited to the expansion of tilth. It affected the very fabric of the countryside, especially in areas of heavy land:

> The plough has been put into the pasture. Hedges have been cut down to the ground and ditches opened up everywhere. Fields which the villagers swore never had been any good, and never would be, have been coaxed into fertility. Spruce copse and oak wood alike have been felled; and even village commons have been ploughed and planted.[61]

## THE COUNTRY HOUSE AT WAR

If wartime changes in the appearance of the countryside were sometimes dramatic, the physical appearance of East Anglian villages altered rather less. There were no resources available to build houses for civilians – indeed, as soon as war broke out a circular was sent to all RDCs by the Ministry of Health instructing that only council houses in an advanced stage of construction were to be completed: work on others was to be discontinued.[62] Road improvements also came to an abrupt end, except where these were deemed strategically important, as around certain air bases. The short-term impact of hostilities on village life – the housing of evacuees, the billeting of servicemen, the removal of signposts and the rest – left no long-term mark on the landscape. Even the more dramatic incidents, such as the complete evacuation of some coastal villages – most notably Iken and Sudbourne in Suffolk – have, with the exception of the Breckland depopulations, passed without permanent physical trace. The impact of war on the rather grander landscape of the country house, however, was generally rather greater, more permanent and almost entirely negative.

Large mansions and their grounds made ideal military hospitals, divisional headquarters and service accommodation, and, given the amount of military activity in the region, it is hardly surprising that large numbers were requisitioned. Some had been occupied in the 1914–18 war, but on nothing like this scale. Langley, Shotesham, Necton, Bayfield, Melford Hall, Cranmer, Blickling, Bradenham, Sudbourne, Weeting, Raynham and Wood Rising Halls were all occupied by the army or the air force.[63] Lynford was used as an officers' hospital, Pickenham by the Red Cross, while Stow Bardolph and Woodbastwick served as convalescent homes for the injured.[64] Stratton Strawless became an RAF HQ, Bylaugh was occupied by the air ministry and served as the HQ for 100 Group, and Sprowston Hall was the Eastern Command HQ, while Didlington served as General Dempsey's HQ in the period leading up to the Normandy invasions and Rackheath was taken over by the 467th Bomber Group, which operated from an adjacent airfield that swallowed up no less than nine of the estate farms.[65] Nearby Haveringland was used as an officer's mess for another airfield. North Elmham housed German POWs, and Lexham evacuees, while its grounds were used as an army service corps dump.[66] Some East Anglian country houses had particularly distinguished war records: Bawdsey Manor, on the Suffolk coast, was occupied by the military as an experimental station from 1937 and was, in consequence, bombed no fewer than twelve times. It was here that Robert Watson-Watt and his team developed the new and immensely important military technology of radar.[67] The four giant transmitter masts, each 360 feet high, have gone (the last was removed in 2000) but underground bunkers and the transmitter block (currently under restoration) remain, together with numerous pillboxes and gun emplacements built into Cuthbert Quilter's artificial cliffs.

Whatever the precise character of military occupation of country houses, their grounds were usually covered with Nissen huts and other military paraphernalia. One visitor, arriving at Blickling Hall in 1942, described how 'we were greeted on our right by a sea of Nissen huts obliterating the orangery and on our left by an amorphous brick NAAFI complex in direct view of the front door of the hall'.[68] Parks were sometimes found military uses even when the associated mansion was not, as at Houghton and Kimberley in Norfolk, where POW camps were established. Indeed, owners tried to limit the military occupation to the grounds, as at Wolterton, where a military camp was established in the park in 1940: the

Figure 41. Flixton Hall in north Suffolk, like many East Anglian country houses, was finally demolished soon after the war (1953). Its site is occupied by farm buildings and its terraced Victorian gardens, by the designer William Andrews Nesfield, survive only as earthworks.

army wished to take over the hall itself but were eventually persuaded that the attic floor would be sufficient to house officers.[69] At Benacre, similarly, the park was covered in military buildings, ammunition dumps and a light railway, but the family continued to reside in the hall, with Polish officers occupying one wing.

By the end of the war many of these places were in a dire state. Heacham Hall was actually destroyed by fire while occupied. More usually, the hall and gardens were badly damaged and sometimes deliberately vandalised – as at Blickling, where bored soldiers attacked Bonomi's Mausoleum in the grounds using a tree trunk as a battering ram.[70] Parks were littered with Nissen huts and other semi-permanent buildings or, when these had eventually been removed, with the concrete bases on which they had stood. Where country houses have survived, few traces of military occupation usually now remain, but there are exceptions, such as the handful of Nissen huts hidden away in various recesses of Thornham Park in Suffolk, or the earthworks of the POW camp in the far north of Houghton Park. Such archaeological remains are important features of these historic landscapes, and perhaps deserve to be treated with more care than they usually receive. But many country houses have themselves become archaeological sites (Figure 41). Military occupation was often the final straw for landed families whose incomes and assets had been contracting steadily in the inter-war years. As we have already noted, more country houses were demolished, and more landed estates broken up, in the immediate aftermath of the Second World War than at any time during the depression years.

Even where country houses were not occupied their parks were often ploughed up, in whole or in part. Because they had been under grass for many years successful cultivation usually involved the application of substantial inputs of lime. Both large parks, such as Holkham, Bylaugh and Kimberley, and smaller ones, such as Bayfield, Barningham or Hoveton, were limed, ploughed and seeded.[71] The entire 1,000 acres of Euston Park on the edge of the Suffolk Breckland was brought into cultivation. Half was used to grow cereals and half sheep fodder, particularly lucerne. There was a serious problem with bracken 'and, had it not been for my 130 boys from Dr Barnado's Homes who were billeted in my house, and who worked hard every evening pulling bracken, I do not know whether the crops would have been visible at all.'[72] Extensive ploughing usually led to the loss of parkland trees, and in addition clumps and belts were often felled to help meet the wartime timber shortage. At Lexham in Norfolk no less than £5,000 worth of softwood trees was cut down.[73] In addition, gardens were neglected through lack of labour, and some formal parterres – where these still survived – were allegedly put to grass to prevent their use for navigation by enemy planes. The present appearance of many designed landscapes in East Anglia was thus radically altered by the Second World War with, in particular, a substantial loss of parkland trees and changes in the character of clumps and belts, where massive clear-fellings were usually followed by extensive invasion by sycamore.

## THE AFTERMATH OF WAR: PLANNING FOR THE FUTURE

The experience of war further encouraged the belief, which had been growing steadily throughout the inter-war years, that State intervention in the agricultural industry was both desirable and necessary. But there was much discussion – even during the war – over what sort of farming should be encouraged. One choice was between traditional mixed farming and large-scale mechanised and specialised production. Astor and Rowntree argued strongly for more specialised farming and saw a further expansion of dairying, based on cows kept on grass leys, and the production of fruit and vegetables as the best way forward, both for farmers and for the nation's health. But small farms needed to be modernised:

> The small farm must adapt and provide opportunities for specialist labour if it is to survive as something more than a place where the wife takes in summer visitors or a misanthrope can retire into unsocial seclusion guarded behind a moat by a nondescript dog and an almost shorthorn bull.[74]

The most desirable balance of cereals and grass was also a matter for debate. Menzies-Kitchen believed that future prosperity was more likely to be achieved from pasture rather than cereals, with an increase in milk production, fat cattle, sheep, pigs and poultry. The existing stock of farm buildings was unsuited to an efficient livestock industry, however, and subsidies would be needed for their improvement.[75] Hall, in contrast, believed that subsidies merely perpetuated redundant systems of production. Farming should be a modern competitive industry, not a 'way of life'. Land needed to be redistributed in larger units, for changes were needed to the farming landscape – field amalgamation, more drainage and reclamation – on a scale that private owners could never afford. All this would be expensive for the taxpayer, but less so in the long run than the continuation of subsidies.[76] Orwin, too, believed that land should be reorganised into units of a size suitable for mechanisation. Fences would have to be removed, drains piped and boundaries straightened.[77]

At the start of 1945 an article in the *Eastern Daily Press* described how the war had laid the foundations for long-term improvement in the countryside, but emphasised that further changes were required. More and better cottages were needed, as well as more up-to-date farms with modern buildings and equipment, and electricity and water supplies needed to be extended.[78] Particularly noticeable was the article's acceptance of the requirement for future planning if the countryside was to remain prosperous: there needed to be improved marketing, a secure prospect of stable prices, closer cooperation between rural and urban industry and an improvement in rural amenities.[79] One solution would be the establishment of national boards for each commodity: 'A united agriculture such as this would be, would have all the advantages and prestige of a great industry.'[80]

The experience of war had thus led not only to a revival in farming fortunes: it also witnessed a fundamental change in attitudes among the farming community. Farmers now accepted government support and intervention, and indeed expected that agriculture would remain a State-led industry: and the post-war Labour government promised to keep guaranteed prices and extend the existing system of advisory services. A faith in technology and modernity and an acceptance of the role of the State went hand-in-hand: the war had seen an increase in both mechanisation and in the application of scientific research to agriculture.

When the post-war Labour government came to formulate farming policy, with the Agriculture Act of 1947, it thus behaved, unsurprisingly, in a highly interventionist manner. The Act, which was to be the 'keystone to planned farming', continued many of the policies of the war years, during which, among other things, price levels had been guaranteed and a National Agricultural Advisory Service had been established (in 1944). The aim of the Act was to promote a stable agricultural sector, to ensure fair returns for farmers, workers and landlords, and all in all to create an 'efficient' system to boost food production.[81] It had two parts, one of which dealt with prices and production, and the other with ways of increasing efficiency. There was to be an Annual Price Review which would state price levels for wheat, barley, milk, eggs, potatoes, sugar beet, beef and pig meat for the year ahead. Grants were made available for drainage, the erection of new buildings and the application of lime, and the price of fertilisers was subsidised.[82] The wheat acreage was to be further expanded.

Continuing food shortages and a desire to reduce foreign imports in order to help in the repayment of war-time debt thus ensured that, for the most part, there was no diminution in the intensity with which land was farmed. The production of livestock also expanded. By 1946 some 8,399 acres in Norfolk alone had been returned to grass, but equally important were the adoption of more intensive methods, and the additional grassland now available because numbers of horses were in steep decline as tractors took over. In central Norfolk the importance of pigs and poultry increased, and dairying rose from 25 per cent of gross output in 1944 to 29 per cent by 1952.[83]

The late 1940s was thus a period of relative affluence in almost all branches of East Anglian farming, not just cereal production. Indeed, return on capital averaged 20 per cent across the region by 1948.[84] The outlook was better than it had been for three-quarters of a century, and price stability through government support stimulated investment and experimentation. Newspaper articles described a range of new machinery which farmers could now acquire, including crop-spraying equipment and beet and forage harvesters. Visitors to the agricultural shows were faced with a variety of tractors and, from 1948, combine harvesters, as well as by a bewildering range of new dairying equipment.[85] Articles in the local press discussed the value of artificial fertilisers, pesticides and herbicides. But as farming became more mechanised, more investment was required if holdings were to be viable: and so it was that the increase in farm size which writers like Hall and Orwin had believed was a precondition for the modernisation of farming in fact became its consequence. Moreover, as farming flourished, land prices rose, further encouraging a growth in the size of farming units. Soon, large farming consortiums began to appear: these were prepared to invest heavily in machinery, enlarge fields, remove hedges and erect large pre-fabricated buildings to support the intensive production and high outputs supported by government. Small and medium-sized family farms sold up, or expanded by absorbing the land of former neighbours. Large landowners capitalised on the booming land market: estates were sold and broken up (above, pp. 77–8).

But – in East Anglia perhaps more than elsewhere – just as important as changes in technology and government policy were changes in farming mentalities. Men like Upcher were enthused by the progress that had been made during the war, when 'With the wonderful machinery available today, bushes were pulled up, ditches cleared out and fences cut down.' 'Ninety-odd acres of wheat in a block – a fine sight.'[86] A new form of modernity was in the air. Attitudes which had formerly characterised smallholders and their ilk, and the pioneers of prairie farming in north-west Norfolk – attitudes which viewed the countryside almost entirely as a place for producing food, and were antagonistic to such things as farmland trees and hedges – were now more widely shared. The ground was being laid for the great transformation of the East Anglian landscape which was to occur in the course of the 1950s, 60s and 70s. Already, by 1950, the rate of hedge removal and field rationalisation was accelerating throughout the region. The kind of landscape which, in the inter-war years, had been largely restricted to areas where smallholdings were dominant now began to appear everywhere. Tractors worked more effectively in larger fields, particularly before the widespread adoption of the three-point linkage made it easier to lift ploughs and other equipment clear of hedges and similar obstacles. More importantly, combine harvesters, machines best adapted to the environment of a prairie, began to come into widespread use. Above all, hedge removal was easier than it had ever been, with bulldozers and mechanical diggers now widely available. In 1956 Bell could already describe how in the area around Benfield in Suffolk: 'The hedges ... are now being rooted up, the ditches piped and filled in. The fields are reverting to 'champion', that is, the big fields of our forefathers.'[87]

The following year hedgerow removal was made cheaper by the provision of government subsidies. In Norfolk alone around 500 miles of hedgerow were grubbed out each year from 1946 to 1955, rising to around 2,400 per year by 1962 and reaching 3,500 miles per year over the next four years.[88] The post-war boom was having damaging effects even where land was not being used as arable: government money was available for improving grassland by ploughing, liming and reseeding,[89] with disastrous consequences for a range of ancient, semi-natural habitats. Small and even medium-sized areas of woodland began to disappear: the *Eastern Daily Press* described how one wood at Thorpe Market, covering thirty-five acres, was clear-felled and ploughed using modern machinery at a cost of £30 an acre.[90]

The new interventionist ethos in the post-war countryside was not, however, restricted to farming. The late 1940s, 50s and 60s also saw important changes in rural settlements, although this is not the place to describe them in detail. Provision of council houses increased; improvements continued to be made to rural roads; and, above all, the electricity grid and mains water spread throughout the countryside, although provision of mains sewage lagged behind in many districts well into the second half of the century. All this represented an increased enthusiasm on the part of the State for the alleviation of the very real problems of rural life: and here, too, we see how the post-war years saw a continuation and intensification of pre-war trends, with a growing acceptance of the efficacy of government intervention. In Pilfold's words, 'The war provided the opportunity for more radical solutions in many fields to be advanced, debated and progressed.'[91] And, increasingly, the solutions involved strategic planning at a national as well as a local level.

On the eve of the war Orwin's study of Oxfordshire had exposed the poor state of rural housing and education, and had urged the improvement of village life through increased social and educational opportunities and better housing and communications. He believed that many traditional crafts had gone for good, and needed to be replaced by small industries: 'A static village is dead and the "preservation of rural England" must not be interpreted in a museum sense.'[92] These ideas were widely accepted as the war ended. Menzies-Kitchen's *The Future of British Farming*, written in 1945, thus emphasised the need for a rural planning policy which encouraged economic diversification: 'The choice in a period of depression should not be between unemployment and agriculture, but between unemployment and new industry.'[93] The most important wartime forum for future rural planning, however, was the Scott Committee – named after its chairman, Leslie Scott, a Lord Justice of Appeal, founder member of the CPRE and an active member of the Town and

Country Planning Institute – which was set up in 1942 to 'consider the conditions which should govern building and other constructional development in country areas consistent with the maintenance of agriculture ... having regard to ... the well-being of rural communities and the preservation of rural amenities.' The vice-chairman was Dudley Stamp, well respected for his work on the Land Utilisation Survey.[94]

In many ways the committee's report shared the opposition of the pre-war CPRE to the intrusion of unplanned mess into rural areas, deploring the 'ramshackle wayside cafes and filling stations which cannot properly claim the dignity of being described as buildings'.[95] It reiterated policies which had been discussed in planning circles throughout the 1930s, especially concerning the poor state of rural housing: 'we regard the improvement of rural housing as an essential prerequisite to a contented countryside.'[96] This would involve much new building, and also the provision of basic services such as electricity, water and mains sewage. The number of tied cottages would be reduced to a minimum, and village life encouraged by the provision of more village halls and playing fields. Although the report envisaged a future in which agriculture would continue to be the main employer in the village, local crafts needed to be stimulated. But larger, industrial forms of production were to be discouraged, and the arrival of commuters and second-home owners was also seen as undesirable. While the majority report advocated an improvement in farm labourer's wages so that they could pay an economic rent, a minority report by Professor Dennison pointed out that only with mechanisation and large farms could British farming hope to compete in the world market – and this would lead to a decline in the demand for labour.[97] The opposing arguments put forward by the majority and minority reports were to dominate thinking on rural issues throughout the second half of the twentieth century. What nobody seems to have envisaged, however, not even Dennison, was the extent to which the industrialisation of farming, the resultant decline in demand for agricultural labour and the steady reduction in the number of small farms would continue, even in East Anglia, and thus erode a distinctively rural way of life. At the same time, improvements in transport and the spread of car ownership opened up the countryside for settlement by an essentially urban workforce, now able to reach their place of employment with relative ease.

But what was perhaps most striking about the Scott Report was its emphasis on how the appearance and aesthetic value of the countryside were intimately connected with its exploitation. Stamp was, after all, a man with a keen knowledge of land-use history:

> We consider that the land of Britain should be both useful and beautiful and that the two aims are not incompatible. In addition to the function of producing food and timber from the land, farmers and foresters are unconsciously the nation's landscape gardeners, a privilege which they share with the landowners.[98]

Many of the ideas of the committee were adopted in the 1947 Town and Country Planning Act, which made planning a statutory duty on local authorities and provided the basis for much of the development of the rural and urban environment in the second half of the twentieth century. Yet what is noteworthy, in this period of agricultural expansion and intensification, is the fact that the Act made little or no attempt to control what farmers did on their own land, in terms of ploughing up ancient grassland and heath, removing hedges, felling trees and woods, and all the other changes to the fabric of the countryside which were developing apace. Agriculture was a factor which had to be taken into account when Development Plans were prepared, but because agriculture was not classed as 'development' farmers could change the use and appearance of their land without constraint.

Those involved in nature conservation also seem, on the whole, to have been unprepared for the scale of landscape change in the immediate post-war years. Many believed that the return to agricultural prosperity would prove short-lived, or would have only a minor impact on the character of the rural environment. It was also generally believed that the widespread acceptance of the importance and efficacy of State planning, encouraged by the experiences of the war, would be brought to bear on environmental as well as on economic matters. As Keith put it in an article in the *Transactions of the Norfolk and Norwich Naturalists' Society* as early as 1942, 'There is much thought being given today to planning a new and better England after the War....' But most conservationists envisaged, in essence, a continuation of the pre-war emphasis on 'islands of preservation'. They wanted to use government planning to create more and more protected areas – national nature reserves and national parks. At a national level the reports of both the Uthwatt and Scott Committees, which came out in 1942, raised this issue; and at a local level committees were formed in both Norfolk and Suffolk, under the aegis of the county naturalist societies, to identify areas particularly worthy of preservation. In the case of Norfolk, the Broads, the remaining unplanted areas of Breckland, various stretches of coastline, some surviving commons and heaths and a number of ancient woods were noted as potential reserves.[99] Some local people were, however, well aware that the 'reserves' policy would be poorly suited to the new, post-Depression agricultural climate, E.C. Keith, for example, arguing in a lecture to the Norfolk and Norwich Naturalists' Society in 1942 that he would 'prefer to see the whole country – this small island – treated as one National Park', and appropriately managed for the benefit of wildlife.[100]

The National Parks and Access to the Countryside Act of 1949, which allowed for the designation and management of National Parks, Areas of Outstanding National Beauty and National Nature Reserves, had a significant impact nationally, but rather less so in East Anglia. The Broads did not become a National Park until the start of the twenty-first century, and the designation of the region's three Areas of Outstanding Natural Beauty (the North Norfolk Coast, the Suffolk Coast and Heaths and Dedham Vale) had to wait until the 1960s. Nine national nature reserves (mostly coastal sites) were designated in the region, more were to follow in the 1950s,[101] and others continued to be created by private trusts, as at Minsmere by the RSPB.[102] But such policies did little to prevent the more general onslaught on the fabric of the countryside which developed in the late 1950s, 60s and 70s. The stage was thus set for the major rural controversies of the later twentieth century, as the demands of a more intensive agriculture increasingly clashed with ideas of environmental and landscape conservation.

# Conclusion

As far as we aware, this is the first published account of the development of the rural landscape of one region of England in the period of the Great Depression. Other similar studies will doubtless follow in the years to come, and some of the arguments advanced here may well be refuted, or at least drastically modified. Nevertheless, the broad outlines of our story will perhaps stand the test of time, and may be of interest not only to other landscape historians, but also to students of rural and agricultural history more generally.

Conventional accounts of the countryside see sharp discontinuities in the 1870s, and again in the 1940s. A landscape of agricultural decline, of weedy fields, outgrown hedges, decaying country houses and dwindling villages is thus neatly sandwiched, in conceptual terms, between periods of prosperity and change. We have told here a more complex story, and one characterised by a far greater degree of continuity. Perhaps the most important aspect of this is the observation that the extent of dereliction and decline in the countryside was never as great as has often been assumed. The neat, tidy landscape of the high-farming years was not suddenly succeeded by wholesale abandonment and desolation. Associated with this is the recognition that in many ways the old Victorian rural order changed only gradually in this comparatively remote region; and that the landscape of country houses, parks, estates and game preservation faded slowly, and not to any significant extent until the inter-war years. But continuities are also apparent at the other end of the chronological period covered by this book, for many features of the countryside associated in the popular mind with the post-war period had in fact made their appearance much earlier in the century. The erection of council houses in rural settlements, for example, was undertaken on some scale before the Second World War. Above all – in some places, and in some areas, at least – the progressive 'rationalisation' of the landscape, with large-scale tree loss, hedge removal and field amalgamation, was already well under way in the inter-war years.

In terms of the rural landscape the period 1870–1939, in Norfolk and Suffolk at least, was characterised not so much by dereliction and decay, but by vibrancy and change. True, conditions for a large proportion of the rural population remained appalling – nothing we have written should detract from that.[1] But new forms of land use – smallholdings, tourism, large-scale afforestation – developed, and have left an indelible mark on the countryside. Such things were only in part a response to the poor state of farming. They also reflected wider social, political and technological changes, especially the increasingly urbanised character of British society as a whole, changes in lifestyles and in the distribution of disposable wealth, and significant improvements in transport. Above all, perhaps, they were a consequence of the growing influence of central government, and of local government, on rural life. Indeed, looking back at the landscape of the early twentieth century from the perspective of the early twenty-first, what is particularly striking is the radical nature of government intervention under administrations of all persuasions: providing council housing, acquiring and planting thousands of hectares of land as national forest, and above all engineering a massive transfer of property to provide for a new class of smallholder. Agricultural depression, in other words, was only one of several influences at work on the rural landscape in this period, and many instances of apparent dereliction, most notably the changing character of heaths, fens and other commons, were in reality a consequence of a decline in tradtional forms of management which had quite different economic causes.

Most landscape historians probably under-estimate the extent of change in the countryside in the years of depression, believing that – with agriculture in the doldrums – there was little money available to make significant alterations to the environment. As we have explained at some length, such a view rests in large part on a misunderstanding of the character of the agricultural economy in this period. But it is also a consequence of the nature of the archaeological evidence. Most East Anglian farms are still dominated by eighteenth- and nineteenth-century farm buildings, and it is true that new facilities, such as cow houses and milking sheds, were often slotted into existing structures, such as stables, rather than being erected afresh. Nevertheless, in some respects present appearances are misleading. Many new buildings were erected in this period, and some completely new forms of building were developed, especially piggeries and poultry houses. But because these were generally constructed of materials less durable than those traditionally employed, they have often failed to survive into the present century. Many were built of wood, galvanised corrugated iron and asbestos. Entirely new farm complexes constructed of such materials, as we have seen, appeared in this period but have since disappeared almost entirely.

Landscapes are not simply the passive physical outcome of social and economic activity: their various elements, in all periods, also carry symbolic meaning. The ways in which they are represented – which aspects of their structure and appearance writers and artists chose to emphasise in their descriptions and depictions – were accordingly structured by specific social and political ideas. The popular perception of the Depression landscape derives from the farming press – mainly dominated by and catering for a class of traditional landowners and farmers; and from the writings of men like Bell and Williamson, for whom the dereliction of the rural landscape served as a mirror for a more general decline in a traditional way of rural life based on landed estates and on large or medium-sized arable or mixed farming enterprises. Such people, not surprisingly, focused their attention on broken fences, collapsing buildings and weedy fields. Other sources, such as contemporary photographs of the farmed landscape, reveal a very different world. Moreover, signs of economic vitality in the rural economy, epitomised above all by the expansion of smallholdings, receive scant attention from those writing in this tradition, for whom such enterprises, and their physical expression in terms of buildings, structures and a newer, bleaker landscape, were evidently regarded as an intrusion as alien in the East Anglian countryside as the expanding resorts of Broadland and the coast, or the sombre pine plantations of Breckland and the Sandlings.

Yet these representations of the countryside were not the only ones produced in this period, and others were structured by different assumptions, needs and prejudices. In an increasingly urban world, in which fewer and fewer people lived or worked in agriculture, the countryside could be invested with a range of new and often quite alien meanings. Topographic writings catered, above all, for a common need to find in the countryside an older world, perhaps even the roots of the nation: a shared inheritance which could foster a sense of national identity. Aspects of the rural environment which were obviously new could easily be categorised as threats to the unspoilt and the picturesque if they were obviously urban and intrusive in character: especially suburbs, new roads and associated structures like garages and bridges, holiday resorts, billboards and other aspects of the 'octopus'. More indigenous forms of change, however, manifested in such things as chicken sheds, smallholdings, corrugated iron and wire netting, village halls and council houses, were more problematic. They were either ignored or, in some cases, seen as another form of rural dereliction.

The observation that representations of the countryside might be structured by ideologies, and by the concerns of an essentially urban readership, is in itself hardly new. But it is one worth emphasising once again, at the conclusion of this study, because it does help to explain why so many aspects of landscape change in this comparatively recent period of our history have been forgotten or misunderstood. The kinds of attitudes to the countryside embedded in many of these writings, moreover, and especially the notion that historical and environmental importance attaches to points and places, rather than to wider landscapes, may well have contributed to the scale of devastation wrought in the countryside by post-war agricultural intensification. That devastation is often viewed simply in economic and technological terms: by the time British farming recovered from the Great Depression, that is, new technology both facilitated a transformation of the landscape and demanded it. And in the urgent situation of post-war food shortages, farmers were given full government support in their attempts to modernise the countryside. But the grubbing of hedges, the felling of trees and the ploughing of ancient grassland also manifested a particular ideology, that of rural modernity, which had been developing in the inter-war years, and which saw the countryside essentially as a factory for the production of food. Those who had controlled the 'traditional' landscape, in contrast, had seen it for the most part as an arena for a more diverse range of activities, including timber production and sport, and as something to be enjoyed for its variety, interest and aesthetics. Only in the last decades of the twentieth century, as food shortages became a memory, as middle-class dominance of the countryside was (even in East Anglia) finally achieved, and as environmental concerns became central to the perceptions of many, did the idea of a countryside with a range of uses once again begin to structure government policy and the activities of agricultural producers. But in many areas of Norfolk and Suffolk this welcome change came too late to save an ancient landscape, intricate, complex and abounding in biological and historic interest, from being destroyed forever.

# NOTES

**CHAPTER 1**

[1] Williamson 2000a, 109–18.
[2] Rowley 2006.
[3] Matless 1998; Cosgrove 1993.
[4] Simmons 2001; Sheail 1976, 1981 and 2002.
[5] Howkins 1991; Howkins 2003.
[6] Brassley et al. 2006.
[7] TNA: PRO MAF 32; Short and Watkins 1994; Short et al. 2007.
[8] Chatwin 1961; Funnell 2005; Wymer 1999.
[9] Catt 1978.
[10] Funnell 2005; Jones and Keen 1993, 260–1.
[11] Williamson 2006, 193–218.
[12] Hodge et al. 1984.
[13] Williamson 2003, 46–52; Williamson 2006, 45–7.
[14] Holderness 1984.
[15] Wade Martins and Williamson 1999.
[16] Allison 1957.
[17] Rackham 1986, 3–5.
[18] Wade Martins and Williamson 1999, 34–43.
[19] Wade Martins and Williamson 1999, 43–6, 57.
[20] Williamson 2006, 153–72; Hodge et al. 1984, 117–19, 132–5, 209–12.
[21] Holderness 1984, 211; Postgate 1973, 315.
[22] Wade Martins and Williamson 1999, 61–7; Theobald 2000.
[23] Silvester 1988.
[24] Darby 1983, 106–19.
[25] Wade Martins and Williamson 1999, 53–4.
[26] Wade Martins and Williamson 1999, 77.
[27] Edwards 1984.
[28] Muthesius 1984.
[29] Grace 1999a.
[30] Joby 2005; Robertson 1988.
[31] Wade Martin and Williamson (1999), 131–53.

**CHAPTER 2**

[1] Perry 1974; Brown 1987.
[2] 'A loss of capital so great, a period of depression so prolonged, the intrusion of so new and disturbing an element in every calculation, could scarcely fail to affect every side of farming.' Ernle 1961, 382–3.
[3] Fletcher 1961.
[4] Perry 1974, 141.
[5] Thompson 1991, 211–40.
[6] Brown 2006, 140.
[7] Perry 1974, 139.
[8] ESRO HA28 50/23/1.8 (12).
[9] Farm memoranda book of the Carter family, quoted in Thirsk and Imray 1956, 101–2.
[10] NRO BR108/12.
[11] Farm memoranda book of the Carter family, quoted in Thirsk and Imray 1956, 101–2.

[12] Brown 2006, 122.
[13] Thompson 1991, 232.
[14] Collins 2000, 2044–5.
[15] NRO BR108/13–38.
[16] NRO BR112/15.
[17] ESRO HA11 c3/23.
[18] Holkham MSA/Au/142–160.
[19] NRO HARE 6760.
[20] NRO HARE 6789/2.
[21] NRO BR143/34.
[22] NRO WLS LXVIII/28/15 479X1.
[23] NRO WLS LXVIII/28 479X1.
[24] NRO WLS LXVIII/45 479X3.
[25] NRO WLS LXVIII/26 479X 3.
[26] Turner et al. 1997, 150.
[27] EDP 30 Nov 1895, 7. Thompson's figure for 1872/3–1892/3 is 21.8 per cent for Norfolk and 30.4 per cent for Suffolk: 1991, 226.
[28] Brown 2006, 122.
[29] Wade Martins 1980, 180 and 183.
[30] ESRO HA505/2/55.
[31] NRO BU 11/472.
[32] Wolterton MS 7/3.
[33] Wade Martins 2002, 188.
[34] Wade Martins 1980, 180 and 183, 124–5.
[35] LRO HA12/D4/23.
[36] NRO Kim 5/10/4–7.
[37] TNA: PRO MAFF 66/8, 9, 11 and 12.
[38] LRO HA12 /D7/1.
[39] TNA: PRO MAFF 66/8–11.
[40] NRO GRSRML.1921.
[41] NRO BR108/18and20.
[42] Parliamentary Papers 1881, 17, 735–748.
[43] Parliamentary Papers 1881, 17, 750–760.
[44] Parliamentary Papers (1884–5), Royal Commission into the Housing of the Working Classes, 30, 588–90 and 593.
[45] Druce 1881, 375–9.
[46] Druce 1882, 64–9.
[47] Druce 1881, 379–80; Druce 1882, 90–101.
[48] Fox 1895, 51, 72.
[49] Haggard 1902, II, 382, 390–2 and 400.
[50] Haggard 1902, II, 449.
[51] NRO HARE 6514.
[52] Hunt and Pam 2002.
[53] Brown 2006, 140.
[54] A set of Norfolk show catalogues is held at the Norfolk showground, Eaton, Norwich.
[55] ESRO GC491/5/7.
[56] ESRO GC491/5/21 and Norfolk show catalogue 1898.
[57] ESRO GC491/5/8 and Norfolk show catalogues 1890s.

[58] ESRO GC491/5/8.
[59] Holkham MS E/F1/60–90.
[60] MAFF Agricultural Returns
[61] Fox 1895, 9.
[62] Norfolk Show catalogues 1888 and 9.
[63] Holkham MS E/F1/60–90.
[64] NRO WLS LXVIII/25/27 478x9.
[65] NRO WLS LX/20 429x7.
[66] Holkham MS E/F1 60–123.
[67] MAFF Agricultural returns
[68] EDP 24 August 1895, 7.
[69] Rew 1895, 31–6.
[70] Moscrop 1886, 566–664.
[71] Moscrop 1886, 594.
[72] Moscrop 1886, 640.
[73] ESRO GC491/5/13.
[74] Norfolk Show catalogue 1897.
[75] EDP 19 Jan 1895, 7.
[76] Fox 1895, 66–72.
[77] Wolterton MS 7/9.
[78] Kains Jackson 1888, 280.
[79] Jenkins 1884.
[80] Moscrop 1886, 588.
[81] NRO WLS LXVIII/15/20 479X9
[82] NRO WLS LXVIII/25/21 479X9 and LXVIII/54/11 479X4.
[83] Norfolk Show catalogue 1885.
[84] LRO HA12 /D9/1.
[85] Read 1887, 1–28.
[86] Read 1887, 8.
[87] NRO Thomas Rose, Report 1894. Gunton, MS NRO, uncatalogued.
[88] NRO WLS LXVIII/28/20/479X1.
[89] Wolterton MS 7/2.
[90] Moscrop 1886, 658–62.
[91] Trist 1971, 7–8; SRO HD238/1.
[92] Haggard 1902, 457.
[93] EDP 7 Sept 1895, 7.
[94] Biddell 1907, 385–402.
[95] ESRO HC502/12.
[96] Carson 1935, 51.
[97] Collins 2000, 208.
[98] EDP 11 June 1900, 10, and 16 July 1900, 10.
[99] Carson 1935, 45–77.
[100] Thompson 1996, 52.
[101] Collins 2000, 208
[102] NRO BR142/1–35.
[103] MERL BRNORF 9/1/50.
[104] NRO BR100/5.
[105] Holkham MS A/Au 141–91.
[106] Based on an examination of a total of 208 sales catalogues in the Norfolk and Suffolk Record Offices.
[107] NRO BR100/5.
[108] TNA: PRO IR58 51/8/31.
[109] TNA: PRO IR58 51/8/51.
[110] TNA: PRO IR58 42/1/36.
[111] TNA: PRO IR58 42/1/37.
[112] TNA: PRO IR58 (Gedgrave 42/2/72, Orford 42/2/73).
[113] TNA: PRO IR58 62/5/76.
[114] Whetham 1970, 70.
[115] EDP 9 Jan 1915, 10.
[116] EDP 23 Jan 1915, 9, 31 July 1915, 8, 28 Aug 1915, 7, 25 Sept 1915, 8.
[117] Whetham 1970, 77.
[118] NRO c/c10/15.
[119] Sheail 1974,147.
[120] NRO c/c10/15, June 1917.
[121] NRO c/c10/15, May 1917.
[122] NRO c/c10/15, June 1917.
[123] NRO c/c10/15, May 1917.
[124] NRO c/c10/15, February 1917.
[125] NRO c/c10/15, February 1917.
[126] Douet 1989, 36.
[127] Dewey 1989, 153.
[128] ESRO GC491/5/19.
[129] Sheail 1974, 151.
[130] ESRO HA11/c4/17.
[131] EDP 6 Jan 1917.
[132] NRO c/10/18, 28 March 1918.
[133] ESRO HA11/c4/17.
[134] ESRO HA11/c4/17.
[135] Douet 1989, 40.
[136] Douet 1989, 40.
[137] MAFF Agricultural Returns.
[138] NRO c/c10/18 330.
[139] NRO c/c10/18 330.
[140] NRO c/c10/18 349.
[141] NRO c/c10/19 450.
[142] Gay 1944, 5–6.
[143] Dewey 1989, 227.
[144] Whetham 1978, 116.
[145] MAFF Agricultural Returns.
[146] NRO BR111/20 and /9.
[147] Carson 1935, 51 and 55.
[148] MAFF Agricultural Returns.
[149] Parliamentary Papers, Royal Commission on Agriculture 1919, Command Paper 473.
[150] NRO BR111/9.
[151] NRO BR143/37.
[152] ESRO HA11/c4/17.
[153] For instance, Thompson 1963, 333: 'A transfer [of land] on this scale and in such a short space of time had probably not been equalled since the Norman Conquest'.
[154] Barnes 1993, 67.
[155] Douet 1989, 72.
[156] EDP 17 April 1920, 10.
[157] NRO LeeW 24/5.
[158] Douet 1989, 72.
[159] Statutes of the Realm 1920 c76.
[160] EDP 3 Jan 1920, 10.
[161] East Anglian Daily Times 12 June 1920, 9.
[162] Douet 1989, 73.
[163] Holkham MS E/F1.

164 Carslaw and Venn 1929.
165 MAFF Agricultural Returns.
166 Bensusan 1927, 42.
167 Whetham 1978, 226–8; Sheail 2002, 111.
168 EDP 15 Feb 1930, 13.
169 Carslaw et al. 1933.
170 EDP 27 Dec 1929, 11.
171 NRO BR112/36.
172 EDP 27 Sept 1930, 10.
173 EDP 12 April 1930, 12.
174 Whetham 1978, 249–53.
175 EDP 5 Jan 1935, 14.
176 MAFF Agricultural Returns.
177 Douet 1989, 155.
178 EDP 28 April 1900, 7.
179 Douet 1989, 155.
180 EDP 5 Nov 1910.
181 Douet 1989, 157.
182 Douet 1989, 157.
183 British Sugar (Subsidies) Bill; Statutes of the
   Realm 1925 c.12.
184 Trist 1971, 159.
185 Douet 1989, 157–159.
186 MAFF Agricultural Returns.
187 Butcher 1941, 323; Mosby 1938, 162.
188 EDP 19 Jan 1935, 14.
189 Douet 1989, 161.
190 Mosby 1938, 170; Butcher 1941, 339.
191 Bensusan 1927, 43.
192 Holkham MS E/F1.
193 NRO 6.10.70.
194 NRO 6.10.70.
195 EDP 20 June 1924,10.
196 EDP 5 Jan 1935, 14.
197 ESRO GC491/5/27.
198 Douet 1989.
199 Carson 1935, 55.
200 MAFF Agricultural Returns.
201 EDP 28 Dec 1935, 10.
202 Bensusan 1927, 57–8.
203 Martelli 1952, 103–4.
204 ESRO HC502/16.
205 ESRO GC491/5/39.
206 ESRO GC491/5/45.
207 NRO MEA 3/11.
208 NRO BR73/76.
209 NRO BR143/274.
210 See footnote 106.
211 ESRO GC491/5/35.
212 Rea 1949, 28.
213 MAFF Agricultural Returns.
214 Quoted in Mosby 1938, 170.
215 EDP 6 July 1935, 12.
216 NRO BR112/36 and 39.
217 Raynes 1934, 117–35.
218 Robinson 1932, 157–65.
219 Boorman 2006.

220 Keith 1954, 53.
221 Whetham 1970, 319.
222 TNA: PRO MAFF 745/281 and 742/256.
223 TNA: PRO MAFF 32/886/289.
224 Bensusan 1927, 41.
225 EDP 12 April 1924, 10.
226 EDP 19 Jan 1924, 6.
227 EDP 25 April 1925, 10.
228 Perren 1995, 41.
229 Martin 2000, 35.
230 Howkins 2003, 75.
231 Butcher 1941; Mosby 1938.
232 Oldershaw and Dunnett 1939, 56–61.
233 Mosby 1938, 213.
234 Bell 1932, 190.
235 ESRO HA11 c3/38.
236 Street 1937a, 71–8.
237 Bell 1932, 40.
238 MAFF Agricultural Returns.
239 NRO BR111/9; Holkham MS E/F1.
240 MAFF Agricultural Returns.
241 Short 1997 and 1989.
242 Foot 1994.
243 TNA: PRO IR 127/8/208 and MAFF 73/28/44; NRO
   DE/TA27 (Terrington St John) and DE/TA32
   (Walpole St Peter).
244 MAFF 73/28/53; NRO DN/TA326 (Rollesby),
   DN/TA232 (Repps with Bastwick), DN/TA363
   (Burgh St Margaret), DN/TA469 (Clippesby) and
   DN/TA731 (Ashby).
245 TNA: PRO IR 127/6/639, 640, 643, 644; MAFF
   73/28/96; NRO DN/TA411 (Forncett St Peter),
   DN/TA139 (Aslacton), DN/TA19 (Moulton St
   Michael), DN/TA501 (Wacton) and DN/TA143
   (Bunwell).
246 TNA: PRO IR 127/5/50–65; MAFF 73/78.
247 TNA: PRO IR 58/51/8/31–3; MAFF 73/38/17.

**CHAPTER 3**
1 Thirsk 1997.
2 NRO WLS LXVIII 54/11 479x4.
3 NRO WLS LXVIII/26/53 and 57 479x1.
4 Faunce De Laune 1886, 213–52.
5 Wood 1919; Mosby 1938, 242–3.
6 ESRO HA11 c23/1.
7 NRO WLS LXVII 54/5 479x4.
8 EDP 19 Nov 1910, 10.
9 ESRO GC491/5/38
10 Douet 1989, 163.
11 Haggard 1902, II, 453, 461 and 477.
12 EDP 13 Aug 1900, 9.
13 ESRO HA515/513/3/2a.
14 NRO BR112/15.
15 Carslaw 1928.
16 EDP 15 March and 19 April 1924, 10.
17 NRO BR73/32.

18 ESRO GC491/5/39.
19 ESRO GC491/5/45.
20 Norfolk show catalogues, 1926 and 1935, Rural Life Museum, Gressenhall; SRO GC491/5/46
21 *EDP* 13 Sept 1930, 12.
22 *EDP* 16 Feb 1935, 14.
23 *EDP* 26 May 1900, 7.
24 TNA: PRO IR58 45153–6.
25 NRO BR73/77.
26 *EDP* 25 Jan 1930, 10.
27 *EDP* 20 June 1925, 10.
28 *EDP* 19 July and 13 Sept 1930, 10 and 12.
29 *EDP* 9 Oct 1935, 15.
30 Mosby 1938, 167.
31 Butcher 1941, 336.
32 Douet 1989, 167.
33 Mosby 1938 183.
34 Butcher 1941, 337–8.
35 Mosby 1938, 183.
36 NRO BR143/259
37 Mosby 1938,183–4.
38 Mosby 1938, 165
39 Mosby 1938, 165.
40 Mosby 1938, 164.
41 *EDP* 7 Sept 1935, 8.
42 NRO BR143/236, 259, 271.
43 Mosby 1938, 165.
44 Bell 1932, 42–3.
45 The collection of photographs taken by the Wisbech photographer Lillian Ream are in Wisbech Museum and were described by Caterina Benincasa in a paper entitled 'Strawberries and sinners' at the Inter-War Rural History Research Group Conference 2007.
46 NRO 143/236 and 256.
47 Cavill-Worsley 1930; Mosby 1938, 243–5.
48 ESRO HC548.
49 Mosby 1938, 245–6.
50 Massingham 1937, 11.
51 Packer 2001, 3; see also Weiver 1981.
52 Bell 1941, 75.
53 Williamson 1940, 40.
54 Moore-Collyer 2001, 85–108.
55 Thirsk and Imray 1956, 26; Frere 1863; Gurdon 1863.
56 WSRO Ac.850.
57 *The Independent Vegetarian Advocate* 11 (July 1891).
58 Marsh 1982, 113–15.
59 *The Independent Vegetarian Advocate* 11 (July 1891); Kelly's *Directory*, 1908, 262.
60 Birtles 2003, 195–201.
61 Birtles 2003, 209.
62 Bird 1909, 631–70.
63 Clarke 1918, 298; 1910, 60.
64 Clarke 1918, 298.
65 Clarke 1918, 299.
66 Clarke 1918, 301.
67 Clarke 1910, 59.

68 Clarke 1910, 66.
69 Clarke 1918, 298.
70 Bird 1909, 645.
71 Butcher 1941, 336.
72 Dymond 1985, 216.
73 Birtles 2003, 205–10; 236–40.
74 Birtles 2003, 235–6.
75 Birtles 2003, 237.
76 TNA: PRO MAFF 25/36.
77 Birtles 2003, 244–7; 268–74.
78 Burchardt 2002a and b.
79 Bone 1975, 654.
80 Bone 1975, 656.
81 NRO c/c10 563 Small Holdings and Allotments committee minute book, 1889–1895.
82 Parliamentary Papers (1890–91) 1, 63: 'Bill to confirm Provisional Order by Norfolk County Council'.
83 Bone 1975, 658.
84 Rowell 1959, 109.
85 NRO c/c10563.
86 Jebb 1907, 216–18.
87 Jebb 1907, 342.
88 Bone 1975, 660.
89 NRO c/c10/566 Small Holdings and Allotments committee minute book 1909–1911.
90 Bone 1975, 661.
91 Smith 1946, 80.
92 NRO c/c10/567 Small Holdings and Allotments committee minute book 1913–1916.
93 ESRO ESCC 1194/1.
94 Parliamentary Papers 5 (cd 2903) *Report on the working of the smallholdings acquired under the Smallholdings and Allotment Act 1908.*
95 Statutes of the Realm 1919 c.59 part 1; Meredith 2006.
96 Statutes of the Realm 1919 c.59 part 2.
97 NRO c/c10/568 Small Holdings and Allotments committee minute book 1916–21.
98 WSRO WSCC 3098/1.
99 NRO c/c10/568 Small Holdings and Allotments committee minute book 1919–1920.
100 ESRO 1194/1.
101 WSRO WSCC 3098/1.
102 Norfolk Property Services, County Land Agent, 'Report' 1927: NRO, uncatalogued.
103 WSRO WSCC 3098/1.
104 ESRO ESCC 1194/1.
105 Upcher 1946, 105; *A Review of Small Holdings etc.*, Norfolk Property Services, Norfolk County Council, 1951; NRO, uncatalogued.
106 Whetham 1978, 301; Lockwood 1998.
107 Trist 1971, 40.
108 NRO c/c10/566 Small Holdings and Allotments committee minute book 1909–1913, September 1910.
109 ESRO HA11 c/417.

[110] NRO c/c10/567 Small Holdings and Allotments committee minute book 1913–1916, July 1914.
[111] *EDP* 7 Aug 1920, 10.
[112] NRO c/c10/568 Small Holdings and Allotments committee minute book 1916–1920, July 1919.
[113] NRO c/c10/568.
[114] Parliamentary Papers 1913, 15, 'Report on Small Holdings', 580–2.
[115] NRO c/c10/568, Feb 1920 Building Committee Report.
[116] NRO c/c10/569 Small Holdings and Allotments committee minute book 1921–1923, Sept 1921.
[117] *Norfolk Chronicle* 19 August 1921.
[118] NRO c/c10/569 Small Holdings and Allotments committee minute book 1921–1923, Sept 1921.
[119] NRO c/c10/571 Small Holdings and Allotments committee minute book April to October 1925, report of June 1925.
[120] NRO Norfolk Property Services, uncatalogued plan.
[121] NRO Norfolk Property Services, County Land Agent, ' Report' 1927: uncatalogued.
[122] NRO c/c10/583, Small Holdings and Allotments committee minute book September 1935–June 1937, March 1936.
[123] NRO c/c10/583 Small Holdings and Allotments committee minute book September 1935–June 1937, December 1936.
[124] NRO c/c10/585 Small Holdings and Allotments committee minute book June 1938–June 1939, June 1938.
[125] NRO c/c10/589 Small Holdings and Allotments committee minute book 1947–50, June 1948.
[126] Parliamentary Papers 1913, 15, 'Report on Small Holdings', 580–2.
[127] NRO c/c10/574, May 1927.
[128] Norfolk Property Services, County Land Agent 'Report' 1927, 3.
[129] NRO CVES 97 and 98.
[130] WSRO WSCC 3098/1.
[131] Norfolk Property Services County Land Agent, 'Report', 1927, 5: NRO, uncatalogued.
[132] NRO c/c10/573, June 1925 and 1926.
[133] NRO c/c10/581 Small Holdings and Allotments committee minute book February 1933–July 1934, June 1934.
[134] NRO c/c10/580 Small Holdings and Allotments committee minute book October 1931–February 1933.
[135] NRO c/c10/581 Small Holdings and Allotments committee minute book February 1933–July 1934, March 1933.
[136] NRO c/c10/568–76.
[137] NRO c/c10/578 Small Holdings and Allotments committee minute book February 1930–October 1930, September 1930.
[138] Ryle 1969, 185–94; Pritchard 1928, 5–7.
[139] Butcher 1941, 331.
[140] Forestry Commission archives, Santon Downham: uncatalogued leases for forest holdings, 1928, 1930, 1935.
[141] Broach 1931, 46–7.
[142] Oral history archive: Thetford Forest Project. Landscape History Group, University of East Anglia.
[143] Forestry Commission archives, Santon Downham. Forestry Commission Annual Report, year ending 30 September 1927, 32.
[144] Oral history archive: Thetford Forest Project. Landscape History Group, University of East Anglia.
[145] NRO c/c10/566, Small Holdings and Allotments committee minute book 1909–1913, October 1911.
[146] WSRO 3098/, July 1922.
[147] NRO c/c10/568 Small Holdings and Allotments committee minute book 1916–1921, September 1916.
[148] NRO c/c10/568 Small Holdings and Allotments committee minute book 1916–1921, September 1916.
[149] NRO c/c10/567 Small Holdings and Allotments committee minute book 1913–1916, June 1914.
[150] NRO c/c10/567 Small Holdings and Allotments committee minute book 1913–1916, June 1914.
[151] NRO c/c10/568 Small Holdings and Allotments committee minute book 1919–1921, April 1921.
[152] Parliamentary Papers 1918 5, 371–80.
[153] WSRO WSCC 3098/1, July 1921.
[154] NRO c/c10/569, October 1921.
[155] WSRO WSCC 3098/1, February 1922.
[156] NRO c/c10/570 Small Holdings and Allotments committee minute book 1923–1924, December 1923.
[157] WSRO WSCC 3098/1, October 1923.
[158] NRO c/c10/569 Small Holdings and Allotments committee minute book 1921–1923, December 1923.
[159] NRO c/c10/572 Small Holdings and Allotments committee minute book 1925–1926, September 1926.
[160] NRO c/c10/572 Small Holdings and Allotments committee minute book 1925–1926, September 1925.
[161] NRO c/c10/572 Small Holdings and Allotments committee minute book 1925–1926, January 1926.
[162] NRO c/c10/572 Small Holdings and Allotments committee minute book 1925–1926.
[163] NRO Smallholdings and Allotments Committee Letter Book, uncatalogued.
[164] NRO c/c10/578 Small Holdings and Allotments committee minute book February 1930–October 1930, September 1930.
[165] WSRO 3098/1, January 1931.
[166] NRO c/c10/580 Small Holdings and Allotments Committee Book 1931–1933, December 1932.
[167] NRO c/c10/580 and 581 Small Holdings and Allotments committee minute book October 1931–February 1933 and February 1933–June 1934.
[168] Sheail 2002, 12.

[169] Bell 1932, 45.
[170] Bell 1932, 140.
[171] www.applesandorchards.org.uk. Accessed 16 April 2008.
[172] Mosby 1938, 183–4.
[173] Silvester 1988.

**CHAPTER 4**
[1] Thompson 1963, 325, 330.
[2] Bujak 1997, 280–92.
[3] Offer 1981, 378.
[4] Bujak 1997, 84–5.
[5] NRO MC3.
[6] LRO HA11 c3/24
[7] NRO KIM 7/8.
[8] ESRO HA 61:436/1260.
[9] WSRO HA 507/3/353.
[10] WSRO HA 535/5/121
[11] Barnes 1993, 20–1.
[12] NRO MEA 2/8.
[13] NRO Hare 5503.
[14] Farm Economics Branch Cambridge University, School of Agriculture 30 1947, 'Land ownership in the eastern counties'.
[15] Rowley 2006, 271–3.
[16] NRO MEA 3/10.
[17] Bateman 1883; ESRO HA1/HB4/5; E500/419/6.
[18] WSRO HA535/4/1–58.
[19] Barnes 1984, 179.
[20] Kenworthy-Browne *et al*. 1981, 221, 227, 237
[21] ESRO HD1192/1.
[22] WSRO HD1180/277; Bujak 1997, 294, 298.
[23] ESRO HA535/5/72.
[24] Barnes 1993, 23.
[25] Wolterton MS 8/102/M.
[26] WSRO HD1186/11.
[27] Barnes 1993, 66–8.
[28] Barnes 1993, 67.
[29] ESRO HC539/B1, HD1346/11, HD526/1/7, HD526/1/10, HD1750/114; Barnes 1993, 67.
[30] ESRO 707/1.2; HD1180/83.
[31] NRO GRSRM 1982 158.7.
[32] WSRO HD1700/8.
[33] Barnes 1993, 80.
[34] HD 1180/80; HD1180/83.
[35] ESRO HA1/HB4/5–7.
[36] ESRO HB416/B1/91/1; 2; 3; 5; LRO 1117/335/1 and 2; Bujak 1997, 307–10.
[37] WSRO HA535 5/125.
[38] ESRO HA 222: 1335/1/2, 3, 4 and 5.
[39] Storey 1973; Kelly's *Suffolk Directory* 1937, 383.
[40] WSRO HA116: 4861/29.
[41] Kenworthy-Browne *et al*. 1981, 214, 215, 230, 250.
[42] Kenworthy-Browne *et al*. 1981, 221, 231, 234, 242, 257, 258, 265, 265.
[43] Kenworthy-Browne *et al*. 1981.
[44] LRO 1117/412/1.

[45] LRO 1117/364/4.
[46] Haggard 1902, II , 385.
[47] Forestry Commision archives, Santon Downham: Downham Hall acquisition report (no catalogue number).
[48] NRO MC3/871.
[49] Perciful 1999, 93; the paternalistic motivations are evident in the statement by Culford's owners, Lord and Lady Cadogan, that they would have 'greater enjoyment of the grounds, garden and Park if they were shared by our neighbours. It is a means of joining us together and making our lives happier and pleasanter': *Bury and Norwich Post* 17 October 1905.
[50] Thompson 1963, 1.
[51] Batey 1995; Ottewill 1989; Brown 1982.
[52] Robinson 1870.
[53] Robinson 1883.
[54] Jekyll 1899; Bisgrove 1992.
[55] *Gardeners' Chronicle* 1888, 328.
[56] *Gardeners' Chronicle* 1890, 278.
[57] Photographs in the Shrubland Hall archive, uncatalogued.
[58] Perciful 1999, 116–7.
[59] *Gardeners' Chronicle* 37, no. 991, 440; Perciful 1999, 114–15; 117.
[60] ESRO HA244 c/26/3; Williamson 2000, 161.
[61] ESRO HA244 D1/H.
[62] ESRO HA244 c/26/3.
[63] ESRO HA244 x/5/1.
[64] Alfred Jodrell's diary: Bayfield Hall, private archive, no catalogue number.
[65] Ordnance Survey 6-inch maps.
[66] NRO BR184/768.
[67] NRO MEA7/12.
[68] NRO MEA3/8, 625X7.
[69] Account books, private archive, Benacre Hall.
[70] Account books, private archive, Benacre Hall.
[71] Based on the evidence of the OS 6-inch maps. Allen 2005, 40–4.
[72] NRO PD459/48.
[73] Hartley 1953, 122.
[74] Uncatalogued note by W.O. Hassall in Holkham archives. We are grateful to the Holkham archivist, Christine Hiskey, for drawing our attention to this gem.
[75] Mosby 1938, 161.
[76] Pevsner 1961, 180.
[77] Pevsner 1961, 163.
[78] Perciful 1999, 116.
[79] ESRO HA79/2/2.
[80] Pevsner and Wilson 2002a, 531–2.
[81] Pevsner and Wilson 2002b, 665; Perciful 1999, 68–70.
[82] Perciful 1999, 60, 119–20.
[83] Pevsner and Wilson 2002b, 612.
[84] Sales Particulars, 1895, WSRO FL 574/13/3; Farquar 1984, 5; Sales Particulars, 1918, WSRO O/GOD 78.4.

85 Sales particulars, in possession of the owners.
86 Williamson 2000, 163–4.
87 Bawdsey Estate Sale Catalogue 1959: ESRO SC032/1; Bawdsey Estate Sale Catalogue 1991: ESRO SC032/8; Guide to Bawdsey Manor, privately published leaflet, n.d., ESRO.
88 *Gardeners' Chronicle*, December 1908, 406–9.
89 *Gardeners' Chronicle*, December 1908, 406–9.
90 Pevsner and Wilson 2002a, 540–1, 580, 633–4; Perciful 1993, 33, 41–2, 46–8, 49–51, 66–7.
91 SRO HA505/2/54; Wade Martins 1980, 55.
92 WSRO HD 934.
93 ESRO 438.
94 NRO MC 3/956–7, 727X2; NRO WKC 5/438, 464X4.
95 ESRO HB 416/B1/91/1 and 5.
96 NRO MEA3/569X1.
97 WSRO HD 1750/114.
98 NRO BUL 11/540/11.
99 Cresswell 1887.
100 Skipper and Williamson 1997, 14.
101 Bateman 1878, 265.
102 Fox 1895, 73.
103 Home 1946, 43.
104 Fox 1895, 72–3.
105 Butcher 1941, 349.
106 Burrell 1914, 25.
107 Williamson 1995, 124–30; Daniels 1988.
108 Mosby 1938, 178.
109 Gilston 1948, 20–3.

**CHAPTER 5**
1 Ryle 1969, 25.
2 Ryle 1969, 25–39.
3 TNA: PRO FC 18/73, 374/22, Vol. 1.
4 TNA: PRO FC 14/36.
5 Sheail 2002, 84–90.
6 TNA: PRO FC 54386/2; FC 374/24.
7 Forestry Commission archives, Santon Downham: Acquisition Files, uncatalogued.
8 Forestry Commission archives, Santon Downham: Acquisition File for Feltwell; TNA: PRO FC L3/3, Vol. 1; L3/3/15; L3/3/9; L3/1/1; Barnes 1984, 51–7.
9 Forestry Commission archives, Santon Downham: Acquisition Files; TNA: PRO FC L3/3, Vol. 1; L3/3/15; L3/1/1.
10 Forestry Commission archives, Santon Downham: Acquisition Files, uncatalogued.
11 Skipper and Williamson 1997, 21.
12 Forestry Commission archives, Santon Downham: Acquisition File, Culford, uncatalogued.
13 Forestry Commission archives, Santon Downham: Acquisition Files, Brandon and Mildenhall, uncatalogued.
14 Skipper and Williamson 1997, 23.
15 Forestry Commission archives, Santon Downham: Acquisition Files, uncatalogued.
16 Forestry Commission archives, Santon Downham: Acquisition Files, uncatalogued.
17 Forestry Commission archives, Santon Downham: Acquisition File, Walk Farm, Tunstall, uncatalogued.
18 Broach 1931.
19 Forestry Commission *Annual Reports*, 1927–1945; Forestry Commission archives, Santon Downham, *Working Plan for Thetford Forest*, Chapter 8.
20 Butcher 1941, 331.
21 *Working Plan for Thetford Forest*, Chapter 8.
22 Forestry Commission archives, Santon Downham, stocking maps, uncatalogued.
23 *Working Plan*, Chapter 10; Forestry Commission *Annual Reports* 1927–1940.
24 *Working Plan*, Chapter 10.
25 Skipper and Williamson 1997, 33–6.
26 Backhouse 1972, 6.
27 Colledge 1989, 6.
28 Ryle 1969, 58.
29 Colledge 1989.
30 Forestry Commission *Annual Report*, 1928, 33.
31 Skipper and Williamson 1997, 50–6; Forestry Commission Archives, Santon Downham: file labelled 'East Anglian Pine Thinning Project'; *Working Plan* 1959, Chapters 11 and 12.
32 Forestry Commission Archives, Santon Downham: 'A History of the Santon Downham Central Depot 1946–1988', unpublished typescript.
33 Edlin 1972, 12–14.
34 Dufton 1952–4, 67–9.
35 'O.J.S' 1934, 673–7.
36 Chard 1959, 154–89.
37 Chard 1959, 154–89.
38 Smith 1952–4, 70–1; Forestry Commission Inspector's Report, Thetford Forest, 1938; 'Working Plan Report', 1960; Ross 1935, 56–64.
39 Wass 1956, 75.
40 Ryle 1969, 265–6.
41 NRO uncatalogued; Allen 2005, 24.
42 Butcher 1941, 332.
43 Butcher 1941, 332.
44 Butcher 1941, 333.
45 Pratt 1927.
46 Haggard and Williamson 1943, 17.
47 Mosby 1938, 175.
48 Butcher 1941, 333.
49 Mosby 1938, 236.
50 Mosby 1938, 238.
51 NRO ECO20, 405X2.
52 NRO ECO1, 405X8.
53 NRO ECO20, 405X8; ECO3, 405X8.
54 NRO ECO38, 405X.
55 NRO ECO26, 405X.
56 NRO ECO28, 405X.
57 NRO ECO28, 405X.
58 NRO ECO29, 405X.
59 NRO ECO29, 405X.
60 Mosby 1938, 238.
61 NRO ECO30, 405X.
62 NRO ECO115, 405X.

[63] Butcher 1941, 238.
[64] Petch 1947a, 106–9.
[65] Dymond 1985, 176–7.
[66] Reid 1986.
[67] Wade Martins 1984, 99.
[68] Ward Lock and Co., *Cromer, Norwich and District* (n.d.), 1.
[69] Ward Lock and Co., *Cromer, Norwich and District* (n.d.), 40.
[70] Scott 1886.
[71] Ward Lock and Co., *Cromer, Norwich and District* (n.d.) Sheringham section, 38.
[72] Rouse 1982, 77–8.
[73] Rouse 1982, 77–8.
[74] Carnie 1899, 85–6.
[75] Rouse 1982, 50–1.
[76] Rouse 1982; ESRO AE150/8/8.3–8.6.
[77] NRO DC15/4/1.
[78] Mosby 1938, 199.
[79] Butcher 1941, 370.
[80] Scott 1942, 25.
[81] Sheail 2002, 36–41, 131–7; Sheail 1977.
[82] Sheail 2002, 131.
[83] Wade-Martins 1987, no. 108.
[84] Abercrombie and Kelly 1935, xi.
[85] Davies 1891, 138.
[86] Davies 1884, v.
[87] Bygott 1923, 151.
[88] Malster 1993, 92–100.
[89] Malster 1993, 91.
[90] Matless 1994, 127–56.
[91] Miller 1935, 12–13.
[92] Dutt 1905, 120–1, 151.
[93] Malster 1993, 108.
[94] Editor's comments, 'Preservation of Broadland', *East Anglian Magazine* **2, 3** (1936), 97.
[95] Carnie 1899, 55.
[96] Kemp 1924, 18.
[97] Rouse 1982, 124–7.
[98] Parkes 1912, 11.
[99] Glencairn Stuart Ogilvie in *Sunday Express*, 23 February 1930.
[100] Kemp 1924, 17.
[101] Abercrombie and Kelly 1935 , 83.
[102] EDP 2 Feb 1895, 7.
[103] The Independent Vegetarian Advocate 11 (July 1891), 43.
[104] Bell 1932, 82.
[105] EDP 31 August 1935, 12.

**CHAPTER 6**
[1] Sheail 2002, 110; Barber 1988.
[2] See, e.g., Rowley 2006, 252–3.
[3] Williamson 1940, 206.
[4] Rew 1895, 31.
[5] Fox 1895, 9.
[6] *EDP* 24 June 1905, 8.

[7] Mosby 1938, 181.
[8] Home 1944, 17.
[9] Butcher 1941, 353.
[10] Clarke 1908, 569.
[11] Butcher 1941, 353–4.
[12] Clarke 1908, 563.
[13] Butcher 1941, 367.
[14] Butcher 1941, 361–4, Appendix II.
[15] Mosby 1938, Appendix I.
[16] Butcher 1941, 364.
[17] George 1992, 193.
[18] Williamson 1997, 98–9.
[19] Wade Martins and Williamson 1999, 67–71.
[20] Jessopp 1887, 6.
[21] Rackham 1986, 191.
[22] Rackham 1986, 223.
[23] Haggard 1902, II, 506.
[24] Haggard and Williamson 1943, 97.
[25] Haggard 1946, 73.
[26] Haggard and Williamson 1943, 31.
[27] Haggard 1946, 57.
[28] The second and provisional editions of the Ordnance Survey 1:10,560 did not record farmland trees. The RAF 1946 vertical air photographs are kept at the National Monuments Record, Swindon.
[29] Haggard 1946, 8.
[30] Tennyson 1939, 13.
[31] Tennyson 1939, 14.
[32] Haggard 1946, 57.
[33] Bell 1932, 40.
[34] Tennyson 1939, 41.
[35] Tennyson 1939, 41.
[36] Butcher 1941, 362.
[37] Butcher 1941, 357.
[38] Mosby 1938, 203–4.
[39] *Proceedings of the Suffolk Naturalists' Society* 3 (1935), xcix.
[40] NRO GRSRML.1921.
[41] Clarke 1908, 563–4.
[42] Clarke 1925, 17.
[43] Butcher 1941, 353.
[44] TNA: PRO IR 18/5861. Tithe files Congham.
[45] TNA: PRO IR 18/5937. Tithe files Fulmodeston.
[46] NRO WLS XVIII/7/1.
[47] NRO HARE 5502–5503.
[48] NRO MEA3/8, 625X7.
[49] Butcher 1941, 361
[50] Butcher 1941.
[51] Butcher 1941, 361.
[52] Wolterton archives, WOLT 3/1/16–19.
[53] WSRO HA507/3/501.
[54] FitzRandolph and Doriel Hay 1926, 114.
[55] Barnes 2003, 292.
[56] FitzRandolph and Doriel Hay 1926, 71.
[57] Barnes 2003, 292.
[58] Bell 1931, 39.
[59] Barnes 2003, 311.

[60] Barnes *et al*. 2007, 395–6.
[61] Birtles 2003, 194–6.
[62] Clarke 1918, 294.
[63] Clarke 1910, 56.
[64] Rodwell 1991, 372–8.
[65] Grubb *et al*. 1969, 175–212.
[66] Norden 1618, 234.
[67] Clarke 1908; Clarke 1914.
[68] Trist 1971, 103, 110; Armstrong 1973; Williamson 2005, 70–5.
[69] White, *Suffolk Directory*, 1885, 20.
[70] Butcher 1941, 352.
[71] Clarke 1908, 567.
[72] Clarke 1908, 567.
[73] Clarke 1918, 306.
[74] Home 1944, 15.
[75] Bird 1909, 645
[76] Clarke 1918, 308.
[77] Clarke 1918, 305.
[78] Clarke 1918, 308.
[79] Haggard and Williamson 1943, 129.
[80] Forestry Commission archives, Santon Downham: acquisition file, uncatalogued.
[81] *Proceedings of the Suffolk Naturalists' Society* 3 (1935–7), lvii.
[82] Clarke 1925, 'Introduction'.
[83] Tennyson 1939, 76.
[84] Joly de Lotbiniere 1928, 673–7.
[85] Joly de Lotbiniere 1928, 674.
[86] Joly de Lotbiniere 1928, 677.
[87] *The Times* 4 May 1935.
[88] Gay 1944, 9.
[89] Gay 1944, 9; Long 1935, 76.
[90] Gay 1944, 10–11.
[91] Keith 1942, 311–18.
[92] Joly de Lotbiniere 1928, 675.
[93] Cadman 1936, 24–6.
[94] Sheail 2002, 94–7.
[95] Forestry Commission archives, Santon Downham, uncatalogued.
[96] Williamson 1997, 92–103.
[97] Dutt 1905, 140, 161.
[98] Bird 1909, 631–65.
[99] Turner 1922, 231.
[100] Boardman 1939, 14.
[101] Boardman 1939, 14.
[102] Petch 1947b, 317–19.
[103] Turner 1922.
[104] Driscoll and Parmenter 1994; 1995.
[105] Driscoll and Parmenter 1995, 3.
[106] Cavill-Worsley 1931, 104–15.
[107] Lambert 1961, 56.
[108] Ellis 1963, 32.
[109] Fowler 1947, 326.
[110] Gay 1944, 4.
[111] Petch and Swann 1968, 263.
[112] Petch and Swann 1968, 263; Simpson 1982, 142: occasional rare records, as at Felixstowe Docks in 1938, probably represent introductions from Europe.
[113] White's *Norfolk Directory*, 104–5.
[114] Southwell 1871, 14–23.
[115] Upcher 1884, 573.
[116] Stevenson 1887, 419.
[117] Gurney 1870, 25.
[118] Southwell 1870.
[119] Stevenson 1870, 17.
[120] Stevenson 1876, 306; Truck 1891, 209–11.
[121] Stevenson 1882, 135.
[122] Stevenson 1876, 306.
[123] Gurney 1870, 22–6.
[124] Petch and Swann 1968, 267; Simpson 1982.
[125] Petch and Swann 1968; Simpson 1982.
[126] Petch and Swann 1968, 266; Simpson 1982, 306.
[127] Nicholson 1914; Petch and Swann 1968, 266.
[128] Stevenson 1882, 779.
[129] Turner 1922, 228–40.
[130] Southwell 1896, 207–14.
[131] Norgate 1876, 195–206.
[132] Crompton 1870, 7.
[133] Fisher 1950, 1–13.
[134] Haggard and Williamson 1943, 128.
[135] Haggard and Williamson 1943, 128.
[136] NRO WLS LXVIII/26 479x3.
[137] Burrell 1914, 24.
[138] Norgate 1878, 458–70; Clarke 1897, 301.
[139] Petch and Swann 1968, 268; Simpson 1982, 389.
[140] Petch and Swann 1968, 264; Simpson 1982, 211.
[141] Petch and Swann 1968, 264, 267; Simpson 1982, 228.
[142] George 1992, 99–154.
[143] Southwell 1896, 207–14.
[144] Rothschild and Marren 1997.
[145] Gay 1944, 3–13.
[146] Sheail 2002, 117.
[147] Keith 1942, 312.

**CHAPTER 7**
[1] Ditchfield 1910.
[2] Howkins 1991, 11.
[3] Howkins 1991, 13.
[4] NRO BR108/12–47.
[5] NRO BR111/28–68.
[6] NRO BR112/13–42.
[7] Groves 1949, 29.
[8] Fox 1895, 77; Rew 1895, 43.
[9] NRO BR108/12.
[10] NRO BR108/26.
[11] NRO KIM5/5/11–39.
[12] Burnett 1966, 92; Mitchell and Deane 1962, 344.
[13] NRO BR112/2 and 5, 9 and 17.
[14] NRO B118/47–85 1895–1950.
[15] ESRO HC548.
[16] Bowley 1921, 171.
[17] Groves 1949, 149.

[18] Burrell 1966, 92–3.
[19] Packer 2001, 87.
[20] NRO BR108/22.
[21] NRO BR108/47.
[22] NRO BR112/13–42.
[23] NRO BR111/50 and 52.
[24] Pedley 1942, 70; 'Report of the Committee to Enquire into the Occupation of Land and the Cost of Living of Rural workers', Parliamentary Papers 1919, 8, 897.
[25] NRO BR112/29 and 32.
[26] NRO BR111/28–68.
[27] Bowley 1921, 171; Pedley 1942, 47; Report of the Committee to Enquire into the Occupation of Land and the Cost of Living of Rural workers', Parliamentary Papers 1919, 8, 883.
[28] Armstrong 1988, 167.
[29] Pedley 1942, 165.
[30] NRO BR108/12.
[31] Jessopp 1887, 117.
[32] Rew 1895, 41.
[33] Haggard 1899, 464.
[34] Parliamentary Papers 1881, Royal Commission on Agriculture, question 51924.
[35] Haggard 1899, 460–1.
[36] Wade Martins 1980, 29.
[37] Rollesby: over 70, 4; 60–70, 7; 50–60, 7; 40–50, 8; 30–40, 10; 20–30, 15; under 20, 15.
Drayton: over 70, 2; 60–70, 4; 50–60, 8; 40–50, 6; 30–40, 4; 20–30, 7; under 20, 7.
Forncett: over 70, 2; 60–70, 5; 50–60, 11; 40–50, 21; 30–40, 12; 20–30, 16; under 20, 25.
Hollesley: over 70, 1; 60–70, 3; 50–60, 6; 40–50, 7; 30–40, 6; 20–30, 7; under 20, 6.
The South Elmhams: over 70, 9; 60–70, 20; 50–60, 17; 40–50, 24; 30–40, 26; 20–30, 35; under 20, 37.
Wickhambrook: over 70, 4; 60–70, 9; 51–60, 9; 41–50, 14; 30–40, 16; 20–30, 20; under 20, 18.
[38] Wild 2004, 107–8.
[39] Baker 1953, 37.
[40] Kelly's Directories.

[41]

| Parish | Date | Total working population | No. agricultural labourers |
|--------|------|--------------------------|----------------------------|
| Rollesby | 1881 | 139 | 76 |
|  | 1901 | 128 | 66 |
| Drayton | 1881 | 138 | 51 |
|  | 1901 | 164 | 39 |
| Terrington St Clement | 1881 | 660 | 295 |
|  | 1901 | 607 | 296 |
| The South Elmhams | 1881 | 390 | 185 |
|  | 1901 | 321 | 168 |
| Hollesley | 1881 | 84 | 53 |
|  | 1901 | 78 | 36 |
| Wickhambrook | 1881 | 110 | 61 |
|  | 1901 | 186 | 90 |

[42] Mosby 1938, 187–8, 191.
[43] Mosby 1938, 187–8, 191.
[44] Abercrombie and Kelly 1935, xii.
[45] Mosby 1938, 188.
[46] Scott 1942, 23.
[47] Glynn and Oxborrow 1976; Thorpe 1992, 125–6.
[48] Haliday and Coombes 1995; Carr 1997, 140–6.
[49] Abercrombie and Kelly 1935, xii.
[50] Scott 1942, 18.
[51] Sheail 2002, 12–43.
[52] Parliamentary Papers (1884–5), Royal Commission on the Housing of the Working Classes 30, 588.
[53] Fox 1895, 17.
[54] Wade Martins 1980, 241–2.
[55] Parliamentary Papers (1884–5), Royal Commission on the Housing of the Working Classes 30, 594.
[56] Rew 1895, 45.
[57] Wolterton MS 8/102/M.
[58] TNA: PRO MAFF 66/8–11.
[59] Parliamentary Papers (1884–5), Royal Commission on the Housing of the Working Classes 30, 593.
[60] Parliamentary Papers 1893, 25, 5–6 Royal Commission on Labour.
[61] NRO BIR 200/3.
[62] WSRO EF510/1/1. We are grateful to John Broad for drawing our attention to these houses.
[63] Linsley 2005, 27.
[64] Linsley 2005, 73.
[65] NRO DC3/5/17.
[66] Packer 2001, 90.
[67] NRO PC29/2.
[68] Linsley 2005, 278.
[69] Pedley 1942, 80–5.
[70] NRO DC5/1/3–7.
[71] Linsley 2005, 84.
[72] NRO DC7/1/34.
[73] NRO DC7/1/34.
[74] NRO DC2/5/1 and 2.
[75] Wolterton MS 8/102/M.
[76] NRO DC3/5/7.
[77] NRO DC7/1/34.
[78] Pedley 1942, 80–5.
[79] Shears 1936, 4.
[80] Linsley 2005, 235.
[81] EDP 15 Sept 1937.
[82] NRO DC5/1/3.
[83] NRO DC9/1/12; DC19/6/8.
[84] EDP 26 Jan 1944.
[85] WSRO EF505/1/59.
[86] WSRO EF505/1/60.
[87] WSRO EF505/1/61.
[88] NRO DC2/3/13.
[89] Pedley 1942, 80–5.
[90] WSRO HA535/5/133.
[91] Moore-Collyer 1999, 108, 121.
[92] NRO DC4/1/19.
[93] Scott 1942, 18.

[94] Pevsner and Wilson 2002b, 740.
[95] Kelly's *Cambridge, Norfolk and Suffolk Directory*, 1916.
[96] Kelly's *Cambridge, Norfolk and Suffolk Directory*, 1916.
[97] Williamson 1993, 60–6.
[98] Kelly's *Cambridge, Norfolk and Suffolk Directory*, 1916.
[99] Williamson 1993, 60–6.
[100] Kelly's *Norfolk Directory*, 1925.
[101] Ede, Virgoe and Williamson 1994, 24–32; Williamson 1993, 67–8.
[102] Ede, Virgoe and Williamson 1994, 37.
[103] Ede, Virgoe and Williamson 1994, 13; Williamson 1993, 69–72.
[104] Hansard, third series, CXCIX, 443–4.
[105] Statutes of the Realm 1870 c75.
[106] Statutes of the Realm 1902 c42.
[107] Kelly's *Directories*.
[108] NRO c/cc22/30, 145; NRO c/cc42, 54.
[109] Pedley 1942, 112.
[110] Ashby and Byles 1923, 43–5.
[111] Wild 2004, 110–12.
[112] Wild 2004, 110–12.
[113] Kelly's *Cambridgeshire, Norfolk and Suffolk Directory*, 1916.
[114] Grieves 1999, 177.
[115] NRO BUL 4/221, 614 X 1.
[116] King 2007, 63–8.
[117] *Eastern Daily Press* 24 Jan 1919.
[118] *The Builder* 116, 7 Feb 1919.
[119] NRO PC29/2.
[120] Weaver 1920, 8.
[121] Weaver 1920, 22–3.
[122] Weaver 1920, v.
[123] J. Burchardt: paper given at University of Sussex 13 April 2007: 'Countryside, Community and Citizenship: the Rural Community Councils and the Idea of the Village Between the Wars'; Burchardt 1999.
[124] Weaver 1920, 1.
[125] *EDP* 18 and 24 Jan 1919.
[126] *EDP* 21 March 1919.
[127] K. Grieves, paper given at University of Sussex 14 April 2007, 'Memorials and inter-war iconography'.
[128] Mee 1940, 153.
[129] Bushaway 1992; Mansfield 1995.
[130] *EDP* 28 March 1919.
[131] Mee 1940, 101.
[132] NRO c/c10/230.
[133] NRO c/c10/230.
[134] ESRO 50/51/1 Jan 1891.
[135] Sheail 2002, 177.
[136] ESRO EF509/1/2.
[137] NRO DC/4/1 Minute book Highways committee, Depwade RDC.
[138] Sheail 2002, 179.
[139] ESRO 95/4, 27 February 1901.
[140] ESRO 95/4, 27 February 1901.
[141] ESRO EF509/1/2.
[142] NRO c/c10/267.
[143] NRO c/c10/267.
[144] ESRO 50/51/3 1911.
[145] ESRO EF505/1/2.
[146] NRO DC7/1/33, DC7/1/31, DC7/1/33, DC5/2/4.
[147] NRO c/c10/239.
[148] Hibbs 1989, 64.
[149] Kelly's *Cambridgeshire, Norfolk and Suffolk Directory*, 1916, Suffolk, 117.
[150] Hibbs 1989, 63, 74, 76.
[151] Kelly's *Norfolk Directory*, 1925.
[152] Abercrombie and Kelly 1935, 48.
[153] Statutes of the Realm 1930 c32.
[154] ESRO 95/8, Dec 1919.
[155] O'Connell 1998.
[156] Taylor 1965, 302.
[157] NRO c/c10/241.
[158] NRO c/c10/478.
[159] NRO RDC NRODC/3/1.
[160] NRO DC2/3/4.
[161] NRO DC2/3/8.
[162] NRO DC2/3/11.
[163] NRO DC5/1/5.
[164] NRO DC4/1/6.
[165] NRO DC7/1/34.
[166] NRO DC2/3/11.
[167] WSRO EF505/1/4.
[168] NRO D4/1/6.
[169] ESRO 95/12 1930.
[170] NRO c/c10/446.
[171] NRO c/c10/478.
[172] NRO c/c10/270.
[173] ESRO 95/8 19 September 1919.
[174] ESRO 95/21.
[175] See, e.g., Wayland RDC minutes, DC 9/1/15.
[176] NRO DC 5/4/2.
[177] NRO DC 19/6/8.

**CHAPTER 8**
[1] Brassley *et al*. 2006.
[2] Howkins 2006, 24.
[3] Wallace 1945, 20.
[4] Wade Martins and Williamson 1999, 76–7.
[5] Bell 1931, 39.
[6] Mosby 1938, 203–4.
[7] Bell 1931, 97.
[8] Bell 1931, 97.
[9] Bell 1931, 39.
[10] Whitehand and Carr 2002; Swenarton 2002.
[11] Bensusan 1927, 39.
[12] Haggard and Williamson 1943, 195.
[13] Baldry 1939; Home 1934; Home 1944; Home 1946; see also Snell 1998.
[14] Jessopp 1887.

[15] Williamson 1940, 37.
[16] Betjeman 1958, 45.
[17] Dutt 1900, 1.
[18] Scott 1942, 110.
[19] Sheail 2002, 30.
[20] Bunce 1994.
[21] Sheail 2002, 103.
[22] Matless 1998, 25–61.
[23] Matless 1998, 20.
[24] Trollope 1980, 117.
[25] Mann 1991, 112.
[26] Daniels 1991, 9–17.
[27] Cosgrove 1993, 281–305.
[28] Howard 1991, 149, 165.
[29] Kneale 1973; Howard 1991, 111, 117, 144.
[30] Scott 2002, 26–49.
[31] Wodehouse 1930, 322.
[32] Hartley 1953, 9.
[33] Clarke 1925.
[34] Clarke 1925, 'Introduction'.
[35] Cleveland 1986, 86–7.
[36] Quoted in Malster 1993, 79.
[37] Taylor 1986, 77.
[38] Scott 1886, 18.
[39] Matless 1998, 64.
[40] Knights 1986, 12–20.
[41] Jessopp 1887, 69 and 71.
[42] Berlyn 1894, 199.
[43] Dutt 1900, 11–12.
[44] Dutt 1905, 85.
[45] Patterson 1909, 41.
[46] Addison 1950.
[47] The Norfolk and Norwich Archaeological Society was founded in 1846 and the Suffolk Institute of Archaeology in 1848.
[48] e.g. Messent 1928.
[49] Dutt 1900, 47.
[50] Dutt 1900, 134.
[51] Dutt 1900, 13.
[52] Mee 1941, 18, 32, 36–7.
[53] Dutt 1900, 59.
[54] Thornhill n.d., 15.
[55] Thornhill n.d., 7.
[56] Thornhill n.d., 31.
[57] Thornhill n.d., 29.
[58] Dutt 1900, 37.
[59] e.g. Vincent 1907.
[60] Anon. 1939, 13.
[61] Addison 1950, 27.
[62] Dutt 1900, 80.
[63] Matless 1998, 10.
[64] Davies 1891, 68.
[65] Matless 1994, 127–56.
[66] Miller 1935, 12–13.
[67] Dutt 1905, 56.
[68] Redstone 1939.
[69] Jones 1990, 253.

[70] CPRE MS: Norwich Office, uncatalogued.
[71] CPRE MS correspondence, Norwich Office, uncatalogued.
[72] Matless 1998.
[73] Sheail 2002, 106.
[74] Matless 1998, 44; Abercrombie 1943, 202–4.
[75] Williams-Ellis 1928.
[76] Stamp 1948, 432 and 438.
[77] Sheail 2002, 22.
[78] For a detailed discussion of inter-war planning see Sheail 1981.
[79] Abercrombie and Kelly 1935, passim.
[80] Abercrombie and Kelly 1935, xi.
[81] Williamson 1940, 93.
[82] Wallace 1945, 20.
[83] Mee 1941, 5.

**CHAPTER 9**
[1] Kent 1988; Gliddon 1988.
[2] Dobinson 1996.
[3] Kent 2005, 180–1.
[4] Foot 2006, 134.
[5] Newsome 2003, 49.
[6] Kent 1999, 186–7; Newsome 2003, 42–58.
[7] TNA: PRO MAFF 38/574.
[8] Bowyer 1979; Freeman 1999, 188–9.
[9] Bowyer 1992, 59–60, 142, 218–21.
[10] Perry and Perry 1999.
[11] Perry and Perry 1999, 267.
[12] Foot 2006, 137.
[13] Kinsey 1981.
[14] Wilt 2001, 2.
[15] Martin 2006, 23.
[16] Hall 1941, 111–12.
[17] Trist 1971, 341.
[18] TNA: PRO MAFF 32.
[19] TNA: PRO MAFF 32 744/725 and 740/316.
[20] Martin 2006, 27.
[21] TNA: PRO MAFF 32 891/112.
[22] TNA: PRO MAFF 32 745/99.
[23] TNA: PRO MAFF 32 720/166.
[24] TNA: PRO MAFF 32 734/147 (Rollesby) and 728/141 (Martham).
[25] TNA: PRO MAFF 32 748/266 (Wiggenhall St Mary), 747/264 (West Walton), 745/261 (Walpole St Peter) and 742/256 (Terrington St John).
[26] NRO c/c10/582, September 1936.
[27] *Farmers' Weekly* 8 Sept 1939.
[28] Douet 1989, 266.
[29] Douet 1989, 268.
[30] Upcher 1946, 102; Birtles 2003, 200–30.
[31] *EDP* 6 July 1940, 3; 7 Sept 1940, 3; 14 Sept 1940, 3; and 5 Oct 1940, 3.
[32] TNA: PRO MAFF 32/734/147.
[33] TNA: PRO MAFF 32 744/725 Tottington and 740/316 Sturston.
[34] Upcher 1946, 101.

[35] TNA: PRO MAFF 32 745/99.
[36] TNA: PRO MAFF 32 708/158.
[37] TNA: PRO MAFF 32 711/162.
[38] TNA: PRO MAFF 32 709/159.
[39] Keith *et al*. 1942, 116–17.
[40] Nicholson 1948, 212–21, 213.
[41] Nicholson 1948, 212–21, 214.
[42] Douet 1989, 271.
[43] ESRO HA11 c4/20.
[44] Ministry of Information 1945.
[45] Upcher 1946, 101.
[46] Upcher 1946, 101.
[47] Trist 1971.
[48] Keith *et al*. 1942, 113–15.
[49] Robinson 1943, 136, 138.
[50] Murray 1955, 112.
[51] MAFF Agricultural Statistics.
[52] TNA: PRO MAF 32 891/111.
[53] University of Cambridge, School of Agriculture, Farm Economics Branch **40** 1953 'Report on Farming 1952'.
[54] MERL TR RAN AD7/12.
[55] NRO BR73/133.
[56] NRO BR73/140.
[57] Martin 2000, 58–9.
[58] Short *et al*. 2006, 5.
[59] Upcher 1946.
[60] *EDP* 28 March 1940, 8.
[61] Warren 1943, ix.
[62] NRO DC 9/1/19.
[63] Allen 2005, 80–2.
[64] Barnes 1993, 34; Bowyer 1979, 166.
[65] Allen 2005; Bowyer 1979, 173–6; Snelling 1996, 16; NRO MC542/80; Barnes 1993.
[66] NRO BR73/180; Barnes 1993, 34.
[67] Kinsey 1983.
[68] Lees-Milne 1992, 30.
[69] Wolterton MS 8/102/M shelf L.

[70] Allen 2005, 64.
[71] Allen 2005, 80–2.
[72] Grafton 1943, 85–7.
[73] Barnes 1993, 34.
[74] Astor and Rowntree 1946, 83.
[75] Menzies-Kitchin 1945, 62.
[76] Hall 1941.
[77] Orwin 1942, 63.
[78] *EDP* 6 Jan 1945, 6.
[79] *EDP* 27 Jan 1945, 6.
[80] *EDP* 10 Feb 1945, 6.
[81] Martin 2000, 70.
[82] Statutes of the Realm 1947 c48.
[83] *EDP* 6 May 1950, 7.
[84] Farm Economics Report **35**, University of Cambridge 1950.
[85] NRO BR143/278.
[86] Upcher 1946, 102.
[87] Bell 1956, 61.
[88] Baird and Tarrant 1970.
[89] *EDP* 10 June 1950, 9.
[90] *EDP* 4 March 1950, 7.
[91] Pilfold 2006, 196
[92] Orwin 1944, 1; Thomas 1939, 274.
[93] Menzies-Kitchin 1945, 11.
[94] Pilfold 2006, 196.
[95] Scott 1942, 25.
[96] Scott 1942, 48.
[97] Scott 1942, 108–17.
[98] Scott 1942, 47.
[99] Riviere 1944, 392–4.
[100] Keith 1942, 315
[101] Evans 1997.
[102] Sheail 2002, 129.

**CONCLUSION**

[1] For the best discussion of the conditions of the rural poor, see Howkins 1991 and 2003.

# BIBLIOGRAPHY

Anon. (1939) *Picturesque Norfolk: A Guide to some of the Beauty Spots of the County*, Norwich.

Abercrombie, P. and Kelly, S.A. (1935) *East Suffolk Regional Planning Scheme*, University of Liverpool/Hodder and Stoughton, London.

Abercrombie, P. (1943) *Town and Country Planning*, Home University Library, London.

Addison, W. (1950) *Suffolk*, Robert Hales, London.

Allen, K. (2005) 'The Development of Country House Landscapes in Norfolk, c.1880–1945', unpublished MA dissertation, School of History, University of East Anglia.

Allison, K.J. (1957) 'The sheep-corn husbandry of Norfolk in the sixteenth and seventeenth centuries', *Agricultural History Review* **5**, 12–30.

Armstrong, P. (1973) 'Changes in the Suffolk Sandlings: a study of the disintegration of an eco-system', *Geography* **58**, 1–8.

Armstrong, A. (1988) *Farmworkers: A Social and Economic History, 1770–1980*, Batsford, London.

Ashby, A.W. and Byles, P.G. (1923) *Rural Education*, Oxford University Press, Oxford.

Astor, Viscount and Rowntree, S. (1938) *British Agriculture. The Principles of Future Policy*, Longmans, London.

Astor, Viscount and Rowntree, S. (1946) *Mixed Farming and Muddled Thinking*, Macdonald, London.

Backhouse, G. (1972) 'Thetford Forest', in H.L. Edlin (ed.) *East Anglian Forests*, HMSO, London, 4–14.

Baird, W. and Tarrant, J. (1970) *Hedgerow Destruction in Norfolk 1946–1970*, Centre of East Anglian Studies, University of East Anglia, Norwich.

Baker, W.P. (1953) *The English Village*, Oxford University Press, Oxford.

Baldry, G., ed. L. Rider Haggard (1939) *The Rabbit Skin Cap*, Collins, London.

Barber, D. (1988) 'The Countryside: Decline and Renaissance', *JRASE* **149**, 81–9.

Barnes, G. (2003) 'Woodlands in Norfolk: A Landscape History', unpublished PhD thesis, University of East Anglia.

Barnes, G., Dallas, P., Thompson, H., Whyte, N., Williamson, T. (2007) 'Heathland and Wood Pasture in Norfolk: Ecology and Landscape History', *British Wildlife* **18, 6**, 395–403.

Barnes, P. (1984) 'The Economic History of Landed Estates in Norfolk since 1880', unpublished PhD thesis, University of East Anglia.

Barnes, P. (1993) *Norfolk Landowners Since 1880*, Centre of East Anglian Studies, University of East Anglia, Norwich.

Bateman, J. (1878) *The Great Landowners of Great Britain and Ireland*, London.

Batey, M. (1995) 'Gertrude Jekyll and the Arts and Craft Movement', in M. Tooley and P. Arnander (eds) *Gertrude Jekyll: Essays on the Life of a Working Amateur*, Michaelmas Books, Durham, 63–70.

Beard, M. (1989) *English Landed Society in the Twentieth Century*, Routledge, London.

Bell, A. (1931) *Corduroy*, Bodley Head, London.

Bell, A. (1932) *The Cherry Tree*, Bodley Head, London.

Bell, A. (1941) 'The Family Farm', in H.J. Massingham (ed.) *England and the Farmer*, Batsford, London.

Bell, A. (1956) *A Suffolk Harvest*, Bodley Head, London.

Bensusan, S.L. (1927) *Later-Day Rural England*, London.

Berlyn, A. (1894) *Sunrise-Land: Rambles in Eastern England*, London.

Betjeman, J.fg (1958) *Collected Poems*, John Murray, London.

Biddell, H. (1907) 'Agriculture', in *Victoria County History Suffolk, Vol. II*, Constable, London, 382–402.

Bird, M.C.H. (1909) 'The Rural Economy, Sport, and Natural History of East Ruston Common', *Transactions of the Norfolk and Norwich Naturalists' Society* **8**, 631–70.

Birtles, S. (2003) 'A Green Space beyond Self Interest: The Evolution of Common Land in Norfolk', unpublished PhD thesis, University of East Anglia.

Bisgrove, R. (1992) *The Gardens of Gertrude Jekyll*, Frances Lincoln, London.

Boardman, E.T. (1939) 'The Development of a Broadland Estate at How Hill Ludham, Norfolk', *Transactions of the Norfolk and Norwich Naturalists' Society* **15**, 14.

Bone, Q. (1975) 'Legislation to Revive Small Farming in England 1887–1914', *Agricultural History* **49**, 653–61.

Boorman, A. (2006) 'Alley Brothers', *Old Tractor* **37**, 28–33; **38**, 28–31; **39**, 20–4.

Bowyer, M.J.F. (1979) *Action Stations: Military Airfields of East Anglia*, Stephens, Cambridge.

Bowyer, M.J.F. (1992) *Action Stations: Military Airfields of East Anglia*, Patrick Stephens, London.

Bowley, A. (1921) *Prices and Wages in the United Kingdom 1914–1920*, Oxford University Press, Oxford.

Brassley, P., Burchardt, J. and Thompson, L. (2006) *The English Countryside Between the Wars: Regeneration or Decline?* Boydell Press, Woodbridge.

Broach, J. (1931) 'Building Operations: Thetford Chase', *Journal of the Forestry Commission* **10**, 46–7.

Brown, J. (1982) *Gardens of a Golden Afternoon: The Story of a Partnership*, Allen Lane, London.

Brown, J. (1987) *Agriculture in England: A Survey of Farming. 1870–1947*, Manchester University Press, Manchester.

Brown, J. (2006) *Farming in Lincolnshire 1850–1945*, Lincolnshire Heritage, Lincoln.

Bujak, E. (1997) 'Suffolk Landowners: An Economic and Social History of the County's Landed Families in the Late Nineteenth and Early Twentieth Centuries', unpublished PhD thesis, University of East Anglia.

Bunce, M. (1994) *The Countryside Ideal*, Routledge, London.

Burchardt, J. (1999) 'Reconstructing the Rural Community: Village Halls and the National Council of Social Service', *Rural History* **10**, **2**, 193–216.

Burchardt, J. (2002a) *The Allotment Movement in England, 1793–1873*, Royal Historical Society, London.

Burchardt, J. (2002b) *Paradise Lost: Rural Idyll and Social Change since 1800*, Taurus, London.

Burnett, J. (1966) *Plenty and Want: A Social History of Food in Britain from 1815 to the Present Day*, Nelson, London.

Burrell, W.H. (1914) 'Physiography and Plant Distribution', in W.A. Nicholson (ed.) *A Flora of Norfolk*, West, Newman and Son, London, 13–33.

Burrell, W.H. and Clarke, W.G. (1914) 'A Contribution to a Vegetation Survey of Norfolk', *Transactions of the Norfolk and Norwich Naturalists' Society* **8**, 743–56.

Bushaway, B. (1992) 'Name upon Name: The Great War and Remembrance', in R. Porter (ed.), *Myths of the English*, Polity Press, Cambridge, 136–97.

Butcher, R.W. (1941) *The Land of Britain: Suffolk*, Geographical Publications, London.

Bygott, J. (1923) *Eastern England*, Routledge, London.

Cadman, W.A. (1936) 'Bird Life at Thetford', *Journal of the Forestry Commission* **6**, 24–6.

Carnie, W. (1899) *In Quaint East Anglia*, Greening and Co., London

Carr, M. (1997) *New Patterns: Process and Change in Human Geography*, Nelson Thornes, Cheltenham.

Carslaw, R.McG. (1928) 'A Successful Poultry Farm 1922–6', *Farm Economics* **5**, Cambridge University, School of Agriculture.

Carslaw, R.McG. and Venn, J.A. (1929) 'Four Years Farming in East Anglia', *Farm Economics* **12**, Cambridge University, School of Agriculture.

Carslaw, R.McG., Kitchen, A.W. and Graves, P.E. (1933) 'An Economic Survey of the Agriculture of the Eastern Counties of England', *Farm Economics* **21**, Cambridge University, School of Agriculture.

Carson, S.H. (1935) 'Half a Century of Changes on an East Anglian Farm', *JRASE* **96**, 45–77.

Catt, J.A. (1978) 'Contribution of Loess Soils to Lowland Britain', in S. Limbry and J.G. Evans (eds) *The Effect of Man on the Landscape: The Lowland Zone*, Council for British Archaeology Research Report 21, London, 12–20.

Cavill-Worsley, P.E.T. (1930) 'A Fur Farm in Norfolk', *Transactions of the Norfolk and Norwich Naturalists' Society* **13**, 104–15.

Chard, R. (1959) 'The Thetford Fire Plan', *Journal of the Forestry Commission* **28**, 154–89.

Chatwin, C.P. (1961) *East Anglia and Adjoining Areas*, British Regional Geology, HMSO, London.

Clarke, W.G. (1897) 'A List of Vertebrate Animals Found in the Vicinity of Thetford', *Transactions of the Norfolk and Norwich Naturalists' Society* **6**, 300–6.

Clarke, W.G. (1908) 'Some Breckland Characteristics', *Transactions of the Norfolk and Norwich Naturalists' Society* **8**, 555–78.

Clarke, W.G. (1910) 'The Commons of Norfolk', *Transactions of the Norfolk and Norwich Naturalists' Society* **9**, 52–70.

Clarke, W.G. (1914) 'The Breckland Sand-Pall and its Vegetation', *Transactions of the Norfolk and Norwich Naturalists' Society* **10**, 138–51.

Clarke, W.G. (1918) 'The Natural History of Norfolk Commons', *Transactions of the Norfolk and Norwich Naturalists' Society* **10**, 294–318.

Clarke, W.G. (1925) *In Breckland Wilds*, Heffer, Cambridge.

Cleveland, D. (1986) 'Some Writers on the Norfolk Broads', in N. McWilliam and V. Sekules (eds) *Life and landscape. P.H. Emerson: Art and Photography in East Anglia 1885–1900*, University of East Anglia, Norwich, 86–7.

Colledge, D. (1989) *Labour Camps: The British Experience*, Popular Publishing, Sheffield.

Collins, E.J.T. (ed.) (2000) *Agrarian History of England and Wales Vol VII*, Cambridge University Press, Cambridge.

Cosgrove, D. (1993) 'Myths, Gods and Humans', in B. Bender (ed.) *Landscape: Politics and Perspectives*, Berg, Oxford, 281–305.

Cresswell, L. (1887) *Eighteen Years on the Sandringham Estate*, London.

Crompton, Rev. J. (1870) 'Presidential Address', *Transactions of the Norfolk and Norwich Naturalists' Society* **1**, 1.

Daniels, S. (1988) 'The Political Iconography of Woodland in Later Eighteenth-Century England', in D. Cosgrove and S. Daniels (eds) *The Iconography of Landscape*, Cambridge University Press, Cambridge, 51–72.

Daniels, S. (1991) 'The Making of Constable Country, 1880–1940', *Landscape Research* **12**, 9–17.

Darby, H.C. (1983) *The Changing Fenland*, Cambridge University Press, Cambridge.

Davies, G.C. (1884, 2nd edn) *Norfolk Broads and Rivers*, Blackwood and Sons, London.

Davies, G.C. (1891) *The Handbook to the Rivers and Broads of Norfolk and Suffolk*, Jarrold and Sons, London.

Dewey, P. (1989) *British Agriculture in the First World War*, Routledge, London.

Ditchfield, P.H. (1910) *Vanishing England*, Methuen, London.

Dobinson, C.S. (1996) *Twentieth-century Fortifications in England II: Anti-Invasion Defences of World War II*, Council for British Archaeology, York.

Douet, A. (1989) 'Norfolk Agriculture 1914–1972', unpublished PhD thesis, University of East Anglia.

Driscoll, R.J. and Parmenter, J. (1994) 'Robert Gurney's 1908/1909 Vegetation Survey of Broadland', *Transactions of the Norfolk and Norwich Naturalists' Society* **30**, 71–9.

Driscoll, R.J. and Parmenter, J. (1995) 'Changes in the Vegetation of Honing Common', unpublished report, Castle Museum, Norwich.

Druce, Mr (1881) 'Report on Norfolk', *Royal Commission on Agriculture*, Parliamentary Papers **16**, 375–9.

Druce, Mr (1882) 'Further report on Norfolk', *Royal Commission on Agriculture*, Parliamentary Papers **15**, 64–9.

Dufton, F.C. (1952–4) 'Thetford-Type Static Water Tanks', *Journal of the Forestry Commision* **8**, 67–9.

Dutt, W.A. (1900) *Norfolk*, Dent, London.

Dutt, W.A. (1905) *The Norfolk Broads*, Dent, London.

Dymond, D. (1985) *The Norfolk Landscape*, Hodder and Stoughton, London.

Ede, J., Virgoe, N. and Williamson, T. (1994) *Halls of Zion, Chapels and Meeting Houses in Norfolk*, Centre of East Anglian Studies, University of East Anglia, Norwich.

Edlin, H.L. (1972) *East Anglian Forests*, HMSO, London.

Edwards, J.K. (1984) 'Industrial Development 1800–1900', in C. Barringer (ed.) *Norwich in the Nineteenth Century*, Gliddon Books, Norwich, 136–59.

Ellis, E.A. (1963) 'Some Effects of Selective Feeding by the Coypu (*Myocasto coypus*) on the vegetation of Broadland', *Transactions of the Norfolk and Norwich Naturalists' Society* **20**, 32–5.

Ernle, Lord (R.E. Prothero) (1961, 6th edn) *English Farming, Past and Present*, Heinemann, London.

Evans, D. (1997) *A History of Nature Conservation in Britain*, Routledge, London.

Farquar, J. (1984) *Arthur Wakerley, 1862–1931*, Sedgebrook, Leicester.

Faunce De Laune, C. de L. (1886) 'Tobacco as a farm crop for England', *JRASE* 2nd series **22**, 213–52.

Fisher, J. (1950) 'Bird Preservation', *Transactions of the Norfolk and Norwich Naturalists' Society* **18**, 1–13.

FitzRandolph, H. and Doriel Hay, M. (1926) *Rural Industries of England & Wales*, vol. 1, Oxford University Press, Oxford.

Fletcher, T.W. (1961) 'Lancashire Livestock Farming during the Great Depression', *Agricultural History Review* **9**, 17–42.

Fletcher, T.W. (1961) 'The Great Depression in English Agriculture, 1873–96', *Economic History Review* 2nd series **13**, 417–32.

Foot, W. (1994) *Maps For Family History. A Guide to the Records of the Tithe, Valuation Office and National Farm Surveys of England and Wales*, PRO publications, London.

Foot, W. (2006) 'The Military and Agricultural Landscape', in B. Short, C. Watkins and J. Martin (eds) *The Front Line of Freedom, Agricultural History Review*, Supplement Series **4**, 132–42.

Fowler, E. (1947) 'The Future of the Broads', *Transactions of the Norfolk and Norwich Naturalists' Society* **16**, 323–7.

Fox, W. (1895) *Royal Commission on Agriculture: the County of Suffolk*, HMSO, London.

Freeman, R.A. (1999) 'Airfields of the Two World Wars', in D. Dymond and E. Martin (eds) *An Historical Atlas of Suffolk*, Suffolk County Council, Planning Department and Suffolk Institute of Archaeology and History, Ipswich, 188–9.

Frere, P.H. (1863) 'Remarks on Mr Gurdon's Letter', *JRASE* **24**, 168–73.

Funnell, B. (2005, 3rd edn) 'Geological Background', in T. Ashwin and A. Davison, *An Historical Atlas of Norfolk*, Phillimore, Chichester, 4–5.

Gay, C.E. (1944) 'The Norfolk Naturalists Trust', *Transactions of the Norfolk and Norwich Naturalists' Society* **16**, 3–13.

George, M. (1992) *The Landuse, Ecology and Conservation of Broadland*, Packard, Chichester.

Gilston, R.B. (1948) 'Brandon Park', *Journal of the Forestry Commission* **19**, 20–3.

Glynn, S. and Oxborrow, J. (1976) *Interwar Britain: A Social and Economic History*, Barnes and Noble, New York.

Gliddon, G. (ed.) (1988) *Norfolk and Suffolk in the Great War*, Gliddon Books, Norwich.

Godfrey, J. and Short, B. (2001) 'Analysis of Record Linkage Over Time', *Agricultural History Review* **29**, 56–78.

Grace, F. (1999a) 'The Growth of Modern Ipswich', in D. Dymond and E. Martin (eds) *An Historical Atlas of Suffolk*, Suffolk County Council, Planning Department and Suffolk Institute of Archaeology and History, Ipswich, 160–1.

Grace, F. (1999b) 'Population Trends, 1811–1981', in D. Dymond and E. Martin (eds) *An Historical Atlas of Suffolk*, Suffolk County Council, Planning Department and Suffolk Institute of Archaeology and History, Ipswich, 106–9.

Grafton, Duke of (1943) 'Experiences in Land Reclamation', *JRASE* **104**, 85–7.

Grieves, K. (1999) 'Common meeting places and the brightening of rural life: local debates on village halls in Sussex after the First World War', *Rural History* **10, 2**, 171–92.

Groves, R. (1949) *Sharpen the Sickle*, Porcupine Press, London.

Grubb, P.J., Green, H.E. and Merrifield, R.C.J. (1969) 'The Ecology of Chalk Heath: Its Relevance to the Calciole-Calcifuge and Soil Acidification Problems', *Journal of Ecology* **57**, 175–212.

Gurdon, J. (1863) 'Co-operative Farming at Assington, Suffolk', *JRASE* **24**, 165–8.

Gurney, J.H. (1870) 'Stray Notes on Norfolk and Suffolk Mammalia', *Transactions of the Norfolk and Norwich Naturalists' Society* **1**, 22–6.

Haggard, H.R. (1899) *A Farmer's Year*, Longmans, Green and Co., London.

Haggard, H.R. (1902) *Rural England*, 2 vols, Longmans, Green and Co., London.

Haggard, L.R. (1946) *Norfolk Notebook*, Faber, London.

Haggard, L.R. and Williamson, H. (1943) *Norfolk Life*, Faber, London.

Haliday, J. and Coombes, M. (1995) 'In Search of Counter-Urbanisation: Some Evidence from Devon', *Journal of Rural Studies* **11, 4**, 433–46.

Hall, A.D. (1941) *Reconstruction and the Land: An Approach to Farming in the National Interest*, Macmillan, London.

Harland, E. (1951) *No Halt at Sunset*, Ben, London.

Hartley, L.P. (1953) *The Go-Between*, Hamilton, London.

Hibbs, J. (1989) *The History of British Bus Services*, David and Charles, Newton Abbot.

Hodge, C., Burton, R., Corbett, W., Evans, R. and Scale, R. (1984) *Soils and their Uses in Eastern England*, Soil Survey of England and Wales, Harpenden.

Holderness, B.A. (1984) 'East Anglia and the Fens', in J. Thirsk (ed.) *The Agrarian History of England and Wales Volume VI, 1640–1750*, Cambridge University Press, Cambridge, 197–238.

Home, M. (1934) *God and the Rabbit*, Rich and Cowan, London.

Home, M. (1944) *Autumn Fields*, Methuen, London.

Home, M. (1946) *Spring Sowing*, Methuen, London.

Howard, P. (1991) *Landscapes: The Artists' Vision*, Routledge, London.

Howkins, A. (1991) *Reshaping Rural England: A Social History 1850–1925*, Unwin Hyam, London.

Howkins, A. (2003) *Death of Rural England: A Social History of the Countryside Since 1900*, Routledge, London.

Howkins, A. (2006) 'Death and Rebirth? English Rural Society, 1920–1940', in P. Brassley, J. Burchardt and L. Thompson (2006) *The English Countryside Between the Wars: Regeneration or Decline?* Boydell Press, Woodbridge, 10–25.

Hutchison, J. and Owers, A.C. (1980) *Change and Innovation in Norfolk Farming*, Packard, Chichester.

Hunt, E.H. and Pam, S.J. (2002) 'Responding to Agricultural Depression, 1873–1896: managerial success, or entrepreneurial failure?' *Agricultural History Review* **50**, 225–52.

Jebb, H. (1907) *Small Holdings*, John Murray, London.

Jekyll, G. (1899) *Wood and Garden*, London.

Jenkins, H.M. (1869) 'Lodge Farm, Castle Acre', *JRASE* **5**, 460–74.

Jenkins, H.M. (1884) 'Report on the Practice of Ensilage', *JRASE* **20**, 126–246.

Jessopp, A. (1887) *Arcady, for Better, for Worse*, London.

Joly de Lotbiniere, H.J. (1928) 'Afforestation in Breckland', *Transactions of the Norfolk and Norwich Naturalists' Society* **12**, 673–7.

Joby, R. (2005) 'Railways', in T. Ashwin and A. Davison (eds) *An Historical Atlas of Norfolk*, Phillimore, Chichester, 3rd edn, 147–8.

Jones, D.N. (1990) 'Planning and the Myth of the English Countryside in the Inter-war Period', *Rural History* **2**, 249–64.

Jones, R.L. and Keen, D.H. (1993) *Pleistocene Environments in the British Isles*, Chapman and Hall, London.

Kains Jackson, H. (1888) 'Experiments in Making Ensilage during the Wet Season of 1888', *JRASE* **25**, 280.

Keith, E.C. (1942) 'The Policy of the Society', *Transactions of the Norfolk and Norwich Naturalists' Society* **15**, 311–18.

Keith, J. (1954) *Fifty Years of Farming*, Faber, London.

Keith, J., Garner, F. and Lewis, I.G. (1942) 'Experiences in Land Reclamation', *JRASE* **103**, 108–24.

Kemp, G. (ed.) (1924) *Concerning Thorpeness: Being a Few Principles with Practical Examples of the Art and Science of Town Planning*, Clay & Sons, Bungay.

Kent, P. (1988) 'The Fixed Defences', in G. Gliddon (ed.) *Norfolk and Suffolk in the Great War*, Gliddon Books, Norwich, 1–17.

Kent, P. (1999) 'Fortifications of the Two World Wars', in D. Dymond and E. Martin (eds) *Historical Atlas of Suffolk*, Suffolk County Council Planning Department and Suffolk Institute of Archaeology and History, Ipswich, 186–7.

Kent, P. (2005) 'First and Second World War Coastal Defences', in D. Dymond and E. Martin (eds) *Historical Atlas of Suffolk*, Suffolk County Council Planning Department and Suffolk Institute of Archaeology and History, Ipswich, 180–1.

Kenworthy-Browne, J., Reid, P., Sayer, M. and Watkin, D. (1981) *Burke's and Saville's Guide to Country Houses, Volume 3: East Anglia*, Burke's Peerage, London.

King, C. (2007) 'The Rise and Decline of Reading Rooms with Particular Reference to Norfolk', unpublished MA dissertation, University of East Anglia.

Kinsey, G. (1981) *Orfordness – Secret Site. A History of the Establishment 1915–80*, Terrence Dalton, Lavenham.

Kinsey, G. (1983) *Bawdsey – Birth of the Beam. A History of RAF Stations at Bawdsey and Woodbridge*, Terrence Dalton, Lavenham.

Kneale, N. (ed.) (1973) *The Ghost Stories of M.R. James*, Folio Society, London.

Knights, S. (1986) 'Change and Decay: Emerson's Social Order', in N. McWilliam and V. Sekules (eds) *Life and Landscape. P.H. Emerson: Art and Photography in East Anglia 1885–1900*, University of East Anglia, Norwich, 12–20.

Lambert, J.M. (1961) 'The Chief Norfolk Habitats', in *Norwich and its Region*, British Association for the Advancement of Science, Jarrolds, Norwich, 51–8.

Lees-Milne, J. (1992) *People and Places: Country House Donors and the National Trust*, John Murray, London.

Linsley, B. (2005) '"Homes for Heroes": Housing Legislation and its Effects on Housing in Rural Norfolk, 1918–1939', unpublished PhD thesis, University of East Anglia.

Lockwood, C.A. (1998) 'From Soldiers to Peasants – Land Settlement Schemes in East Sussex', *Albion* **30**, 439–62.

Long, S.H. (1935) 'The Norfolk Bird Sanctuaries', *Transactions of the Norfolk and Norwich Naturalists' Society* **14**, 71–8.

MAF (1925) *Land Settlement for England and Wales, Being a Report under the Smallholdings and Allotment Acts 1908–1919*, HMSO, London.

Malster, R. (1993) *The Broads*, Phillimore, Chichester.

Mann, M.E. (1991) *Tales of Victorian Norfolk*, Morrow, Bungay.

Mansfield, N. (1995) 'Class Conflict and Village War Memorials', *Rural History* **6**, **1**, 67–87.

Marsh, J. (1982) *Back to the Land*, Quartet, London.

Martelli, G. (1952) *The Elveden Enterprise*, Faber, London.

Martin, J. (2000) *The Development of Modern Agriculture: British Farming since 1931*, Macmillan, Basingstoke.

Martin, J. (2006) 'The Structural Transformation of British Agriculture: The Resurgence of High-Input Arable Farming', in B. Short, C. Watkins and J. Martin (eds) *The Front Line of Freedom*, *Agricultural History Review*, Supplement Series **4**, 16–35.

Massingham, H.J. (1937) 'Our Inheritance from the Past', in Clough William-Ellis (ed.) *Britain and the Beast*, Dent, London.

Massingham, H.J. (ed.) (1940) *England and the Farmer*, Batsford, London.

Massingham, H.J. (ed.) (1945) *The Natural Order*, Batsford, London.

Mathias, P. and Davis, J. (eds) (1996) *Agriculture and Industrialisation*, Oxford University Press, Oxford.

Matless, D. (1994) 'Moral Geography in Broadland', *Ecumene* **1**, 127–56.

Matless, D. (1998) *Landscape and Englishness*, Reaktion Books, London.

Mee, A. (1940) *The King's England: Norfolk*, Hodder and Stoughton, London.

Mee, A. (1941) *The King's England: Suffolk*, Hodder and Stoughton, London.

Meredith, A. (2006) 'The Women's Smallholding Colony at Lingfield, 1920–1939', *Agricultural History Review* **54**, 105–21.

Messent, C. (1928) *The Old Cottages and Farmhouses of Norfolk*, Hunt, Norwich.

Menzies-Kitchin, Dr A.W. (1945) *The Future of British Farming*, Pilot Press, London.

Middleton, T. (1923) *Food Production in War*, Oxford University Press, Oxford.

Miller, D. (1935) *Seen From a Windmill: A Norfolk Broads Revue*, Heath Cranton, London.

Ministry of Information (1945) *Land at War*, HMSO, London.

Mitchell, B.R. and Deane, P. (1962) *Abstract of British Historical Statistics*, Cambridge University Press, Cambridge.

Moore-Collyer, R.J. (1999) 'Aspects of the Urban–Rural Divide in Inter-War Britain', *Rural History* **10**, 105–24.

Moore-Collyer, R.J. (2001) 'Back to Basics: Rolf Gardiner, H.J. Massingham and "A Kinship in Husbandry"', *Rural History* **12**, 85–108.

Mosby, J.E.G. (1938) *The Land of Britain: Norfolk*, Geographical Publications, London.

Moscrop, W.J. (1886 ) 'Report of the Farm-Prize Competition of 1886', *JRASE* **22**, 567–664.

Murray, K.A.H. (1955) *Agriculture*, HMSO, London.

Muthesius, S. (1984) 'Nineteenth-Century Norwich Houses', in C. Barringer (ed.) *Norwich in the Nineteenth Century*, Gliddon Books, Norwich, 94–117.

Newsome, S. (2003) 'The Coastal Landscapes of Suffolk During the Second World War', *Landscapes* **4**, **2**, 42–58.

Nicholson, H.H. (1948) 'Field Drainage and Increased Production', *JRASE* **109**, 212–21.

Nicholson, W.A. (ed.) (1914) *A Flora of Norfolk*, West, Newman and Son, London.

Norden, J. (1618) *The Surveyor's Dialogue*, London.

Norgate, F. (1876) 'Notes on the Nesting Habits of Certain Birds', *Transactions of the Norfolk and Norwich Naturalists' Society* **2**, 195–206.

Norgate, F. (1878) 'Notes on Norfolk Mammalia', *Transactions of the Norfolk and Norwich Naturalists' Society* **2**, 458–70.

O'Connell, S. (1998) *The Car in British Society*, Manchester University Press, Manchester.

'O.J.S.' (1934) 'Forest Fires in 1933', *Journal of the Forestry Commission* **13**, 9–16.

Offer, A. (1981) *Property and Politics 1870–194: Landownership, Law, Ideology and Urban Development in England*, Cambridge University Press, Cambridge.

Oldershaw, A.W. and Garner, H.V. (1944) 'Light Land Experiments at Tunstall, Suffolk', *JRASE* **105**, 98–114.

Oldershaw, A.W. and Dunnett, F.W. (1939) 'A Field-by-Field Survey of East Suffolk', *JRASE* **100**, 56–61.

Oldershaw, A.W. (1941) 'Experiments on Arable Crops at Saxmundham', *JRASE* **102**, 136–55.

Orwin, C.S. and Darke, W.F. (1935) *Back to the Land*, P.S. King, London.

Orwin, C.S (1942) *Speed the Plough*, Penguin, Harmondsworth.

Orwin, C.S. (1944) *Country Planning*, National Institute of Agricultural Engineers, London.

Ottewill, D. (1989) *Edwardian Gardens*, Yale University Press, New Haven.

Packer, I. (2001) *Lloyd George, Liberalism and the Land*, Boydell and Brewer, Woodbridge.

Parkes, W.H. (1912) *Thorpeness*, repr. Meare Publications, Aldeburgh (2001).

Patterson, A. (1909) *Man and Nature on Tidal Waters*, Methuen, London.

Pedley, W. (1942) *Labour on the Land*, P.S. King and Stephens, London.

Perciful, S. (1999) 'Arts and Crafts Influences on East Anglian Gardens', unpublished PhD thesis, University of East Anglia.

Perren, R. (1995) *Agriculture in Depression 1870–1940*, Cambridge University Press, Cambridge.

Perry, H.and Perry, E. (1999) *Tottington: a lost village in Norfolk*, George Reeve, Norwich.

Perry, P.J. (ed.) (1973) *British Agriculture 1875–1914*, Methuen, London.

Perry, P.J. (1974) *British Farming in the Great Depression: An Historical Geography*, David and Charles, Newton Abbot.

Petch, C.P. (1947a) 'Reclaimed Lands of West Norfolk', *Transactions of the Norfolk and Norwich Naturalists' Society* **16**, 106–9.

Petch, C.P. (1947b) 'Fenlands of West Norfolk', *Transactions of the Norfolk and Norwich Naturalists' Society* **16**, 317–19.

Petch, C.P. and Swann, E.L. (1968) *Flora of Norfolk*, Norfolk and Norwich Naturalists' Society, Norwich.

Pevsner, N. (1961) *The Buildings of Suffolk*, Penguin, Harmondsworth.

Pevsner, N. and Wilson, B. (2002a) *The Buildings of England, Norfolk I: Norwich and North East*, Yale University Press, London.

Pevsner, N. and Wilson, B. (2002b) *The Buildings of England, Norfolk II: North-West and South*, Yale University Press, London.

Pilfold, W. (2006) 'Dudley Stamp, the MAF and Rural Land Utilisation Planning', in B. Short, C. Watkins and J. Martin (eds) *The Front Line of Freedom*, *Agricultural History Review*, Supplement Series **4**, 194–203.

Poole, K. and Keith-Lucas, B. (1994) *Parish Government, 1894–1994*, National Association of Parish Councils, London.

Porter, R. (ed.) (1992) *Myths of the English*, Polity Press, Cambridge.

Postgate, M.R. (1973) 'Field systems of East Anglia', in R.A. Baker and A.R.H. Butlin (eds) *Studies of Field Systems in the British Isles*, Cambridge University Press, Cambridge, 281–324.

Pratt, E.K. (1927) 'The East Anglian Timber Willow', *Journal of the Forestry Commission* **88**, 80–6.

Pritchard, H.A. (1928) 'Forest Workers' Holdings', *Journal of the Forestry Commission* **7**, 5–7.

Rackham, O. (1986) *The History of the Countryside*, Dent, London.

Raynes, F. (1934) 'Two Decades of Lightland Farming', *JRASE* **95**, 117–35.

Rea, E. (1949) 'Silage for self-sufficiency', *JRASE* **110**, 28

Read, C.S. (1883) 'Agriculture', in W. White, *History, Gazetteer and Directory of Norfolk and the City of Norwich*, Sheffield, 69–76.

Read, C.S. (1887) 'Large and Small Holdings', *JRASE* **23**, 1–28.

Redstone, L.J. (1939) *Our East Anglian Heritage*, Methuen, London.

Reid, A. (1986) *Cromer and Sheringham: The Growth of the Holiday Trade 1877–1904*, Centre of East Anglian Studies, University of East Anglia, Norwich.

Rew, H. (1895) *Royal Commission on Agriculture: the County of Norfolk*, HMSO, London.

Riviere, B.B. (1944) 'Nature Reserve Investigation in Norfolk', *Transactions of the Norfolk and Norwich Naturalists' Society* **15**, 392–4.

Robertson, A. (1988) 'Railways in Suffolk', in D. Dymond and E. Martin (eds) *An Historical Atlas of Suffolk*, Suffolk County Council, Ipswich, 108–9.

Robinson, G.W. (1943) 'The Use of Lime', *JRASE* **104**,136–44.

Robinson, H. (1932) 'Messrs S.E. and J.F. Alley's Mechanised Farming', *JRASE* **93**, 157–65.

Robinson, W. (1870) *The Wild Garden*, John Murray, London.

Robinson, W. (1883) *The English Flower Garden*, John Murray, London.

Rodwell, J.S. (1991) *British Plant Communities Volume 2: Mires and Heaths*, Cambridge University Press, Cambridge.

Ross, J.M. (1935) 'Study of Pine Shoot Moth Damage', *Journal of the Forestry Commission* **14**, 56–64.

Rothschild, M. and Marren, P. (1997) *Rothschild's Reserves*, Harley Books, Colchester.

Rouse, M. (1982) *Coastal Resorts of East Anglia*, Terrence Dalton, Lavenham.

Rowell, C.W. (1959) 'County Council Smallholdings 1908–58', *Agriculture* **60**, 109–14.

Rowley, T. (2006) *The English Landscape in the Twentieth Century*, Hambledon Continuum, London.

Ryle, G. (1969) *Forest Service: The First Forty-Five years of the Forestry Commission in Great Britain*, David and Charles, Newton Abbot.

Scott, Lord Justice (1942) 'Report on the Committee on Land Utilisation in Rural Areas', Command Paper 6378, HMSO, London.

Scott, C.S. (1886) *Poppy-land: Papers Descriptive of Scenery on the East Coast*, Jarrold and Sons, London.

Scott, R. (2002) *East Anglian Interludes: Artists at Walberswick 1880–2000*, British Art Dictionaries, London.

Sheail, J. (1974) 'The Role of the War Agricultural and Executive Committees in the Food Production Campaign of 1915–18 in England and Wales', *Agricultural Administration* **5**, 141–53.

Sheail, J. (1976) *Nature in Trust: The History of Nature Conservation in Britain*, Blackie, Glasgow and London.

Sheail, J. (1977) 'The Impact of Recreation on the Coast: The Lindsey County Council (Sandhills) Act, 1932', *Landscape Planning* **4**, 53–72.

Sheail, J. (1981) *Rural Conservation in Inter-War Britain*, Clarendon Press, Oxford.

Sheail, J. (2002) *An Environmental History of Twentieth-Century Britain*, Palgrave, London.

Shears, R.T. (1936) 'Housing the Agricultural Worker', *JRASE* **97**, 1–12.

Short, B. (1989) *The Geography of England and Wales in 1910*, Historical Geography Research Series **22**, Bristol.

Short, B. (1997) *Land and Society in Edwardian Britain*, Cambridge University Press, Cambridge.

Short, B. and Watkins, C. (1994) 'The National Farm Survey of England and Wales 1941–1943', *Area* **26**, 288–93.

Short, B., Watkins, C. and Martin, J. (eds) (2006) *The Front Line of Freedom: British Farming in the Second World War*, Agricultural History Review, Supplement Series **4**.

Silvester, R. (1988) *The Fenland Project, No. 3: Norfolk Survey, Marshland and the Nar Valley*, East Anglian Archaeology **45**, Norfolk Archaeological Unit, Dereham.

Simmons, I.G. (2001) *An Environmental History of Great Britain*, Edinburgh University Press, Edinburgh.

Simpson, F.W. (1982) *Flora of Suffolk*, Suffolk Naturalists' Society, East Bergholt.

Skipper, K. and Williamson, T. (1997) *Thetford Forest: Making a Landscape 1922–1997*, Centre of East Anglian Studies, University of East Anglia, Norwich.

Smith, J.J. (1952–4) 'Rabbit Clearance in Kings Forest 1947–51', *Journal of the Forestry Commission* **8**, 70–1.

Smith, N.R. (1946) *Land for the Small Man*, Morningside Heights, New York.

Snell, K. (1998) *The Regional Novel in Britain and Ireland, 1800–1990*, Cambridge University Press, Cambridge.

Snelling, S. (1996) *Over Here: The Americans in Norfolk During World War Two*, Breedon, Derby.

Southwell, T. (1870) 'Fauna of Norfolk: Mammalia and Reptilia', *Transactions of the Norfolk and Norwich Naturalists' Society* **1**, 71–82.

Southwell, T. (1871) 'On the Ornithological Archaeology of Norfolk', *Transactions of the Norfolk and Norwich Naturalists' Society* **1**, 14–23.

Southwell, T. (1896) 'The Wild Birds Protection Acts of 1880 and 1894, as Applied to the County of Norfolk', *Transactions of the Norfolk and Norwich Naturalists' Society* **6**, 207–14.

Stamp, D. (1948) *The Land of Britain: Its Use and Misuse*, Longmans, London.

Stevenson, H. (1870) *The Birds of Norfolk*, London.

Stevenson, H. (1876) 'Ornithological Notes', *Transactions of the Norfolk and Norwich Naturalists' Society* **2**, 306.

Stevenson, H. (1882) 'Ornithological Notes', *Transactions of the Norfolk and Norwich Naturalists' Society* **3**, 779.

Stevenson, H. (1887) 'Ornithological Notes', *Transactions of the Norfolk and Norwich Naturalists' Society* **4**, 125–39.

Storey, G. (1973) 'Culford Hall', in E. Carr, B. Rutterford and G. Storey (eds) *People and Places: An East Anglian Miscellany*, Terrence Dalton, Lavenham, 93–200.

Street, A.G. (1937a) *Farming England*, Batsford, London.

Street, A.G. (1937b) 'The Countryman's View', in Clough Williams-Ellis (ed.) *Britain and the Beast*, Geoffrey Bles, London, 122–32.

Strong, R. (1996) *Country Life 1897–1997*, Country Life Books, Boxtree, London.

Swenarton, M. (2002) 'Tudor Walter and Tudorbethan: Reassessing Britian's Inter-War Suburbs', *Planning Perspectives* **17, 3**, 267–86.

Taylor, A.J.P. (1965) *English History 1914–1945*, Oxford University Press, Oxford.

Taylor, J. (1986) 'Landscape and Leisure', in N. McWilliam and V. Sekules (eds) *Life and Landscape. P.H. Emerson: Art and Photography in East Anglia 1885–1900*, University of East Anglia, Norwich, 73–82.

Tennyson, J. (1939) *Suffolk Scene: A Book of Description and Adventure*, Blackie, London.

Theobald, J. (2000) 'Changing landscapes, changing economies: holdings in Woodland High Suffolk, 1600–1850', unpublished PhD thesis, University of East Anglia.

Thirsk, J. (1997) *Alternative Agriculture: A History From the Black Death to the Present Day*, Oxford University Press, Oxford.

Thirsk, J. and Imray, I. (1956) *Suffolk Farming in the Nineteenth Century*, Suffolk Record Society, Ipswich.

Thomas, F.G. (1939) *The Changing Village*, Thomas Nelson and Sons, London.

Thompson, F.M.L. (1963) *English Landed Society in the Nineteenth Century*, Routledge and Kegan, London.

Thompson, F.M.L. (1991) 'An Anatomy of English Agriculture, 1870–1914', in B.A. Holderness and M. Turner (eds) *Land, Labour and Agriculture 1700–1920*, Hambledon, London, 211–40.

Thompson, F.M.L. (1996) 'Agriculture and Economic Growth in Britain', in P. Mathias and J. Davis (eds) *Agriculture and Industrialisation*, Oxford University Press, Oxford, 40–67.

Thornhill, E. (n.d) *Historical Rambles in East Anglia*, Lee, Exeter.

Thorpe, A. (1992) *Britain in the 1930s: The Deceptive Decade*, Blackwell, Oxford.

Trist, P.J.O. (1971) *A Survey of the Agriculture of Suffolk*, Royal Agricultural Society of England, London.

Trollope, A. (1980) *Can You Forgive Her?* Penguin, London.

Truck, J.G. (1891) 'Note on the Great Bustard in Suffolk', *Transactions of the Norfolk and Norwich Naturalists' Society* **5**, 209–11.

Turner, E.L. (1922) 'The Status of Birds in Broadland', *Transactions of the Norfolk and Norwich Naturalists' Society* **11**, 228–40.

Turner, M.E., Becket, J.V. and Afton, B. (1997) *Agricultural Rent in England and Wales*, Cambridge University Press, Cambridge.

Turner, P. and Wood, R. (1974) *P.H. Emmerson, Photographer of Norfolk*, Gordon Fraser, London.

Upcher, H.M. (1884) 'President's Address', *Transactions of the Norfolk and Norwich Naturalists' Society* **3**, 564–633.

Upcher, H. (1946) 'Norfolk Farming', *Transactions of the Norfolk and Norwich Naturalists' Society* **16**, 97–105.

Vincent, J. (1907) *Through East Anglia in a Motor Car*, Methuen, London.

Wade-Martins, P. (ed.) (1987) *Norfolk From the Air*, Norfolk Museums Service, Norwich.

Wade Martins, S. (1980) *A Great Estate at Work*, Cambridge University Press, Cambridge.

Wade Martins, S. (1984) *A History of Norfolk*, Phillimore, Chichester.

Wade Martins, S. (1988) *Norfolk, A Changing Countryside*, Phillimore, Chichester.

Wade Martins, S. (1991) *Historic Farm Buildings*, Batsford, London.

Wade Martins, S. (2002) *The English Model Farm*, Windgather Press, Macclesfield.

Wade Martins, S. and Williamson, T. (1999) *Roots of Change, Agricultural History Review*, Supplement Series **2**.

Wallace, D. (1945) *The Noble Savage*, Collins, London.

Ward Lock & Co. (n.d.) Illustrated Guide Books, *Cromer, Norwich and District*.

Warren, C.H. (1943) *This Land is Yours*, Eyre and Spottiswood, London.

Wass, J.G. (1956) '*Fomes Annosus* in East Anglian Pine Sample Plots', *Journal of the Forestry Commission* **9**, 75.

Waterson, M. (1994) *The National Trust: The First Hundred Years*, BBC publications, London.

Weaver, L. (1920) *Village Clubs and Halls*, Country Life, London.

Weiver, M.J. (1981) *English Culture and the Decline of the Industrial Spirit*, Cambridge University Press, Cambridge.

Whetham, E.H. (1970) 'The Mechanisation of British Farming 1910–1945', *Journal of Agricultural Economy* **21**, **3**, 314–20.

Whetham, E.H. (1978) *The Agrarian History of England and Wales Vol. VIII, 1919–1939*, Cambridge University Press, Cambridge.

Whitehand, J.W.R. and Carr, C.M.H. (2002) *Twentieth-Century Suburbs: A Morphological Approach*, Routledge, London.

Wild, T. (2004) *Village England: A Social History of the Countryside*, Tauris, London.

Williams-Ellis, C. (1928) *England and the Octopus*, Geoffrey Bles, London.

Williamson, A. (1995) *Henry Williamson, Tarka and the Last Romantic*, Alan Sutton, Stroud.

Williamson, H. (1940) *The Story of a Norfolk Farm*, Faber, London.

Williamson, T. (1993) 'The Norfolk Nonconformist Chapels Survey: some preliminary results', in N. Virgoe and T. Williamson (eds) *Religious Dissent in East Anglia*, Centre of East Anglian Studies, Norwich, 59–72.

Williamson, T. (1995) *Polite Landscapes: Gardens and Society in Eighteenth-century England*, Alan Sutton, Stroud.

Williamson, T. (1997) *The Norfolk Broads: A Landscape History*, Manchester University Press, Manchester.

Williamson, T. (2000) *Suffolk Parks and Gardens: Designed Landscapes from the Tudors to the Victorians*, Windgather Press, Macclesfield.

Williamson, T. (2003) *Shaping Medieval Landscapes: Settlement, Society, Environment*, Windgather Press, Bollington.

Williamson, T. (2005) *Sandlands*, Windgather Press, Macclesfield.

Williamson, T. (2006) *England's landscape: East Anglia*, English Heritage and HarperCollins, London.

Wilt, A.F. (2001) *Food for War*, Oxford University Press, Oxford.

Wodehouse, P.G. (1930) *Very Good, Jeeves!* Republished in *Life With Jeeves*, 1986. Penguin, Harmondsworth.

Wood, A. (1919) *The Development of the Tobacco-Growing Industry in Great Britain*, British Tobacco Growers Society, London.

Wright, J. (1993) 'Population Change, 1851–1951', in P. Wade Martins (ed.) *An Historical Atlas of Norfolk*, Norfolk Museums Service, Norwich, 134–5.

Wymer, J. (1999) 'Solid Geology', in D. Dymond and E. Martin (eds) *An Historical Atlas of Suffolk*, Suffolk County Council Planning Department and Suffolk Institute of Archaeology and History, Ipswich, 16–17.

# INDEX